From Cotton Picker to Store Keeper

THE BROOKSHIRE GROCERY COMPANY STORY

From Cotton Picker to Store Keeper: The Brookshire Grocery Company Story
Jim S. Powell

First printing, 2020.

Published by W.T. Way Publishing
Tyler, Texas

Printed in the United States of America.

Produced with the assistance of Fluency Organization, Inc.

FLUENCY
TELLING STORIES THAT MATTER

Proceeds from the sale of this book support the BGC Partners Care Fund, a voluntary emergency fund partners can contribute to throughout the year to help each other through hardships and emergency situations.

BGC PARTNERS CAREFUND

Table of Contents

To my wife, Ann, my greatest supporter, inspiration and proofreader. Ann's encouragement, advice and loyalty have been never-ending for over 62 years.

To my daughter Scharlanne Powell Crozier, who designed the cover for this book, and to my granddaughter Callie Ann Crozier for additional proofreading. Both have added endless joy and excitement to my life.

To all of the devoted partners at Brookshire Grocery Company, past and present, who have contributed their talents and resources in making Brookshire Grocery Company the vibrant and successful organization it is today.

THE W.T. WAY

CORE**VALUES**

- "Jump Over The Counter" Service Excellence
- Do The Right Thing
- Competitive Grit
- Do Your Best Every Day
- The Team Matters
- Results-Driven With A Future Focus

W.T. Brookshire

BGC
BROOKSHIRE
GROCERY COMPANY

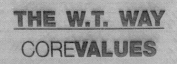

About the Author

Jim S. Powell, a native of Chandler, Texas, enjoyed over 40 years in the advertising/marketing field at Brookshire Grocery Company before his retirement in 1999. He last served as BGC's Senior Vice President–Advertising and on the Board of Directors from 1992-2005. He is a graduate of the University of Texas at Austin, receiving a Bachelor of Journalism degree in 1958. He also received a Master of Arts degree from East Texas State University in Commerce, Texas. Jim is also a graduate of Chandler High School and Tyler Junior College.

When he went to work for Brookshire Grocery Company on September 1, 1958, the Company had 13 Brookshire's retail stores. At the time of writing this book, BGC has 181 retail stores under four banners. Presently his daughter and granddaughter are partners in the Company, making it the third generation of his family serving BGC.

Throughout the years several BGC leaders influenced his life, namely Pat Prestwood, his first boss, Wood T. Brookshire, Company founder, and Wood's sons Bruce and S.W. "Woody" Brookshire. The author also had the privilege of getting to know and working with four of Mr. Wood's talented grandsons—Tim, Brad, Britt and Mark.

The author lives in Tyler with his wife, Ann. They have been married over 62 years. He is a member of the Chandler Historical Society and a Smith County Master Gardener. In addition to gardening he enjoys antiquing and finding collectibles with his daughter and granddaughter, some of which he sells at a local antique mall.

He is the author of four books. Three of them, *Feed Sack Fashions, Them's Funny Looking Catfish* and *Way Back When*, present touching snapshots of a young boy's experience growing up in a rural East Texas community in the 1940s. His fourth book, *The Mystery of The Totem Trees*, is a children's mystery fiction.

Introduction

Third- and fourth-generation family members who are direct descendants of the Company's founder, Wood T. Brookshire, are leading Brookshire Grocery Company today. Very few family-owned companies make it to the third or fourth generation of leadership.

J. W. Marriott, founder of the Marriott chain of hotels, once said, "It's the little things that make the big things possible." This could very easily describe the business journey of Brookshire Grocery Company.

When Wood Brookshire opened his first store in 1928, he had a cherished aspiration of being successful in the grocery business. With hard work and the assistance of his faithful wife, Louise, and several devoted employees, he saw his dream gradually become a reality.

Throughout the journey that shaped this Company, Mr. Wood stressed being competitive and giving outstanding service. He often said that if we have a little volume, we would make a little money. This Wood Brookshire philosophy has been reiterated so many times in the Company that it is one of the Core Values which the Company still practices.

In writing this book I was compelled to sometimes rely on hearsay for what actually happened, since Mr. Wood

Brookshire and many of his family members and acquaintances are deceased. However, the book is based on research, facts, recollections, Company publications and interviews. Dialogue is based on conversations that did take place, and whenever possible, incorporates actual phrases used by the speakers.

My purpose in writing this book is to reflect on my feelings and love for Wood T. Brookshire and Brookshire Grocery Company.

Jim S. Powell
September 2020

CHAPTER 1

"Gone to Texas"

Texas gained its independence from Mexico on April 21, 1836, when Sam Houston's army won a quick battle against General Santa Anna and his Mexican forces at San Jacinto. Texas had already voted to become the Republic of Texas on March 2, 1836. Then, in December of 1845, Texas was annexed into the United States of America.

News of Texas's independence and statehood traveled fast via word of mouth. Early newspapers, especially throughout the southern states, caused an influx of individuals and caravans of Anglo-American families heading to Texas from Missouri, Tennessee, Arkansas, Alabama and Kentucky. They were seeking a place to prove themselves on the vast new frontier with new ideas, new beginnings, new jobs, new money and new opportunities for their families.

Joining this group of opportunity seekers journeying to East Texas in 1856 was the Hillary Hackman Brookshire family, including P. Jasper Brookshire, a six-year-old youngster who was born in Giles County, Tennessee, in 1850. The family packed up their belongings, joined other families and traveled the long journey from the state of Tennessee to San Augustine, Texas.

Prior to the Civil War, San Augustine was one of the top cotton shipping centers in Texas. As the Anglo-American migration to Texas increased in the early 1800s, San Augustine and nearby Nacogdoches (considered the oldest town in Texas) became a favorite stopover for Anglos entering Texas. At the time, the two towns were perhaps the most civilized places to live in Texas. They were connected by the Old San Antonio Road, also known as the Spanish Camino Real (The Royal Road), often translated as The King's Highway. Tennesseans had begun migrating to Texas in the 1830s. Sam Houston and Davy Crockett, two fellow Tennesseans who helped Texas fight for independence, arrived in Nacogdoches in the 1830s. At one time Sam Houston lived in San Augustine, and Davy Crockett was known to visit the town often.

San Augustine County is in extreme East Texas, only 23 miles from the eastern state border of Louisiana. It was also one of the first counties to be formed in the new Republic of Texas and became the county seat in 1837. The town's churches helped bring religious freedom to Texas. San Augustine's Christ Episcopal Church was organized in 1848, and the present building was completed in 1870.

When the P. Jasper Brookshire family left Tennessee, they were not thinking about the long, tough journey to Texas. They were probably dreaming about laying the foundation for a major step in creating an inspiration and advancement for their family. The rich and fertile land of East Texas and the cheap land grants were perhaps what lured them to East Texas. Fish, wildlife, berries and wildflowers abounded in the area. The fertile land was also well suited for cotton and corn crops.

No record of the Brookshire's journey from Tennessee to Texas remains; however, they perhaps joined other families traveling by covered wagons drawn by oxen. In the 1800s traveling long distances in caravans was a much safer way to travel. Traditionally the children from six years of age and up and many adults walked three-fourths of the way to Texas. The caravan's journey included miles of forest dirt roads with often-soggy mud. They perhaps averaged only 20 miles per day.

The caravan of wagons usually camped at night near a small stream or creek so they could have water for themselves and the animals. The women washed their clothes and bathed their children and themselves. All of their cooking was done on open fires using Dutch ovens and deep cast iron skillets with tight-fitting covers and handles. Historical accounts of other caravans recorded that settlers along the way were usually friendly and helpful, often giving the traveling families food for their meals and for the oxen.

At this time, there were no bridges, so the wagons and oxen had to be ferried across rivers and larger creeks by existing ferry operators. The oxen, sometimes frightened by the water and the ferry, had to have a sack placed over their heads in order to get them onto the flat wooden ferries. The Sabine River was the last river the Brookshire family ferried across before entering Texas from Louisiana.

After living and farming in San Augustine for perhaps less than a year, the Brookshire family moved approximately 45 miles to a section of land east of the present city of Lufkin, Texas, in Angelina County. At that time, the future town of Lufkin was known as Denman Springs, a settlement that was a little bit more than a clearing when a railroad surveying crew crossed Angelina County planning the route for a railroad in 1881. The settlement was renamed Lufkin in 1882. The railroads brought the rapid expansion of people and business to the Lufkin area and to other towns across Texas.

Probably the first major project of the Brookshire family was to build a house. During that period most new East Texas families used the abundance of local timber to construct a one- or two-story rough timber house with a middle breezeway. This commonly was called a "dogtrot" house because dogs could trot from the front yard to the backyard through the breezeway.

As a young adult, P.J. Brookshire, who was later nicknamed "Uncle Jap," began dealing in the buying and selling of oxen, horses, mules and cattle. In 1870 a yoke of oxen sold for $150, a heifer for $18.75, a cow for $26, a bull for $90 and a steer for $22.50. An average workhorse sold for $150, and a good saddle horse brought $200. In addition to buying and selling livestock, P.J. continued farming, especially growing cotton. Cattle and cotton production continued to dominate farm operations throughout the nineteenth century in East Texas.

In all of his endeavors Uncle Jap exemplified much toughness, eagerness and enthusiasm until his death on November 23,

1934. He had been a Texas resident for 78 years. Representative Martin Dies Jr., a Texas politician and Democrat member of the United States House of Representatives, delivered the eulogy at Uncle Jap's funeral in Lufkin. It was said that the funeral was attended by more people than had ever attended a funeral in Angelina County at that time. Representative Dies said, "It could certainly be said of Uncle Jap that he lived well, laughed often and loved much. Uncle Jap always looked for the best in others and gave the very best he had." Dies continued, "While Uncle Jap was the relentless foe of evil and wickedness, he possessed a rare understanding and sympathetic tolerance of the weakness of others."

P. J. "Uncle Jap" Brookshire, Wood T. Brookshire's father, and his wife, Fannie. On the farm where Wood was reared in Angelina County near Lufkin, Texas.

His son Wood T. Brookshire, founder of Brookshire Grocery Company, was born in 1904 and was the fourteenth of Uncle Jap's 16 children. At the time of Wood's birth, his father was 65 years old, and his oldest brother, Austin, was asked to raise him. As a lean and tall youngster, Wood lived the hardy life of an average East Texas farm boy on his father's Angelina County farm. As a child, he attended a one-room schoolhouse in the nearby farming community of McKendrie. Although Wood attended grade school, he joined some of his brothers and sisters to take a leave from school in spring and fall to plant, hoe and pick cotton. In the early twentieth century, one-room schoolhouses were commonplace throughout rural East Texas. A single teacher would typically have students in the first through the eighth grade. The younger students sat in the front of the class, and the older students sat in the back. Usually the students were taught reading, writing, arithmetic, history and geography. Learning in a one-room schoolhouse was often a community effort with older students assisting the teacher in helping the younger students with their lessons.

The McKendrie school building was the combination of a church and school. The wood floor was heated in the winter by a wood-burning potbellied stove. Standing behind the building were two outhouses—one for the boys and one for the girls. A well of water located near the school building supplied fresh drinking water for the students. A bucket, rope and pulley were used to draw up the water. Students all shared the same dipper to drink from.

Wood commented, "My teachers were above average for

their day." He also recalled, "On many occasions, I had to miss classes at school in order to help harvest crops, like picking cotton for my father." Wood rode horseback to Lufkin to attend high school. He was physically tough from farm life and was also an unusually fast runner. In 1921 as a junior in high school, he started playing football on the Lufkin Panthers' football team. In fact, he played in the first football game he ever saw, and later wound up being captain of the football team.

The one-room schoolhouse/church in the McKendrie farming community near Lufkin, Texas. Wood attended school here for 1st–8th grade.

This "Cotton Picker," the nickname Wood adopted for himself, received an education in the schools of Angelina County, graduating from Lufkin High School in 1923. Following high school, he continued his education by studying business administration for two years (1924-1925) at Baylor University in Waco, Texas.

Wood recalled, "I received most of my business training from my father who imbued in me the fundamentals of hard work, honor and integrity"—characteristics he instilled in his life, business and employees. These qualities have influenced Brookshire Grocery Company's success for almost 100 years.

Some food innovations of the early 1900s were condensed canned soups, Hershey chocolate bars, Wrigley Doublemint gum, Nabisco Oreos, Life Savers and Moon Pies. The Life Savers candy was introduced in 1912 as a candy that could withstand the summer's heat. Since it was shaped like a life preserver, it was named Life Savers. In 1917, it was rumored that a coal miner asked for a snack "as big as the moon." A bakery placed marshmallows between two graham crackers and called it the Moon Pie.

Average Cost of Grocery Items in 1900-1920s

Flour (5 lb)	$0.12
Milk (1/2 gal)	$0.14
Bacon (lb)	$0.14
Eggs (doz)	$0.21
Butter (lb)	$0.26

Insights into Wood T. Brookshire:

Quotes from Former Brookshire Grocery Company Partners

"Mr. Brookshire always set an example. In the early days we all worked hard in the stores. One Saturday night after we closed the store, he asked me to go sweep the alley behind the store. I was tired when I started sweeping. The more I swept, the more upset I got about having to do such a manual job late at night. Just when I made up my mind to stop sweeping, I looked up and saw Mr. Brookshire coming to help me with a broom in his hand!"

"When I was a part-time employee at sixteen years old, Mr. Brookshire reached out and pointed his finger very hard on my breastbone to get my full attention. He talked to me about giving good customer service. All I could manage to say was, 'Yes Sir, Yes Sir, Yes Sir.'"

CHAPTER 2

Wood's First Store

As already stated, Wood T. Brookshire referred to himself as the "Cotton Picker." It was a well-suited nickname since he had hours of experience as a young country boy hoeing and picking cotton on his father's farm.

Prior to 1920 very little had happened in the world of food distribution. However, A&P had opened its first grocery store in 1912. Unlike the small mom-and-pop stores at the time, the A&P had no telephone, no credit lines and no delivery options.

America's true first self-service grocery store in the country opened in 1916 in Memphis, Tennessee. It was the brainchild of businessman Clarence Saunders, who started the Piggly Wiggly grocery chain. By the end of the year, there were nine Piggly Wiggly stores in the Memphis area. Prior to the self-service store, a customer selected an item and had to wait for a store food clerk to secure it for them. Sometimes this became time-consuming and frustrating for the customer, and it required several store clerks to select the items.

Self-service streamlined the grocery shopping experience by saving the customer time and money. It also cut operating costs and lowered prices. However, self-service presented its own problems. One problem was the lack of communication between the customer and those who worked in the store.

Wood's earliest exposure to the grocery business came in 1921, when at sixteen years old he started working part-time on Saturdays and during summers at the Brookshire Brothers store owned by two of his brothers, Austin and Tom. The store was located on the courthouse square in Lufkin, Texas. Wood started working in his brothers' store in order to seek advancement and escape the cotton patch and the hot Texas sun. He gained valuable grocery store experience working in the store. After these two brothers paid for their store, they had net cash capital of $165 in the bank. This was the first store of the Brookshire Brothers retail grocery chain.

By 1928, eight Brookshire brothers and sisters, including Wood, had invested in the partnership of Brookshire Brothers. The original "Brookshire Brothers" included Austin ("Auss"), Houston ("Huss"), Tom, Bryan ("Jack"), Lee and W.T. ("Wood").

Wood, at the age of 21, married Helen Louise Rhein on September 1, 1926. A grandson said he always enjoyed hearing the love story of his grandparents. Mimi, the name he called his grandmother, was raised in a strict Catholic family with two of her brothers eventually becoming Catholic priests. Conversely, Papaw, his grandfather, was raised in a very conservative

Protestant family! When they met and fell in love, they were assured of their two families conflicting denominational beliefs and fearful of the lack of support for a potential wedding. Therefore, they eloped! They were confident of their love and commitment to each other.

Louise's family had moved from Illinois to Nacogdoches County, Texas, when she was a young girl. She graduated from Nacogdoches High School and attended Stephen F. Austin State Teachers College. Louise's grandfather, John Schmidt, was in the retail business and was the founder of the Mayer Schmidt department store in Tyler, Texas. Mayer Schmidt sold men's and ladies' clothing and had opened in a new building on the northwest corner of North College Avenue and West Ferguson Street in 1893 on the courthouse square in downtown Tyler. The store advertised to be "The Fashion Center of East Texas."

In 1926, with a wife to support, Wood left Baylor and became a "store keeper" when he joined his brother Tom, opening a Brookshire Brothers store in Kingsville, Texas, located 350 miles south of Lufkin. Wood said, "Our business growth in Kingsville was very fruitful; however, Tom and his wife, who had worked many long hours over a period of several years, decided to sell the South Texas store to enjoy a long needed rest and to fulfill their ambitions to travel."

In 1928 at the age of 24, Wood and his wife, Louise, returned to East Texas from Kingsville. Wood commented, "Louise and I started searching for a community in which we would be glad to rear our family. We were expecting our first child in December." Wood further commented, "I looked over several East Texas towns, and I can't pick out the magnet that pulled me to Tyler. Louise and I were both impressed by Tyler at that time, a good, stable, farming community." Wood concluded, "We decided we would like to live here where we found the folks in Tyler to be congenial. It was just a good country town."

Wood Brookshire's Self-Service grocery store located on Spring Avenue in downtown Tyler. Grand Opening was September 1, 1928.

This was the decade when gas stoves, electric refrigerators, radios and automobiles were first being produced. In 1927 Henry Ford watched his 15 millionth Model T Ford roll off the assembly line. It was also during a period that Tyler was becoming a more progressive city. The local *Tyler Courier-Times* daily newspaper and the *Tyler Journal* weekly newspaper provided the Brookshires an avenue for advertising their business. As an example of the city's growth, Tyler Junior College had been founded in Tyler two years prior to their arrival to provide higher education in the East Texas area. Wood and Louise were impressed with the opportunities Tyler offered, and they also could have been influenced by the fact that Louise's grandfather had a business in Tyler.

East Texas was fundamentally an agriculture-based economy with cotton as its money crop until around 1932. Cotton was grown on small farms by individual farmers like the Brookshire family in the Lufkin area or by tenant farmers. According to the *Texas Almanac* in 1925, over 50,000 bales of cotton had been produced in Smith County. Tomatoes for "green-wrap" shipping were also grown in abundance in the area. During this period farmhands bought groceries from mom-and-pop country stores that were widespread throughout East Texas. The stores were small and very limited in selection. Most groceries were bought on credit that was paid off after the crops were harvested. Unfortunately, if the cotton crop was poor, due to bad weather conditions or boll weevils, the debt went unpaid.

Wood saw the coming change from service-credit-delivery retailing to self-service "cash and carry" mass merchandising. So, taking a leap of faith, on September 1, 1928, Wood, with a mere $300 in his pocket and a trust in God to bring forth profits, joined with W.A. Brookshire, a first cousin, in opening a Brookshire Brothers Self-Service Grocery Store on Spring Avenue on the east side of the square in downtown Tyler. The partnership they set up was designed to serving the Tyler area with excellent service and low prices. Their store was wedged in among other downtown retail establishments, including the Arcadia Theater, which had opened in 1925. The Arcadia showed the first talking motion picture in Tyler in February 1929. Spring Avenue offered retail stores and the theatre very limited off-street parking.

Wood said, "Before I opened the store, I went all over Tyler and introduced myself to everybody I met. I told them I would appreciate a chance to serve them." His act of asking people for their business paid off, because the new store met with instantaneous results and sales were excellent that first day of business. An article in the September 2, 1928, issue of the *Tyler Courier Times* described the grand opening of the store: "Large numbers of people seen trailing in the store and then seeing them coming out with large packages indicated that they had taken advantage of the special bargains offered by the new concern."

A former partner who helped develop the Company's produce operations shared the following memory of the first Brookshire store. "My daddy was in the produce business and sold produce to Mr. Brookshire at the first store. I was six years old when it opened in 1928, and I thought it was the biggest store I had ever seen in my life. I remember Mr. Brookshire standing behind the little counter. I think the inventory in produce there was probably some apples, onions, potatoes and maybe some homegrown tomatoes. I went with my daddy to help deliver these few items to the store."

A former customer of the first store recalled, "Back when steaks were 10 cents a pound and $19 would buy a month's worth of groceries, I began swinging by Brookshire's on my way home from work to pick up groceries for my mom and dad.

"Inevitably, company founder W.T. Brookshire would be there manning the long, narrow store that soon would become the cornerstone of one of the largest family-owned grocery chains in the country.

"Every time he'd see me, he'd ask if I'd been to church that Sunday. I would always answer 'yes sir,' because that was the way my family was. We went to church.

"After serving in World War II, my wife and I settled near Tyler, and we continued the family tradition of shopping at Brookshire's. I liked Mr. Brookshire because he was a strong Christian man. I respected him and what he did."

Wood's Grand Opening advertisement contained the following slogans:

"You are cordially invited to pay our store a visit and see for yourself our attractive special prices. Get our attractive feed prices before you buy. We will handle all kinds of country produce. No thrifty housewife can overlook the above prices."

Some of the opening day specials in the advertisement were:

Bananas (lb)	$0.05
Lettuce (nice head)	$0.08
Lemons (doz)	$0.22
Lard (8 lb bucket)	$1.08
P&G Soap (10 bars)	$0.36
Calumet Baking Powder (1 lb)	$0.21
Pure Cane Sugar (18 lb)	$1.00
Primrose Flour 48 lb (sack)	$1.69
Vari Best Peaches (2 1/2 can)	$0.19

Admiration Coffee (3 lb container) $1.35

Camels, Chesterfields, Lucky Strikes,
Old Golds Cigarettes (carton) $1.12

In Wood's first grocery store customers had a choice of 600 to 800 items. The Food Marketing Institute estimates today the average supermarket stocks 40,000 to 50,000 items with some averaging thousands more. This was the initial store of the present Brookshire Grocery Company (BGC).

Just as today, Wood's customers picked up something to place their groceries in as they entered the store. Back then it was a wooden basket that the customer hung on her arm as she walked around the store selecting her items to be purchased. These baskets were rectangular oak splint containers having the bottom and sides from woven or braided splints, crossed at angles. For the convenience of customers, the baskets were located in a slanted wooden bin near the entrance of the store.

The coincidence began simply enough when two young mothers had their babies in those baskets as they shopped for groceries in Wood Brookshire's new long and narrow wood-floored grocery store. One of the young women was Louise Brookshire, Wood's wife. The other was a woman who would prove to be a Brookshire customer for 70-plus years.

The customer said, "There I was, in the store with my tiny baby, wondering how in the world I was going to shop and hold her at the same time. I just tucked her into one of those tiny shopping baskets they used to have and saw across the way that Louise Brookshire had done the same thing with her tiny son." The two mothers began comparing notes on their children whenever they met in the store.

On many occasions Wood would greet the customer as she entered the store, help her locate items, check and bag her groceries, "jump over the counter" and take her groceries to her car. Customers were delighted with the personalized service they received at the new store.

Wood Brookshire in his first store on the courthouse square in Tyler, Texas. Wood is behind the counter wearing a Lufkin High School football letter sweater in September, 1928.

Retail food stores of the 1920s were typically small. Wood's store was only 25 feet wide by 100 feet deep, with an upstairs storage area and an unfinished basement. It was necessary to carry all surplus stock either upstairs to the second floor or downstairs to the basement. His store was narrow so the customer could easily go from wall to wall selecting from the high, almost to the ceiling, shelves. A convenient "can grabber" had to be used to secure hard to reach items on the top shelves. It was a long trigger pull tool with rubber ends. Hanging exposed light bulbs lit the store. This type of lighting was typical in retail stores of the 1920s.

All the fixtures in this first store, with the exception of an enclosed glass candy case, were designed by Wood and built by local carpenters. The wall shelving fixtures, divided in sections, held the major food items needed in the household except refrigerated items, since refrigeration was still fairly new and not widely used in retail stores in the 1920s. The store stocked cheese, and smoked and cured meats. Wood used a cheese cutter that sat on a counter. During the 1920-30s a hoop of cheese rested on the cutter at room temperature. The customer selected the exact amount of cheese she desired, and the cheese was cut, weighed and wrapped. The cutter resembled a turntable with a large hinged blade that pulled down to cut the cheese. He also sliced the cured and salt bacon that was sold in his store.

Candy, gum and other impulse items were placed at the counter. Wood had his special "store bought" candy case at his check stand. Baby Ruth candy bars can be seen in a photo of his first store. Other candy that was available included Milky Way, Abba-Zaba, Oh Henry chocolate bars, Haribo Gold Bears, Reese's Peanut Butter Cups and Dubble Bubble Gum that had just been introduced.

Fresh meats had to be purchased at a butcher shop because of the lack of commercial refrigeration. On many occasions eggs and milk were delivered door-to-door by local farmers. Ice was also delivered to homes to refrigerate oak iceboxes that kept food cool.

Wood had five friendly employees in his first store. He challenged them by saying, "In your job just do the small things and apply good common horse sense which is so necessary to our success." Louise served as her husband's partner and bookkeeper, using a ledger book. When Wood "rang-up" a bill of groceries, it was with a pencil and paper.

Wood was called "Mr. Do-It-All" because he was the buyer, stocker, checker, sacker, floor sweeper, and meat and produce man. He was also in charge of advertising in the local newspaper. He said, "I went to work in my first store at 6 a.m. every Saturday morning and usually did not leave until 1 a.m. on Sunday morning." The long Saturday hours did not stop him from being in church on Sunday mornings at the First Presbyterian Church in Tyler. It was reported that people used to stand outside the door to his store on Saturdays to watch that "young Brookshire boy" working because he hustled so hard, gave good service and treated everyone so well that his reputation spread as an exceptional businessman in Tyler.

Although it was not realized at the time, this was the first of many stores to be opened in Texas, Louisiana and Arkansas by Wood Brookshire and his associates in the years to come.

The young Brookshire couple plunged wholeheartedly into the activities of the Tyler community. Louise modeled graciousness, thrift, love for her family, absolute integrity and independence for all to see. She made many contributions of time and talents to her family, to the Company, to her church and to the Tyler community. She and Wood became members of the First Presbyterian Church soon after they moved to Tyler. They had a favorite pew in the church, which their family occupied every Sunday. Wood and Louise donated the carillon bells in the First Presbyterian Church's bell tower. These bells continue to grace the church and its neighborhood to call hearers to worship.

On December 3, 1928, the Brookshire's first son, Bruce Glenn Brookshire, was born. Two years later, Shirley Wood "Woody," their second son, was born on November 8, 1930. Mr. Wood knew from the time Bruce and Woody were born that he could not contemplate any line of endeavor for his two sons other than joining him in the grocery business when they became young men.

Grand Opening newspaper advertisement for Wood Brookshire's first store on September 1, 1928.

Wood firmly believed and practiced the concept that if you take out of the community, you must put back into it. He believed this included not only money and time, but also leadership. He expressed his feelings by stating, "I feel an obligation to our customers as I hope my minister feels in his efforts to minister to me. If God has endowed me with any talents at all, it has been in the field of serving my fellow man with his food needs. If I fail to give the best I have, I would prove an unworthiness of the good fortune that has been mine."

Perhaps the most interesting figures from the 1920s are those on income and food expenditures. Of the average per capita income in the 1920s, close to 40% of it was spent on food. To the sociologist, the decade of the 1920s may have been the "Roaring Twenties," but for Brookshire's it was the beginning of self-service, mass marketing and the birth of a developing grocery business that became the successful Brookshire Grocery Company of today.

When Wood opened that first store in 1928, Calvin Coolidge was the U.S. President and penicillin had just been discovered. First-class stamps cost 2 cents, the New York Yankees would again win the World Series title and the first television set was sold for $75, featuring a 3"x4" screen.

For a young man from a rural East Texas farming family with 15 siblings, limited education and limited funds, Wood had developed a strong desire to succeed in serving others in the grocery business. He always emphasized that one made and kept customers by remembering their names and giving them friendly service. He once said, "I believe in and enjoy doing 'the right thing' of giving excellent service to our customers because I feel like it is one of the ways of practicing the Golden Rule that God set before us to follow." That would prove to be one of the cornerstones of Brookshire Grocery Company.

By the end of the Roaring 1920s the world had been introduced to many new ideas and inventions unlike anything it had ever seen.

The Company's advertising slogan for the 1920s was: **"It is your opportunity to save and obtain the best qualities to be had."**

New grocery items introduced in the 1920s were Kool-Aid, Pez, Dubble Bubble gum, Baby Ruth, Popsicles and canned foods. The Baby Ruth candy bar was introduced in 1920. Although the name sounds like the great American baseball legend Babe Ruth, the Curtiss Candy Company traditionally claimed it was named after President Cleveland's daughter Ruth Cleveland.

AVERAGE COST OF GROCERY ITEMS IN THE 1920S

Bread (lb)	$0.09
Kool-Aid (pkg)	$0.10
Milk (gal)	$0.35
Bacon (lb)	$0.47
Coffee (lb)	$0.52
Butter (lb)	$0.55

INSIGHTS INTO WOOD T. BROOKSHIRE:

Quotes from Former Brookshire Grocery Company Partners

"Mr. Brookshire believed in giving everyone a fair shake, and he certainly practiced what he preached."

"Mr. Brookshire purchased Bloodhound plug chewing tobacco at our store. He would always say, 'This is not for me. It is for Mama.'" Bloodhound was advertised as a "Dog-gone Good Chew."

"I think Mr. Brookshire was the most amazing man I have ever met—and I have been around a long time and have met a lot of amazing people. He was a big, husky guy. He never met a stranger, and he never had a customer he didn't speak to."

CHAPTER 3

"Black Gold" Gushes

Nationally, food retailing entered the 1930s in a state of shock due to the stock market crash in 1929, followed by the Great Depression that lead to the failure of 86,000 businesses and 9,000 banks. While the decade was filled with many hardships, it was also a decade of several historical events. Amelia Earhart became the first woman to fly solo across the Atlantic Ocean, and the Empire State Building opened, becoming the tallest building in the world. Also, Jesse Owens, an African-American track star, won four gold medals in the 1936 Olympics in Berlin to the consternation of Adolph Hitler.

Locally the Brookshire Brothers store that opened in 1928, was experiencing a period of growth due to the fact that on October 14, 1929, oil was discovered in Van, Texas. This small East Texas town, only 27 miles west of Tyler, launched into an oil boomtown overnight, ultimately creating additional business not only for Van, but also for other East Texas areas including Tyler. Oil had previously been found in the Brookshire Brothers trade area near the North Central Texas town of Mexia in West Texas and also near the Southeast Texas town of Beaumont.

The 14 Tyler area mom-and-pop country stores were beginning to become a thing of the past in the 1930s since they were mainly set up for credit and were restricted in size. Usually family-owned, they also had limited employees and a small amount of business volume. Self-service "cash and carry" stores like Brookshire Brothers were taking over the industry offering lower prices and a wider selection of merchandise.

Wood Brookshire and his two sons, S.W. "Woody" (left) and Bruce (right) in 1933.

During most of the 1930s, Wood was in partnership with five brothers—Austin, Houston, Tom, Lee and Bryan, operating several stores in East Texas under the Brookshire Brothers banner.

Less than a year after the Van discovery and also after the start of the Great Depression, another tremendous economic boost for East Texas occurred. On September 3, 1930, with the discovery of oil by "Dad" Joiner in Joinerville, Texas, the Daisy Bradford #3 oil well became a gusher of black gold. "Thousands crowded their way to the site of Daisy Bradford No. 3, hoping to be there when and if oil gushed from the well to wash away the misery of the Great Depression," noted a Kilgore, Texas, historian. The oil flowing profusely from the well without being pumped created great excitement throughout the East Texas area, and men and families flocked there to find jobs in the oilfields. This discovery, just 26 miles east of Tyler, resulted in the largest and most prolific oil reserve ever discovered in the contiguous United States. It turned quiet little East Texas communities into boomtowns, making millions for oil producers.

Just when the country as a whole was experiencing an economic depression, East Texas suddenly found itself in the midst of a population boom and with oil, a great new resource of wealth. Area residents who owned just a portion of land also suddenly found themselves dramatically changed from poverty to riches. By an act of fortune, Tyler was located midway between the two oil fields to the west and to the east.

The oil boom brought a variety of new businesses and many job opportunities for people in the East Texas area. The discovery immediately brought option dealers, wildcatters and prospectors sinking exploratory oil wells throughout the countryside. This activity created several oil fields to the area east of Tyler around Kilgore and Gladewater. New towns, if one could call them towns, sprang up almost overnight. Honky-tonks, cafés, gambling places, houses of ill repute and barbershops (which offered baths) abounded in each town, although many took up shop in tents and temporary buildings.

The boom brought in con artists, prostitutes, thieves and other criminal activity. In the 1940s Gregg County, which contains the cities of Longview, Kilgore and Gladewater, was the only wet county between Dallas and Shreveport, Louisiana. Because of the criminal activity in the area, the National Guard had to be called to East Texas in 1931 to help keep peace because of the rough atmosphere of roughnecks, lease hounds, oil spectators and camp followers! At one time, downtown Kilgore, located only 26 miles east of Tyler, had more than 1,000 active oil wells clustered in a tight area. More than 30,300 oil wells have been drilled within the 140,000 acres of the East Texas oil field.

Both of these discoveries started additional population growth in Tyler since a large percentage of the people and new businesses made their way there. Hotels and boarding houses were full, and cafés and retail stores were busy. Many families moved to Tyler and built homes in order to escape the rough and tough atmosphere created in some of the oil boomtowns. In 1930 Tyler's population had grown to 17,112.

S.W. "Woody" (left) and Bruce (right) with their mother, Louise, in 1933.

H.L. Hunt, a Texas oil tycoon and Republican political activist, was one of the most influential men who moved his family to Tyler in 1931 from El Dorado, Arkansas. A rumor said that trading poker winnings for oil rights, Hunt ultimately secured oil titles to much of the great East Texas oil field. In 1936, Hunt had approximately 400 oil wells in East Texas, almost every one of them a major producer.

According to Brad Brookshire, Wood's grandson, Hunt and his family first resided in an apartment on the second floor above Brookshire's Store #1 on South Broadway Avenue in Tyler. This store was the replacement for the Spring Avenue Store #1. In 1933 Hunt built his two-story home he called Mayfield Estate on East Charnwood Street in Tyler's Azalea District.

Joseph Zeppa, president of Delta Drilling Company and head of one of the world's largest oil drilling businesses in the country, and other members of the Zeppa family also made

Tyler their home during the oil boom. Delta Drilling, founded in 1931 in a downtown apartment in Longview, Texas, was later based in Tyler. For several decades many Delta employees made the Tyler area their home.

Tyler also had several independent oil producers who played a major part in the search for oil, wildcatting in areas where major companies did not want to make investments on a smaller scale.

There is a residential area in the Azalea District partly surrounding Bergfeld Park on South Broadway in Tyler that is known for a neighborhood of historic homes and stately mansions that were built in the 1930s when oil brought enormous wealth to Tyler.

Men and families flocked to East Texas to find work in the oilfields during the oil boom years that started in 1930. Oil played a vital part in the establishment and the growth of Brookshire Grocery Company. Almost overnight, the discovery of oil transformed East Texas from a farmland into a growth area of boomtowns and caused the region to be recognized worldwide. Many oil companies opened facilities in Tyler, pushing the population to near 30,000 by 1940. The local oil industry became somewhat weaker, but the timing of the oil booms saved Tyler from the worst of the Great Depression.

Tyler's prosperity during the 1930s was summed up in the May 29, 1936 issue of the *Tyler Journal* newspaper. An article described how the people of Tyler had virtually escaped the effects of the Depression, calling attention to the phenomenal expansions in industry, business, highways and education. The

Tyler City Directory of 1936-37 even had the bragging rights to claim Tyler as "The Oil Capital of the World."

Despite the national food retailing business entering the 1930s in somewhat of a state of shock, the Brookshire Brothers stores experienced tremendous growth during the decade, primarily because of the East Texas oil boom. As the oil business boomed, so did the Brookshire Brothers organization. It grew to include 32 Brookshire Brothers locations throughout East Texas, including stores located in Lufkin, Henderson, Nacogdoches and Tyler.

The original "Brookshire Brothers," who operated several grocery stores throughout East Texas. (left to right) Austin, Houston, Tom, Bryan, Lee and Wood organized the Brookshire Brothers chain in the 1930s.

In 1931 Wood moved his Spring Avenue store to a location in the 200 block of South Broadway, about two blocks from his original store. The new store was larger and in a more convenient location for his customers and offered more parking. It was at this location that Wood made one of the major decisions of his career by adding fresh meats to his offerings. He said, "Oil field men like meat, so I am going to make it available for them and other customers at my store." This addition was a huge success. Shoppers—who previously had to make a trip to the butcher shop to purchase fresh meats—could now buy fresh meats while doing their grocery shopping.

A June 25, 1932, Brookshire Brothers newspaper advertisement contained these Saturday Specials:

Watermelons (lb)	$0.01½
Fresh Corn (6 ears)	$0.10
Cheese (lb)	$0.15
Half or Whole Ham (lb)	$0.15
Iowana Sliced Bacon (lb)	$0.18
Hospital Tissue (3 rolls)	$0.19
Lemons (doz)	$0.23
Special Blend Coffee (3lbs)	$0.49
White Crest Flour (24 lbs)	$0.70

In this advertisement Wood wrote, "To those of you who have given us your valuable business, we are very grateful to you. To those of you who have not been a regular customer, we extend to you a special invitation to make a Brookshire Bros. store YOUR store when purchasing your next bill of groceries. We have four big stores located for your convenience. We invite your inspection. Come see for yourself and compare prices—You will be convinced that Brookshire's 'Sells For Less.' Come see us Saturday or any day of the week. We give you the 'Best For Less.'"

The advertisement also invited the readers to "Listen to our (radio) program over KGKB daily at 9:45 a.m. and Monday, Wednesday and Friday at 8 p.m."

Bread was not an advertised item in the Brookshire Brothers 1932 ad, even though bread was a much talked about grocery product in the early 1930s. Around 1928 an automatic bread slicing and bread packing machine was invented. Chillicothe Bakery in Ohio ran the first sliced bread advertisement, calling the loaf "Sliced Kleen-Maid Bread." Two years later, in 1930, Wonder Bread, the first commercial bread manufacturer, was one of the first to sell pre-sliced bread nationwide. Sliced bread made it easy for people to eat bread since they didn't have to spend time slicing it themselves, and they loved the uniform slices. Bakeries began advertising the pre-cut loaves as, "the greatest forward step in the baking industry" since the bread was sliced and wrapped. This prompted Americans to coin the phrase, "The best thing since sliced bread."

Americans' love of pre-sliced bread didn't stop the government from banning it. In January 1943, the pre-sliced bread marvel disappeared from the grocery store shelves. The U.S. Food Administration banned all commercial bakers from selling any pre-sliced bread, deeming it necessary to help conserve resources for World War II. The ban was to conserve the thicker wax paper that the Federal Drug Administration said bakeries had to use because sliced bread went stale faster than whole loaves. The ban didn't last long. The government repealed it three months later, probably due to the ban's unpopularity, saying the savings were not as much as expected.

Wood Brookshire (left) opened a store on the corner of South Broadway Avenue and Front Street in Tyler in 1939. It was the first air-conditioned food store in East Texas.

Wood Brookshire could be called a "dreamer," and he was known to take chances when he saw opportunities. In 1938 Wood and W.A. Brookshire swapped their shares and withdrew from the Brookshire Brothers organization, taking with them the four Tyler stores. The next year in 1939 Wood became venturesome enough to want to operate three stores on his own. He took control of three of the four Tyler stores in exchange for his shares in the partnership. The three stores were # 1 South Broadway, #2 East Bow Street and #3 East Erwin Street. This transaction became the cornerstone of Brookshire Grocery Company, bearing the trade name Brookshire's Food Stores. It took courage for Wood to go into business by himself. Running a business by himself was certainly another leap in faith. The two companies are no longer related except by the Brookshire name.

Part of the reason Wood decided to pull out of the partnership he operated with W.A. was his two sons—Bruce and S.W. (Woody). Wood had a great ambition to become a better father and a strong desire to give his two sons a future opportunity to grow in the grocery industry.

One early morning that year Wood received the shocking news from the Tyler Fire Department that a devastating fire had destroyed his store on South Broadway, eight years after it opened. This was the best of the three stores. "Our South Broadway store has just burned down. This is a sad day for all of us," he sadly informed Louise, eleven-year-old Bruce and nine-year-old Woody. Losing one of his three Tyler stores was an overwhelming shock both emotionally and financially to the family.

Woody, Wood's son, commented on the fire, "I suppose my earliest recollection was the fire that destroyed Dad's store. Looking back, that had to be the most trying time for Dad in this business. Had it not been for his tenacity and 'stick-ability' he would have gone under. That store was the only one making a profit, and what made things worse was that the receipts from the day before were also in the fire. You see, in those days you hid the money in some merchandise somewhere in the store. I remember Dad going to where the money was and finding a glob of melted pennies held together from the heat of the fire. Of course, the paper money was all destroyed. I also remember that there was a lot of bath soap melted in the fire, and rather than throw it away, Dad salvaged it for us to use at home. I thought we never would use up all that stuff."

One of Wood's grandsons said that he heard that the Brookshire family also ate some canned goods from the destroyed store with the paper labels completely burned off.

Rudolph Bergfeld, Wood's friend who founded Tyler's Bergfeld Reality Company in 1882, gave Wood $200 to restock the burned store. (The $200 in purchasing power in 2020 would be equal to $3,709.31, a difference of $3,509.31 in 81 years.)

Over fifty years later after a new store grand opening, Bruce and Woody had lunch with one of the Brookshire Grocery Company retail leaders at a restaurant in Plano, Texas. The partner recalled, "I sat there for two hours at least and listened to Bruce and Woody talk about how the Company was started. They talked about the fire and how the Ivory soap smelled like smoke for years. I learned so much about the foundation of Brookshire's that day!"

The next day after the fire, Wood didn't hesitate in saying, "The store has to be rebuilt." He started making plans to replace the store by analyzing the monies he would get from insurance, taking stock of his savings and perhaps taking out a loan from the bank. The new replacement store opened in 1939 at the corner of South Broadway and West Front Street. It had the distinction of being the first air-conditioned food store in East Texas and was considered one of the most modern food stores in the area. The building that housed the first air-conditioned food store still stands in Tyler, although it has been renovated and no longer looks like it did when Brookshire's occupied it.

In 1937 one of Wood's local competitors was the M System Store #2, headquartered out of San Angelo, Texas. It was located on North Bois D'Arc Ave. in Tyler. Jewel Mauldin, the M System store manager, later became a Tyler store manager for Wood.

In October 1939 Wood decided to expand his business by opening Store #4, the Company's first store in Longview. This new store, located on South Fredonia Street, contained almost 4,000 square feet of floor space. His four store managers were C.B. Hardin, Pat Prestwood, Jewel Mauldin and Zack Nutt. These early managers played instrumental roles in the growth of the Company in years to come, and all become vice presidents and stockholders in the organization, with one eventually being named president.

In the 1930s Wood demonstrated his concern for those associated with him by making it possible for his four store managers to share in the profits of their stores. Wood considered this profit-sharing concept to be one of the wisest moves he ever made in his career. From the origin of the plan, the Company began to grow. This profit-sharing concept is still a policy of the Company. Commenting about the profit-sharing plan, Jewel Mauldin, one of the recipients, said, "I remember well that Mr. Brookshire began dividing profits with us even before he owned a home. He was renting at the time, but he still wanted us to share in the profits. So, we got a percentage of the profits made by each store." Pat Prestwood, another one of the recipients, once said, "When bonus time came and the Company was low on cash, Mr. Wood would hand me a bonus check, ask me to endorse it and hand it back to him. In return he would give me a Brookshire Grocery Company stock certificate."

With four stores Wood found it necessary to establish an office and bookkeeping department. Therefore, the Company's first general office was established in late 1939. It was a 25' x 50' relatively crude sheet metal building located near the railroad tracks just off East Front Street in Tyler. It was devoid of heating and running water. The floors were covered with cardboard to keep the cold air from coming through the cracks in the winter. It was heated with clay bricks filled with charcoal—a means commonly used in those days to charcoal meats. Pat Prestwood once commented, "Since our office was located at the railroad tracks, it became convenient for railroad tramps who traveled the rails to sleep under the office at night using cardboard from the railroad boxcars for beds." In addition to serving as the central office, the building was also used as a surplus dry-grocery storage for the Company stores. In this modest building, as primitive as it seems to modern standards, Wood Brookshire managed to set up his first office.

The *Tyler-Courier Times Telegraph* newspaper featured the following editorial about BGC in 1933: "Efficient merchandising methods, alertness and a unique understanding of the public's needs and desires pushed the firm already to the top, and one store after another appeared in East Texas with the name 'Brookshire' above the doorway.

"Now the firm is moving its headquarters store into an edifice worthy of the business traditions on which its greatness is built, a handsome stone-faced structure at South Broadway and East Front carrying the most modern features of construction and arrangement—a credit to all Texas.

Brookshire Grocery Company original store managers and stockholders. (Left to right) C.B. Hardin, Pat Prestwood, Zack Nutt and Jewel Mauldin.

"Wood Brookshire, a young man in years but old in his wisdom of his chosen calling, is one of the businessmen who are the genius of growing Tyler. He has identified himself with the life of the city and the city wishes him well in his new surroundings. His example is worth much to the future of the community." This editorial from the *Tyler Courier-Times Telegraph* may have said it best as to why the Company saw so much success in the 1930s decade.

During the later 1930s Bruce and Woody were growing up

as youngsters and soon assisted in their dad's stores. Wood had a great ambition to become a better father to his sons and to give them the opportunity for growth in the food industry.

The Company slogan in the 1930s was **"The Best for Less."**

Some food innovations of the 1930s were Bisquick, Ritz Crackers, Nestles Chocolate Chips and Kraft Macaroni & Cheese. According to General Mills, Bisquick was invented in 1930 after one of their top sales executives met an innovative dining car chef on a business trip. The chef stored his pre-mixed biscuit batter on ice in the kitchen, enabling him to make fresh biscuits quickly on the train every day. General Mills developed the idea, and Bisquick started appearing on grocers' shelves in 1931.

Average Cost of Grocery Items in the Mid-1930s

Bread (lb)	$0.12
Eggs (doz)	$0.18
Bananas (4 lbs)	$0.19
Milk (gal)	$0.26
Bacon (lb)	$0.37
Sugar (5 lb)	$0.49

INSIGHTS INTO WOOD T. BROOKSHIRE:

Quotes from Former Brookshire Grocery Company Partners

"Mr. Brookshire taught me to be a man. He set a good example of being tough but very fair. He asked me to do a good job and expected that from me. He challenged me to always try to do something good for people and especially for our customers. Mr. Wood said, 'If anyone comes into the store and wants anything for my church, you let them have it.'"

"I remember Mr. and Mrs. Brookshire would attend our annual gathering at the Recreation Park. He always thanked us warehouse and transportation workers and always made us feel special. He would always say how he built his institution with his God-given endowed gifts, with great people and his vision for success. He always challenged us to give our best and the best would be returned to us."

CHAPTER 4

Enduring World War II

Following the economic depression of the 1930s, the 1940s brought about the greatest change and biggest growth that the retail food industry had ever experienced. However, when 1942 arrived, the nation was still shocked over Japan's surprise attack that bombed and devastated Pearl Harbor on December 7, 1941. Now suddenly our country was engulfed in World War II. President Franklin D. Roosevelt summed it up when he gave his famous radio speech about "a day that will live in infamy." Immediately, sadness, shock and sorrow penetrated our nation, engulfing everyone in a sense of disbelief.

Wood and his four leaders, and the nation as a whole, pondered and worried about what effects the war was going to have on our nation. Locally, Wood told his leaders, "Boys, I have no idea what the effects of the war will be on our grocery business. However, I know it's time for us to gear up now that we have a war to win and a challenge to serve and take care of our customers through the tough times ahead."

The civic leaders of the cities of Tyler and Longview came to the rescue by making a vigorous and determined effort for the government to locate an army-training center in this area of East Texas. Their effort was rewarded when the announcement came that such a center named Camp Fannin Texas, a World War II Army infantry replacement camp and a German prisoner-of-war Internment Camp, would be constructed between the two cities. The training center was named in honor of Colonel James Walker Fannin of the Texian Army of the Republic of Texas. He was a hero during the Texas Revolution's battle at the Goliad massacre on March 27, 1836.

Construction on Camp Fannin began on December 1, 1942, on 14,000 acres of wooded hills 12 miles east of Tyler on U.S. Highway 271. Local retail businesses in the Tyler area immediately began to get a boost when construction workers started arriving. Many of the building materials were purchased locally. Almost 3,000 civilians worked on the camp's construction at an estimated cost of $5 million.

Even before the camp was completed, soldiers could be seen in downtown Tyler and the surrounding Tyler area. Barracks were yet to be completed at the camp, so the soldiers were housed in the Blackstone Hotel, Alamo Courts Motel and the Bluebonnet Courts Motel. During this period Tyler Commercial College provided army staff radio-operation training as a Signal Corps school to over 2,000 army staff between April 1942 and July 1943. A local resident said soldiers could be seen downtown near Brookshire's Store #1, marching down to and from Tyler Commercial College and the Blackstone Hotel.

Construction on the camp was completed in the spring of 1943. Camp Fannin employed approximately 30,000 civilians from 1943 to 1946, many of them new Tyler residents. Hundreds of people moved to Tyler to live, especially wives whose husbands were permanently stationed at Camp Fannin. This created a greater demand for eating establishments and for food stores, giving grocery stores like Brookshire's a boost in sales.

The camp was in operation from May 29, 1943, until it was converted to a separation center and declared surplus in January 1946. It had trained more than 200,000 soldiers during the three-year span. At any one time there were about 30,000 to 40,000 soldiers going through infantry training.

A *Tyler Morning Telegraph* article recalled in 1944 how one of the thousands of soldiers who received their basic training at Camp Fannin before being shipped overseas to Europe claimed that Texas was so hot "you could fry an egg on the cement." In addition to the heat, trainees had to adjust to high humidity, ticks and chiggers.

Camp Fannin functioned like a city with its own activities. It had a movie theater, a library, a newspaper, the Service Men's Recreation Center, a football team and the Station Hospital with beds for 1,074 patients. Tyler area musicians, acting civilians and Camp Fannin soldiers jointly produced several camp musicals. During the war several movie stars and musicians entertained at Camp Fannin.

One of the favorite family pasttimes in the 1940s was "Sunday Driving." Families would load up in their car and head out to local places for a leisurely afternoon. One of the enjoyable drives was to do an auto tour of Camp Fannin on the certain Sunday afternoons that tours were offered. The camp supplied a World War II Tour brochure that mapped a self-guided driving tour.

After the war ended, many of the veterans who received training at Camp Fannin returned to Tyler to live, some returning because they thought East Texas was an ideal place to live and raise a family. Others returned because they had sweethearts or wives living here. Business opportunities attracted others.

During the war many items that had been a part of Americans' daily lives were completely absent. In order to fairly distribute food, the government implemented rationing. Beginning in the spring of 1942, Americans were unable to purchase sugar without government-issued coupons. Then vouchers for coffee were issued in November. By the spring of 1943, meat, cheese, fats, canned milk, canned fish and several other processed foods were on the list of rationed foods. Several non-grocery items were also rationed including gas, tires, nylons, silk, bicycles and typewriters.

Ultimately during the war every American was issued a series of numbered "War Ration Books" and could buy only an allotted amount of the rationed items. During this time, a person could not buy a rationed item without giving the grocer the proper stamp for the item from the ration book.

The shortages and rationing during the war made for very

hard times in the grocery business; however, Brookshire's store managers provided better customer service than the larger food chains. C.B. Hardin, store manager in Tyler, described it this way: "During the war it was about as hectic as it could possibly be trying to run a grocery store. The shortages of merchandise, regulations, rationing and shortage of labor all made it quite difficult."

On many occasions during the period of government rationing, Brookshire's store managers helped the people who really needed the rationed products the most, especially young mothers with small children and the elderly. Zack Nutt, store manager in Longview, also made a comment about the shortages and rationing. He said, "We would put some items back like bacon and coffee for our regular customers. If they hadn't been able to get in the store when the items first came in, we felt we had to take care of them. We used to save canned milk and baby food for babies. I still have people come up to me and thank me for saving things for them during the war."

Ela Sheppard, who opened her Flowers by Ela flower shop in Tyler in 1941, continually praised Wood Brookshire for taking care of her and her young baby during the war. "Mr. Brookshire saved me rationed canned milk for my baby. He knew about how much I needed per week, and he'd always have it saved in the storeroom for me when I shopped for my weekly groceries. I don't know how I could have made it through those tough times without him." Wood once said, "It's not one big thing we do for our customers, but the thousands of little things."

During World War II the nation survived mandatory

rationing for the greater good of allowing resources to the war effort. Most Americans didn't complain about the conditions they were experiencing, realizing that during wartime everyone had to sacrifice and pull together for the good of our country.

The war brought lasting progress to Texas and to Tyler. Downtown Tyler was often crowded, especially on weekends, with hundreds of off-duty G.I.s creating a demand for refreshments, food, groceries and entertainment. A Tyler resident said, "It wasn't unusual to see soldiers and their wives shopping regularly for groceries in the Brookshire store." They also had downtown entertainment with five movie theaters around "the Square"—the Tyler, the Liberty, the Majestic, the Arcadia and the Palace.

With the discovery of oil and the establishment of Camp Fannin in the 1940s, the Great Depression seemed to have faded into memory. Tyler's population grew from 28,279 in 1940 and then to 38,968 in 1950, adding additional grocery shoppers.

The 1940s gave birth to the shopping center concept. In February 1949, Bergfeld Shopping Center, located one and three-fourth miles from downtown Tyler—just off South Broadway—had its grand opening. According to Julius L. Bergfeld Jr. in an October 14, 2017, article in the *Tyler Morning Telegraph*, his grandfather, J.A. Bergfeld, envisioned developing a shopping center outside of Tyler's downtown patterned after Highland Park Village in Dallas, which was built in the 1930s. His great-grandfather Rudolph owned the land. A first of its kind for Tyler, Bergfeld Center became the second oldest shopping center in the state and the oldest in East Texas.

According to Julius, J.A. was one of the local leaders who felt Tyler should grow to the south. At that time, the area at the south end of town was known as the airport. The era of aviation had begun in Tyler after World War I when an Air Corp veteran kept a landing strip and small bi-plane on a grassy field between Donnybrook and Broadway Avenues, just south of Bergfeld Center. He took passengers for small flights over the city.

In January 1949, on a 65-acre tract of land considered to be out "in the country," J.A. built Bergfeld Shopping Center with two buildings running along both sides of east Eighth Street just off South Broadway. As a five-year-old child, Julius also recalled the excitement of opening night and compared it to a "carnival atmosphere" where everyone in town came to see.

Also opening in January of 1949 was Brookshire's Store #9, one of the first retail stores in the Bergfeld Shopping Center. Brookshire Grocery Company has had a store in the center ever since. The *Tyler Morning Telegraph* grand opening advertisement read, "Tyler's Newest, Largest and Most Modern Food Store." Wood Brookshire took a gamble or perhaps another leap of faith by venturing out to a new, unproven shopping center away from downtown and near a cemetery. While the new store was under construction, Wood looked across the street at the Rose Hill Cemetery and told three of his leaders, "This new store out here may be where we bury ourselves." Fortunately, this statement was far from true because the store became one of the leading stores in the Company.

As the 1940s began, BGC had 35 employees and the future looked brighter than ever for the Company. Recognizing the potential for additional growth, Wood hired Edward M. "Mr. Eddy" Mayes as his first office employee. Mr. Eddy later became the Company's first secretary-treasurer. He was affectionately called "The man who signs the checks." Wood praised Mr. Eddy by saying, "I have hired the right man for the job."

During the 1940s the supermarket concept achieved great success, and many new inventions were released. It was during this decade that the fluorescent tube lights tripled the lighting in the Brookshire stores. They were first publicly displayed at the Chicago World's Fair in 1939. Before the 1940s the food stores were lit with a few globed incandescent light bulbs.

Another essential equipment development for supermarkets was the shopping cart with baskets and wheels. The new cart permitted portability of larger purchases. The new concept came about one night in 1936 when Sylvan Goldman, owner of the Humpty Dumpty supermarkets in Oklahoma City, invented the design of the two-basket grocery shopping cart that became popular in the 1940s. He took a wooden folding chair and placed a basket on the seat and another basket under the chair. He then put wheels on the legs, coming up with the idea of a shopping cart that would enable customers to move more groceries. From that idea, he and a mechanic designed the first metal shopping cart with two removable baskets.

At the time, some considered the new invention a "flop" because only the elderly used them. In an interview Goldman said, "I went to our biggest store—there wasn't a soul using our new basket carrier, despite the fact that an attractive girl was posted at the entrance offering the new cart. The housewives, most of 'em, decided no more carts for me. I have been pushing the baby carriages, and I don't want to push anymore. At each store where carts were available I installed a covey of young middle-aged men and women. I instructed them to wander about incognito, filling their folding carriers. I told this young lady that was offering carts to customers to say, 'Look everybody is using them—why not you?' She did, and they did."

Still another equipment development during this decade was the improved heavy duty National cash register. It featured itemization with a stub receipt, serving as an adding machine and cash register. This new register gave the Brookshire customers more confidence because now they had a receipt. The early nickel, bronze and marble mechanical cash registers did not give receipts. The employee was required to ring up every transaction, and when the total key was pushed, the drawer would open, and a bell would ring on the register indicating the transaction was complete.

In the late 1940s male checkers began to appear behind the check stands manning the new cash registers in the early BGC grocery stores. Later, female checkers became the primary checkout people in the stores.

A past BGC publication mentioned that a checker is the best good-will ambassador in the Company's retail stores. She's the come in-er, the comeback-er, the hello-er, the goodbye-er, the greet-er, the meet-er, the smile-er or the I haven't seen you in a long while-er. A checker is the name know-er, an item show-er, a trash stow-er and a buggy tow-er.

A checker is an old man pleaser, a kid teaser, a Coke lugger, a neck hugger, a cart shover, a people lover, a penny saver, a hand shaker, a sack flopper, a gripe stopper, and a knee knocker when she thinks she might have made a mistake. A checker's being on "center-stage" in view of the public is not an occasional thing for BGC checkers—it's an all-the-time thing!

Needless to say, the 1940s was productive and exciting, yet a trying time in the history of BGC. Despite the war, one of the turning points of BGC's history occurred in the 1940s when five additional stores were added with locations in Tyler, Longview, Winnsboro, Gladewater and Kilgore, bringing the total stores in BGC to nine.

Post-war Tyler was recovering from the war, and families began enjoying fun times together when a major entertainment attraction had its grand opening in September 1947. It was the Star-Lite, Tyler's first drive-in theater. The open-air attraction was located on the Old Kilgore Highway (East Erwin Street) opposite Stewart Airport.

The grand opening advertisement stated, "Bring all the family out and let 'em see a movie under the stars at East Texas's largest drive-in theater." The theater was equipped with 465 in-car speakers. The advertisement further read, "Just put the speakers in your car and turn the sound to your desire. All grounds are hard-topped. No mud! No dust!"

The Company slogan in the 1940s was **"The Best Food for Less."**

Some food innovations of the 1940s were Cheerios, M&M's, Nutella and corn dogs. M&M's were first made in 1942 for American soldiers in World War II. They were ideal for the soldiers since M&M's did not melt easily, withstanding various climates. During World War II there was a shortage of cocoa, but there was a plentiful supply of hazelnuts. Therefore, pairing the cocoa with hazelnuts and creating Nutella was a unique way of extending the use of chocolate.

Average Cost of Grocery Items in the Mid-1940s

Bread (lb)	$0.10
Milk (gal)	$0.26
Coffee (lb)	$0.34
Sugar (5 lbs)	$0.38
Bacon (lb)	$0.53
Eggs (doz)	$0.59

Insights into Wood T. Brookshire:

Quotes from Former Brookshire Grocery Company Partners

"Mr. Brookshire taught me to practice kindness and understanding"

"Mr. Brookshire believed that fairness should be practiced with everyone who did business with the Company."

"To me, Mr. Brookshire was one very down-to-earth, nice guy. He had the ability to visit with anyone regardless of their age, race or background."

"Mr. Brookshire would visit our Store #9 at 9 a.m. every Saturday morning. He would circle around the store and spit tobacco on the floor. He would come back to the store about one hour later to see if anyone had cleaned up the tobacco. Of course, the floor had been cleaned because the store manager would ask one of us employees to go find the spot and clean it up as soon as Mr. Brookshire left the store."

CHAPTER 5

Rocking and Rolling

By the 1950s, the population in the nation was really booming and moving forward mainly due to the "baby boom." The transition to supermarkets was complete, and the migration to shopping centers had begun. It was in the 1950s that there was an extreme growth in supermarkets and one of the most revolutionary changes in the grocery industry. The supermarket became an American symbol, reflecting America's characteristics of innovation, opportunity, efficiency, variety and abundance.

Locally, the 1950s were seen as a growth time for Brookshire Grocery Company, and by the end of the decade, seven more bright new Brookshire stores had opened in Texas. Mr. Wood's words of wisdom were, "The success and leadership we now enjoy have been built upon more genuine, friendly service to those who honor us by visiting our stores more than any competitor in our field. Our slogan is 'Better Foods For Less,' and it is our aim and purpose to make this slogan a vital, living reality."

Throughout this decade, BGC introduced significant changes in stores, which reflected the move towards more innovation and efficiency. The new stores were larger and offered air-conditioning, ample parking, more self-service sections, larger frozen food sections, expanded self-service meat departments and new streamlined equipment. They also had automatic doors, in-store music, electrically lighted exterior store signs, free parking and check cashing services for customers.

The stores were also designed with eight large glass front windows that accommodated huge silk-screened signs featuring items on sale. Sixteen large 3-1/2'x4-1/2' paper window signs, completely covering the large windows, were sent via company trucks to each store twice a week. One set of signs contained the Monday-Wednesday advertised special items, and the second set contained the Thursday-Saturday specials, corresponding with the bi-weekly newspaper advertisements. The window signs could be printed on seven different colors of paper with as many as six different colors of ink.

BGC's distribution center had a unique window sign area where the large signs were sketched, stenciled and printed using a silkscreen process. On a normal run during the 1950s, around 650 sheets of paper per week were sent out to the stores; however, on occasions as many as 1,400 signs promoting grand opening and special promotions were sent out during a period of a week. Signs were removed on Saturday night at closing since all of the stores were closed on Sunday.

Wood Brookshire, affectionately known as the "Cotton Picker" from a farm in Angelina County, Texas, was experiencing, along with other supermarket owners, a growth in super marketing that was considered to be the most revolutionary and constructive change in any business at any time. After the war, the popularity of automobiles in many households created a greater demand for additional store parking.

In the 1950s the shopping cart greatly improved. The new design consisted of a bigger basket cart with a baby seat, drink holder and plastic on the handles. The popularity of the new designed shopping cart caught the attention of Queen Elizabeth and Prince Philip when the English royal couple was in Washington in 1957 on a Royal Tour visiting President Eisenhower. They toured a supermarket in nearby Maryland. The shopping cart with the collapsible little seat amused the Queen. It was reported that she said, "It is particularly nice to be able to bring your children here." Having more children in the supermarkets changed branding, creating a new wave of placing food items at kids' eye level to help woo their parents to purchase.

After graduating from Tyler High School, Bruce Brookshire (Wood's oldest son) attended the New Mexico Military Institute, a public Junior College in Roswell, New Mexico. His additional education included attending The University of Texas at Austin. It was at The University of Texas that he met his future wife, Peaches Parker. They were married August 30, 1950. Thereafter, Bruce interrupted his education to come home to Tyler to work alongside his father and his younger brother Woody, who had also decided to end his college education and take leadership roles in the family grocery business. They both had years of experience that began when they were youngsters.

Bruce started his grocery career as a young boy, working in the back room of one of his dad's stores where his duties included "plucking chickens" and sweeping floors. Bruce was named store manager of BGC's Store #10 in Corsicana, Texas in 1951.

Woody started his grocery career as a clean-up boy and sack boy at one of the Tyler stores. He graduated from Tyler High School, attended the New Mexico Military Institute, Tyler Junior College, The University of Texas at Austin, Trinity University and Michigan State University. He was a staff sergeant in the United States Air Force, serving in the Korean Conflict. Woody married Ann Howard just after she graduated from Southern Methodist University in 1953. He served as assistant manager and store manager of Store #12 in Marshall, Texas, in 1956-1957. He then was promoted to a district manager.

When Bruce and Woody joined the Company in the early 1950s, three active Brookshire men were leaders in the Company and on the board. In order to avoid the confusion of addressing the three Mr. Brookshires, company partners started calling them by first names—Mr. Wood, Mr. Bruce and Mr. Woody. It certainly made things simpler!

A produce warehouse was set up in 1951 in a rented building separate from the office and dry storage building. Prior to the 1950s the Brookshire stores were stocking mainly local seasonal produce and bananas. Beginning in the 50s, the

Company's produce buyer would take the produce orders from each store, purchase the produce at the Dallas market and sort the items according to each individual store's order. Then he hauled the fresh local, regional, and national produce to the rented warehouse and shipped it via truck to each individual store.

In 1953 BGC hit a milestone with the opening of its first warehouse on the corner of Front and Dean Streets in downtown Tyler. The new facility included an office area and dry grocery and fresh produce warehouses. The Dean Street building was conveniently located adjacent to the railroad track, an important factor since the majority of dry groceries was being shipped by rail.

The first Brookshire Grocery Company produce and grocery warehouses and office built in Tyler in 1953 on East Front Street and Dean Street.

This Dean Street location is where I joined the Company in 1958 after graduating from The University of Texas at Austin. I immediately became aware that Mr. Brookshire had great faith in the honesty of people, and he believed that fairness should be practiced with everyone who did business with the Company—customers, vendors and employees. When Mr. Wood was interviewing me for a job in advertising, he emphasized, "Always remember when dealing with others that we want every penny due us; however, if you accept a cent that is not due us, you will be fired."

This move to the new location reduced operating costs and lowered the price of goods in the retail stores. Jewel Mauldin, a pioneer store manager and stockholder, commented, "The warehouse offered our company a big advantage. At the time, we were almost forced to put in our own warehouse to be competitive. Another company pretty much had a monopoly, and we couldn't get a good variety of goods...when we could, we had to pay a high price."

The new produce warehouse allowed the Company to maintain a higher standard of quality of fresh fruits and vegetables. Bananas are a good example of maintaining quality. A lot goes into getting bananas into the customer's hands when they are just right. A lot of people are involved in this process. In the 1950s BGC's warehouse purchased bananas from the United Fruit Company located in New Orleans. Later in the 1970s, BGC purchased bananas from the Dole Banana Company, one of the world's largest suppliers of bananas. At that time, Brookshire trucks picked up the bananas in Gulf Port, Mississippi.

Depending on the time of the year, the bananas came from three different Central America countries: Ecuador, Guatemala or Costa Rica. In the 1950s, after the stalks of unripe bananas were harvested and washed, they were placed in large wooden boxes for shipment on cargo container ships to New Orleans and via trucks to Brookshire's warehouse in Tyler.

The banana boxes were personalized with the Brookshire's logo. In later years these wooden boxes were replaced with cardboard boxes. During this shipping process the bananas were kept at 55 degrees.

Brookshire's received the green bananas about 10 days after they were harvested. Since the bananas were still green, forced ripening was required. At the Brookshire produce warehouse they were placed in temperature-controlled rooms for five to seven days. As long as the temperature was kept at 55 degrees, the bananas didn't begin their ripening process. Ethylene gas and hydrocarbons were fed into the rooms, which triggered the ripening of the bananas. The temperature was turned up to 62 degrees for 24 hours before the bananas were delivered to the stores. Occasionally, one of the boxes of bananas would arrive with a surprise tucked away in it—a colorful snake that had made its journey all the way from Central America!

The new grocery warehouse replaced wholesale grocery salesmen who took orders at each individual store. BGC could now buy in large quantities directly from the packer or manufacturer like the larger grocery chains in the U.S. The grocery warehouse also made it possible to have more control on the pricing structure and created a more efficient delivery system to the stores. At the time it was assumed the new facility could serve fifty retail stores. Within a decade this assumption was proven incorrect.

Approximately ten people worked in the new dry grocery warehouse in 1957. The starting salary for a five-and-one-half-day workweek, or when work was completed, was $1.00 per hour. Five days were spent unloading railroad boxcars, stacking the merchandise in the warehouse, filling orders for the retail stores on four-wheeled carts and loading the merchandise on the trucks. This work was done by hand. No machinery was available. Some of the warehouse merchandise was heavy, like a 24-can case of No. 2 ½ canned peaches, Gaines 60-pound bag of dog food and Imperial Sugar's 60-pound sacks. Brad Brookshire, chairman and CEO said, "As a youngster I can remember going to the old warehouse in downtown Tyler and seeing bales of sugar stacked to the high ceiling."

The corrugated tin warehouse was cold in the winter and hot in the summer. One employee said that every Saturday morning the warehouse crew used red floor sweeps and brooms to "sweep every inch" of the warehouse. Payday in the warehouse was at the end of the day on Friday afternoons. The warehouse manager recorded by hand the names and hours worked by each employee in a ledger notebook.

In the mid-fifties BGC started honoring all full-time employees with a special Christmas gift check in December. This was set up as a "usual custom," but not a policy of the Company. The gift check to the employees was based on length of service and salary. In a 1960 letter attached to each Christmas gift check, Mr. Wood stated, "This is another way we have of dividing with you the fruits of our labors together—another way we have of expressing to you our gratitude for the application of your God-given talents for the advancement of Brookshire's Food Stores in your community." This annual Christmas gift check has been awarded to partners every December since its inception.

By the end of the 1950s, BGC had expanded to 16 stores located in 11 cities throughout Northeast Texas. At this time there were almost 400 employees and ten BGC stockholders, including Wood and his two sons. Later BGC began calling its employees "partners" because they joined each other as a team in sharing risks and profits of the Company.

The Company slogan in the 1950s was **"Better Foods For Less."**

Some food innovations of the 1950s were Minute Rice, Ore-Ida frozen potato products, Duncan Hines Cake Mix, Kraft Cheese Wiz, Swanson TV Dinners and Jif Peanut Butter. According to General Foods Corp., Minute Rice was invented in 1941 when Ataullah Ozai Durrani took a portable stove to the office of one of their executives. He cooked the rice he had invented in 60 seconds!

AVERAGE COST OF GROCERY ITEMS IN THE MID-1950s

Bread (lb)	$0.16
Milk (1/2 gal)	$0.48
Sugar (5 lbs)	$0.52
Bacon (lb)	$0.65
Eggs (doz)	$0.67
Coffee (lb)	$0.87

INSIGHTS INTO WOOD T. BROOKSHIRE

Quotes from Former Brookshire Grocery Company Partners

"Mr. Brookshire always dressed in a dark suit and tie and conducted semi-annual business meetings with store managers. Traditionally, after a prayer, he stood before us with his right hand tucked in his buttoned coat. He recognized top achievers by asking all store managers who had experienced a 3% increase in sales to stand, while the underachievers sat quietly thinking, 'I'm going to be standing next time'! One of his favorite challenges to us store managers would be, 'I want you boys to get out there and fight your competition until you are as shitty as a bull.'"

"Mr. Brookshire cautioned me, 'Son don't mess with the help or with my money, and you can work for me as long as you want to.'"

"Mr. Brookshire was a wonderful, wonderful guy whether he was dressed in a business suit and tie or his casual khakis."

CHAPTER 6

A New Era

The Sixties saw the assassinations of President John F. Kennedy, U.S. Attorney General Robert F. Kennedy and Civil Rights leader Martin Luther King Jr., as well as the Vietnam War, the Civil Rights Protests and the Cuban Crisis. The Cuban Crisis was created in 1962 when the Soviet Union (USSR) began building medium-range nuclear-armed missile sites in Cuba, less than 100 miles from our Florida shores. This crisis was seen by America as one of the most important confrontations in the Cold War that existed at that time. We came close to a nuclear war. On October 22, 1962, President John F. Kennedy went on national television and told the American people he had ordered a blockade of Cuba. The blockade was to prevent the Soviet Union from completing a shipment to Cuba of parts for ballistic missiles that could strike the U.S. This action created a tense time during a thirteen-day political and military standoff.

As the crisis developed, there was a rush on batteries, guns and groceries. Some Americans both nationally and locally started stockpiling groceries in the event of a war with Russia. Some thought that the extra groceries in their homes could be a means of survival if a war occurred. Of course, this helped volume in Brookshire Grocery Company stores. Most people were shocked and depressed about the situation and did nothing or didn't know what to do!

Ten Brookshire partners, including me. and all the members of the 49th Armored Division of the Texas National Guard were called to active duty in October of 1961 when their division was mobilized. BGC held our jobs until we returned. Our government considered this a time of emergency when the security of our country was at stake. One of the men said, "The communists insist that our way of life must collapse. We must all do our best to help protect our freedom."

This dangerous conflict ended when an agreement was met between the two superpowers. The Soviet Union agreed to remove the Soviet missiles from Cuba, and America agreed not to invade Cuba. After a scare, the grocery business went back to normal, and the deployed partners went back to work.

The first issue of "Brookshire Briefs," a publication, or "house-organ," published by and for the employees of BGC appeared on June 10, 1960. It was printed on one simple sheet of 8 ½"x11" paper, moving to an 8 1/2"x13" format in 1963. The Company did not have a printing press, so the "Briefs" was printed on a mimeograph machine, a popular duplicating machine that produced copies from a stencil, now superseded by a photocopier.

In keeping with BGC's strong Christian beliefs and the fact that a prayer opens every BGC meeting, the early issues of the "Briefs" contained a Bible scripture verse under a "Strength from the Bible" heading. The "Briefs" were published for many years until the name was changed and the partner publication was renamed "Off The Shelf," then, "The Core."

Since the Company began in 1928, BGC partners were required to sign in and out in a "Time Book" kept in each store and office department. This book was used to calculate the hours a partner worked each week in order for the Company to pay him or her. This problem was solved in October 1963, when the Company installed time clocks in all 20 stores, the general office, the grocery warehouse and the produce warehouse. Using the time clocks, BGC's payroll system was completely automated, offering faster service to all partners. Partners were excited because they considered this a giant step into the technology age!

Courtesy Clerks ("Sack Boys") in white shirts and black bow ties in the 1960s.

The Sixties was also a decade when the American housewife, and indeed the entire world, had given the stamp of approval on the supermarket. Self-service had become a more cost-effective means of retailing in grocery stores, and the shopping experience was improved by additional refrigeration and the use of packaging materials like polyethylene. The self-service concept had proven itself with efficiency, sales, profitability and manageability. In addition, the packaging of items in the supermarkets began to feature attention-getting designs, helping increase their sales.

"A company is like a tomato," Wood Brookshire once said. "When it gets ripe it ceases to grow. The only process nature had developed for a ripe tomato is the rotting process. When a company gets ripe, it gets complacent. We must grow to avoid that." Proving what he preached, the decade of the Sixties saw the greatest expansion the Company had ever experienced with the addition of 15 retail stores and the replacement or remodeling of an additional eight stores.

One of these "new" stores was an old building in a small East Texas downtown store with limited square footage. Sometimes opening a Brookshire's store in an old location was a way to enter a new market while a new store was planned for the town. One day a checker in this old store yelled for the store manager and said, "Come to the front quick. A lady has her foot hung in the floor." Sure enough, the customer had her high heel wedged into a hole in the old concrete floor. The store manager had to remove her foot from the shoe in order to free the shoe! This is typical of why the Company had plans to eventually replace old stores with new buildings.

Also, BGC took a monumental step and investment in 1961 by crossing the state line and opening two stores in Shreveport, Louisiana. One was Store #17, the first store outside of Texas, and 33 days later Store #18 opened. It took courage for the Company to move into the Shreveport market with several established supermarkets already in the city. The Company didn't become successful overnight. It took time to build the business, getting the Brookshire name before the people.

Years later, Bruce Brookshire recalled, "When we entered Shreveport, those first two stores lost more money than our very best eight stores made. We were fifth in the share of market in Shreveport, but we were determined to stay with it. We are now first in share of the Shreveport market because of our devotion to excellence." Today Shreveport is one of the greatest markets that BGC operates in.

A partner at #18 in Shreveport wrote, "Since I joined the Company in October I have learned to love, honor, respect and work for Brookshire Food Stores. Each morning, as I pass the site where our new store is being constructed, a feeling of happiness and pride occurs to know that I am a part of this wonderful organization. That can truly be felt. I do not wish to be just a number of a group, but I want to know and realize that I have a job to do in helping my company expand to the highest."

In 1965, a "How I Win Customers and Increase Sales" company-wide partner contest was held. Excerpts from the four winners were:

"I see Mr. Brookshire in his humble beginning some thirty-eight years ago. When a person would come into his store, he would treat that person in a true and genuine manner—not a pretending attitude. My smile, my hello and my willingness to serve must come from a heart that really means it. A customer can tell when I am sincere, and she can tell when I am just going through a formality. Our thoughts should be, 'Not what this store can do for me, but what can I do for this store and its customers.'"

"I try to know the majority of our customers by name. In extending my departing invitation to the customer to come again, I try to put a sincere meaning behind it. Being neat, clean and well-groomed is also a helpful aid in winning customers. Cleanliness in the store is an essential must in keeping customers and in helping increase sales."

"I must always feel that satisfying each and every customer who walks in the door every day is my most important reason for being there. By doing this I must be courteous, friendly and pleasant—not just sometimes but each time I see them. I must cultivate the habit of remembering names with faces, not only the ones who buy the most, but also to the ones I don't see in the store very often."

"The question has been asked, 'How do you win customers and increase your sales?' At our store we use courtesy, friendliness and a real feeling that we want to serve folks who shop in our store. Instead of making the customer feel we 'expect' them to shop with us, we make them feel at home and pleased that they shopped with us."

BGC's 34th anniversary was celebrated in September 1962. In a message to all partners Wood Brookshire stated, "It is my hope that all the days that lie ahead will be filled with a full measure of God's richest blessings as have the past 34 years." He continued, "This 34th anniversary has been made possible by all of us using our God-given talents as partners working and growing together. The promise of tomorrow is in our hands. I have often made you the promise that if you give Brookshire's the best that you have, the best will come back to you."

BGC's stores had doubled in square footage over the past 20 years and were now averaging approximately 15,000 to 16,000 square feet. The demand for new items hitting the market had also increased, with store inventories now consisting of 5,000 to 7,000-plus items. The Company was "bursting at the seams" and had outgrown its warehousing space that it had secured only 15 years earlier on Dean Street in Tyler.

In 1967, after much travel, research and inspections of the most efficient and modern supermarket warehousing facilities in the United States, the Company started construction on the 175,000 square-foot distribution center located on 35 acres of land on Loop 323 in south Tyler. The southern portion of Loop 323 had been completed in 1958. The BGC complex included a 26,000 square-foot section to house the general offices. At the time, this location was considered to be on the outskirts of the city.

The gigantic move of the warehouses and office across town involved moving millions of product units and took over a month to accomplish relocating the merchandise, machinery and employees. Dry groceries and produce inventories were built up at the new center, while those at the old warehouse on Dean Street were depleted. It could possibly be considered the largest move in East Texas history.

One of the produce employees said, "To illustrate the magnitude of the moving task, one must consider the problem of handling and moving bananas, just one of those 6,000 items to be moved. The new warehouse had six specially designed banana rooms, each built to house the fruit from the green to the ripening stages. The six rooms contained a total of about 120,000 pounds of bananas or about a quarter of a million individual bananas."

In a booklet describing the new facility Mr. Wood stated, "We of Brookshire's are deeply grateful for the support of our friends, loyal customers and fellow employees which has made this new distribution center necessary and possible. This structure was designed and built to meet the food needs of our customers at the lowest cost possible. We humbly dedicate this new center to the God of our creation and to friends, customers and employees. It expresses fully our confidence in the present and future of the beloved areas we serve."

During the 1960s most of the dry grocery shipments, especially the heavy items, were delivered to the new warehouse inside Cotton Belt Railway boxcars. Cotton Belt had a spur track that ran directly into the warehouse, accommodating eight boxcars at one time. The boxcars, which were protected from the weather, made unloading in a controlled environment much more pleasant for the Brookshire partners. It took the

Cotton Belt trainmen from one to two hours to do the switching in and out of the full and empty boxcars. Throughout the 1960s and 1970s the added growth of truck transportation, aided by the billions of dollars in federal funding spent on the Interstate highways system led to the decline of railroad transportation of goods to BGC in the 1970s to 1980s. Therefore, the rail tracks were removed from inside the warehouse.

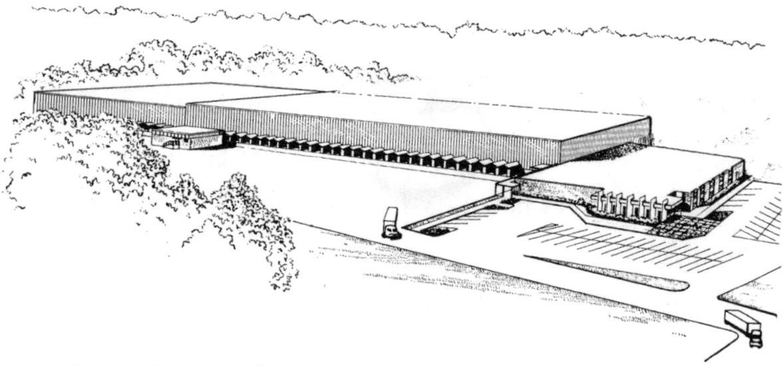

Completed Tyler Distribution Center with Brookshire's Corporate Office on Loop 323 in Tyler, 1969.

In this new warehouse the break room was a place for partners to relax, visit, and have a Coke or cup of coffee. The break room was always filled with talking and laughing and groups playing dominoes. Traditionally, when two teams of two sat down and begin slapping dominoes on the table as fast as they could count, a domino game was about to begin. The games were usually loud and very exciting as each player used various slang words and phrases during the contest. Even though the slang was very humorous, each player's expression showed his seriousness about the game.

Rivalry between teams of the warehouse domino players

continued to grow stronger each year. Bragging on his domino playing, one of the players commented, “I’m the greatest. I never get tired of winning.” He jokingly added, “There needs to be a domino school around here because I would send them both to learn how to play.”

One of his opponents then responded, “I’m the best, and I enjoy playing you two boys because you’re so easy to beat.”

One player said, “Playing dominoes is very relaxing, helps me to concentrate better and serves as a fantastic pastime enjoyment.” Needless to say, when you walked by the break room, you could hear a lot of commotion. The noise was just the domino players having a friendly game during their short break time.

In the 1950s Mr. Brookshire would regularly visit the dry grocery warehouse on Dean Street. He would make his rounds checking on the warehouse and visiting with all of the employees. During lunchtime the employees often removed the handle from one of the flatbed four-wheeled warehouse carts, creating a temporary domino table since the old warehouse did not have a breakroom. On many occasions, Mr. Brookshire felt right at home sitting down and joining the group for a good competitive game of 42 or dominoes. He had a regular partner he called the “snuff dipper.”

Heretofore the Company had been held together for 41 years by the leadership and strength of a great man, the head of the Brookshire family and the controlling stockholder of the Company. In March 1969, 41 years after he opened his first store, in a shift of leadership, Wood T. Brookshire resigned as president, becoming chairman of the board of Brookshire Grocery Company. Bruce G. Brookshire, Wood's eldest son, was promoted to president of the Company, and Wood's youngest son, S.W. (Woody) Brookshire, was promoted to executive vice president.

In an excerpt from the speech delivered by Mr. Wood in 1969, when he moved from company president to chairman of the board, he said, " I have in my feeble way endeavored to build a foundation upon which you can grow and expand this business to the limits and beyond this United States. I firmly believe, with the team you have developed, you can safely guide this organization through, and overcome, any adverse conditions the future might hold...I hope when the Master calls me home, I can look down on this good earth, as did the astronauts as they circled the moon. And I hope as I watch your progress, your achievements and your service to your fellowman, I can proudly say, 'Those are my boys.'"

Mrs. Louise Brookshire also expressed her feelings about the Company when she remarked, "Wood had infinite faith that the company he established would grow into a working institution and growing organization. He was relentless in his pursuit of the success of the company that bore his name."

The decade of the 1960s was also significant for BGC because in 1960 the Company began the Profit Sharing Retirement Trust Plan for employees in order to give them the opportunity to share in the profits of the Company, as well as a way to save regularly. Mr. Wood stated, "Growth, increased sales and profits are desirable and necessary for any business. But beyond that point, the most gratifying factor in the success and growth of our Company is the increased opportunity for personal financial gain and the advancement of the loyal, efficient and aggressive people that are associated with us."

In 1969 "Woody" Brookshire (left) was promoted to Executive Vice President of Brookshire Grocery Company. Bruce, his brother, was promoted to President.

By the close of the 1960s BGC had grown to 31 supermarkets, including eight in the state of Louisiana. Much of the Company's growth was attributed to the fact that Wood always stressed, "Do the right thing, and do your best every day." Wood was also quoted as having said many times, "It's not one big thing we do for our customers, but the thousands of little things. We work with our store managers to train them to serve people as we would have them serve us, as if we were in their store."

The Company slogan in the 1960s was **"The Big Friendly Store For Everybody."**

Some food innovations of the 1960s were Pop-Tarts, Doritos, Starburst, Chips Ahoy, Gatorade, Sprite and Ruffles. Sprite was first developed in West Germany in 1959 as Fanta Klare Zitrone (Clear Lemon Fanta) and was introduced in the United States by the Coca Cola Company in 1961 under the current name of Sprite, as a competitor to 7up.

Average Cost of Grocery Items in the 1960s

Bananas (lb)	$0.10
Flour (5 lbs)	$0.49
Eggs (doz)	$0.55
Bacon (lb)	$0.79
Ice Cream (½ gal)	$0.79

Insights into Wood T. Brookshire

Quotes from Former Brookshire Company Partners

"In the 1960s Mr. Wood followed a regular routine when he visited Store #9 in Tyler. He could be seen crossing the parking lot dressed in his dark suit, tie and black felt hat. He

always entered the store at 7:30 a.m., picked up a package of chewing tobacco and walked over to the produce counter to make sure the turnip greens were fresh. If they were, he spoke to everyone, paid for the tobacco and exited the store."

"In the 1960s my store was in an old downtown East Texas building, and I had limited help in the store with only two checkers. So, my wife would help me stock the store on Sundays while the store was closed. Mr. Brookshire visited my store one morning while Woody Brookshire was in the store. Woody told his dad how hard my wife and I were working in the store. I thought they might send me more help. But Mr. Brookshire walked over and punched me on my chest bone with his index finger three times and said, 'It takes a hell of a lot of work to get anything done.'"

"Mr. Brookshire was a man of vision, an innovative thinker."

CHAPTER 7

Special Company Ventures

The United States was still in the process of recovering from World War II during the 1960s, and the threat of a Cold War existed. However, in the 1970s people became more relaxed and started thinking about bettering themselves. For about six months people even started adopting pet rocks. Maybe things got a little too relaxed when some people started "streaking"—running in public naked. During this decade, post-Vietnam War inflation and recession took its toll on some supermarkets; however, the grocery industry as a whole continued to grow in size and in innovative ideas and Brookshire Grocery Company proved to be no exception.

In the 1970s BGC almost doubled its size. The Company started the decade with 31 retail stores in two states and ended with 59 stores in three states. The Company's tremendous growth during the Seventies included several new ventures. The first one happened in the fall of 1971 when BGC opened four more supermarkets in Tyler under the name of B-Mart. They were purchased from Cecil Lasater, a local competitor who operated under the name of Lasater Food Stores. One reason he sold to BGC was the fact that Brookshire's was so competitive in its advertising. These four additional stores brought the Brookshire's number of stores in Tyler to ten.

Grand Opening of Brookshire's Store #44 in Overton, Texas, in the 1970s. "Woody" Brookshire welcomes the customers.

Mr. Wood would often remind me about staying competitive on our advertised prices. Sometimes this friendly reminder would be on a telephone call to my home at 7 a.m. on Thursday when the newspaper ad changed. Needless to say, I hated to hear that phone ring because he would always remind me to not let those "peckerwoods" beat us on advertised prices.

The second undertaking happened in the summer of 1972 when the Company expanded its operations into the convenience store industry by opening a Zippy B convenience store in Longview, Texas. Another Zippy B was opened in Tyler later that year. The Zippy B's were designed to offer shoppers the services of fast checkout, close-in parking and more store hours. The Zippy B's bright, colorful décor and distinctive layout offered a new approach to convenience store design and shopping. Because of Brookshire's ongoing policy of closing on Sundays, a big volume day for convenience stores, the two original Zippy B's were sold in 1974. A third Zippy B is presently open in Natchitoches, Louisiana.

Crossing the state line in 1975 into Arkansas, opening Store #48 in El Dorado created the third Company venture. The store was purchased from A&P. In the Seventies, A&P stores had become outdated, and their effort to combat high operating costs resulted in poor customer service. Brookshire's clean stores and friendly service quickly gained attention from the people in El Dorado, providing the Company a "firm foot in the door" to expand in Arkansas.

The fourth exciting venture was the 1974 opening of the new Brookshire Recreation Park on the southeast end of Lake Palestine on FM 346, about 20 miles south of the BGC Distribution Center.

Mr. Wood loved hunting and fishing for recreation. He had a burning desire to develop an employee recreation area on a lake in East Texas where all BGC partners could go free of charge and enjoy nature, the lake, boating, camping, swimming, picnicking and especially fishing. After the building of Lake Palestine was announced, Wood spent many hours dressed in his khakis and driving his Ford Bronco searching for undeveloped land for sale that would have lake accessibility after the lake was constructed. With a blueprint of the future lake in hand, he found the ideal property located on Lake Palestine and purchased 205 acres from a local farmer in 1973.

The Park is open year-round seven days a week. The new area offers an opportunity for relaxation and pleasure to all Company partners, families and guests. It is located in a beautiful East Texas setting surrounded by pine trees and offers visitors a place to chase butterflies, run through the fields, splash in the water, go fishing, ride a bicycle, go boating, play in the park, experience camping or barbecuing…whatever they fancy!

In addition to camping, fishing and swimming, the recreation area provides picnic tables, barbecue pits and grills, a large pavilion with an attached cooking area, electricity, water and places for softball, volleyball and horseshoes. It has campsites, restrooms and shower facilities, a fishing pier, boathouses, a boat ramp and a fenced playground for small children.

Mr. Wood once stated, "We have always had a desire for our employees to share in the fruits of our labor together. Almost everyone enjoys an outing in the country. So, we felt we could provide a facility to make it possible for all of the families associated with us to enjoy a fishing trip, picnic or stroll in the woods to enjoy nature. This would help keep their minds clear,"

Mr. Wood, a true backer of the project in both moral and physical support, spent a great deal of time planning and overseeing the layout, design and construction of the lake property. After the dam was built, the boathouses and fishing pier were completed and the lake was filled with water, he decided it was time to harvest the cedar trees on the property. These trees would be used later to create fishing beds that would attract crappies, a popular lake fish in East Texas. He asked two warehouse employees to help him with the project. Thus, they cut the cedar trees and stocked them to dry.

Wood T. Brookshire, founder of Brookshire Grocery Company, 1904-1977.

After a few months, Mr. Wood came to the warehouse and picked up his favorite two partner "helpers," men who worked regularly in the warehouse. He asked them to go with him in his Bronco to the lake to sink the trees near the pier. They tied local iron ore rocks to the trees to weigh them down. The trees failed to properly sink into the water. At that time, the weather was a cool 42 degrees. One of the guys removed his billfold and jumped into the cold water. Mr. Wood shouted, "I didn't intend for you to do that."

However, after swimming and diving, the partner successfully sank the trees. The next day the partner who jumped into the cold water came to work at the warehouse sick with a sore throat. Later that morning Mr. Wood called the guy and asked him to meet him on the grocery warehouse dock. Mr. Wood said, "Son, you're sick and I'm here to take you to the doctor." He did just that and paid for the doctor visit. The partner was thankful, but still doesn't know who told Mr. Wood he was sick.

The supervisor of BGC's upscale recreation park has kept it safe, well-manicured and family-oriented for the past 20 years. He stated, "We have approximately 12,000 visitors each year, and we expect that number will only continue to grow as more and more partners find out about the Park."

A partner said, "It's a family time when we are at the Park. We have stayed in several State Parks, and this Park ranks at the top of our list."

The fifth exciting venture occurred in the fall of 1975 when BGC began the construction of a wildlife museum and replica of a country store in the lobby area at the Tyler Distribution Center. The wildlife museum contained animal trophies that Mr. and Mrs. W.T. Brookshire had harvested on their three hunting trips to Africa and other trips to Alaska and North America. Long before the construction of the museum Mr. Wood shared, "I have dreamed of someday giving those who have never had the opportunity to see nature's wild animals up close a chance to do so."

In the 1970s getting an up-close look at exotic animals and artifacts from around the world was a rarity. He and Louise were permitted to harvest some African animals based on their plans to help future generations observe wildlife in a museum atmosphere. The World of Wildlife and Country Store Museum, dedicated to Louise and Wood Brookshire, officially opened in early 1975. The museum was a popular attraction for school, civic, church and family groups as well as many individuals who toured it.

As the 1970s came to a close, BGC made two additional new ventures in Shreveport, Louisiana, that prepared the Company to move ahead in added food related endeavors. They were the opening of the stand-alone Tasty Bakery, the Company's first effort in manufacturing. It enabled the Company to operate a full-scale retail bakery plant that would service various bakery departments in Brookshire stores throughout the Shreveport area. Also, the Company opened Brookshire's Cafeteria, offering BGC the opportunity to diversify business interests. A second cafeteria was opened in Shreveport in 1984, and the names were changed to Tasty Cafeteria. After trying these new ventures, all were closed at a later date.

Another milestone occurred in 1975 when a 71,000 square-foot addition was added to the Company's Tyler Distribution Center. The new expansion added additional length to aisles and enabled the warehouse to accommodate four more boxcars inside the warehouse, bringing the total to 12.

The entire warehouse had to be reset. The dry grocery warehouse used a Towveyor system for filling orders for the retail stores. The system consisted of an 859-feet tow line chain that constantly moved, just under the floor level. It ran down every main aisle and to every dock door where items were loaded onto trucks for shipment to stores. The warehouseman pulled the order on a buggy, hooked the buggy to the chain and magnetically keyed the buggy as to what door to stop.

There were several innovations made by the Company in the Seventies. In March of 1973, BGC took a giant step in preparing the Company for the future, installing a new National Cash Register Century 200 computer in a specially designed area in the distribution center's office. The 200 series had a flexible base for expansion of a variety of processing and performance capabilities. The new computer had disk packs capable of storing up to 60 million characters, enabling the Company's Data Processing Department to handle its duties with greater efficiency.

The computer's "Metro Marker," a device that printed adhesive price tags, was introduced in all stores. Unlike the ink stampers being used, the Metro Marker printed the price on an adhesive sticker and adhered it to the product, all in one motion, an improvement for the retailer and the customer. The old price marker ink stamper took a great deal of time in turning the small metal disks that changed the prices to be stamped on the merchandise, and the stamped price could not be removed from the product.

Also, some of the Brookshire stores started installing new electronic registers that were capable of being upgraded to include automatic scanning of prices, trading stamp disbursement and scales for fresh produce. The computer-assisted checkout offered customers' greater speed, efficiency and accuracy while providing other benefits such as easier inventory control and less risk of checker error.

Since BGC had not been pleased in the sales results of the two new stores in Shreveport, a decision was made to start offering S&H Green Stamps at these stores as an extra incentive for customers to shop at Brookshire's.

Trading stamps such as the S&H Green Stamps had hit their zenith in the 1960-70s. The Sperry and Hutchinson Company first introduced S&H Stamps in 1896. BGC knew that trading stamps generally would cost them about 2 % of sales. The Company hoped to make up the difference in the cost of the stamps by the increased business the stamps generated. The S&H Green Stamps were small paper stamps with a gummed backing for sticking in saving books. They were given to the customer at the checkout counter after groceries were purchased. This was the first type of loyalty program that predated the current "Thank You" loyalty card at Brookshire's.

In addition to grocery stores, trading stamps were also issued at gas stations, dry cleaners, department stores and other retailers. Customers used the old "lick 'em and stick 'em" method to adhere the stamps onto savings books. Filled booklets could be exchanged for merchandise at redemption centers or by mail. Customers could exchange their books for household goods, appliances, furniture, tools, sporting goods, toys or anything used around the home.

The trading stamp incentive program proved to be successful in these two stores, plus additional Shreveport stores. The S&H Stamps and Gold Bond Stamps were used as sales incentives in other stores in the Company.

I can very well remember those days. Before BGC issued trading stamps in any store, I designed and ran an unusual newspaper advertisement. It portrayed a hand holding a price marker that was currently being used in our stores. The headline on the ad proclaimed, "This is the only stamp you will find at Brookshire's." Mr. Wood called me in his office and held up a copy of the newspaper ad. He said, "Son, in the future don't ever make a public statement about what we are going to do or not going to do." A lesson I shall always remember since we did end up using another stamp!

Confidentiality of store sales and company volume figures has always been considered very "sacred" to everyone in the BGC organization. An example of the importance of this confidentiality occurred one morning at the store in Mexia, Texas. The story goes that a BGC district manager received a phone call on his car phone from Bruce Brookshire, chairman of the board. Mr. Brookshire asked him, "Are you at the store?"

The answer was, "Yes, sir, Mr. Brookshire. I am."

Bruce said, "Good. Go get on the store phone and call me back from the office."

The district manager did as instructed and called him back. Bruce said, "Now, I want you to get down on your knees near the counter where no one can see your lips. OK, now tell me what the volume was at the store yesterday. Remember, you have to really be careful with volume figures because someone could read your lips from the parking lot."

As Bruce and Woody Brookshire both began learning the grocery business at young ages, so did their sons. Bruce's older son, Tim, at age nine rode his bicycle from his home for several blocks to the Bergfeld Brookshire's store in Tyler to work in the produce department where he earned $3 a week. He worked in various areas of the Company as a youngster and later joined the Company full-time. After serving several capacities in the retail stores, Tim was promoted to store manager of the Company's Store #1 in the Green Acres Shopping Center in Tyler in 1975. In 1978 he was promoted to District Grocery Supervisor. He was later promoted to Personnel Training Manager, pioneering that position for the Company.

Woody's oldest son, Brad, began working for the Company when he was in the third grade. He went to summer school in the mornings and worked at Store #1 in Tyler in the afternoons. His dad paid him 2 cents per bag to bag ice. He bagged it himself in the produce department and then took it on a cart to the freezer. Afterwards, he went to TG&Y and purchased baseball cards with the money he had earned and chewed all the gum that was with the cards. While Brad was still in grade school, Woody was a district manager. In the summer Brad would ride with his dad to visit stores. While Woody talked to the store manager, he had Brad working in produce shucking onions. Brad said it was fun being with his dad, even though he had to shuck onions.

As a youth in 1970 Brad worked in the warehouse in Tyler. He also worked as a stocker in several of the stores and in July

1977 joined the Company full-time as a manager trainee. He was named store manager of Store #42 in Monroe, Louisiana, in 1978. In 1980, Brad transferred to the Tyler Distribution Center in Tyler as warehouse manager trainee and later that year was named Assistant Warehouse Superintendent.

Bruce's younger son, Britt, also began working for the Company as a youngster. He said, "I was encouraged by my dad and grandfather to begin working in the Company at an early age in the summer of 1963 at age eight. I worked at Store #9 in Tyler every day peeling onions in the back produce room by the coolers. Additionally, I learned to mop the back produce room and bathroom. I was not paid by the Company directly due to child labor restrictions. I was paid from the front pocket of my dad at 50 cents an hour!"

Britt also served in several Company stores as a courtesy clerk, stocker and checker before working in the warehouse in Tyler. After completing college, Britt joined the Company as a manager trainee. He became assistant manager of Store #9 in Tyler and later was transferred to Store #1 in Tyler as assistant manager before being named store manager of Store #45 in Longview in 1980.

Woody's son, Kirk, worked in the Company as a youngster in 1969 and 1970. His dad paid him $1 an hour. He also worked in the warehouse in 1974-75. He did not make Brookshire's a career choice.

Karen, Woody's daughter, had her first experience working for BGC when she was 14 years old. She said, "It was the summer of 1970. My dad took me to work with him at the warehouse.

Because I was under 16, he paid me out of his own pocket. My best remembrance of my hourly wage was $1-2 an hour. I was a timid girl and remember being very nervous in the beginning. I was to help Reba Rayford in the front office. My duties were to answer the switchboard and sort store coupons. My additional duty was to greet salesmen and to notify the buyers of their arrival. More than one buyer was surprised to learn that my granddaddy was the founder of Brookshire's. I knew that I was not to mention or take advantage of that fact."

Mark, Woody's youngest son, started to work in the Company for $1 per hour during the summers when he was ten years old. He worked from 8 a.m. to noon peeling onions in the produce department of Store #9 in Tyler. He said they had to double-up the apron he wore so it would not drag the floor! His father paid his salary. He officially joined the Company in 1982 and served as an assistant store manager in four stores prior to becoming a store director.

In May 1975 BGC held the first company-wide meeting of all 2,200 Company partners and their spouses or dates. They joined with Company officers at Harvey Hall Convention Center in Tyler. Some of the main events in the meeting were the awarding of service pins, recognitions, prizes and speeches. From then on the Company started having two separate annual company meetings, one in Tyler and one in Shreveport.

Sometimes creative efforts don't work out as planned, or they just plain backfire. Such was the case with two different experiments conducted by the Company in the 1970s. As mentioned before, Mr. Wood was a "dreamer" and was always challenging the Company leaders to seek new ideas and ways the Company could better serve its customers.

At one point, a decision was made that BGC should get into the cattle business—buying, raising and having company cattle slaughtered for beef to be sold in the Company's retail stores. After all, East Texas had transformed from a large farming area to ranching and raising cattle. The Company planned to use the land surrounding the Employee Recreation Park and lease several more acres of grazing land for the cattle venture. Around 800 young steers in addition to a large variety of cows and bulls were purchased over several weeks at the livestock barns in the East Texas area.

Several partners in the Company became involved in the cattle business including the Company's meat buyer, who was credited with suggesting the idea. Also, the grocery warehouse manager, men from the grocery warehouse, the Recreation area manager and even a representative from the accounting department were involved.

Taking care of and feeding hundreds of cattle became a big unanticipated problem. One of the men said, "Surviving that first winter was a killer for BGC's cattle business." He continued, "We spent a great deal of time feeding the herd over 100 bales of hay, in addition to range cubes and keeping out salt blocks."

The accountant said, "I was challenged with counting or inventorying the cattle once a week, not a simple task." He continued, "It seems that I came up with a different number each time I tried to count them because they were all squirming around. I just had to choose a number."

At one point, one of the Company leaders said, "This is definitely not the thing we should be doing!" Therefore, the BGC cattle business lasted a little over a year and 1,100 head of cows, calves, steers and bulls were sold at local livestock auctions.

One of the BGC "cattlemen" stated, "The biggest job we had was trying to match the right calf with its mother as we loaded them in trucks to transport them to the auctions. Fortunately, we made only one mistake that resulted in two mismatches. A buyer in Trinidad, Texas, called and said his cow and calf was not a match. We quickly went to Trinidad and took care of that situation, and never heard about the other cow and calf that didn't belong to each other!"

S.W. "Woody" Brookshire, W.T. Brookshire and Bruce Brookshire at the Grand Opening of Store #51 in Tyler.

In the spring/summer of 1976, an idea supposedly conceived by Wood Brookshire, since he considered himself a cotton picker, was adopted. The brainstorm of growing quality vegetables for resale in the retail stores was implemented. At the time, many held a somewhat "wait and see" feeling; however, the consensus of the Company was "we don't know until we try it."

Some fertile farmland just two miles north of the Brookshire Employee Recreation Park was leased. The land was cultivated, and seven acres of tomatoes, two acres of squash, one acre of bell and banana peppers and a small plot of peas were planted. "Everything grew profusely, and we had bumper crops to harvest," according to the experiment's leader who was a BGC warehouse employee chosen by Mr. Wood with some "farm boy's" expertise. It appears finding workers to harvest the crops was a tremendous chore, since the veggies were maturing at the same time local farmers were seeking help in picking their crops. "At one point we were using an elderly husband and wife with a handful of youngsters ranging from 8 to 12 years old," the leader recalled.

The veggies were sold in the stores as "locally grown." However, even though their quality was very good, they were not professionally packaged and did not have the attractive appearance of products from the Dallas produce market where BGC's fresh veggies were purchased. As a result, the experiment was not considered a success and was not tried again. The general consensus was, "Well, we gave it our best effort, and it didn't work."

The BGC Employee Profit-Sharing and Retirement Plan

demonstrated the strong commitment the Company made for the future of its partners. In 1978 the Company enhanced the Plan by selling company stock to the Plan, making every Brookshire partner who is a member a stockholder in the Company.

As in life, sometimes when things are going great, a tragedy strikes! This happened to BGC in the early 1970s when the Wills Point, Texas, police chief called the store director and told him to get to his store immediately. Upon arrival, the store director saw his store being completely destroyed by fire. The manager said the fire was so hot that, "The store's iron beams were twisted like Christmas candy."

Fire Marshall investigations discovered that someone had driven a pick-up truck loaded with two barrels of gasoline to the store's front door. The truck's gas pedal had been rigged so that the truck would go forward when it was put in forward gear. The barrels of gas also contained timers. The timer on the first barrel went off immediately after the truck forced its way through the front doors and entered the store. The second barrel's timer went off near the meat market in the rear of the store's sales area.

No clues were discovered as to who had committed this horrible act of violence. However, the store manager told the police chief a local competitor had been wanting him to raise prices in his store, which he refused to do. The manager even received a note that said, "Get up with your prices or get out!" Also, when the store manager opened the store one morning a few days before the fire, he found broken glass on the floor. He noticed little bullet holes in a front plate glass window. The bullets from a 22-rifle had entered the store and knocked out a row of lights over one of the grocery gondolas.

At this point, the chief of police determined the note writer should be considered a suspect. All Brookshire retail store supervisors were called to Wills Point to assist the FBI and local police in searching for a possible second vehicle that could have been involved in the explosion. They spent the day with several teams of two in each vehicle searching almost every road in Van Zandt County, reporting any suspicious looking vehicle to the authorities.

No arrests were made because none of the investigations turned up a suspect. However, several months later an unofficial report was revealed that the culprit had been arrested in Mexico.

Then, in August of 1975, another store fire occurred at Store #20 in Terrell, Texas, only a few miles from the Wills Point store. This caused BGC officials to wonder if the second fire was connected to the Wills Point fire. Or was it just a coincidence? Since damage from that fire was caused by the electrical box, apparently the two fires were not related. However, the damage was extensive enough to close down the store operations for several months. The Company's prior success in Terrell made it obvious that rebuilding the store as soon as possible was imperative. During the reconstruction, full-time partners were assigned to work in other stores in the area. This was the third store fire that had occurred in the Company's history.

Pat Prestwood, one of the first store managers and an original BGC company stockholder, made a statement that summed up what happened to the Company in the Seventies.

Prestwood said, "Mr. W.T. Brookshire told us the Company was going to grow, but we never dreamed it would get as big as it is today." In the Seventies, it grew by opening 28 new stores and remodeling several stores, bringing the total operating stores to 59.

When asked about BGC's future, Bruce Brookshire, president, said, "I believe our Company's future will be bright as long as each of us as individuals works toward what I call 'Five Shining Goals.' We must have a passion for perfection, a desire to work, duty toward our jobs, honesty and economy—all of us must practice good economy in every area. I think by applying these principles, we will rise above trying times."

The Company slogan in the 1970s was **"The Happy Food Stores."**

New food innovations in the 1970s were Hamburger Helper, quiche, fondue, fajitas and Jell-O Salads. Hamburger Helper was introduced in 1971 in response to higher meat prices created by a meat shortage. It allowed a housewife to stretch a pound of ground beef into a meal for four or five.

Average Cost of Grocery Items in the Mid-1970s

Bananas (lb)	$0.12
Eggs (doz)	$0.59
Bacon (lb)	$1.29
Milk (gal)	$1.32
Butter (lb)	$1.33
Coffee (lb)	$1.90

Note: With the recession in the mid-1970s (due in part to the rising grain and oil prices) inflation surged, and many food items became more expensive.

INSIGHTS INTO WOOD T. BROOKSHIRE:

Quotes from Brookshire Grocery Company Partners

"When I moved to Tyler in 1975, I first met W.T. Brookshire at 4 a.m. in the BGC office. I was up working early getting some letters and preparing for a store re-set. I turned the corner by the old executive break room, and there he was, bigger than life! Much bigger than the statue out in front of the building. I introduced myself and he asked, 'Are you a big shot?' I replied, 'No, sir. I am not.' He told me to have a good day, and he was gone. I did not breathe for two hours."

"A memorable incident involving Mr. Brookshire occurred at a Store Manager's meeting at the Employee Recreation Park. I was probably 21 or 22, and this was my first store manager's meeting outside. He got right to the point! He had found a Safeway sack in the trashcan at the lake. He was wearing us out about loyalty, emphasizing that he had spent a lot of money on some place we could take our families free

of charge. He was really hurt! Then, it started to rain—not just a rain—but a flood! No one moved an inch. We all just stood there in our red coats getting drenched. I think almost all the crowd felt some kind of betrayal to that individual."

"Mr. Wood Brookshire truly believed in, and valued, people."

WOOD T. BROOKSHIRE

March 1, 1904 – April 17, 1977

Partners collectively mourned the death of the Company founder, Wood T. Brookshire, who passed away April 17, 1977, at the age of 73. A man from modest beginnings, Wood remained humble throughout his life in spite of his tremendous successes. Wood was revered by all who knew him as a Christian, citizen, businessman, husband, father and grandfather. He demonstrated stewardship in life through each and every relationship and responsibility he encountered.

"My grandfather was larger than life with a magnetic personality. People generally liked to be around him. To me, he was the ultimate grandfather figure, always giving advice and counsel. People in the community respected him. He was CEO of the Company for 40 years, working extremely hard into his 60s before backing away and making way for the next generation of leadership. He loved to travel with my grandmother. He was totally devoted to his wife, and I don't think they ever spent a night apart. He was very competitive, didn't like to lose and had a 'whatever it takes' mentality. Customer service was always top of mind. He was obsessive about providing great customer service and surrounding himself with great people in the Company. He always took interest in me as a grandson and knew what was going on in my life. That was pretty special.

"Papaw's fierce, competitive nature in the business allowed him to rise above larger competitors such as A&P, Safeway and Piggly Wiggly by giving the best service and the customers the best price possible." — B. Tim Brookshire, grandson

"I remember coming back one day from a deer lease around Kerrville with my grandparents, probably in the late 60s. At the time, there were very few, if any, four-lane highways in the state. My grandfather decided to pass the car in front of us. As he pulled into the oncoming lane, another car was coming right at us. Instead of slowing down and getting behind the car in front of us, he swerved into the shoulder of the opposite lane, and then finished passing the car! He was nonchalant about it. He was fearless, determined and not afraid to take risks. He started our Company the year before the Great Depression. While most people who had one store stayed at one store, my grandfather continued expanding and growing the Company through the decades." — Brad Brookshire, grandson

"Papaw was a man of great wit, with a forthright personality. He was community-minded and very generous to worthwhile causes. He was a big man in stature and could be quite intimidating with his command of any room. On many occasions, upon leaving one of the grocery stores, he would take his right index finger and firmly poke the male employee directly on the sternum to emphasize his directive. What a lasting impression this would make, although I'm not sure this would ever be tolerated in today's society! Papaw liked to tell a good story. Many times, he would vividly recount the details to the grandchildren about how he started Brookshire Grocery Company. I loved hearing the story from him. His eyes would light up as he told us about the boldness it took to step away from the plans of his six brothers and initiate his own company in Tyler." — Britt Brookshire, grandson

"My Papaw was certainly a guiding light in my life. He was a principled man with lots of wisdom to share with his grandchildren." — Karen Brookshire Womack, granddaughter

"Papaw was a good speaker and a very sharp dresser. Unless he was at leisure in his khaki clothing, he wore a suit, dress shirt, tie and even cuff links. Papaw had a great personality. Once as a youngster I was returning from South Texas with him. We stopped by the side of the road to buy fresh peaches just outside of Fredericksburg, Texas.

Papaw asked the man, 'What is the price of a bushel of peaches?'

The man replied, 'They are $2 per bushel.'

'Oh my, that is too much money because I'm just a poor old country boy,' Papaw said quickly.

Then the man said, 'I can tell that by the fancy car you are driving!'" — Mark Brookshire, grandson

Mark also said that his Papaw was very compassionate. He remembers going on a turkey-hunting trip with him to South

Texas when Mark was twelve years old. Suddenly three turkey gobblers appeared. His Papaw whispered, "Mark, shoot 'em." Mark aimed with his shotgun, shot and missed all three! With a word of encouragement, his Papaw said, "Don't worry, my sweet little man. You can get them next time."

"My grandfather was a visionary businessman, a smart and tough leader and an inspirational family man who put his faith first, family second and business third." — Kirk Brookshire, grandson

When Wood Brookshire died, those who knew and respected him and his business organization felt his passing. A portion of the letter received by the Brookshire family from a customer in Kilgore, Texas, expressed the sentiments of many people:

"It has been said a man's shadow…may fall where he may never go. I think that must be true of the husband and father you recently lost. For as long as there has been a Brookshire's store in Kilgore, I have become aware of the unfailing courtesy of each employee and of their evident happiness in their jobs. Groceries I can get anywhere, but men who build a better community are a town's greatest asset. Mr. Brookshire was one of these."

That was a great tribute to the founder of BGC, but it was also a great tribute to the Brookshire organization he built and to the employees who kept the Company running efficiently.

The following words are excerpts from a letter written as a tribute to the Company founder W.T. Brookshire at the time of his death by his son, Bruce G. Brookshire.

"Wood Brookshire was a blend of a spirited, aggressive business leader and a compassionate, understanding, patient and loving counselor, coach, husband and father.

"He possessed loving loyalty to God, fierce loyalty to family and friends, and high moral standards in his personal life and business ethics. He was an example of free enterprise at its best. Raised from a poor, penniless cotton farm boy with very humble beginnings and by hard work, extreme honesty, thriftiness and dedication to his customers he became a successful business leader. He believed sincerely that he should serve his fellowman by selling him food at the highest quality and lowest price. He was a hard-driving and ambitious man who possessed intense competitiveness to strive for perfection."

Coach Floyd Wagstaff, a respected long-time coach at Tyler Junior College and a member of the Texas Sports Hall of Fame said, "All of the Brookshires are my good friends. W.T. was the best man I ever knew—'The Old Country Boy.'"

Dr. Wylie Clyde, a Tyler dentist, said, "Wood Brookshire, Louise and their sons, Bruce and Woody (as youngsters) paid me visits. I remember Mr. Brookshire well. He would always come in with his suit coat on. One time I asked, 'Mr. Brookshire, do you want to take your coat off?' He joked, 'No, I've got holes in my elbows.'

"He was always a gentleman," Dr. Clyde said. "That's what I remember about him most."

Mr. Wood was quite a character, and I considered him my granddaddy. I was honored that on many occasions Mr. Wood called me "son." Mr. Wood taught me to be a better man, to always be fair about my dealings with everyone, to be honest and to stay close to my Christian values.

I had the unique privilege of delivering some necessary items to Mr. Wood and visiting him before his death in the hospital. He was weak but, as usual, he had a few words to share with me and a company partner who was with me there by his bedside. I shall always remember the advice he gave us. In his unique way he said, "Boys, I can leave this world saying that I was always true to my wife. Now, let that be a lesson to you young men!"

CHAPTER 8

Challenges and Opportunities

The 1970s were viewed as a time of great prosperity and growth for Brookshire Grocery Company. However, the 1980s recession, along with inflation and unemployment that struck the United States, seemed to put a cloud on the nation's horizon and many businesses. Despite the recession, growth remained constant at BGC by adding 27 stores, enlarging the Tyler Distribution Center and expanding the Company's geographic region. By the midway point of the decade, the Company had 75 supermarkets in operation.

BGC's warehouse and office complex in Tyler has always been a secure place for partners to work, protected by a chain-link fence and a guard gate. Guests to the main office were required to check in with a front lobby receptionist. That said, it was quite unusual one day in the mid-1980s when a very casually dressed man was seen wandering in one of the office halls. A BGC office partner asked him, "Sir, are you looking for someone?"

The man's shocking reply was, "Yes. I'm Sam Walton, and I'm looking for Bruce Brookshire. Is he around?" He was proudly escorted to Bruce's office.

Like a flash of lightning, news spread that Sam Walton, the founder of Walmart, was a visitor and had entered the office complex undetected! Later, it was determined Mr. Sam had entered through the employee entrance. After he and Bruce had a friendly visit, Bruce asked one of the men from my department to drive Mr. Sam to the Tyler airport. While they were traveling on SSW Loop 323 in Tyler, Mr. Sam looked at some vacant property and said, "That would be a good place for one of my Sam's Warehouse Clubs." That new concept had opened in 1983. Yes, that is exactly the spot where Sam's Club was constructed a couple of years later. It's a small world after all!

At a glance, BGC's "Zap Mr. Inflation" newspaper advertisements in the 1980s looked like Brookshire's was promoting *Star Wars* movies. However, those outer space-looking characters popping up in Company ads called shopper's attention to the ways Brookshire's helps them fight inflation. The ads urged shoppers to look for the "Zap Mr. Inflation" characters in the stores to remind them how to fight rising food prices and save money by purchasing advertised specials and Plain Label and Hy-Top—Brookshire's brand of products at the time.

BGC's vice president–retail grocery operations learned about a new supermarket warehouse concept at a national grocers' conference he attended. He shared his experience with Company leaders, and Woody Brookshire asked him and some of his peers to "check-out" the warehouse store in Kansas City, Missouri, to see the concept in action. The new supermarket warehouse retailing involved selling a large amount of food and groceries at deeper discounts than in a conventional supermarket. It offered lower prices with a little or no-frills shopping experience and with less customer service. The Kansas City store was considered to be one of the first of its kind in the U.S.

Under Woody Brookshire's leadership, BGC decided to consider opening a store under this new concept. Company partners visited with the Kansas City store and the warehouse concept company as a possible supplier, along with having joint meetings with Malone and Hyde—a warehouse store supplier headquartered in Monroe, Louisiana. The leadership team chose the Malone and Hyde program along with the Super 1 Foods name with a bright green and yellow color selection.

Alexandria, Louisiana, was selected as the location for the first store because it was outside the present Brookshire's trade area. A suitable and inexpensive location was a vacated 38,639 square-foot lumberyard. Brad Brookshire was challenged with becoming the project manager in developing this new endeavor. The remodeling was completed, but unfortunately at 4 p.m. before the store was opening, the entire file system containing the dry groceries was wiped out. Scanning was new at that time, and the new store had a stand-alone IBM system. Store employees worked all night rescanning items into the system to have the store ready to open the next morning. The grand opening was a success. BGC was pleased with the new store's volume, and two

Super 1 Foods stores, #602 in Monroe, Louisiana, and #603 in Bastrop, Louisiana, both in recycled stores, were later opened.

In 1987 BGC made the largest acquisition in its present history when it purchased seven former Safeway stores in East Texas and Shreveport. The quick turnaround of converting these seven stores to Brookshire's in only a few days was a success story that was accomplished by BGC's dedicated partners from several departments working around the clock. BGC's real estate department, working with leaders from both companies, put the buyout plan together.

Safeway agreed that BGC partners could visit each of the seven stores while final plans of the purchase were being completed. A team of eager BGC partners with notebooks, tape measures and cameras in hand visited each of the Safeway stores. Partners from construction, sign and décor, refrigeration, retail operations, IT services and the sign company who did exterior signs for BGC hit the stores to establish a budget and put a fixture plan together. The partners returned home, created a budget and layout plan and immediately started securing the proper supplies to accomplish the plan of turning the Safeway stores into fresh new Brookshire's within a few days.

The task began immediately after BGC became the owners. It took dedicated teamwork for such a massive in-house task to be accomplished on a limited budget. All outside signage was replaced, the in-store curtain wall (the space from the top of cases and fixtures to the ceiling) was removed, walls were prepped for painting and all the Safeway brand merchandise was removed from the shelves, including all perishable items. Plans were made to use sales reps from Brookshire's major suppliers and the store's new employees to help restock the shelves and gondolas. A special series of Grand Opening advertisements were also designed. With all these tasks accomplished, seven new Brookshire's opened, and ex-Safeway employees and local citizens were offered jobs. Partner promotions for most of the management positions were made. This was the first of many turnaround stores to come, all done in a few days. I will always remember this Company project because my wife still reminds me that we had to give up a week's all-expenses-paid trip to London! I did not believe that it was right for me to be on vacation while my team was working diligently with others to get those seven stores open in such a short time.

"The Redcoats." Brookshire's store managers wearing red sport coats and black bow ties, 1981.

In the 1980s BGC placed more and more interest on customer convenience. With a constant desire to serve the customers better, BGC made several moves with this in mind, such as adding fresh fish counters and floral shops. Bakery and deli operations were added in many stores, and BGC became committed to adding computer-assisted scanning checkout systems in some stores. In addition, the Company made the decision to open all stores on three major holidays each year including New Year's Day, Fourth of July and Labor Day. Store hours were extended, and some stores stayed open 24 hours per day, Monday through Saturday.

While these major decisions were discussed and approved by the Board, the obvious question about opening the stores on Sunday came up. This was not an easy decision for the Board to make. Everyone knew Mr. Wood's strong conviction about not opening the stores on Sunday, based primarily on his strong Christian belief that the Bible taught Sundays should be a day of rest.

Through the years the Company had publicly stated why its stores were closed on Sunday. In 1977 a poster said, "We Close Our Stores On Sunday! Although many of our competitors open on Sunday, Brookshire's still believes its employees deserve a day of rest—whether they choose to worship, visit relatives, relax or whatever."

In a 1960s BGC employee booklet a policy statement said, "It is the policy of Brookshire's that stores are not open on Sundays. It is believed that employees and customers should attend the church of their choice, and normal work or grocery buying should not be done on Sunday. In rare instances, it will be necessary to inventory on Sunday; in that case employees will be paid additional salary for such work."

The discussion about BGC changing the "closed on Sunday" policy brought back memories for some Board members about what they were taught growing up in East Texas in part of the Bible Belt. The general belief among many Christians during that time was that no outside labor was to be done on Sunday. Games and activities that could ordinarily be enjoyed without a care in the world on any other day of the week were a definite no-no on Sunday. Some were taught that Sunday entertainment should not involve playing cards or dominoes, going fishing or seeing a picture show. These activities, including not working out of the home, were considered sinful to do on Sunday. Shopping on Sunday was not an option because most stores were closed.

Typical of that mindset, a friend relayed an experience his grandfather had on a Sunday when he almost ran out of gas in rural East Texas in the 1950s. The story goes he had driven several miles trying to find a gas station that was open. As a last resort he stopped at a little grocery store with gas pumps outside. After seeing the "closed" sign on the door, he walked next door to the owner's house. He pleaded with the owner to please let him have some gas. The owner said, "Sorry, sir. As God commanded, I don't work on Sunday—it's a day of rest." But the owner, after pondering awhile, finally said, "You know, I need to unlock one of those pumps." He unlocked the pump and disappeared into his house. My friend said his grandfather pumped gas into his car, left money on top of the pump and drove off. Everyone was happy, since the car owner had gas and the station owner didn't disobey God and work on Sunday!

For over 50 years BGC stores operated under the "Never

on Sunday" concept, even though most competitive stores were open on Sunday. However, the Super 1 Foods that opened in Alexandria, Louisiana, on May 1,1984, had always been open on Sunday. So, making the choice to open the other Company stores on Sunday was a major decision that presented many pros and cons from BGC Board members who would ultimately vote yes or no on the decision of Sunday opening.

The Brookshire family relationships were not always peaceful. In fact, Bruce Brookshire, chairman of the board and Woody Brookshire, vice chairman of the board, shared different opinions that developed into a dispute over the Sunday opening subject!

Storefront of Store #62 in Ashdown, Arkansas, displaying large window signs in the 1980s.

At the time, the two new stores in Plano, Texas, were suffering from lack of volume because they were closed while all their competitors were open for business on Sunday. In fact, being closed on Sunday was making the Company less competitive in other larger markets. After much prayer, discussion and debates, the Board voted to change the over fifty-year-old policy of closing stores on Sunday to opening them for business.

Several company leaders who helped make the decision to open all BGC stores on Sunday were in attendance in Plano anticipating a big day on the first Sunday that the two stores were open for business. That particular Sunday happened to be Mother's Day. Traditionally, business on Mother's Day was the lowest volume Sunday of the year for supermarkets since many families celebrated Mother's Day eating out in restaurants. Consequently, true to form, business on that Sunday was slow and very disappointing with the lack of customers shopping in the stores. Needless to say, it was not what all BGC partners wanted to see. However, future Sunday opening results were very fruitful throughout the Company.

Several promotions occurred with top management in the 1980s. In September 1980 company officials named C.B. Hardin, one of the first store managers, to company president, and in 1985, the veteran grocer became vice chairman of the board. James Hardin, C.B.'s son was named executive vice president–operations in 1980 and in 1985 succeeded his father as president of the Company and served as president and CEO until he retired in 2000.

When he was named president, James Hardin said, "My desire for BGC is for us to continue to operate the best supermarkets in the United States. I want this company to be a place of business where partners will thoroughly enjoy their work and where customers will find it a pleasure to do shopping."

Bruce G. Brookshire was named chairman of the board and chief operating officer. In 1984 B. Tim Brookshire, Bruce Brookshire's son, was named vice president–personnel and Brad Brookshire, Woody Brookshire's son, became vice president–distribution/Super 1 Division.

An addition of a 29,750 square-foot meat warehouse at the distribution center in 1980 was another major step for BGC since it enabled the Company to buy meat in larger quantities at lower prices. It also created an avenue for the Company to buy meat from more companies, not just those that provided delivery service. New construction at the Tyler base included new office facilities, a new sign and display shop and a new bakery manufacturing plant. An additional 11,500 square feet of freezer space was also added to the warehouse operation.

In the 1980s the Company introduced a "We're Listening" comment form in all retail stores, a way of hearing from customers. For example, a unique customer critique about the TV commercials the Company was currently running was received from a grandmother who was a customer at Store #26 in Bossier City, Louisiana. She commented that she found something about the commercials she didn't like, and she was registering a complaint. She wrote, "The commercials are good, but they don't have any of my store's people in them. As far as I am concerned, my store employees are the best! I get tired looking at those men in the commercials. Why didn't you put some of those good-looking men from Bossier City on those commercials? They're better than the ones you used!" It's unknown how this question was answered.

The first Spirit of Christmas Food Drive was held in 1982 with a goal of helping thousands of people throughout the communities served by BGC stores. That year, partnering with Tyler's Rose City's Kiwanis Club for approximately six weeks leading up to Christmas, all Brookshire's and Super 1 Foods stores collected non-perishable food items to be donated to local service organizations and food pantries for distribution. Pre-assembled grab bags were made available to purchase and donate to the drive, and monetary contributions were made using scan coupons at checkout. Funds collected were used to purchase additional food items for the drive. The food drive assisted 93 families that first year. BGC has always been committed to help hunger relief in the communities that they serve. In 1998 the 37th annual food drive assisted more than 18,000 households in 150 communities.

The first Brookshire Grocery Company Charity Golf Tournament was held in Tyler in 1988. In 2019 the 31st annual tournament raised a record-breaking $625,000 with more than 675 golfers competing on four East Texas courses. In 2019 BGC donated proceeds to more than 100 non-profit organizations in more than 150 communities served by BGC. Since the tournaments inception more than $6.5 million has been raised and contributed to non-profits in communities served by BGC stores.

By the end of the 1980s, BGC was operating 89 stores and had more than 6,500 partners.

The Company slogan for the Brookshire stores in the 1980s was **"The More For Your Money Grocery Store."**

The Company slogan for the Super 1 Foods stores was **"The Ultimate Supersaver."**

Snack foods and drinks dominated the new food innovations in the 1980s. New items included Cool Ranch Doritos, Diet Coke, Fruit Roll-Ups, Jell-O-Pudding Pops, poppy seed dressing and Totino's Pizza Rolls.

AVERAGE COST OF GROCERY ITEMS IN MID-1980S:

Bread (lb)	$0.50
Eggs (doz)	$0.91
Hamburger Meat (lb)	$0.99
Milk (gal)	$2.16

INSIGHTS INTO WOOD T. BROOKSHIRE

Quotes from Former Brookshire Grocery Company Partners

"Mr. Brookshire was very conservative, especially with electricity in the office. Often, he would catch a light left on in a meeting room. His reaction to anyone around, including his administrative assistant, would be, 'Do you have stock in TP&L (Texas Power and Light company)? Let's turn the lights off!'"

"Mr. Brookshire was a great man. He was also a particular man—insisting that everything must be correct or suitable in every detail."

"Mr. Brookshire always had an 'open-door' policy for employee-partners. My brother was a BGC produce manager in the mid-1960s in Longview, Texas. He always told a story of how Mr. Brookshire listened to his problem and solved it. My brother and his store manager's personalities clashed. At some point my brother was demoted to a job in the dry-grocery department with a reduction in salary. He was upset, so he decided to drive to Tyler and visit with Mr. Brookshire about the situation. Mr. Brookshire listened to all the details and said, 'I tell you what. You find out what salary the produce manager who replaced you is making, and let me know. I will make sure your salary will be the same.' My brother did just that and got a raise. In fact, later his salary was raised again when he reported to Mr. Brookshire that the produce manager got a raise."

S. W. "WOODY" BROOKSHIRE

November 8, 1930 – February 20, 1986

The Company was saddened by the loss of S. W. "Woody" Brookshire, vice chairman of the board and chief operating officer, who died at the age of 55. Woody was the youngest son of W.T. and Louise Brookshire, founders of Brookshire Grocery Company.

Woody was admired and deeply respected by all who knew and worked with him. His wisdom, vitality and leadership in innovative and progressive steps in the Company will be missed. As chief operating officer he led the Company in many new endeavors. After his untimely death, partnering with several vendors, BGC honored Woody by sponsoring the addition of "Angler's Pavilion," a special events facility at the Texas Freshwater Fisheries Center near Athens, Texas. Woody was an avid fisherman, hunter, outdoorsman and a supporter of wildlife conservation.

"My father had a great, fun-loving personality, and my friends enjoyed being around him. Not only did he teach me how to be a better person, but also he taught me to hunt and fish and to play sports, especially tennis, that he also loved. He taught me how to work and have fun. Both have had a lasting influence on my life." — Mark Brookshire, son

"Woody Brookshire, my father, set a great example for me through his work ethic. He was an early riser, worked hard and was very dedicated. He exemplified honesty and integrity, and he was very loyal to the Company and to his family. My dad had respect for others and valued their opinions. He was very humble, down-to-earth and authentic. He could talk just as easily with the President of the United States as with anyone, and people felt comfortable around him. He tried to be a genuinely good person, and people admired him for that." — Brad Brookshire, son

"My father was a combination of my grandfather, a visionary businessman, and my grandmother, an intensely loyal wife. He was a smart businessman and a kind and compassionate father." — Kirk Brookshire, son

"When my dad took me to work with him, he expected me to be a reasonable, hard-working employee. Under no circumstances was I to exploit my last name. He himself exemplified these qualities. My dad taught me that there should be a difference between work and play. He never brought his work home, and the weekends were usually family time. Woody Brookshire loved his family." — Karen Brookshire Womack, daughter

I asked a former partner the question, "What leaders influenced you most during your BGC career?" He replied, "The gentleman who took me under his wing at a very early age was S.W. 'Woody' Brookshire. He took a liking to me and was my teacher for many years. I've never been more thankful for an individual than him. There are many others that I worked with and for, but Woody was the one I leaned on the most."

Woody was an operations leader who inspired all partners to reach out with new ideas. The main thing he taught me was to make decisions and stick to them. Woody said, "Some will be good and some not so good. Don't worry about the outcome. The main thing is to be creative and make them!"

CHAPTER 9

Approaching a New Decade

Two major world happenings occurred in the early part of the 1990s. The U.S. Armed Forces joined other U.N. members in participating in the Gulf War that was waged in the Middle East against Iraq. In 1991 the Cold War ended when the USSR was dissolved.

Locally, Brookshire Grocery Company's tremendous growth continued in the 1990s, not only in the number of stores and trade areas but also in many areas of operations, including technology, distribution and manufacturing.

Major growth was fueled in the 1990s by five acquisitions, including the purchase of the SouthWest Dairy Plant in Tyler, the 463,000 square-foot Malone and Hyde distribution center in Monroe, Louisiana, and the 491,000 square-foot SouthWest Foods complex north of Tyler that housed additional warehousing and offices. In the 1990s BGC also purchased 12 former ThriftMart stores primarily in Central Texas and nine former Harvest Foods stores in Arkansas and Louisiana.

The Tyler Distribution Center received a 113,000 square-foot frozen food warehouse in order to meet the demand for more frozen foods in the stores. In addition to grocery and ice cream freezers, the new facility also housed offices, maintenance and support areas and included a drink plant and an ice plant.

An ice cream plant opened at SouthWest Foods complex in 1997 and began manufacturing Goldenbrook Farms ice cream. According to a member of the newly-formed ice cream committee, "BGC's decision to get into ice cream manufacturing was because of the excessive butterfat left over from our milk operations. People were beginning to prefer low fat and skim milk, so the Company was always looking to sell off butterfat. We could profitably make ice cream out of that butterfat. We also had plenty of room for the plant at our SouthWest Foods facility."

BGC's Advertising Department was asked early in the process to develop a marketing plan for the new ice cream. "I can remember being involved early in the process to pick a name for the ice cream. We wanted a name that was sophisticated and didn't sound like any of our in-store brands," the Advertising representative said. Ultimately the name was chosen from a list of suggestions from advertising partners.

The Advertising Department continually conducted focus groups testing recipes, and the ice cream plant would formulate and tweak the recipes to get it right until all focus groups selected Goldenbrook over competitive brands. The goal was for it to consistently match or beat out the top ice cream brand currently being sold in BGC stores.

The Advertising Department worked on the design of the carton in phases. After BGC executives approved the name, "Goldenbrook Farms," a logo and font style for the name was locked down. Once that was approved, carton design came next. Three were presented to the committee, and one was chosen. Advertising and marketing plans were approved, and Goldenbrook Farms ice cream was introduced to the public in early 1997. Today's carton does not include the word "Farms." It is just Goldenbrook.

The Company also advanced technology by adding company-wide email and launching its first website. BGC improved and updated vehicle maintenance with computers and hand-held scanning wands for the Company's almost 600 vehicles.

Brookshire's Loyalty Card program, known today as the Thank You Card program, launched in 1998. The program was first introduced as a test in Monroe and West Monroe, Louisiana. It made it possible to offer loyal customers discounts on certain items and for the Company to track customer's transactions and target offers based on their shopping habits.

The Loyalty Card frequent shopper program equips partners to know who their customers are and what they want. It also provides the means to reward customers for their patronage.

To offer customers more one-stop shopping conveniences, pharmacies, delis, bank branches and fuel centers began popping up at various company stores. BGC's first fuel center was opened at Store #39 in Flint, Texas, just south of Tyler, in the Nineties.

Brookshire University, offering career enhancement courses to employee-partners, was established and opened in 1996. In only four years the University had grown to offer 40 courses, with class enrollments totaling more than 20,400 since the program's inception. To attend the Brookshire University courses, a partner must have been in good standing with the Company, and the class he or she registered for must have been relative either to his or her current job or to the next position in the career path. Courses were offered at no expense to the partner, and partners received their regular pay rate for class attendance. In 2014 there were 208 Brookshire University Leadership degrees awarded and 563 Eagle degrees awarded to BGC partners.

These third-generation Brookshire family members were elected Presidents of BGC in 1999. They are (from left) B. Tim Brookshire, Mark Brookshire, Brad Brookshire and Britt Brookshire.

An exciting partner benefit was added in 1993 when "The Partners' Place" was established on the grounds of the BGC Recreation Park. It's a quaint two-bedroom home, standing among shade trees and colorful blooming crepe myrtle trees. The house is fully furnished and is hailed to be "Where a new day begins." As the slogan says, "The Partners' Place serves as a refuge for all BGC partners needing a place to stay during an emergency situation or family crisis." The house is readily available whenever needed. The white frame house was moved from property on Highway 31 in Chandler, Texas, where a new Brookshire's store was going to be constructed.

For example, when the home of a partner at one of BGC's Tyler manufacturing plants was destroyed by fire, about the only thing he did not have to worry about was where he and his family were going to live until they could find a new home. The Partner Place became his family's free home until they could find a permanent home.

Not every venture that BGC tried worked. The Company opened several Super 1 Foods stores in the Dallas/Ft Worth metro area in the late 1990s and early 2000s. Some were new buildings, and others were replacements for nearby Brookshire's locations. The Company realized they could not compete in the Dallas/Ft Worth area because of the high cost of advertising in the market and other concerns. The Company left the area when they sold all metro area stores to the Fleming Company who re-branded them as Rainbow Foods. BGC took the funds from the Fleming sale and purchased 17 Winn-Dixie stores and six Albertsons in 2002.

At the end of the decade James Hardin relinquished his responsibilities as Company president to four long-term leaders, stressing the need of continuing solidarity in the Company. The four newly appointed presidents became the third generation of the Brookshire family to lead the Company. James said, "These young men have a wide array of talents."

Brad Brookshire was named president–corporate development, leading the Company's real estate, manufacturing, distribution and construction areas. Brad is a graduate of Southern Methodist University with a degree in business. Brad stated, "We will remain progressively conservative in our approach to business. It's an operating philosophy that has brought us this far and will not fail us in the future. I look forward to an exciting company future." Brad had most recently been serving as executive vice president–corporate development.

Britt Brookshire was named president–retail operations, overseeing all Brookshire's and Super 1 Foods operations. Britt has a degree in management and finance from Texas Christian University. Britt said, "It is an honor to be elevated to this position." Britt had been serving as executive vice president–retail operations.

B. Tim Brookshire became president–human resources and financial group, leading the Company's information technology departments. Tim earned a bachelor's degree in business management from Texas Christian University. Tim said, "Our vision for the future is to maintain the moral integrity of all future leaders who are promoted. I will work hard to be a firm and fair custodian of high moral values in our company."

Tim most recently served as executive vice president–human resources.

Mark Brookshire was named president marketing, directing the Company's merchandising, communications and procurement efforts. Mark earned a bachelor's degree in economics from Southern Methodist University. Mark said, "What an exciting time as we look to the next millennium and the possibilities it brings for continued opportunities and success—both for our partners individually and our company as a whole. It's humbling to be a part of history in the making." Mark had recently been serving as executive vice president–marketing.

Brad, Tim, Britt and Mark would continue to serve on the Company's executive committee, each serving as chairman and rotating on an annual basis.

Fear hung over our entire nation as plans were made to transition from 1999 to the year 2000. It was anticipated that a widespread computer programming glitch would cause havoc as the year changed from 1999 to 2000. The expected problem was called Y2K. Computer users, programmers and the general public feared that computers would stop working at midnight on December 31, 1999.

When complicated computer programs were being written in the 1960s through the 1980s, engineers used a two-digit code in which the "19" was left out. Instead of allowing four digits for the year, many computer programs only allowed the two digits. A majority of BGC partners had absolutely no clue how computers worked, thus many worried about what would happen, not knowing the problem had been solved before it arrived by computer programmers in many ways.

As the last few days of 1999 approached, there was some minor overstocking and hoarding of groceries just in case glitches happened. The media advised residents, "Have enough supplies in the house, but don't overreact and overstock your pantry. Just use common sense and plan ahead." Some couples ran their bathtubs full of water on New Year's Eve just in case they needed the water to flush toilets in their home if a Y2K glitch occurred! After Y2K did not result in a problem, it was often called a big hoax.

The Company—which by the end of the decade included 133 stores in three states, five manufacturing plants, distribution operations in Tyler and Monroe, and more than 10,000 partners—entered the new millennium with a goal of paving the way for future growth.

Average Cost of Grocery in the 1990s:

Apples (lb)	$0.72
Eggs (doz)	$0.99
Bread (loaf)	$1.29
Ground Beef (lb)	$1.60
Milk (gal)	$2.78

INSIGHTS INTO WOOD T. BROOKSHIRE

Quotes from Former Brookshire Grocery Company Partners

"Mr. Brookshire was an honest Christian man, and he expected his employees to be honest and hard working."

"With his index finger pointed strongly on my breast bone, to get my attention, he would remind me to treat the customer fairly."

"Mr. Brookshire always said, 'Take care of your customers. If you have a fire in your back room, you be sure and take care of your customer first.'"

CHAPTER 10

Moving Forward

The year 2000 was the start of the new millennium. It arrived without any of the computer glitches that people feared would happen at midnight on December 31, 1999. However, a terrible tragedy occurred on September 11, 2001. when Al-Qaeda, an Islamic terrorist group, coordinated four airplane attacks against the United States, destroying the World Trade Center in New York City and damaging the Pentagon in Washington D.C. This devastating aggressive action is considered to be the single deadliest terrorist attack in human history. It resulted in 2,977 deaths, over 25,000 injuries and long-term health problems and $10 billion in property and infrastructure damages.

This attack affected the grocery business by triggering a greater interest in comfort foods like meatloaf, chicken potpies, mac 'n cheese and anything reminding us of home. It appears when people are stressed, the foods they turn to remind them of family and friends.

In October 2000, Brookshire Grocery Company began shipping and receiving products at the Company's new 300,000 square-foot perishable warehouse located at the Tyler Distribution Center. Logistics partners relocated 283,000 cases of merchandise (7,451 pallets) to the new facility in just three days.

During this decade BGC received several awards. The Texas Retailers Association named BGC the 2007 Food Retailer of the Year during an annual awards ceremony in Houston. BGC was selected from some 200 major Texas retailers for its role in shaping issues impacting the state's food industry.

For four consecutive years (2006-2009) *Texas Monthly* magazine recognized BGC as one of the "Best Companies to Work For in Texas." The magazine began the awards program in 2006. One hundred companies were on the list in 2009 with BGC recognized in the large business category consisting of companies with 250 or more employees.

In a 2005 move that helped bind more closely BGC's four operational divisions—retail, distribution, administration and manufacturing—BGC's board of directors elected Marvin S. Massey Jr. as chief executive officer and chairman of the Company's executive committee. In 2006 Brad Brookshire became chairman of BGC's board.

In 2007 Rick Rayford, executive vice president of corporate development, was named president and chief operating officer of BGC. His promotion came a few weeks following the announcement that Chief Executive Officer Marvin S. Massey

Jr. would retire in 2008.

B. Tim Brookshire, Brad Brookshire, Britt Brookshire and Mark Brookshire, who served as presidents over respective areas of operations since 1999, remained in strategic roles on the Company's board of directors with Tim as chairman and the others as vice chairmen.

BGC moved forward with 29 acquisitions during this decade, greatly increasing the Company's trade area and creating many opportunities for partners. Purchases included four former Delchamps stores in Louisiana and six former Albertsons stores in Natchitoches, Louisiana, as well as Jackson, Mississippi, and Tyler. This was BGC's first venture into the state of Mississippi. On February 11, 2010, after a decline in market grocery shares against Kroger and Walmart (two very strong competitors in Jackson), Brookshire's made the decision to sell the stores and exit Mississippi, thus dropping the state of Mississippi from the Company's operating area.

Western boundaries were extended with the purchase of 17 former Winn-Dixie stores and five Levels stores in North, Central and West Texas. Two Winn-Dixie stores were also purchased in South Louisiana. Thousands of partners from across the Company pulled together as a team to complete the transformation.

The Company didn't just simply change the store signs and put new locks on the doors of the newly acquired 17 stores, formerly operated by competitors. Company executives launched the most aggressive and creative pro-active approach that had ever been implemented in the Company after a group of acquisitions. The team effort of extra dedication and hard work paid off, and the stores began opening in a couple of weeks after the acquisition.

Next, the Company launched a massive publicity effort aimed at familiarizing the people with BGC before the stores opened. Brad Brookshire, president–corporate development group, sent emails and flyers throughout the Company asking partners for the names and addresses of friends, family and acquaintances in these new towns so he could personally invite them to shop with BGC.

For the towns where a store was being converted into a Brookshire's, the Company hosted breakfast and luncheon meetings and invited local government, school, church and community leaders to attend. Hundreds of local dignitaries received packets containing an explanation of Brookshire's approach to customer service, a biography of their new store director and coupons for products. More importantly, they received a personal introduction and an invitation from the four Brookshire Grocery Company presidents to be BGC's guests. After the stores opened, a partner said, "New customers are arriving with an air of sheer excitement about BGC's style of customer service."

During this decade the Company introduced three new concepts, including two Olé Foods, a banner merchandised primarily for Hispanic customers. After disappointing results, these two stores were later closed. Another new concept was the Express Lane, a fuel center-convenience store. The Company now operates four of these convenience stores. An ALPS "always low-price store" was opened and later became a Brookshire's. The ALPS has been considered a forerunner to the present Spring Market stores.

To allow partners to share more in the Company's ownership, the Employee Stock Ownership and 401(k) Plan was established in 2002. Building on the original Profit-Sharing Plan, the program provided several improvements. It offered partners more diversified investments and gave them the opportunity to place up to 50% of their pay in tax-deferred savings. Plus, they could see the value and number of shares of Brookshire stock in their accounts. The Company also increased its match of the partners' contributions to half of the first 4% they contribute.

New grocery items introduced in 2000-2010 included White Reese's Peanut Butter Thins, York Thins, Kellogg's Frosted Mini Wheats and Skinny-Dipped Dark Chocolate Almonds.

Average Cost of Grocery Items in 2001

Flour (5lb)	$0.89
Peanut Butter (18oz)	$0.98
Bananas (3lb)	$1.00
Ground Beef (lb)	$1.49

INSIGHTS INTO WOOD T. BROOKSHIRE

Quotes from former Brookshire Grocery Company Partners

"Mr. Brookshire saw excellent customer service as a marketable commodity."

"Mr. Wood was a businessman who believed in God."

"Shortly before Mr. Brookshire passed away, Mrs. Brookshire drove him to my Tyler store. Since he was in a wheelchair, she parked sideways parallel to the sidewalk in front of the store so it would be convenient for him to sit in the car and visit with me. She called me outside to visit with Mr. Wood. He said, 'Son, I appreciate the good job you are doing running this store. Always remember, if you put people first, profits will follow.'"

"Mr. Brookshire would visit my Tyler store regularly. He would come into the store, walk around checking store conditions and visiting with all of the employees. He would leave the store without discussing anything he found wrong. I knew Mr. Brookshire was pleased with what he saw if my supervisor did not arrive at my store within an hour to ask me to take care of a problem."

HELEN LOUISE BROOKSHIRE

March 11, 1909 – November 22, 2006

Family and friends mourned the death of Louise Brookshire, 97, co-founder of Brookshire Grocery Company and widow of Wood T. Brookshire. Mrs. Brookshire exemplified a sweet, gracious and infectious spirit to all who knew her. She had a special love for children, and especially enjoyed being a docent for groups of children who visited the Brookshire's World of Wildlife Museum and Country Store. She also demonstrated an enduring love for her family members. Louise and Wood were avid hunters. They enjoyed participating in three African safaris and many hunting trips on the YO Ranch in South Texas. She had been an active member of the First Presbyterian Church in Tyler for over 70 years.

"My grandmother was an intensely loyal wife, mother and grandmother whose kind and loving nature was apparent to all." — Kirk Brookshire, grandson

"My grandmother was my personal idol! I cherished any and all the time I spent with her. I learned strength and determination from her example. Simply put, she was my role model. She never apologized for her beliefs, and she was led by her faith in God." — Karen Brookshire Womack, granddaughter

"My grandmother was a very special person and a true lady in the highest regard. She had impeccable manners and was extraordinarily gracious. The thing I remember most was

her unconditional love for her family. She was very loyal to her family, particularly to her husband. She was also devoted to her sisters and had a lot of fun with them. She set incredible examples for her grandchildren to follow. My grandmother was instrumental in founding the Company with my grandfather and remained fiercely loyal to the Company throughout her life. She helped establish and continued to be actively involved in the Brookshire's World of Wildlife Museum and Country Store, a passion she shared with my grandfather. It was another way they gave back to their community, offering a free educational opportunity for tens of thousands of visitors each year to experience and learn more about the world and its creatures. To honor her legacy, we established the Louise Brookshire Spirit Award in 2004. This award recognizes outstanding women in BGC leadership who demonstrate my grandmother's qualities of integrity, professional work ethic, service to partners, a high level of energy and unwavering loyalty to BGC."
— Brad Brookshire, grandson

"Mimi, as we lovingly called my grandmother, was a sweet-dispositioned, Southern woman. She was a great encourager and soulmate to my grandfather. She loved the outdoors and was the constant companion to Papaw on travels abroad to Russia, Alaska, England, Paris and many United States cities. She learned to love hunting and went on three safaris to Africa. She agreed to live in the bushveld of Kenya, Tanzania and Mozambique in South Africa for six weeks! During these hunting expeditions, many of the prized trophies were ultimately harvested for the benefit of the Brookshire's World of Wildlife Museum and

Country Store. She boldly stated that on these safaris, *she* was the better shot!" — Britt Brookshire, grandson

Louise Rhein Brookshire, co-founder of Brookshire Grocery Company, 1909-2006.

"Mimi remembered best her family home located inside the family compound in Nacogdoches, Texas. Mimi grew up loving her mother's wonderful cooking and valuing her handmade window curtains and dresses. Her favorite meal was salmon croquettes, German sour pork roast, green peas, mashed potatoes, handmade noodles and marble cake." — B. Tim Brookshire, grandson

"Mimi was so loyal and had a deep love for Papaw and for her family. She was real and true and had no pretense. She loved the simple things in life. Yet, she was a strong, resilient woman. To lose her son and then the love of her life, she faced it bravely and honored them well. She loved to laugh and really took an interest in the person in front of her. She was genuine and generous." — Mark Brookshire, grandson

Mrs. Brookshire was a joy to work with on both the Brookshire's World of Wildlife Museum and Country Store projects. The animals were very dear to her heart, and I received an extra treat hearing her safari stories every time we worked together. She was a lovely and extremely talented lady.

CHAPTER 11

Opportunity and Growth

Highlights of top world news during the 2010-2019 decade included protestors in Hong Kong clashing with police, fire consuming much of the 850-year-old Notre Dame Cathedral in Paris, the U.S. soccer team winning the World Cup and the U.S. House of Representatives impeaching President Donald Trump. Locally, the T.B. Butler Publishing Company (*Tyler Morning Telegraph* newspaper) honored Brookshire Grocery Company with the T.B. Butler Award as Tyler's most outstanding citizen of 2012.

In May 2010 BGC launched its Brookshire Grocery Company WWII Heroes Flight, taking 38 veterans on an all-expenses-paid trip to Washington D.C. to see the memorial built in their honor and other sites. The trip was designed to honor veterans for their service and sacrifices. The 18th flight with 24 veterans occurred in May 2019. The Company has taken more than 480 veterans from Texas, Louisiana and Arkansas since establishing the program.

The Heroes Flight included visits to the WWII Memorial, Arlington National Cemetery and the Air and Space Museum. Visits were also made to memorials honoring the U.S. Marines, Navy, Air Force, Abraham Lincoln, Franklin D. Roosevelt, Martin Luther King Jr. and Vietnam and Korean War veterans. The groups also toured the U.S. Capitol. "Our nation and the world would be very different today if it were not for the incredible bravery and sacrifices of the Americans who served in WWII," said Brad Brookshire.

A group of Heroes Flight veterans shown in front of the nation's capitol.

One of the Flight 19 participants said, "I'm a marine who served in the Korean War. I was thrilled when I was invited to participate in Brookshire's Heroes Flight. It was an unbelievable experience from the time we gathered in Tyler until we returned. It was like a family reunion with the other veterans. What an extra treat it was to be accompanied on the trip by a group of Brookshire partners as our tour guides and, of course, the most impressive Tyler Junior College Apache Belles. We absolutely didn't want for anything because it was already taken care of. It was an unbelievable trip of a lifetime! Thanks to Brookshire's for honoring us veterans."

May 2010 marked a historic day for BGC, Smith County and the City of Tyler as the Company announced a $300,000 donation to help restore five fire-ravaged buildings in downtown Tyler—one of them the home of BGC's first store, opened in 1928 by Wood Brookshire. The restoration represented a time when BGC has come full circle to remember where it all started. The county used BGC's donation to help restore the brick facades of the storefronts, retaining their original look and feel. Some bricks from this first store have been used on an accent wall in the FRESH store in Tyler.

BGC opened the new store banner called FRESH by Brookshire's in Tyler on March 10, 2011. The store was designed to give an upscale shopping experience and features a scratch bakery and many organic items. The store area offers dozens of chef-prepared entrees, authentic Japanese ramen and Vietnamese pho counters, a taco bar, brick-oven Neapolitan-style pizza, an artisanal bakery, dry-aged beef and full-service meat and seafood counters. FRESH by Brookshire's also has a charcuterie with cheese selections, fresh produce with a large variety of organics, a full-service floral shop, a gourmet coffee bar, hand-crafted gelato, patio dining, outdoor café, live music and an on-site park with children's playground.

(Left to right) Brad Brookshire, B. Tim Brookshire and Mark Brookshire at the Grand Opening of FRESH by Brookshire's in Tyler, Texas, on March 10, 2011.

The FRESH store opened and immediately started evolving as a favorite destination in East Texas for an extraordinary food shopping experience with vast culinary and wine selections, along with special events and entertainment for the entire family. The new FRESH concept store has been certified by LEED (Leadership in Energy and Environmental Design), a nationally recognized standard for high-performance green buildings. The *Progressive Grocer* magazine named FRESH by Brookshire's Store of the Month in November 2013. The store was featured on the cover with a story inside.

The first FRESH 15 Road Race was held on March 1, 2014, and continues yearly. The USTA-certified 15-kilometor Road

Race sponsored by BGC is held every March in Tyler and draws runners from all over the region and the nation. The race day also includes a 5-kilometor race and the Lil FRESHie 1K, a race for kids 12 and under. The race focuses on the runner experience, offering the best swag, a safe spectator-filled course and an awesome post-race party with music and refreshments. Money raised in the run is donated to Tyler non-profit organizations. In 2019, 4,400 runners from 22 states and three countries participated. Since the race began, it has raised over $500,000 for charity.

Brookshire's and Super 1 Foods host a half-marathon, 5K and Kids 1K named Heroes Run in Shreveport, Louisiana, benefiting local first responders and military heroes. The 2016 race had 1,500 participants and raised $40,000 for charity. In 2019 more than $70,000 was raised.

Over 16,000 runners along with thousands of volunteers and spectators have participated in the FRESH 15 Run in Tyler and the Heroes Run in Shreveport. So far, these two races have raised more than $1 million for charity.

One of the recent race participants said, "The race was really awesome. It was a lot more excitement and fun than I expected. All of the participants were so supportive. The people along the path were very encouraging and cheering as I passed by them. All in all, the experience was uplifting!"

BGC was selected by *Progressive Grocer* magazine as its 2011 Outstanding Independent Regional Retailer of the year. The magazine featured BGC on the cover with an eight-page special section spotlighting how the Company continues to operate on the "people first" philosophy that has been its cornerstone since 1928.

In 2011 two prominent elected government representatives visited BGC in Tyler, Texas. Governor Rick Perry visited the Tyler Distribution Center on March 8 where he discussed the state's budget during a press conference. U.S. Senator John Cornyn visited the new FRESH by Brookshire's on March 22 during the store's grand opening celebration where he held a press conference to discuss national fiscal concerns.

The Company established the Women's Fellowship Forum in 2012 to support the development of women at BGC and increase their visibility in order to provide opportunities for career development. There were approximately 175 members the year it was formed, who ranged in various positions, including corporate and store-level, part-time and full-time. They would gather several times a year to network with each other and BGC leadership. They would also learn more about career development and hear speakers on everything from time management to character.

In 2012 Danny Glover, actor and film director, filmed a scene from his upcoming movie *Chasing Shakespeare* at Store #604 in Ennis, Texas. The scene was shot in the dairy section and featured the actor selecting a large quantity of eggs.

The partners were excited about the whole experience, including the fact that they got to meet a celebrity. "The historic buildings in downtown Ennis and other areas in Ellis County have attracted an increasing number of filmmakers in recent years," said #604's store director. Three Oscar-winning films including *A Trip to Bountiful*, *Tender Mercies* and *Places in the Heart* were also filmed in the Ellis County area.

In 1989 a scene from *Steel Magnolias*, another popular movie, was filmed inside Brookshire's Store #29 in Natchitoches, Louisiana. In 2007 a scene from *Premonition*, starring Sandra Bullock, was filmed inside Brookshire's #78 in Shreveport, Louisiana.

BGC celebrated two milestones with The University of Texas at Tyler when the school named BGC the 2014 Patriots of the Year recipient. The Patriots of the Year award is given to an individual or individuals who have "made enduring contributions to the advancement of the university and the community," according to a statement from UT Tyler.

The other milestone was the groundbreaking to officially start the construction of the W.T. Brookshire Hall, located in the Ben and Maytee Fisch College of Pharmacy on the campus at UT Tyler. Since that time, W.T. Brookshire Hall has grown to a stately three-story $26.5 million building.

The building was designed to encourage student-faculty interaction, support the college's innovative teaching methods and include a variety of student-centered classroom and faculty spaces. It includes classrooms, study areas, modern pharmacy and compounding laboratories, student lounge, research labs and the Covalent Café.

In 2015 BGC commenced a new chapter in Company leadership. After more than four decades with the Company, CEO Rick Rayford retired from the Company, passing the torch of CEO to Brad Brookshire. "We appreciate Rick's 44 years of service to this company and the legacy he leaves behind," Brad Brookshire said.

The new chairman and CEO, who started working for the Company part-time as a teenager, has since served many leadership roles in the Company. In fact, for 30 years before becoming chairman of the board in 2007, Brad worked his way through various Company positions.

In late 2014 the BGC Board of Directors voted to start privately exploring the possibilities of selling the Company to another grocer. As a result, BGC started attracting a lot of attention from other supermarket operators and private equity investors as the Company leaders explored the potential sale. During the following months there was speculation that the Company was seeking a buyer.

In October 2015, multiple agencies reported the Company was exploring the sale. At the time, the Company had several manufacturing facilities and 152 stores with estimated annual sales of about $2 billion, according to analysts familiar with the situation. A report in the *Dallas Morning News* suggested that BGC could receive more than $1 billion in the sale.

At the time, BGC was working with investment bank JPMorgan Chase & Co. on an auction that would attract peers to possibly purchase the Company. The association with JPMorgan attracted three larger grocery companies, including Albertsons Companies. Albertsons in 2013 had acquired United Supermarkets' 54 stores throughout Texas. In 2015 Albertsons had a $9.2 billion takeover of Safeway. Perhaps they were interested in acquiring another company. Other prospective buyers were reported to be Kroger and H-E-B companies.

A memo issued to BGC partners acknowledged the fact that BGC was seeking a potential deal. The Company also made this statement to partners: "It is our goal to preserve and strengthen Brookshire Grocery Company's business and heritage."

The Company received a bid from a major food store company and bids from two private equity investors. The BGC Board of Directors rejected all three of the bids, concurring they were all too low.

Brad Brookshire was named Chief Executive Officer of Brookshire Grocery Company in 2015.

In 2018 Trent Brookshire, a fourth-generation Brookshire, was promoted to Chief Operating Officer.

In late November, Brad Brookshire announced in a letter to the Company partners that the BGC Board of Directors had voted to discontinue the sale process. He said, "I am pleased that the board of directors of the Company has decided this morning to discontinue the sale process of our Company. The Company is no longer for sale, and we can now focus on the things that matter most—our customers and partners. I personally want to thank each one of you for sticking with us during these past few months of difficult uncertainty."

Kevin Eltife, Chairman of The University of Texas System's Board of Regents and a former mayor of Tyler and member of the Texas Senate, spoke at the Grand Reopening of Store #51 in Tyler shortly after the Company announced it was no longer for sale. "I've never seen such an outpouring in this community about a corporate citizen that we could possibly lose to a larger company. There's a reason for that. There's not been a more generous family in this community than the Brookshire family. There's not been a better corporate citizen in this community than Brookshire Grocery Company. And that includes the employees who are partners in this company.

"When I was mayor, I remember how many times we called on Brookshire Grocery Company when we needed help for the poor, for the needy, for all parts of Tyler—not just South Tyler but north, south, east and west. You are the fiber of this community. You are what makes Tyler such a great place to live."

In 2015 the Company donated $15,000 to update the BGC-themed exhibit at the Discovery Science Place in Tyler. The exhibit was first installed in 2004. Renovation highlights included a working monitor and scanner at the check stand, as well as touch screen monitors. The exhibit is a hands-on learning center that features a small-scaled grocery store and interactive games and activities to teach children about nutrition and budgeting. The NuVal nutritional scoring system used in BGC stores was added to product tags at the mock store to educate children on how to make healthier nutritional choices.

The updated exhibit now includes a "farm-to-table" aspect to show visitors how fresh produce moves from farms to grocery stores, and ultimately to their homes and dinner table. In the past 11 years the Company has contributed more than $50,000 to the Discovery Science Place for the creation and maintenance of the exhibit.

Several communities in BGC's market area experienced severe weather in May 2015. At least one partner in the Van, Texas, area lost her home. Two residents died and dozens were injured, but no BGC stores were damaged.

One of the tornados that hit Van and the surrounding area was classified as a EF3, with wind speeds anywhere from 136-165 mph. Roughly 30 percent of the town was damaged or destroyed, with approximately $40 million in damage.

BGC partners from the six cities in the surrounding area volunteered to help. More than 700 hours were volunteered the first week. Partners did everything from sorting donated goods, to cleaning up debris, to preparing and distributing food and beverages to the community and volunteers.

Initially the Company donated $7,000 in food, bottled water and other supplies. The Company also created "We Stand With Van" shirts to sell as a fundraiser in BGC stores around Van. The shirts sold for $10, with about $7 of every sale going to a relief fund. Stores also had a $1 scan coupon that customers could purchase at the register to donate to the American Red Cross.

In June 2016 BGC purchased 25 Texas and Louisiana stores from Walmart (formerly their Walmart Express brand). The

20 stores in Texas and five stores in Louisiana were rebranded as Spring Market. The new name represents and honors the Company's great history which began with its first store location on Spring Avenue in Tyler. Partners from across the Company and supplier sales reps worked to open the stores in just a few weeks, beginning in late July. These stores resulted in 25 store director promotions, 50 promotions for other leaders and hundreds of jobs in new communities for the Company. Spring Markets are all about small-town stores serving local communities. These stores stand for friendly service, quality products, affordable convenience, and a pleasant shopping environment.

Spring Market is a distinct brand with a format designed uniquely for this new concept. These stores offer many of the same products as the Company's other store brands, including produce, market, dairy, bakery, grocery and health and beauty care items. Each location includes a fuel center, and some stores sell beer and wine. When the 25 new stores opened, it brought BGC's store count to 177, the most in the Company's history. "We're going to have more than 25 Spring Market stores," Brad Brookshire stated. Sure enough, another Spring Market, located in Arkansas, opened in 2020, the only one without a fuel center.

In 2017 BGC sold its manufacturing plants in Tyler to Missouri-based Hiland Dairy Foods. The sale included BGC's ice cream plant and dairy and water plants. Brad Brookshire said that this decision to sell made sense on a number of levels, and the assurance from Hiland that they will retain the employees, supply our stores with the same great products and expand these operations at the plants in Tyler confirmed that this would be a good fit. In its statement, the CEO of Hiland Dairy said they were committed to growing the facilities and investing capital dollars to expand product capabilities.

An exciting time occurred for BGC's pharmacy operations in 2017, as the Company continued to streamline the prescription refill process through a new central fill facility. The Company's former bakery plant near Tyler was converted into a pharmacy central fill facility. The facility features premier high-speed automated machines that use robotic arms to dispense medication, along with automated prescription packaging machines. A conveyor belt carries orders through the entire refill process and can hold several hundred orders at a time.

The central fill operation allows prescriptions to be filled more efficiently and at a fraction of the in-store cost. By reducing the in-store pharmacy workload, partners can focus more on serving guests and patients. Partners now have more time to interact with customers and address their needs. These services are critical to the success of BGC's pharmacy operations and include Medication Therapy Management, immunizations, point-of-care testing and other health initiatives.

In 2018 BGC continued to move toward a unified leadership involving an appropriate alignment of responsibilities and improved outcomes. An important organizational change in retail included naming Trent Brookshire chief operating officer. Trent had more than 15 years of service with BGC, and represents the fourth generation of the Brookshire family in the Company leadership. He is the great-grandson of Wood

T. Brookshire, the grandson of S.W. "Woody" Brookshire and son of Brad Brookshire, chairman and CEO. There are very few companies who make it to the fourth generation.

I asked Trent, "How does being a family-owned grocery company set BGC apart from other independent and chain retailers?" He answered, "The word 'family' really says it all. In a family there is a level of authentic care that cannot be manufactured or replicated. At BGC that care extends to our partners, our vendor-partners, our customers and the 150 communities we are proud to be a part of. A family business offers a level of heartfelt care for people that no national or international can compare with."

Trent was also asked, "What is your vision for the future of BGC?" He said, "My vision for the future of our Company is for our stores to keep getting better to the point that we are best in class, not only in our current markets but in many more to come."

In 2018 BGC acquired eight Winn-Dixie supermarkets in Louisiana to become a part of the Company's Super 1 Foods stores. The stores went under a brief transition period and were opened in a matter of several days. "We are excited about this opportunity to grow and expand in the Acadia region," said Brad Brookshire.

The regional vice president for Winn-Dixie in Alabama, Mississippi and Louisiana said, "We are pleased to have found a strong partner in Brookshire Grocery Company, who shares our focus on customers and who respects and values their employees." He continued, "We know Brookshire Grocery

Company very well and are confident that the eight stores being transferred will see continued success in their communities."

Since becoming chairman and CEO of BGC in late 2015, Brad Brookshire started working with Company leaders on a campaign to renew the Company's focus on W. T. Brookshire's 1928's founding principles. Therefore, in 2018, the Company started moving forward by combining today's best business practices with Mr. W.T.'s core values. Today, the Company refers to these core values as "The W.T. Way." In 2018, the Company introduced these Core Values:

"Jump Over The Counter" Service Excellence (We strive to deliver a higher level of service every day because it is our duty to make the difference in the lives of our customers, partners and communities.)

Do The Right Thing (BGC partners are expected to be people of character. We aim to conduct ourselves with utmost honesty and integrity while treating everyone with respect.)

Competitive Grit (We are constantly trying to improve the customer shopping experience and will diligently persevere in the face of competition.)

Do Your Best Every Day (We demand excellence of ourselves and others each workday.)

The Team Matters (We value our partners. Their individual commitment to the team effort drives BGC's success.)

Results-Driven With A Future Focus (Results matter. Our company's future depends on the results we obtain today.)

In order to help ensure the core values remain ingrained in BGC's culture, signs were placed in store break rooms and corporate areas. Leaders were tasked with reviewing the core values at meetings that begin with prayer and celebrating partners for actions that reinforce the core values.

The following incident is an example of how Wood Brookshire's "jump over the counter" service value is still alive in Brookshire's stores after 92 years. A nurse from the Ochsner LSU Health Hospital in Shreveport, Louisiana, got off work on April 6, 2020 at 8 p.m. (during the COVID-19 pandemic) after many days of 12-hour shifts. She went to Brookshire's on Barksdale Blvd. in Bossier City, Louisiana, to get some groceries she needed. She said, "I didn't even know they closed grocery stores at 8 because of COVID-19, so I went to Brookshire's on Barksdale, got there about 8:15 and tried to go in. I'd just got off work, so I still had my scrubs on. Anyway the guy says, 'We're closed.' So I turned around, hung my head and walked back to my car. The guy comes running out to get me. They let me shop, even ran around the store getting things on my list for me. I couldn't believe it! It was so amazing to me."

A customer at the Canton, Texas, Brookshire's spoke about a time when a young father with children, who was in front of him in the checkout line, didn't have enough money for his entire order. Before this customer could pull out his wallet to help, the courtesy clerk bagging the man's groceries reached into his own wallet and paid the difference. The same customer also said, "You can go into some corporate stores and you are just a billfold to them. There's no friendliness, and the atmosphere is cold. It's not like that at Brookshire's. You are important here." The "old-fashioned service" the customer referred to is part of

BGC's over 90-year legacy. "Jump over the counter" service is much alive in BGC's stores today!

Another example occurs when "Mr. Bob" steps off the city bus and enters the doors of Store #627 in Lafayette, Louisiana. He does not turn to select a grocery cart or pull out his grocery list like other guests. Instead he stands and waits, knowing store partners will soon be at his side. Mr. Bob is blind and needs assistance to shop for his groceries.

"I always get the help I need, and I do need help with certain things. People are always friendly and courteous, while still being professional," he said.

A cashier and the front-end manager always step up to help Mr. Bob. As soon as he comes in the door they go right to him. They go out of their way to make sure he is taken care of. They escort him around the store to make sure he gets everything he needs. They even make sure he catches the store's sales and coupons while they shop.

When they finish shopping, partners take Mr. Bob to the checkout and sack his groceries, making sure he has everything he needs before waiting for the city bus to return.

The cashier said, "To 'jump over the counter' means to go out of your way to do what's best for the customer. It's something I've always done and will continue doing."

The front-end manager added, "It's making sure the customers come first. It makes me feel good inside because I always want to help people."

"It makes me feel wanted," Mr. Bob said. "What else can I say?"

Wood Brookshire once said, "There are many reasons why each partner does a better job. When a person puts out good work he or she is (1) helping Brookshire's beat competition, and thereby providing better jobs. (2) gaining a feeling of achievement and personal satisfaction."

"I am convinced that our focus on our core values is reigniting the passion and vision of my grandfather. We are on the right path to create the bright future he envisioned for us. I believe our core values will continue to inspire and guide us as we take BGC to the next level for our customers, partners and communities," Brad Brookshire said.

The Company launched a new Leadership Academy, with the first group of store directors completing the program in February 2018. The purpose of the Academy is to help ensure store leaders in the Company's four banners are hearing from senior management with one voice.

Store directors hear firsthand from Chairman and CEO Brad Brookshire, along with other senior leaders and subject matter experts. Sessions cover everything from business acumen and food safety to HR law and team building, along with the Company's history, values and culture. The Leadership Academy takes place over two to three days at the Company's corporate office.

On September 1, 2018, the Brookshire Grocery Company celebrated its 90th anniversary. Partners across the Company served birthday cake to customers on a Saturday. Chairman and CEO Brad Brookshire kicked off the day's celebration by visiting Store #9 in Tyler, a descendant of one of the original

Brookshire's store locations.

In observance of the 90th anniversary Brad celebrated with a "90 Stores in 90 Days Challenge" and personally visited 90 of the BGC stores in 90 days. He said the challenge gave him the opportunity to talk face-to-face with hundreds of partners in various roles, departments and communities across the region. He learned what many partners loved about their jobs and the Company, along with some of the challenges and areas where the Company can do better. He said, "I was able to talk directly with many of BGC's customers and continue to learn from their feedback."

In 2019 BGC was recognized on *Forbes'* inaugural list of America's Best-In-State Employer in Texas. The selection was based on an independent survey from a vast sample of more than 80,000 people working for companies employing at least 500 people. Participants were asked to rate their willingness to recommend their employer to friends and family. The Company also received a designation as one of the cleanest grocers in the nation by *Consumer Reports*.

A new venture occurred in Tyler in 2019 when Pizza Hut opened its first kiosks in a grocery store in the United States. Two kiosks were opened, one in a Brookshire's and one in a Super 1 Foods store. Each Pizza Hut kiosk offers a menu with hot and ready items that include personal pizzas, pastas, hot wings, Parmesan bites, pretzel bites and Hershey's chocolate chip cookies. Both are open daily from 11 a.m. to 7 p.m.

In 2019 BGC employed more than 14,000 employee-partners and operated more than 175 stores throughout Texas,

Louisiana and Arkansas under the Brookshire's, Super 1 Foods, FRESH by Brookshire's and Spring Market banners.

The Company slogan during this decade was **"Share Meals—Share Life."**

INSIGHTS INTO WOOD T. BROOKSHIRE

Comments from Former Brookshire Grocery Company Partners

"Mr. Brookshire reminded me that it takes the best combined efforts of all of us for Brookshire's to continue to have the warmest spot in the hearts of the people we endeavor to serve."

"Mr. Brookshire always taught us store managers to be very confidential with store sales. Once I delivered some lamb chops to the Brookshire home, located near my store. After Mr. and Mrs. Brookshire invited me into their home, Mr. Wood said, 'Mama, will you please go into the other room for a minute?' After she left the room he said, 'Now, son, tell me how much volume you did yesterday!'"

"Mr. Wood was a great fellow. I never will forget how he pushed us to do better. Back then, the average sales per week were $25,000. Mr. Wood told me once, 'Jim, if you can't pick 100 pounds of cotton a week, then

turn in your sack.' He meant for me to sell $100,000 worth of groceries, but he was joking. He was good at that. He wanted me to build better sales."

"Mr. Wood came into the store once when I was really busy and swept the front sidewalk. After he was finished he put the broom up, waved at me and left. He just had a way of getting along with people. He also knew how to buy. He knew how to negotiate with the suppliers to get as good of a deal, or better, as the other grocery stores."

"Mr. W.T. was a dynamic leader and someone all of us had great respect for. His sons, Bruce and Woody, were wonderful people and great leaders. They taught many of us in this business a great deal."

BRUCE GLENN BROOKSHIRE

December 3, 1928 – April 16, 2010

BGC mourned the death of Bruce Glenn Brookshire, oldest son of W.T. Brookshire, founder and emeritus chairman of the board of BGC. Bruce's vision and leadership as chairman of the board for over 30 years helped the Company grow to 156 stores at his death. His magnetic personality and infectious smile were well known to the community and to company partners. In the Company he was affectionately known as "The Prune Peddler." Slogans Bruce not only created, but also were philosophies by which he strived to live were:

"We have a SMILE in store for you."

"Pay obsessive attention to each customer."

"We don't sell just food; we sell warm, friendly, courteous customer service!"

Honesty and uncompromising integrity were tenets of his business dealings throughout his life.

Britt Brookshire, Bruce's son, recalled how his father taught him to live his life. He said, "As a child, my father exampled to me the daily long hours of work that the competitive grocery business required. Then, as an adult, he taught me the value of honorable work. Eventually as an employee and executive of BGC, my dad continually emphasized that working hard at any task, great or small, at the best of my ability was what God required of us. Therefore, Colossians 3:23 'In everything you do, do your work heartily as unto the Lord, rather than to man,' was a little lesson my father taught me.

"My father was very 'people oriented.' He strived to treat everyone fairly regardless of their job responsibility, title, race or economic level. I'm so grateful for this lesson as it molded me professionally and personally.

"Dad was insistent that our actions be of utmost honesty and with pure integrity. He spoke many times of this notable quality. I remember it being his corporate measuring stick of character."

Bruce's eldest son, B. Tim Brookshire, said, "The lessons learned from my father are extensive and span the course of his wonderful life. Most lessons were observed through his own life and how he lived and treated people. He led by example and was forgiving, generous and patient with those he worked with. Other paramount lessons were those of honesty and integrity and honoring a promise. My father also encouraged me to give generously and help those who had nothing.

"One Thanksgiving my brother Britt and I were looking forward to our annual deer hunt in South Texas. Before leaving for the hunt, Dad announced that we would make a shopping trip to our Bergfeld Brookshire's store. He said, 'Load up those carts, boys. Pile them up with everything you would like to eat for Thanksgiving.' We were delighted. Cart after cart after cart was loaded, but then our shopping trip had a diversion. His loaded blue Chevrolet was driven to the Salvation Army where we gave everything to the needy people there. 'Boys, always remember that we don't own anything—we are only stewards of blessings for a while. These good people at the Salvation Army need to eat a nice Thanksgiving meal too, and we are going to provide it.' Dad's best lesson was about a lifelong example of stewardship. A good name is to be more desired than riches. Thank you, Papa, for leading by example. You were right—it is more blessed to give than receive."

One retail leader said, "Mr. Bruce was an outstanding and compassionate leader in our company. When I was a district manager, he would call me almost every Thanksgiving morning and wish me and my family a Happy Thanksgiving."

Bruce was a people person and taught me to take care of the partners who worked under me. He always encouraged me to reward them when they did a good job and to prepare them for promotion.

CHAPTER 12

An Unusual Year

The year 2020 was a very unique year. It was the only year anyone was likely to live long enough where the first two digits of the date matched the second two digits. This is the first time this has happened since 1919. It will not occur again until 2121. Anyone alive in 2020 would have to be at least 101 in 2121!

In March 2020, Brookshire Grocery Company announced the second location of its culinary-focused FRESH by Brookshire's concept in Fate, Texas. Groundbreaking for the new location was scheduled for the end of the year with completion anticipated by late 2021. "We are excited to be bringing the next generation of our incredible FRESH by Brookshire's shopping experience to the community of Fate," said Trent Brookshire. The new store marks a milestone in the Company's over 92-year history.

In August 2020 BGC was certified as "A Great Place to Work." The certification is from August 2020-August 2021.

Great Place to Work's mission is, "To build a better world by helping every organization become a Great Place to Work for All." Some of the benefits BGC will receive from the certification include helping recruit cream of the crop talent and helping build pride among the workforce.

Exterior view of FRESH by Brookshire's, 2020.

Each year BGC partners contribute over 20,000 hours volunteering in the communities they serve. Also, the annual vendor-supported Brookshire Benefit Golf Tournament, Fresh 15 Run in Tyler and the Heroes Run in Shreveport, Louisiana, continue to raise thousands of dollars each year supporting causes the Company feels most deeply about: education, hunger relief, family well-being, military personnel and first responders. In addition, Company partners are involved in many worthwhile activities to raise money supporting local causes. Partners adopt families for Christmas and also participate in local blood drives, cook-offs, sports festivals, cooking schools, corporate challenges, Light House for the Blind, Relay-for-Life, Kidsfest,

Adopt-A-School, Habitat for Humanity, Special Olympics, livestock auctions, Food Banks, Check-out Hunger, United Way and The Salvation Army. They also support community and national events and local fundraisers to help those in need after natural disasters.

Since 1980, BGC has spent 365 days a year recycling cardboard. Over 27,000 tons of corrugated boxes are used in BGC's operations annually. This equals to approximately 459,000 trees. This massive number of boxes would end up in landfills without partners' support of BGC's recycling program. Because of their efforts, over six million trees have been saved from destruction since 1980! The recycling program reduces BGC's expenses, creates revenue and most importantly makes a difference in the environment. "We are fulfilling our responsibility to be a good corporate citizen by taking care of the environment, and I am proud of our results," Brad Brookshire said.

In 2020 a devastating worldwide pandemic, starting in China and spreading to the rest of the world, hit our nation. Pandemics are a global outbreak of a disease, happening when a new virus emerges to infect people and can spread between people sustainably. Because there was little or no pre-existing immunity against the new virus, it spread worldwide very fast. Coronavirus disease 2019 (COVID-19) caused a devastating respiratory illness. Symptoms included fever or chills, cough (dry or productive), fatigue, body aches, muscle or joint pain, shortness of breath, sore throat, headaches, nausea, vomiting, diarrhea, nasal congestion and loss of taste or smell. As this book goes to print, this disease has killed over 200,000 Americans and 973,000 worldwide.

The COVID-19 pandemic stay-at-home order took effect in Texas, county by county. It went into effect in Tyler and Smith County on March 27, 2020. The order allowed for essential activities, businesses and services to continue while all retail stores, restaurants and even schools had to be closed. As a designated "Essential Employer," meaning services deemed as critical to the infrastructure of our nation by both federal and state governments, BGC stores continued to remain open for business.

Throughout the COVID-19 pandemic, meetings were held in all areas of BGC to determine how to handle this serious situation that had never been encountered in the modern world. Brad Brookshire, chairman and CEO said, "We are in this together, and it is important to remain calm. As friends and neighbors, let us continue to come together to support one another and be kind."

Abiding by the COVID-19 guidelines for essential businesses and following recommendations from the Centers for Disease Control and Prevention (CDC) created a new normal for partners and customers at all BGC stores. The Company immediately increased the frequency of sanitizing shopping carts, handrails, baskets, keypads, countertops, etc. Cart wipes were available at the front door of every store. Stores posted signs at the entrance encouraging several recommended measures, including social distancing of six feet apart and the importance of washing hands regularly. Partners wore company-provided facemasks and gloves to keep the virus from spreading and started having their temperature taken at the start of their shifts to ensure no fever was detected. The Company had always had high standards when it came to having clean stores, but the pandemic created even higher standards with additional cleaning and sanitation steps.

In order to meet the increase in sales and additional demands, BGC hired an extra 2,500 partners, bringing the total to 16,000 in the 181 stores including Brookshire's, FRESH by Brookshire's, Super 1 Foods and Spring Markets.

Exterior view of a Super 1 Foods, 2020.

BGC's top priority has always been the health and safety of its partners and customers. The Company started monitoring the COVID-19 situation in early January and continued to implement best practices and procedures to adapt its business model during the unprecedented time that lay ahead. When the virus hit, Brad Brookshire said, "We had protocols and procedures in place to protect our partners and customers while in our stores. We were prepared for this pandemic, and are continuing to evaluate our protocols every day as expert guidance becomes available."

Due to increased demand, all stores shifted to modified store hours of 8 a.m. to 8 p.m. so employees could catch up on replenishing shelves and cleaning. Later, the 8 a.m. opening was changed to 7 a.m. Closing store hours ranged from 7:30 p.m. to 10 p.m., based on the location of the store.

All Brookshire's, FRESH by Brookshire's and Super 1 Foods stores in Tyler started offering free next-day pharmacy delivery to senior citizens Monday through Friday.

The Company suspended the practice of allowing customers to bring reusable bags into the store. Because senior citizens were more susceptible to the disease, the Company asked for the customers' help in reserving the first two hours of the day that the store was open for senior citizens and critical emergency responders to shop.

The Company also requested that senior citizens be allowed to move to the head of the checkout line throughout the day. Additionally, the Company offered a temporary 5% daily discount to customers age 60 or over with a valid ID. During the first nine weeks of the discount program, BGC was able to save recipients over $7.1 million dollars. From March through July, recipients saved $13.4 million on grocery items. The discount was extended to July 31 and then to September 8. It was extended again as this book went to press. The Company also waived fees for all guests on curbside orders.

Decals were placed on the floor at the checkout to help customers practice social distancing. As an added layer of protection, clear partitions between the customers and partners were installed at checkouts and pharmacy counters.

A Company spokesman said, "We saw a huge influx of business due to societal fear. People felt uncertain because of a fear of the unknown. They wanted to stock up and hold up in their homes to be safe. People first started with paper products and sanitizers, progressing to the staples like milk, eggs, bread and cases of water. Last, it moved to meal solutions like frozen meals."

Most of the BGC stores received daily deliveries, partners stocked throughout the day to replenish and the Company worked with suppliers to address any outages that stores experienced. In order to serve all customers, limits were placed on some items. Customers were encouraged to buy for preparedness and not stockpiling. The following items were limited: ground beef, fresh chicken, milk, eggs, rice, beans, canned soup, Ramen, bread, water, paper items, sanitation and cold/flu items.

BGC stayed busy throughout the pandemic in an effort to protect customers and partners alike. In April 2020, over 15,000 masks were available for partners, and other measures were added to continue to keep customers and partners safe. The *Tyler Morning Telegraph* printed a story about BGC's furnishing masks for all employees, inspiring many readers to express their appreciation for this effort.

In recognition of and gratitude for the spirit of the partners shown through this difficult time, the Company implemented several monetary rewards to partners. In March the Company awarded a special half-week's discretionary pay to all partners. Also, in March a $1 per hour pay increase was awarded to partners in retail stores and logistics. This increase was good until the end of April. It was extended three more times through September 11. About a month later, in a continued effort to help its employees during COVID-19, BGC gave more than 14,000 retail employees each a second bonus up to a half-week's pay. In addition, the Company implemented an extra 5% partner discount in stores, provided on-site meals and developed a compensation for those partners who were directly affected by COVID-19. In appreciation of partners' service during the COVID-19 pandemic, BGC also gave gift cards to all 16,000 partners amounting to $1.5 million.

A total of approximately $21 million in assistance was awarded to the partners. Family means everything to BGC, and the Company wanted to do something special for its partners and their families. The Company is incredibly appreciative of everything partners are doing to take care of customers and communities and for upholding the Company's safety procedures while serving the customer's needs.

Earl Campbell, nicknamed "The Tyler Rose," was a University of Texas Longhorn running back and graduate, an eight-year NFL player, a 1977 Heisman Memorial Trophy winner and a John Tyler High School graduate. He had these comments for BGC partners about the pandemic: "I remember the incredible opportunity I had serving as a BGC partner (in high school). I remember the hard work it took sacking groceries, stocking shelves and working in the produce department.

Exterior view of a Spring Market, 2020.

"You as a BGC partner, like never before, have stepped up to help during this pandemic. You have served every need in your community, and it is noticed!

"BGC believes in taking care of their partners, which they have done throughout this crisis. BGC has invested more than $8 million dollars (at the time) back to you all in appreciation bonuses, hourly pay increases, extra employee discounts and much, much more. Follow your company guidelines—wear your masks to help protect you and your customer. After all, you are showcasing BGC's core values—making it a stronger company and a brighter future.

"We would like to sincerely thank you for what you have been doing for BGC. We are going to get through this, and I would like to say a very sincere thank you!"

In April BGC started offering a 5% percent daily discount on store brand products for critical and emergency service providers through July 7. The discount was extended through September 8 and once more as this book went to press. The discount was for all emergency first responders (EMS, fire department, and law enforcement officers), hospital personnel and active-duty military (including National Guard and Military reserve). "We believe it is important to show appreciation to those who are serving on the front lines caring for our neighbors," said Brad Brookshire.

As a Christian company, BGC had traditionally prided itself on observing Christmas and Easter holidays by closing all stores on those holidays. However, the Company decided as an essential business that it is dedicated to serving their customers during such an unprecedented time. All BGC stores were open on Easter until 5 p.m. "Our founder, Wood T. Brookshire, believed it was his God-given calling to serve humanity through the grocery business. By opening our stores on this holiday, we are serving God by serving man during these difficult times. It was not an easy decision to break from our 92-year history of closing on Easter, and we do not take it lightly. We are incredibly thankful for our partners' continued dedication and selfless service to our customers during this trying time, and we are glad they will be home with their families for Easter dinner," said Brad Brookshire.

April 12, 2020, was the most unique Easter Sunday in our nation's history with the stay-at-home order in place. Because of COVID-19 Christians in the East Texas area celebrated Easter

Sunday without indoor services in any church. One church held Easter services outdoors where members were instructed to stay in their cars. Still another church's pastor and his wife handed out printed devotionals, candy, prayer cloths and even communion-to-go at a drive-by event in the church's parking lot. The parking lot was used as a meeting area for another church. Church members were asked to socially distance themselves while the sermon was delivered. One church asked its members to use cell phones to text one another hymns and Bible scriptures. Many other Easter services were held virtually by way of Facebook Live or other streaming services. A Tyler pastor summed up the COVID-19 situation by saying, "The one thing we will all take away from this historic time of distancing is this: We will never again take for granted the magnificent blessing of gathering together to worship our Creator."

Many people in America began to recognize that grocery store employees were also working tirelessly on the front lines during the pandemic. Even as sales in other retail areas declined, grocery sales nationwide skyrocketed.

BGC donated $1 million and matched customer donations up to $500,000 to food banks in the Company's region. The million was split between Texas and Louisiana food banks in BGC communities. This effort helped the food banks provide for people who lost jobs and income. It is estimated that the $1.5 million funded about 16 million meals. This giving spirit follows the statement Wood T. Brookshire made 92 years ago when he shared, "I firmly believe if you take out of the community, you must put back into it time, leadership and money."

Texas Governor Greg Abbott named Brad Brookshire to serve on his strike force committee to reopen the state's economy that suffered tremendously during COVID-19. The strike force included various working groups on economic recovery and a special advisory council made up of business leaders representing the state's regions and industries. Brad served on the strike force's special advisory council. He said, "I was proud to be a part of this historic effort to help Texas get back to work, school and their normal routines as safely as possible.

"The council had regular calls to discuss how to safely reopen Texas," Brad continued. "As an essential business, our stores remained open throughout the pandemic, which gave us a unique opportunity to help other businesses."

Governor Greg Abbott's Phase 1 lifting the stay-at-home order in Texas on May 1, 2020, began to reopen parts of the state's economy. Certain businesses were allowed to open, at only 25% of occupancy, which later changed to 50%.

On Saturday, April 25, NBC's *Saturday Night Live* late-night talk show did a parody commercial for items you can get during the pandemic at what appeared to be a Brookshire's Food and Pharmacy. The show used "Bartenson's Grocery Store" with the font, red and green colors and logo with the signature green leaf exactly the same as the Brookshire's logo. The two-minute and 28-second sketch was viewed almost one million times on the *Saturday Night Live* Facebook page.

The commercial started with the two actors saying, "Chicken, eggs, milk, soap and bread might be flying off the shelves, but customers might want to buy some items that were extremely in stock. So much so that the store might want to get rid of them." They showed a few fake items like mint Pringles, fluoride bananas, Boy Scout cookies, oat milk pizza and Hawaiian pizza. They did say, "The store is dependable, and we want to give you what you want, but first you have to buy what we have."

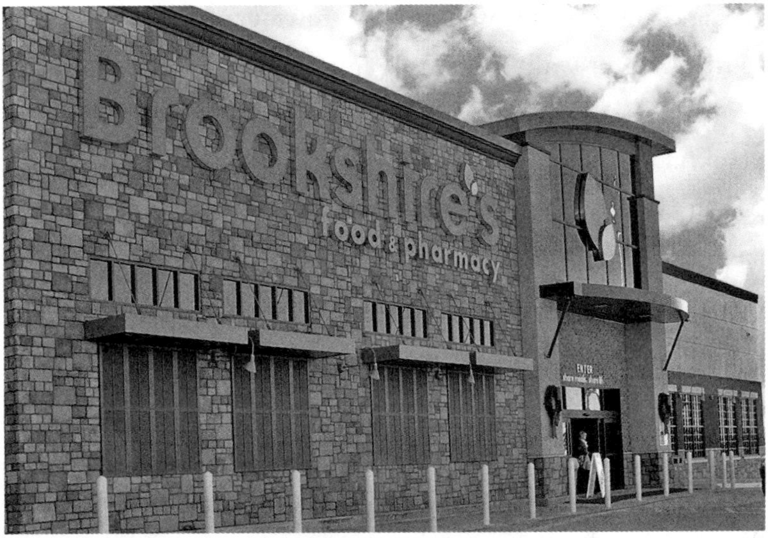

Exterior view of a Brookshire's food store, 2020.

An account of the parody commercial and Brookshire's response to it appeared in an article in the *Tyler Morning Telegraph* newspaper shortly afterwards. The following is a recap of the newspaper's story: On April 28, Brookshire Grocery Company's Chairman and CEO Brad Brookshire and Chief Operating Officer Trent Brookshire dressed up the same as the two *SNL* actors. They posed like the comedy duo and recreated three Bartenson's commercials on Facebook and Instagram using the Brookshire's Food and Pharmacy logo.

The caption with the photos from Brookshire's said, "From your friends at Brookshire Grocery Store, we all wanted to let you know that we are out of stock of Mint Pringles, Dasani Clorox, Pepto Bismol Oreos and Peeps Soup. But don't worry, we have substitutes."

The response from social media was positive. One of the viewers said, "We LOVE our small-town grocery store and are so thankful for y'all! FYI we are in Comanche, Texas."

Another comment was, "Great job, Brad and Trent. So thankful for all that you do for this community."

"It's great that with everything else going on, you can still have fun. Thanks for what you have done for our community," was another comment.

Still another person said, "Love Brookshire's and Super One. Don't get like other stores. That's why I shop you guys."

The decline in the oil economy during the pandemic had an adverse effect on the nation, including East Texas. Efforts to limit the spread of the coronavirus had major cities around the world on lockdown, air travel was seriously curtailed and millions of people worked from home, leading to fewer commuters on the road. Hardly anyone was driving. Thus, the price of crude oil dropped to more than 80% than it was at the start of the year. This reduction led to cheaper prices of gas at the pump, a boon for consumers. The price in Tyler went to less than $1.30 per gallon for regular unleaded gas.

In early May the COVID-19 crisis sent U.S. unemployment surging to 14.7%, a level last seen when the country was in the throes of the Great Depression and President Roosevelt was assuring Americans, saying, "The only thing to fear is fear itself."

One person summed up the feelings of staying-at-home when he stated, "Our lives have been put on hold during this pandemic. It is an uncanny feeling sitting at home, looking for things to do. We can only look forward to looking at magazines, television, the newspaper and the mail. It is weird, indeed!"

We could not have known that this COVID-19 virus would happen. But it did happen, and we knew that we would never again be certain of anything!

As long as this pandemic exists, all Brookshire stores will continue to follow CDC guidelines. They will also strive to keep on the store shelves items that the customers need and want.

Some new food products hitting the grocery shelves in 2020 were Pop Tarts Sugar Cookies, Pillsbury Bark Mix, Kellogg's Eggo Bites Mini Pancakes, Starbucks Cold Brew Coffee and Goldfish Veggie Crackers.

Insights into Wood T. Brookshire

Quotes from Former Brookshire Grocery Company Partners

"'Give excellent customer service' was reiterated so many times by Mr. Brookshire that it became a firmly held belief in the Company that this is what has made our company successful"

"Mr. Wood believed in being fair and impartial to partners, customers and vendors"

"Mr. Brookshire always promised fair treatment, and he gave it! The Company follows his example by doing the same today."

CHAPTER 13

Memories of Louise Brookshire

The following are recollections Louise Brookshire wrote about her family and childhood:

Family

I am a third-generation German. I was born in my parent's home in Belleville, Illinois, on March 11, 1909. The doctor, along with his nurse, came to our home for the delivery. My Pappa had to dig them a path out on the front walk because the snow was waist-deep.

My mother's name was Anna Louise Schmidt, and my father's name was Cassimir Constance Rhein. He was calm, sure and certain with the advice he gave us children. My name was chosen from my mother's name, Anna Louise, and from my mother's best friend named Helen Louise. So, I was named Helen Louise. I was the oldest of six children.

My grandfather Schmidt, born in Boos, Germany, was all German in habits and traditions. He was very successful in the cotton trade before getting into the department store business. My grandmother, Elizabeth Schmidt, was a precious person. She was the postmistress in Nacogdoches when she and Grandpa married. She was gifted in sewing, cooking and managing a household with several housekeepers, some brought over from Germany after Grandpa made a fortune in buying cotton.

My father owned a retail shoe store in Belleville, Illinois. Then he owned a wholesale shoe company in St. Louis, Missouri. My family moved to Nacogdoches, Texas, when I was a young girl, and my father was Secretary-Treasurer of the Mayer and Schmidt Department Store in Nacogdoches, which was owned by his father-in-law. Then, my family moved to Webster Groves, Missouri, then back to Nacogdoches.

All of our family members owned homes in Nacogdoches, clustered around Grandma and Grandpa Schmidt's home.

Church

As a youngster I attended Sunday class at the Catholic Church in Nacogdoches where my mother was church organist. Mama was Catholic, and Pappa was Lutheran. There was no Lutheran church in Nacogdoches.

My family used paper fans at church in the summer months. All of the church's windows were open.

Education

I attended kindergarten in the Old Stone Fort—a historical building in Nacogdoches. I attended grade school in Webster Grove, Missouri. I had trouble learning my 3 X's table at the Catholic Holy Redeemer School, taught by Catholic nuns.

I graduated in 1925 from Nacogdoches High School where I played center on the girls' basketball team. I recalled an unusual experience that occurred during my graduation exercises. We graduates were all sitting on the stage and were called to receive our diplomas. We were seated in alphabetical order, and my name was not called—since my diploma was the one that had fallen on the floor! I did receive my diploma with special attention and an apology.

We took our lunch to school, and we girls sat on old, huge Indian mounds under a large oak tree to eat lunch. The mounds were historical and are still on the campus of Nacogdoches High School. My favorite high school cheer was, "Seniors of '23 were good, and the Seniors of '24, but the best ones alive, are those of '25, and the best for evermore."

After high school I attended Stephen F. Austin State Teacher's College since it was in my hometown. I majored in Home Economics because I liked it!

Entertainment

A very proud moment in my childhood was when I received lots of home-grown flowers (there was not a florist in town) that were thrown on stage (a custom then) as I played the piano.

As young children we made leaf houses, and we loved to burn leaves each fall. Everyone burned their own leaves in their yard. It was so nice to smell and see them burn.

I enjoyed cutting out paper dolls from old dress pattern books from Pappa's store.

My talents as a youth were sewing by hand and roller-skating on the sidewalk and driveway around my grandparent's house.

Pappa always took us to see the circus when it came to town, and he also took us to see the circus unload at the railway depot at 5 a.m. My Grandpa took all of his family to Galveston to the big Hotel Galvez once a year during the summer.

On July 4th we had a few fireworks—Roman candles and sparklers. A 5-cent ice cream cone in the summertime was special. On Halloween there were no masks and costumes. We wrapped in old sheets and walked around the neighborhood.

When we lived in Missouri my brothers and I each had our own sleds. There was lots of snow, and we had fun. We made snowmen using Pappa's old coats and hats.

The movies were silent with captions after each picture. The Saturday matinee was only 10 cents.

Our family went to Pappa's store on Sundays after church, and while Pappa wrote letters, we children loved to roam all over the store. We were only allowed to look. Pappa had a battery-run radio. It was something unbelievable to us kids. My favorite radio programs were *Amos 'n' Andy* and *Ma Perkins*.

Life at Home

My Mama was a most talented pianist. When she was able, she would go into the sitting room and play the lively grand piano for a long time. I can hear her now! Mama sewed the dresses for us girls. We also had a family dressmaker who made dresses for us girls and Mama. Ready-made dresses came later from Pappa's store. Mama always baked our cakes. We had only one bakery in town, and it did not bake cakes or cookies, only bread.

When I was a child our house had heaters that burned coal. Very few homes burned coal. My Yankee father followed this practice. Later we had gas heaters.

Louise "Mimi" Brookshire: wife, mother, grandmother and great-grandmother in 2001.

My father taught me to drive in a Hudson Super-Six seven-passenger touring car. [A 1923 Hudson Super-Six advertisement said, "It's the revolutionary thing to do."] Papa would bring all six of the children a Hershey bar every Saturday. This was a great treat for us. We made a bar of candy last a long time. There was not a lot of store-bought candy available.

Women's make-up was unheard of. Mum deodorant was first introduced in 1923. What a help! It was so beneficial.

I can recall two World War I memories. I remember having seen President Woodrow Wilson in a parade in St. Louis in 1918. He was riding in an open car. We were at Pappa's shoe company when we saw the parade. I also helped sew squares together to make quilts for the little children in Belgium during the war.

I have a story about standing up against the odds for something I really believed in. I really resented some of my friends trying to call my family "German lovers." They said we all kept German flags in our front doors and windows. We did not! I have always treasured my German heritage. I never have had hatred for another person. Maybe anger, when we were criticized. I never did learn German, because the German language was not allowed to be taught in high school.

Christmas

Santa brought our Christmas tree. We saw it first on Christmas morning sitting on a music box. We had an artificial tree because it was a German custom. Our Christmas trees were decorated with ornaments from Germany with lots of tinsel. There were no electric lights on the tree because we had no electric power. We had candles in little holders on the tree. It was a real chore to light all of them. We decorated the entire house with paper chains we had made, and we put sprigs of real holly around all of the pictures.

We had a sweet family service at Christmas with many lighted candles. Mama, Grandma and the aunts spent weeks prior to Christmas making Christmas cookies, German summit waffles, springers, lebkuchen [a traditional German baked Christmas cookie], filled raisin cookies and fruit cakes.

Mimi

The following are recollections about Mimi, the name the six grandchildren called Louise Brookshire, their grandmother:

"One of my funny memories of my grandmother was related to one of our stores. After her 92-birthday lunch, Brad and I drove her over to see the new store in Kilgore. Mimi and I were in the floral department of the store, and I was conversing with the florist. Before I knew it, Mimi was gone on the store scooter. Brad found me and asked where Mimi was! Luckily, we found her a few aisles over. The store, unlike our stores in Tyler, sold beer and wine. Both my grandparents very much disapproved of any alcohol! We were able to direct her to the front of the store before she discovered these particular aisles. Brad and I laughed, and I said she probably would have run into the displays with her scooter. Of course, she would NOT have made any apologies. — Karen Brookshire Womack, granddaughter

"Mimi was extremely proud of her German heritage. Through the years she shared stories about her family, making sure that all six of her grandchildren realized that it was also their heritage. She and Papaw were teetotalers, and I really respected them for the stand they took on that subject. She loved to receive little gifts; however, the giver received the greatest joy by the way Mimi showed great excitement and appreciation for the gift, regardless of its value. Making you feel good was a wonderful trait she had." — Mark Brookshire, grandson

"My grandmother loved holidays, especially Christmas and Halloween. She would throw a Halloween party for her great-grandchildren every year and have so much fun doing it. Family was extremely important to her—truly the only thing that really mattered. She had unconditional love for all family members. However, she was fully capable of giving a very strong opinion at times. My grandmother was famous for her cherry tarts, and she made them for her family every Christmas. They were a favorite family tradition and a highlight of the holidays. Her cherry tarts were unbelievable and truly a labor of love." — Brad Brookshire, grandson

"When Papaw turned 65 his sons Bruce and Woody announced that he was being retired from the Company. They presented both Papaw and Mimi with their own Weatherby magnum big game rifles and encouraged them to pursue their hunting passions around the world. Papaw enjoyed hunting but was impaired with both his eyesight and hearing.

"Papaw and Mimi carried over their competitive natures

from business to hunting expeditions in Africa. One day while hunting near the Okavango Delta in East Africa, their hunting party was tracking a large herd of water buffalo. Papaw insisted on sitting by a stock tank alone, reasoning that the herd would eventually wind up there for water at the end of the day.

"Mimi pleaded with him to let her sit beside him for safety. He, of course, objected to that. He said, 'Mama you will just wind up getting hurt.' Later in the afternoon Papaw did not see or hear the herd as they approached the stock tank. He was run over from behind by a water buffalo. As he came to, he was able to take the buffalo, which he declared was his favorite African animal taken. Mimi was proclaimed the best hunter in the family, taking the larger of most African trophy pairs. In fact, it was on one of the South Texas trips that Mimi had the distinction of harvesting two buck deer with one shot." — B. Tim Brookshire, grandson

"As much as my grandmother Mimi loved animals, she was impatient with pests. Squirrels were a great nuisance to her. She despised squirrels on her roof and was so bothered by their nesting in the eaves of her roofline, or worse, getting into her attic. Therefore, she devised a plan to rid her property of squirrels by engaging me to pop them with my BB gun to the payment of $1 each. It became such a fun project at her home; soon she added the pop of a blue jay (who robbed her robin's nest eggs) for .25 cents and a few sparrows for .10 cents. She knew how much I loved bringing my BB gun over for an afternoon of 'pest control.'

"In Mimi's later years she would welcome the great-grandchildren for lemonade and cookies on her back porch or host a Halloween gathering for the four generations of the Brookshire family. She loved Easter egg hunts and Halloween costume parties. She would wear a bold Queen Bee hat as her costume every year." — Britt Brookshire, grandson

CHAPTER 14

The 3-B Farm

The Brookshire family owns the 3-B Farm in Noonday, Texas, just 11 miles south of Tyler. The 120-acre farm is located on a rolling hillside with a barn, windmill, caretaker house, swimming pool and a farmhouse with a huge screened porch overlooking a beautiful lake. The driveway into the property is lined with a white fence and an abundance of shade trees. The farm was purchased in 1958 and named 3-B Farm after Wood Brookshire and his two sons, Bruce and Woody.

Grandson B. Tim Brookshire said, "The 3-B farmhouse itself is a tribute to Papaw and Mimi and their thrifty nature. Original plate glass windows from their downtown store were saved and used for the great room of the farmhouse, as were the wooden store shelves now covered with wallpaper. Many South Texas deer and turkey mounts were hung in the great room. Spending countless summer nights in sleeping bags on the porch listening to frogs and thinking about the glass eyes of the mounted animals inside was awesome."

When the secondhand air-conditioning unit had to be replaced in the farmhouse, it was noted that when it was installed in 1958 it was a 1935 model, another example of Wood's thrifty nature.

Tim also recalled, "Papaw and Mimi built a huge barn on the property and announced to the family that we were getting into the horse business."

The 3-B Brookshires. (Left to right) S.W. "Woody" with Wood T. and Bruce at the 3-B Farm in 1959.

As announced, in the early 1960s the grandparents made the move to get into the registered quarter horse business at the 3-B Farm. It was a sideline to their grocery business. According to his grandson, Kirk, his grandfather's pride and joy was a registered quarter horse stallion named Sugar Bull, which he purchased for $35,000. Mr. Wood also purchased several mares which produced colts sired by Sugar Bull. At one time every pasture at the farm had horses in it. Mr. Wood became an active member of The Texas Quarter Horse Association. The quarter horse business was not a good investment opportunity for the "Cotton Picker," so all of the horses were sold.

Mr. Wood received a great deal of enjoyment driving his grandchildren around the horse pastures in his Ford LTD. He would laugh and ask them to pick out their favorite horse followed by, "Which horse is yours?" Kirk said he remembered the enjoyment he had riding the quarter horses.

Wood and Louise enjoyed walking leisurely around the lake for exercise in the brisk mornings or late afternoons, enjoying the ripples in the lake, the chirping of birds and the scenic East Texas countryside covered with blooming spring and summer wildflowers, and at times, enjoying the sweet aroma of fresh cut hay.

Mr. Wood received enjoyment and much satisfaction from catching a "mess of fish"—catfish and crappie—from the lake at the 3-B Farm. In 1990 Kirk Brookshire caught a 4lb-4oz crappie, a State of Texas record.

The grandchildren have fond memories of the 3-B Farm. Recently, Mark carried me on a tour of the farm which I had not seen since my retirement 20 years ago. Looking at a photo on the wall, Mark told me about the fun the grandchildren had riding in a wagon pulled by two Shetland ponies. Other grandchildren sent me their memories of the 3-B Farm.

Granddaughter Karen wrote, "My Papaw was a real jokester with his grandchildren. He had nicknames for all of us. He loved the farm he purchased, and that became his retirement project. Many fond memories of my childhood involve that farm. I have continued enjoying it and sharing it with my children and grandchildren."

Grandson Kirk recalled, "When I was a youngster, I received a great deal of enjoyment visiting the farm. It was like a menagerie of farm animals. What a thrill it was to be surrounded by pheasants, peacocks, turkeys, chickens, sheep, goats, cows, pigs and horses."

Grandson Tim added, "Weekends were devoted to farm life—picking up nails from the barn construction, throwing hay in the loft for a penny a bale and catching fish."

Grandson Britt recalled this childhood fishing memory: "Papaw loved the 3-B Farm. On a hot summer day he would drive us in his Ford LTD to Noonday for an afternoon of fishing. He drove with the windows down as he chewed Beech-Nut tobacco and spit out the window! He was quite a character! Fishing was a real art for him. He would carefully demonstrate the 'art of baiting a hook.' I remember specifically how he would take the crust of a slice of bread and mold the soft bread around the hook of the fishing line. Then he dropped the hook in the water briefly to soak the bread, remolding the bread firmly around the hook once again. Only now was the hook prepared, and he would drop the line six feet down into the water to guarantee a good catfish would be caught.

"My grandfather rarely spoke to us driving out to the farm in his Ford. However, turning at the former Noonday Hotel he would spit into his Maryland Club coffee can and answer all of our questions. Later, I tried that same Beech-Nut chewing tobacco with disastrous results. He always sent 'Mama' into the store to buy his chewing tobacco for him.

"One day at the farm Papaw was barreling across the pasture in his Ford rounding up horses as fistfuls of dried Bermuda grass collected under the engine compartment. While we were driving back to town, the car caught fire at the first four-way stop at the Loop. The newspaper crew was conveniently there to record the event."

The 3-B barn located on the Brookshire family's 3-B Farm in Noonday, Texas in the 1960s.

Grandson Brad recalled some very special memories of his grandparents and time spent at the 3-B Farm through the years. He said, "Growing up, we really enjoyed doing things like riding horses, camping out, frog-gigging, fishing and setting trot lines in the lake. It was great because the farm was close to Tyler and easy to get to. In 1984 a swimming pool, cabana, tennis court and kids' playground were added, and this area was named Camp Louise. These amenities greatly enhanced the property and the experience for the whole family. 3-B Farm was truly a sanctuary and incredible gathering place."

The 3-B Farm was an ideal gathering place for having family functions, entertaining friends and hosting Company events. The farm became the perfect location for a Brookshire clan reunion in 1976. According to grandson Tim, "My Papaw had many brothers and sisters, who had large families and interesting careers of their own. Throughout his life he wanted a way to get all the Brookshire family back together to allow everyone an opportunity to enjoy and get to know each other. In 1976 he and my grandmother decided on July 4th they would host a large family reunion at the 3-B Farm. Over 100 people attended with everyone wearing red, white and blue. A square dance was called on the porch while others ate watermelon, pitched horseshoes, swam in the lake, played 42 or rode horses."

A large sign above the farmhouse door read, "WELCOME YOU-ALL. COME IN FOR GREETING OF CLAN." For this festive July 4th occasion, Mr. Wood wore a white shirt with a red, white and blue necktie, and Mrs. Brookshire wore a red checkered dress and red leisure shoes.

Wood passed away the following April after achieving his goal of seeing his family for one last time.

INSIGHTS INTO WOOD T. BROOKSHIRE

Quotes from Former Brookshire Grocery Company Partners

"Mr. Wood would get his hair cut in the Bergfeld Shopping Center on Saturdays, then he would come supervise me across the parking lot at Store #9. I feel fortunate to have been able to work for the founder of the Company. I have been blessed."

"Traditionally Mr. Wood, as a year-end bonus, presented store managers and market managers a new suit of clothes at Christmas. He would instruct us where to go to select the suit."

CHAPTER 15

World of Wildlife Museum & Country Store

Because the Brookshire's World of Wildlife Museum and Country Store in Tyler became such a tourist attraction, it deserves its own chapter.

In the fall of 1975, Brookshire Grocery Company began construction of a wildlife museum in the lobby of the office at the Company's Tyler Distribution Center. The museum was to be a testimony to Louise and Wood T. Brookshire, representing their joys of life, the grocery business and the great outdoors.

Those of us working on the museum were not worried about finding the animal trophies because Mr. and Mrs. Brookshire, the Company founders, had harvested the animals on three different hunting trips in 1967, 1969 and 1971 to Africa, Alaska and North America. At that time animals were mounted and scattered throughout the halls in the distribution center office area. In fact, a full mounted zebra's rear end greeted me each time I exited my office into the hall.

I had the privilege of chauffeuring Mr. and Mrs. Brookshire to and from the Love Field Airport in Dallas for their three trips to Africa. They always dressed in their very best "Sunday-Go-To-Meeting" clothes for the airplane trips, including a suit, tie and hat for Mr. Wood and a special dress, purse and shoes for Mrs. Brookshire. I recall on one of the trips Mr. Wood asked me to stop in downtown Dallas so he could purchase a new felt hat for the trip. Once at the airport, I assisted them with their luggage and walked them out to the apron or ramp so they could board the plane. At the time, I would look up at that huge airplane and dream of the time I would be able to get on an airplane and travel anywhere like the Brookshires. Those dreams did come true many times for me!

Louise and Wood Brookshire came upon this ostrich nest on their safari to Kenya, Africa.

When huge crates from Jonas Brothers Taxidermy in Denver started arriving unannounced to the BGC grocery warehouse in the early 1970s it caused a great deal of excitement among the crew in the warehouse. After all, it wasn't every day that something other than sugar, flour, coffee and canned goods backed up to the warehouse's unloading doors. Excitement mounted after the first shriek from a warehouseman's shock as he peeked into a crate containing a wild African lion. Another shocker was seeing tables made from elephant feet! Everyone had to take a gander as other crates were unloaded.

Long before construction on the museum, Wood Brookshire had dreamed of someday giving those who had never had the opportunity to see nature's wild animals up close a chance to do so. In the 1970s the local Caldwell Zoo was open; however, many East Texas youngsters didn't have an opportunity to go to the zoo.

Construction on the museum began by removing four large plate glass windows from the lobby in order to create four dioramas featuring animals in their natural habitats. A local wildlife artist was commissioned to design and paint the four museum murals.

One diorama consisted of a life-size Alaskan polar bear, along with an Eskimo hunter. It wasn't unusual for inquisitive youngsters to ask, "Is that a real Eskimo?" After the initial shock, the tour guides explained that it was just a dressed-up mannequin and his face wasn't real. It was a mask! The children were always shocked to learn that adults in Alaska made masks for people to protect their faces against the freezing exterior temperatures. Little did they know that it was actually a female mannequin adorned with a fake Mouton coat that had gone out of style and was donated to the museum to be used to dress the Eskimo!

One day Mrs. Brookshire placed some plastic penguins in the diorama with the polar bear. We had some complaints from museum visitors that penguins and polar bears did not mix. They were right; the polar bears are in the Arctic Circle, and the penguins are in Antarctica. In Mrs. Brookshire's opinion that didn't matter because they "looked good" together. One day the penguins suddenly disappeared. Not a soul in our Company knew what happened, and I'm not telling! After the museum moved to a larger location, two beautiful mounted adult penguins were donated to the museum.

Another diorama contained three bears: the black bear, the smallest and least aggressive of the North American bears, the huge grizzly bear and the coastal or brown bear from Alaska. The other two dioramas contained African animals including a lion, grey zebra, wart hog, giraffe, kudu, impala and an ostrich, along with ostrich eggs.

Expanding the museum had been discussed for several months because the Company still had numerous mounts that needed to find a home. An area connected to the lobby had been selected; however, no starting date had been decided. Then, one Friday morning in 1976, Woody Brookshire came to me and said, "Okay, Jim. I hope you are ready because the carpenters will be here next Monday to begin the construction of the museum in the area adjoining the office lobby, and you are in charge, along with my mother." Needless to say, I immediately called Mrs. Brookshire, grabbed my assistant (along with partners from my advertising group and guys from the construction department), and we started putting things into "high gear!" At the time, it seemed like an impossible task, since we did not have any previous experience with museums. Later, I traveled and talked to several museum curators and brought back ideas that we could incorporate into our museum.

Several other dioramas with scenic wallpaper backdrops were created in the new downstairs room adjoining the lobby. They featured the moose and caribou in the North American Trophy cubical. An African Trophy cubical, a Fish nook and a Texas cubical (where the highlight was a large rattlesnake ready to strike) were in the downstairs area.

In another area a large python became the "eye-catcher" of the youngsters when they toured the downstairs area of the museum. Evidently, it was an attraction that Mrs. Brookshire didn't like. One day she said, "Jim, get rid of that ugly snake. Our museum is not a place for that thing because it scares the kids. I don't want to ever see it again!" Yes, as she requested, we moved the snake, but the Company still has it stored "high-up" out of reach and out of sight!

A unique feature of this new museum area was linking the museum to the grocery business by creating a replica of an old 1920s style country store, built from repurposed wood and corrugated tin from old East Texas barns and sheds. The bright red hand-painted sign on the front of the store read, "Brookshire's Grocery Store." The store contained several pieces of antique equipment used in stores of this time period. In addition, replicas and original products sold in the early stores of the past were displayed, some on a vintage wooden bread rack. A vintage screen door with a bread sign posted on it welcomed all guests. Woody Brookshire asked all of BGC's suppliers for donations of vintage products and equipment to help us create the store from scratch. Their response was overwhelming!

Upon its completion, the museum was named Brookshire's World of Wildlife Museum and Country Store, and it was open free to the public. The museum became a favorite attraction for local residents, school children tours, out-of-town visitors and anyone visiting the BGC office complex. "We have been quite pleased with the popularity of the museum," said Woody.

The Country Store located inside the Brookshire's World of Wildlife Museum and Country Store.

In November 1977 Jimmy Dean, a multi-talented country singer, TV show host, actor and entrepreneur who built one of America's favorite sausage companies, visited BGC's office and the museum. Woody Brookshire, one of Dean's friends, accompanied him while he was visiting the complex. At the museum Dean talked with visitors and partners, signing autographs, taking photos and doing a television interview sitting in a vintage chair on the front porch of the Brookshire's Grocery Store. His interview was produced and aired by Channel 7 television in Tyler. Dean was known for his unique way with words, and he shared his famous quote with everyone. He said, "Sausage is a great deal like life. You get out of it what you put into it."

As the museum's popularity grew, the impact of additional visitors on the complex caused a problem. In fact, as one partner put it, "It caused too much commotion on the complex."

To solve the problem, in 1990 BGC purchased adjoining property and office building, located south of the distribution center. An addition was added to the existing office building, making it a 3,248 square-foot facility to house the museum and country store.

Ultimately, the museum featured a wide assortment of over 450 animals from various parts of the world, many donated and 200 from the Brookshire family. The museum was created and dedicated to Louise and Wood Brookshire, and it would not have existed without them.

All of the animals that were located in the original office reception area were moved to a new home in the much larger

Wildlife Museum. Several dioramas and cubicles were specially designed to showcase and enhance animals on display. A huge American black bear welcomed guests as they entered the museum. All children were reminded of the museum's one rule, "We look with our eyes, and not with our hands!"

In addition to the animals mentioned previously, some more popular American animals in the new building were the caribou, mountain lion, elk, Kodiak bear, porcupine, walrus, red fox, bobcat, mink, lynx and rattlesnake. Perhaps the oldest item is a set of African Ankole cattle horns. The horns, measuring 61" from tip to tip and 32" at the base, are well over 150 years old.

It is interesting how some of the items, animals, reptiles and fish found a home in the museum. For instance, the black leopard and her cub died of natural causes. It was assumed they did not survive the birth of the cub. They were donated to the museum and BGC had them mounted for display. The small white tail deer baby fawn has another sad story. A Texas Parks and Wildlife Ranger delivered the baby to the museum. He said, "This little East Texas fawn was killed by fire ants, and I thought you might like to have it mounted for your museum." The baby otters on display in the museum were found in the wild, and they did not survive the efforts of a Texas Parks and Wildlife volunteer. However, their brother River did survive and found a home at the Ft. Worth Zoo.

The Brookshire family went on a vacation in 1945 to Sequoia National Park in California. While there they picked up some giant pinecones. Louise Brookshire brought them home, never dreaming that someday they would be placed in a museum that bore her name!

A beaver dam found in the wild was reconstructed in the museum to accompany a beaver. A fishing pole beavers had used as building material was found when the dam was being dismantled. The pole was placed with care in the new dam in the museum.

The alligator came from a small town in Eastern Louisiana. This story started with a phone call to me at home early one Saturday morning. The caller identified himself and said, "Mr. Powell, I have you an alligator for your museum."

Completely shocked, I asked, "What did you say?"

He replied, "Woody Brookshire asked me to get you an alligator, and I have it. Can you pick it up?"

I asked, "Where is it?"

He answered, "It's downtown in a cattle trailer in Eastern Louisiana."

After I got over the shock, I called our area district manager in Monroe, Louisiana, and asked him to go to the little town and pick up the gator, take it to our distribution center in Monroe, wrap it in plastic, put it in the freezer and have one of our trucks bring it to Tyler over the weekend. Early the following Monday morning I received another alligator shock with a phone call to my home. The call was from the Smith County Health Department. A lady said, "Mr. Powell, I hear you have an alligator in the freezer at the Brookshire warehouse. Is this true?"

I knew she had me, so I answered, "Yes." Then, she reminded me that it was strictly against the city's health rules and the gator must be removed immediately. We wasted no time in removing him from the freezer and carrying him to a taxidermist.

The unusual string of large-mouth bass hanging in the museum was all caught on Lake Palestine, the lake where the Brookshire Employee Recreation Park is located.

On each of the three safaris to Africa, Mr. and Mrs. Brookshire took trinkets like ribbon, hair bows, candy and crayons and traded them for hand-made jewelry that was displayed in a special case in the museum. Also included in the case were hand-carved animals, "lunch box" gourds, wooden spoons, mugs, a wooden pillow rest, camel bells and hand-painted batiks (cloth material painted with dye that soaks through to the other side, making the design visible from both sides of the cloth).

The country store offered nostalgia seekers a world of their own, displaying a wide assortment of items from a past era. It offered a look back in time to the grocery industry. The store, although it contained some items over 100 years old, was much like Wood Brookshire's first store in 1928. Near the entrance to the store was a storefront of a barn, with a hayloft constructed from recycled lumber. It was used as a backdrop for a refurbished 1926 Model T Ford truck, similar to those used to deliver groceries to stores in the 1920s. A goat standing on a bale of hay on the truck seemed to say, "I'm in control here." A vintage "filling station," gas pump, complete with a lighted globe, stood at the store's entrance.

Many items in the store were Brookshire family items donated by Mr. and Mrs. Brookshire. Most early stores did not have air-conditioning or heat, so in the winter the wood burning stoves kept stores warm. Louise and Wood Brookshire used the potbelly black cast iron stove located in the country store in a deer lease cabin the couple enjoyed on the YO Ranch in South Texas. The chairs near the stove were from Wood Brookshire's childhood home near Lufkin, Texas. Mr. Brookshire said, "My family enjoyed sitting in these chairs and visiting around our fireplace on cold winter nights."

One of the family's prized donations was a quilt that belonged to Mrs. Brookshire's grandmother. The red, gold and white quilt is over 100 years old. Mrs. Brookshire's treadle Singer sewing machine she purchased in the 1930s when Bruce was a little boy was on display. Mrs. Brookshire said she used it until the 1980s. In a prominent location in the store was a large, white porcelain scale used near the cash register in one of the Brookshire stores during the 1950s.

A cheese cutter, similar to the one Wood used in his first store, sat on one of the store's counters. Prior to the self-service stores, storekeepers used a can grabber like the one on display to reach items on higher shelves.

The store had a wide assortment of other vintage items, including such things as a large coffee grinder, tobacco cutter, wall-hung telephone, paper holder, string holder and a vintage Nabisco wooden cookie display rack. One could also see a unique candy display case with a top compartment for ice that kept chocolate candy from melting.

Also included in the store was an egg sizer, hanging meat scales, a 1921 IBM meat slicer, seed and grains wooden display counter, a "dial your sewing needle" case, an oil cloth display rack, wooden vinegar barrel with spigot, hanging broom holder and a large variety of food items including large lard cans, coffee cans, peanut butter tins, canned items and packaged goods.

Store items were featured on vintage wooden and glass display cases. The wall shelving in the store was secured from an old East Texas grocery store in Sacul, Texas.

Some interesting readings from five old editions of *Reader's Digest* could also be found. Two of the earliest *Reader's Digest* are included in the five—April 1922, Vol. 1, No. 3 and May 1922, Vol. 1, No. 4. Other editions include May 1926, August 1926 and October 1926.

A fenced playground and picnic area adjoining the museum became a highlight for many visitors, especially those with children. Trees shaded much of the playground, and a variety of playground equipment offered hours of enjoyment for families. Additionally, an antique International Harvester tractor, a vintage LaFrance fire truck placed under a pavilion and a vintage red railroad caboose gave the children added enjoyment. Adding the fire truck and caboose to the playground was a strong desire of Bruce Brookshire. Bruce located the fire truck in one of the northern states, and he heard there was caboose for sale in Louisiana.

Bruce called me one morning and said, "Jim, drop what you are doing. I want you to go with me to Ruston, Louisiana. We're going to buy a caboose for the playground." We drove to Ruston's rail yard and were able to select a rusty caboose, with windows boarded, from three others sitting on the side tracks. We had to use a little imagination to visualize what it might look like after it was reconditioned. The caboose was restored and was named "The Prune Peddler's Choo Choo" in honor of Bruce since he liked to be called "The Prune Peddler."

In 1995 an additional space was added to the museum, featuring a unique gift shop and larger boys' and girls' restrooms. The new museum gift shop replaced a very small gift and candy area in the country store. The new gift shop offered a glance back to the past with its furnishings, including vintage wooden display wall shelving units from an old grocery store in Commerce, Texas. The "show piece" of the store was a huge glass- fronted 10' candy counter from Durant, Oklahoma, with glass sections featuring vintage "penny candy." A collection of large Lance candy jars on display racks offered old-fashioned candy sold by the piece, just as it was done in old stores. The gift shop also offered a large selection of gift items related to wildlife and country stores.

Additional restroom space was the main motivation that caused the construction of the new addition. The original building was an office space; therefore, there were only two small restrooms, one for boys and one for girls. This became quite a problem when a busload of school children "had to go!"

In 2004 the museum had a population explosion and underwent extensive renovations needed to display more than 200 animals and artifacts donated by the Wayne Scogins family from Marshall, Texas, and from Dr. and Mrs. Dan H. Eames of the Galveston, Texas, area. A full-sized bison and numerous species were added to the museum's collection.

In 2015 the museum's playground was completely remodeled

and expanded with new playground equipment. Also, three age group appropriate areas were created. Canopies were added, creating protection from the weather for the children.

Over a period of years, the museum received several TripAdvisor's Certificates of Excellence awards. They were awarded because of the excellent comments the museum received.

The museum was a popular attraction for the school, civic, church and family groups toured it for the 42 years it was open. It became a favorite destination for guests from Texas, other states and other countries. From 2012-2016 the museum had 301,757 visitors. Average yearly attendance was 60,351. These figures do not include hundreds of guests who used only the playground.

The museum and playground were shut down on September 1, 2017, after an accidental ammonia refrigeration release occurred in a nearby Company warehouse. The accident resulted in the evacuation of the warehouse and 11 partners receiving treatment in local hospitals for exposure to the chemical.

In October 2018, the Company announced that the museum's playground equipment would be moved to BGC's FRESH by Brookshire's store. In January 2019, two playgrounds opened at FRESH. The Park, a playground designed for older children, ages 5-12, opened near the store's north entrance. The fenced and shaded area would be open daily until dusk.

A playground for Lil' FRESHies, ages 2-5, opened on the patio. It is open during store hours.

One person wrote, "I am so sad the place closed. At least

Brookshire's moved the playgrounds to FRESH, which are AWESOME! What will they do with the animals?"

The museum received hundreds of positive comments when it was open. Here are three of the comments:

"I have met my daughter and granddaughter there many times, and they thoroughly enjoyed both the museum and the playground. The kids talked about it days later."

"The museum is a great place for all ages. The museum is educational about many kinds of animals and the way life was lived in a bygone era. The playground offers lots of wonderful equipment by age grouping."

"The museum has lots of great animals for the kids to see. There is also an old vintage store, which is great for them to experience. Warning: there is a gift shop! But there is a great playground that has just been redone, and the kids love it. Thanks to Brookshire's, it is all FREE!"

Brad Brookshire, chairman and CEO said, "The Company is presently working on plans to move the museum. It will reopen and be very similar to the museum that closed."

INSIGHTS INTO WOOD T. BROOKSHIRE

Quotes from Former Brookshire Grocery Company Partners

"Mr. Brookshire instilled in me, as a store manager, that you made and kept your customers by remembering their names and giving them friendly, courteous service in the store."

"I remember that unflinching determination was one of Mr. Wood Brookshire's strongest characteristics."

"Mr. W.T. Brookshire stressed being competitive and giving outstanding service. He would say if we had a little volume, we would make a little money...and he was right!"

CHAPTER 16

The Dream That Became a Reality

Wood Brookshire, Brookshire Grocery Company founder, once challenged Company partners, "The future of Brookshire's looks bright and fruitful to me and for all of us. With an aggressive devotion to the duty assigned to you, and with God's help, we cannot fail. I promise to you if you give the best you have, the best will come back to you. I pledge to you the best I have; could you give less than your best to me?"

"People first; profits will follow" was much more than a catchphrase for Wood Brookshire—the motto defines who he was as a leader for almost 50 years. It's a statement that forcefully describes the fundamental operating philosophy that has helped BGC be successful. Not only has that philosophy applied to customers, but just as importantly, it has applied to all the partners working for the Company today.

It's hard to know what Wood T. Brookshire would think of BGC today. He would probably be extremely happy to see how his dreams have become a reality, considering how the company he founded has prospered and grown in the past 92 years. I'm sure he would be pleased that other members of his family are working in the Company and expecting to see their dreams, desires and goals—and those of their fellow partners—become realities as well.

I asked Trent Brookshire, chief operating officer and a fourth-generation Brookshire in the Company, what his great-grandfather would think of his company now. Trent answered, "I think he would be really proud that his vision of serving others through the grocery business is being carried out today by our partners. Ninety-two years after he founded our Company, W.T. Brookshire's passion for service is still at the heart of who we are and how we operate as a Company."

Cliff Brookshire, another fourth-generation Brookshire in the Company, believes his great-grandfather would be most proud of the people at BGC today. "Whether they have been around for their entire career or for a summer job, BGC's people make all the difference in our business. They help us win the daily battle of retail, and I know they would impress W.T. if he could see the Company today."

In discussing the history of BGC with Brad Brookshire, chairman and CEO, he mentioned things his grandfather probably couldn't have imagined when he opened his first store in 1928. Brad said, "I think Papaw would be proud that after

92 years our company is still thriving, growing, and relevant, and that third and fourth generations of his descendants are still actively involved. He would be amazed that we have 181 stores, serve over 150 communities and offer employment opportunities for 16,000 partners. I know that he would be proud that the principles he and my grandmother founded our Company on serve as the core values and compass that guide our decisions and actions more than nine decades later. He would also be surprised that we have four banners. During his lifetime all stores were Brookshire's. Our price impact banner, Super 1 Foods, was established seven years after his passing, and the FRESH and Spring Market banners have been introduced in just the past ten years. I know that my grandfather would be proud that our company is still respected as a community partner and that we give back and have so many good people working in our Company."

I am sure Mr. Wood would be surprised that from his first 1953 corrugated metal office building and small storeroom the Company would now be operating three distribution facilities, two based in Tyler, Texas, and one in Monroe, Louisiana, with more than 2 million total square feet, and a company fleet of 72 tractors and more than 300 trailers.

He had the vision for BGC to be the premier regional grocery retailer in the markets the Company serves. For 92 years the Company has made steady progress toward this vision. However, the Company realizes that there is much more work to be done in the future, guided by BGC's vision, mission and W.T. Brookshire's Core Values.

After visiting with Brad, I wondered what Tim and Mark Brookshire, two of the other family board members, would have to say about their grandfather. Mark said, "I know my grandfather would be very proud of the first-class grocery company that Brookshire Grocery Company is today, with professionals in all departments."

Tim said, "After celebrating the 92nd anniversary of our company, I believe he would be pleased to know that many of his founding principles are still in place today. His insistence on honesty and integrity, providing legendary customer service, being a fierce competitor, treating partners fairly, giving back generously to the communities we serve and allowing key people to own stock are all principles that we know are important today. Even during a health pandemic, we are holding true to all these founding principles."

It was interesting what I found out from Karen Brookshire Womack, Mr. Wood's only granddaughter. Her initial memory of being a member of a "food store" family, what the family called themselves back then, dated back to the former warehouse on Front Street. She said, "It was a treat to go to Daddy's office to see Papaw and Daddy. They always had time for the four of us. Truth be told, the real treat was getting to go in the buyer's office and see what new samples were there." Karen also mentioned that her Papaw would be proud that his legacy lives in all of his grandchildren and great-grandchildren.

Since this book is basically the story of Wood T. Brookshire, to get a real feeling of who he was, one should read this letter he sent to Karen when she was in college in 1974:

Dear Precious Karen:

I am enclosing my check in the amount of $22.50 that you might have a little spending money. May you use it wisely for whatever measure of good it can mean to you. I know you will greatly appreciate this even though it be small since you are conscious of the Scotch instincts of your ole tight-wad Papaw.

Karen, since you have left the warm, feathered nest of your dad and mother, you are now out on your own building a foundation we hope someday will make you the pride of all who share the name Brookshire. From the fine record you have made as a beautiful, sweet, wholesome, precious little girl in this community, you have generated much pride in your ole Papaw and Mimi as I know you have in your noble dad and blessed mother.

In remembering the temptations that came to me in leaving my Christian mother and noble dad for college, I feel an obligation to counsel with you from my years of experience. The temptations that were common in my day are ten times greater with your generation. I am so proud and so thankful that I did not deviate from the teachings and example of my blessed mother and rugged dad. Conscious of all evil and degrading influences today, I cannot help but challenge you to remain steadfast and strong in your unusual qualities for good that have made you one of the most respected and admired young ladies Tyler has ever produced.

Your parents have taught you to walk by the side of God. It has been said that, "One man and God is a majority." There may be times when you would be the only one not conforming to the group. You can see so long as you are on the side of all that is right, good, clean and wholesome, you are not alone.

May you always remain the sweet, precious little granddaughter we have loved so devotedly since God gave you to all of us.

Sincerely,
Papaw

B. Tim Brookshire, a third-generation Brookshire family member, can say so much better than I what the Brookshire family history entails.

"More than anything we are thankful that our family, like so many other first- and second-generation immigrant families from other countries, staked everything to move here. They brought their families here and what few worldly possessions they owned. They believed in the history of America and realized that it offered freedom from oppression and the opportunity to have a better life through hard work and free enterprise. None came with any promises or inheritances of any kind. While bringing their unique cultures and customs here, all learned the American way of life, learned the English language and assimilated into the time-honored American culture. All have transformed and changed the landscape of East Texas and America in magnificent ways. They were honorable, God-fearing and generous people. We are thankful for their history and for memories of them, and we pledge to carry on these timeless traditions on their behalf."

Having had the privilege of working for almost 20 years with Wood T. Brookshire, the "Cotton Picker" turned "Store Keeper," I feel I learned much about him, basically discovering what a great inspirational leader and dedicated Christian man he was. He taught me basic leadership skills and the satisfied feeling you receive in serving and helping your fellow man.

Mr. Wood, who was reared on an East Texas farm, spent the majority of his adult life creating and developing a family-owned food retailing organization that has become the epitome of offering quality service to the consumer.

Wood spent almost 50 years in founding, developing, leading, working and conducting business using specific core values that have remained an important part of the Company's guiding principles, since his first store in 1928. These basic core values from the "Cotton Picker" are the reason why Brookshire Grocery Company is recognized today as one of the primary independently-owned retail food chains in America.

As this book ends, I want to share a lasting challenge from a speech Wood Brookshire, the "Store Keeper," once made:

"I have found that there are two kinds of people on earth today—the people who lift and the people who lean. In which class are you? Are you easing the load of overtaxed lifters who toil down the road—or are you a leaner who lets others share your portion of labor, worry and care?"

In Appreciation

There are many people to thank for assisting me in writing a book of this nature. Their support, suggestions and especially stories from Brookshire Grocery Company's past were invaluable. I especially want to thank Brad Brookshire who offered me encouragement and guidance. Without him this book would not have been a reality. In addition, a sincere thanks to the other five Brookshire grandchildren—Tim, Britt, Kirk, Mark and Karen.

Also, thanks to several current BGC partners who assisted me with information and these former partners who offered me enlightening stories from the past.

Charles Cooper Jr.
Charles Davis
Dee Merritt
Evan Nielsen
Gary Thiemann
Hugh Kirksey
James Womack
Jerry Carrico
Jerry Nick
Louis Mathis
Nancy Horton
Nathan Williamson
Rick Rayford
Ruth Young
Sylvia Wilson
Thomas Pagitt
William Aiken

References

BOOKS:

Minding the Store, Stanley Marcus, Little Brown, 1974.

Tyler & Smith County, Texas An Historical Survey, Robert W. Glover & Linda Brown Cross, Tyler-Smith County Bicentennial Committee, 1976.

Images of America—Tyler, Robert E. Reed Jr., Arcadia Publishing, 2008.

The Big Rich: The Rise and Fall of the Greatest Texas Oil Fortunes, Bryan Burrough, Penguin Books, 2009.

NEWSPAPERS:

The Dallas Morning News

The Tyler Journal

The Tyler Morning Telegraph

The Tyler Courier Times

The Lufkin News

*Tyler Morning Telegrap*h, "Kilgore Oil Discovery Helped Shape Early East Texas Life," January 24, 2016.

tylerpaper.com

OTHER SOURCES:

Wikipedia

1870 Catalogue of Goods

Smith County Historical Society

Camp Fannin Association

Tyler City Directory 1930-1931

Tyler City Directory 1936-1937

Tylertexasonline.com-tyler-texas-vital statistics

Thepeoplehistory.com

Morris County Library, Morristown, New Jersey

Reuters

KLTV Television

PREFACE

Never did I imagine in April 1989 what would happen when I recorded a radio program entitled "A Day with Jesus at Your Side." I couldn't have guessed that it would be the beginning of an ongoing series of stories about a fictional woman named Fran who invites Jesus to accompany her to work. I intended then—as I do now—to help us understand the reality of the presence of Jesus in our lives and to live in that reality.

Like most of you, I know that Jesus is with me all the time because I am his child and his Word tells me that his Spirit is in me and he is with me always. But all too often I live as though Jesus resides in heaven, I reside down here, and we talk to each other occasionally when time allows. The glorious truth of the Christian life is that I don't have to live my life on my own, doing the best I can and sending up emergency prayers when I'm stuck. I am empowered to live the life of Jesus because he died and rose again to give me that power.

So I wanted to find a way to make this power-giving presence of Jesus more of a reality for me and for my listeners. After the first program, I sensed I had found a good way to do this. My listeners related to Fran, so I did another similar program. The popularity of these stories confirmed what I already knew: people learn best from storytelling. That's why Jesus taught in parables.

Since then I've changed the title to "Fran and Jesus on the Job" and continued these episodes. It makes sense to translate these stories into book form, and that's why this book is in your hands right now.

This is a different book, and it's a bit risky. I have thought much about the appropriateness of writing dialogue for Jesus. Certainly my words are not inspired like the words of Christ in the Bible. The words that Jesus speaks in this book are, except in those cases where the dialogue is straight from the Bible, what I have imagined that he would speak. I have tried very hard to closely and clearly tie Jesus' words in this book to biblical truth. But I am not infallible and neither are my words. To make sure you know how I feel about the dialogue I've written for Jesus, we've typeset those words in boldface so as to set them off from all other dialogue.

The risk of writing a book like this is worth it because of the great potential to help many people understand better what it means to daily "walk with the King" and be aware of his presence, his voice, and his guidance in the everyday struggles of life. I am convinced that our greatest opportunity for witness, wherever we are, is the life we live. When people can see the life of Jesus in us, we will start to change our worlds. And when each of us changes our small world for Jesus, we will as a body affect the whole world.

But I also want this book to help others relate to him more personally. In addition to being our Savior and Lord, he is our brother, our friend, our life, our joy. He wants to have a close daily walk with each of his children. What a difference it makes when we understand that and practice his presence.

As you get to know Fran, you will see that she gets into a different predicament in every chapter. I recognize that few of us have a life full of so many different experiences, but I'm not writing a novel. This is a book designed to teach principles in a story format, so each chapter addresses a major area of biblical truth that we need to incorporate in our lives.

I've used the everyday experiences of a single working mom as my story line, but the ideas apply to all of us. I believe men and women—single and married, with or without children, at home or in an office—will relate to Fran, because her struggles are universal. The stage happens to be on the job, but the lessons are ones we all need to learn. To help you apply what Fran is learning, I've included questions at the end of each chapter for personal meditation or group discussion. You can certainly skip over them if you like.

Fran's story does not parallel my own story and is not based on any one person I know. All the names and people are right out of my imagination, so if you think I'm writing about someone you know, it's just a divine coincidence. But undoubtedly my experiences as a workplace woman with more than twenty years in corporate America have influenced this book. Also, I interact with lots of women through my ministry and believe I have a fairly good handle on what you face when you go into that world each day.

I hope you like Fran and enjoy reading her story. If the radio response is any indication, you may find yourself chuckling and crying through some of these pages as you relate to her.

While the book is designed for easy reading, it is not written to simply entertain. More than anything, I pray that it will help you move into a new and much more vital relationship with Jesus Christ, learn how to apply his Word to your daily life, and spend more time in his presence. If so, I've succeeded.

1
Facing the Fear of Job Hunting

"Oh, dear, I don't have anything appropriate to wear," Fran says out loud to herself as she pulls one outfit after another from her closet and throws them on the bed. "I don't have any career clothes; after all, I've been a mommy for the past eight years. My clothes won't do at all for the workplace!"

Frantically she considers her whole wardrobe, and the longer she looks, the more frustrated she feels. Finally she reaches for the phone and dials her good friend, Lynn, who lives a couple of blocks away.

"Hello, Lynn, this is Fran. Listen, I don't have anything to wear for this job interview tomorrow. I've gone through everything I own, and there's nothing suitable for the office. Oh, Lynn, what am I going to do?" Fran is almost at the point of tears.

"I think I have the perfect outfit for you," Lynn replies.

"Do you really think it would look good on me? But I feel bad borrowing your clothes." Lynn, as always, is eager and willing to help Fran in any way possible, and she insists that her beige suit will be just the ticket.

"Okay, I'll come down there and bring a few blouses along. I hope it looks good because I've got to come up with something, and I can't afford to go buy a new outfit for this interview. But Lynn, suppose I get the job? What am I going to wear to work every day?

These casual slacks and shirts I wear all the time around here just won't do."

The more Fran thinks about the problems she faces reentering the job market, the more overwhelmed she feels. But Lynn encourages her to come on over, and she'll help her.

"What a good friend she is," Fran says, as she hangs up the phone. "I don't know what I would have done without her this last year, with Jim gone. She's one of the few friends who has been there for me all the time."

The sudden death of her husband was a terrible blow to Fran and her family. Hardly a day goes by even now that she doesn't recall and relive that awful moment when the phone rang and a police officer told her that Jim had been in a bad accident. She knew—somehow she just knew—that he was dead, even though the officer didn't say that to her.

Instead, he came to her home and took her to the hospital. Her mom watched the kids while her dad went with her in the police car. All the way to the hospital, she bombarded the officer with questions and learned that Jim had been in a head-on accident with a drunk driver. It had happened at about nine-thirty in the evening as Jim was returning from an executive board meeting at church.

As is so often the case, the drunk driver was hardly scratched, but Jim was crushed in the automobile. He was wearing his seat belt, but even that didn't help. When they arrived at the hospital, a young doctor took her aside and confirmed what she already knew. They had done everything they could to save Jim, but in reality he was dead on arrival. The doctor was very kind but at a loss to know what to say.

Fran simply couldn't comprehend it. She refused to believe Jim was dead and told the doctor that he was somehow mistaken. She insisted on seeing him, and, though he tried very hard to dissuade her, she would not take no for an answer. She had to see for herself before she could believe that Jim was gone. About ten minutes after she arrived at the hospital, her pastor and his wife were there beside her, where they found her dad trying to talk her out of seeing Jim's body before it was cleaned. Fran turned to Pastor Brad Gates and Elizabeth. "Pastor, tell them to let me see Jim. I have to see him now."

No amount of persuasion could change her mind, and finally Brad and her father accompanied her into the room where Jim's body lay. It was barely recognizable, but that didn't matter to Fran. She was somehow comforted by being with him. She asked them to give her a few minutes alone with Jim's body, where she said her good-byes to him, things that she would never share with anyone.

The following days became hazy in Fran's memory. She has never been able to straighten out the blur of people coming and going, plans being made for the memorial service, trying to explain their father's absence to Alice and Andrew, sleepless nights alone in her bed, the unbearable pain in her heart, the loving concern of her friends and family, the gifts of food that filled the kitchen with good smells but made her nauseous. All the feelings and sounds and events just ran together in her memory.

The one thing she does remember well is her rage and anger—at the drunk driver, at Jim for staying late at the meeting (she learned from Brad that he had stayed afterward to help with a special project), and at God. How could God allow her husband to be killed? Her good and faithful husband who loved her and the kids and loved God with all his heart—how could this happen to Jim?

There was so much for her to learn and experience in the twelve months following Jim's death. They were, of course, the hardest days she had ever lived, and she prayed to God that never again would she have to face such a tragedy. But during the past year, Fran had learned more about walking with God than in all of her previous thirty-one years.

The sleepless nights and the anger inside drove her to Jesus. She learned how to talk to him without any pretense, any facades. She learned he could handle whatever she had to say, for he understood and could comfort her.

She began to understand the reality of the presence of Jesus in her life, minute by minute. Oh, sure, Fran had been a Christian since she was ten years old. She remembers well the day she decided to "give her heart to Jesus," as her Sunday school teacher put it. It was real to Fran, and she left that class that day knowing her sins were forgiven and that she was a new person. But at age ten, her understanding and experience were limited.

Through the years she had tried to be a good Christian, and she and Jim had built a Christian home. She considered him the greatest blessing in her life because he really loved Jesus and was active in their church. And he really loved Fran. They had met in college, and she knew right away he was the one. While their marriage had its difficult stages, it was, Fran knew, a really good one compared to most others.

But in the past year, without Jim, Fran learned that being a good Christian was impossible for her to do. She came to understand the truth that the Christian life is not something we can live on our own. It is, instead, the life of Christ lived through our bodies. As she got to know Jesus better and better, spending more time with him, talking with him about everything, she realized that, because he was with her at all times—indeed, indwelling her body with his Spirit—she had the strength to deal with whatever came along.

Jim's insurance policy allowed her to stay home with the kids the first year, but now that income was coming to an end. She had to go back into the job market in order to support her family. Just six months before his death, Jim had wanted to buy mortgage insurance, which meant Fran's house would now have been debt free. But she had objected to the monthly payment, saying they couldn't afford any more insurance.

How many times Fran has blamed herself for not agreeing with Jim on that decision. Now she has to worry about whether she can afford to stay in the house. Unless she gets a very good job, she expects to have to sell it and move into an apartment. It would be much better for the children if she didn't have to move them, but she knows that decision is facing her soon. She can't keep up these mortgage payments much longer.

Fran has a liberal arts degree and worked for four years after she and Jim were married, before Andrew was born. She had been an account representative at an advertising agency, so this seemed like the logical place to look for a job now. About a month ago, Fran got her résumé together, had it printed, and started scouring the newspaper ads to find a suitable job. She was shocked to discover that there weren't many in her field, so she began contacting all the agencies in town and asking if there were any openings. It was pretty discouraging; most of them wouldn't even talk with her. Some said to send her résumé, and they'd put it in their files for future openings. Right!

But finally she got through to one human resources director who actually had an opening and agreed to interview her tomorrow. Now, as the time drew near, the butterflies in Fran's stomach fluttered wilder and wilder. Walking over to Lynn's house, fear started to grip her. *I've been away from the workplace so long, I'm out of touch. They're not going to want to hire me. I'm sure they want someone with recent experience. Oh, I'll probably end up with some entry-level job making minimum wage. My résumé is not very impressive.*

She kept letting those negative thoughts whirl around in her mind, getting more and more depressed by the moment. Suddenly she felt a voice saying to her, ***"Why are you allowing yourself to think things which are not true or lovely?"*** Fran looked around to see who had spoken, but realized she was alone on the street.

Then she put two and two together. "Oh, Lord, is that you?" Fran was just beginning to recognize Jesus' voice and was gradually becoming comfortable with the knowledge that he was by her side all the time. Because she had been getting to know Jesus better and better during the past months, his voice was becoming clearer and clearer to her. But she still often wondered if it was really him talking.

"You heard my thoughts, did you?" Fran says to Jesus as they walk toward Lynn's house. "Well, I'm just trying to be realistic, Lord. It is not going to be easy for me to find a job; there are lots of people more qualified than me, and I don't have recent experience. After all, for the past eight years I've been a mommy."

"Yes, but don't you realize that, as a mom, you have developed some wonderful skills in organization, time management, and problem solving?" Jesus says to her.

"I have?" Fran replies, as the conversation continues. "Like what?"

"Fran," Jesus says, ***"think of the time you used to waste before your children were born. You've learned how to organize the family, as well as your own time. And you've been in charge of several large functions at church. What about the fund-raising drive you headed up for the Cancer Society? That was a major undertaking. Don't underestimate the benefits of all this experience. It's not like you've turned into a blob over the last eight years."*** Jesus looks at her with a smile.

They continue walking together. "Do you think I should talk about that in my interview tomorrow? Won't he think I'm crazy? He's interested in job experience," Fran responds.

"They're interested in creativity and ability," Jesus replies.

By now they've reached Lynn's house and Fran rings the doorbell. "Okay, Lord, if you say so. I'll give it a try."

"Hi, Fran, come on in." Lynn opens the door in her usual cheerful way.

"Lynn, this is so nice of you to offer me your suit

for tomorrow. I hope it looks as good on me as it does on you," Fran says, as she gives Lynn a hug.

"Oh, it will. Try it on." Lynn hands the suit to Fran.

Sure enough, the suit looks great on Fran, and one of her blouses goes with it perfectly. Lynn raves over the combination and assures her friend that she's going to look great. "You'll knock 'em dead tomorrow, Fran. Just you wait and see. Come on, let's have a cup of tea before the kids get home." They sit down in the kitchen to talk.

"Lynn, you just can't imagine how frightened I am about this interview. It's been eight years since I've had any contact with the business world; I never figured on having to do this—at least not for a long time. In the back of my mind I thought I might do some kind of work when the kids got older, but Jim's death changed everything."

"But, Fran, you make a wonderful impression on people. It will be obvious to this guy tomorrow that you're very qualified and would make an excellent employee. I know you're going to get the job," Lynn assures Fran.

"Lynn, you're always an encouragement. Thanks. But I really doubt that I'll get the job. . . ." As the negative words start to come out, Fran feels that inner nudge again. She looks over her shoulder to see who touched her, but realizes it was Jesus.

"Don't get into that negative talk again, Fran," Jesus says to her in his quiet way.

"Okay, Lord," she responds, "I'll stop it. I forgot."

Fran turns to Lynn, who is waiting for her to continue. Lynn, of course, is unaware of Fran's conversation with Jesus, but the conversation was real. Fran heard Jesus' voice.

"Well, there's no need to talk about all the reasons I won't get the job, is there, Lynn?" Fran abruptly changes the direction of her conversation. "I know God is in control, but, frankly, it is a bit scary."

"Of course you're afraid. Anybody in your shoes would be. Interviews are frightening for everyone. But you'll do fine."

"Will you pray for me, Lynn?" Fran asks. "The interview is for 10:00 in the morning. It would really help to know someone's praying for me right at that time."

"Sure I'll pray. And you know what—I'll call the prayer chain in our Sunday school class and get them praying for you, too."

"Do you think they would?" Fran asks. "I mean, I haven't been back to the class in a long time. You know I just don't feel comfortable in a couples' class anymore; I don't fit in anywhere."

"They'll be glad to pray for you, Fran. Don't worry. And call me tomorrow as soon as you get home. I want to hear all about it."

As Fran leaves with Lynn's suit, she thanks her again. On the walk home she says to Jesus, "Lynn is one of the best gifts you've given me this past year, Lord. So many of my former friends just stopped calling or inviting me anywhere after the first couple of weeks. But not Lynn. She has listened to me for hours and cried with me and taken me places and made me get out of the house. . . . What a good friend she is."

"Yes," Jesus answers, ***"Lynn has been very sensitive to your needs. So many people don't know what to say to someone who has lost a loved one, so they just fade away."***

"All they have to do is listen," Fran replies, pensively.

As Fran walks the two blocks home, she begins to think again about the interview tomorrow. "I wonder what kinds of questions he'll ask me, Lord? I really ought to be prepared. You know me, I'm not good at quick answers. Oh, dear, I'm probably going to make a fool out of myself. And this is the only job interview I've come up with in one month of looking!"

"There you go with those damaging, discouraging thoughts again. Don't you remember what you've been learning from Philippians 4 about your thought life? Now is the time to practice that principle."

"I know I'm not supposed to think about things that are not lovely or true or of a good report . . . , but honestly, Lord, let's be realistic. . . ."

"Do you think the Word of God is not realistic, Fran?" Jesus asks. He has such a way of pinning her down, quietly and gently, but Fran knows when she's backed into a corner.

"Of course, the Bible is realistic. It's just that sometimes—"

"Sometimes you don't want to exercise the discipline needed to practice the principle; would that sum it up pretty well, Fran?" Jesus succinctly pinpoints the problem.

"Well, how do I do that, Lord? I mean, the negative things I'm thinking are true, and I just can't ignore them," Fran says in frustration.

"They may or may not be true, but they certainly aren't lovely. Now, here's how you do it. Instead of thinking all those discouraging thoughts, replace them with the right thoughts. You were wondering what

questions you would be asked tomorrow. What can you do to be prepared?"

"What can I do? I guess I could write out the questions I think I'll be asked and try to come up with the best response. But, honestly, it's been so long since I've interviewed that I'm not sure what he'll ask," Fran replies.

"Well, who could help you?" Funny how Jesus often prods her to think correctly and come to some good decisions.

"Who could help me? Hmm . . . Jim's uncle George is a vice president for the bank. Maybe he'd help me. Yeah, I bet he'd be glad to help me. I'm going to call him as soon as I get home and ask if he'll give me an hour tonight to role-play with me. That would really be wonderful." With that thought, Fran runs the rest of the way home.

She finds George's number in the directory and calls him at once. Thankfully, he's in his office. "Hi, Uncle George, this is Fran." After explaining why she's calling, her uncle invites her to come over this evening and offers to do all he can to help her. He seems very happy that she called and asked him.

He and Aunt Ginny have been very kind throughout the past year, keeping the kids many times and having them over for dinner or a Saturday lunch. Repeatedly they have said that they don't want to lose touch with Jim's family and children. They loved him very much, and it was almost like losing their own son when he died. Jim's mom died when he was a teenager, and Aunt Ginny had been a substitute mother to him.

Aunt Ginny calls later and insists they all come over for dinner, and she'll play with the kids while Fran and George talk about the interview. The evening is a real encouragement to Fran. Uncle George gives her some good advice, telling her what the latest interview techniques are and doing some role playing. He tries to be as tough as he can on her, and Fran is amazed to see how well she can handle his questions.

"Now, remember, don't be afraid to say, 'I don't know,' or 'I've never given that any thought.' Don't try to bluff an answer," Uncle George advises her. "But don't be afraid to say what you really feel."

After she gets home and puts the kids in bed, Fran sits down and writes out some responses to the questions she might get. "You know, Lord," Fran says to Jesus, "talking to Uncle George was a good idea. Thanks for bringing that to mind."

"Well, I often work through people to answer your prayers. But you must remember that until you stopped those negative thought patterns and got your thinking back in line with Philippians 4:8, I couldn't get through to you with the positive idea. Learning to think correctly is an important principle, and the more you practice it, the more you'll see what a difference it can make."

"Guess I'm a slow learner, but I'll keep working at it," Fran assures Jesus. Finally her eyes and mind are going to sleep on her, so Fran shuts down for the evening and goes to bed, setting the alarm a half hour earlier so she doesn't have to rush tomorrow morning.

The next morning she has some quiet time with Jesus, asking him once again to calm her fears and give her the confidence to know that he will take care of her, no matter what happens. "But, Jesus, I have to tell you, I am scared. There's no other word for it. I'm sorry."

"Oh, Fran, there's no need to apologize for the feelings you have," Jesus assures her. ***"That is a normal***

reaction to a stressful situation, and it doesn't mean that you aren't trusting me. Just keep remembering, even in the midst of this intimidating and frightening situation, that I'm right there with you. I'll be beside you throughout the whole interview."

With that assurance, Fran starts her important day. She and the kids pray together over breakfast. Alice's sweet prayer touches Fran's heart: "Dear Jesus, please help mommy today. She needs this job and she's scared. . . . And help her hair to do right. Amen."

Fran can hardly keep from laughing, as she realizes Alice heard her fussing about her hair not looking right. Well, why shouldn't you pray about your hair? Jesus cares about everything, and her child's simple faith encourages her again.

Fran arrives ten minutes early for the interview, and Mr. Richardson keeps her waiting ten minutes. She fumbles through the magazines in the reception area, not really looking at them, with sweaty palms and her heart beating a mile a minute. ***"Remember, I'm right here,"*** she hears Jesus say to her. ***"Why don't you quote that passage you've been memorizing?"***

Fran puts a magazine aside and begins to recite Psalm 139 in her mind. "O Lord, you have searched me and you know me. You know when I sit and when I rise; you perceive my thoughts from afar. You discern my going out and my lying down; you are familiar with all my ways. Before a word is on my tongue you know it completely, O Lord." Her memory starts to fail her at that point, so she just starts all over again.

She's startled to hear the receptionist call her name. "Ms. Langley. Ms. Langley."

"Yes, yes," Fran stands up as she hears her name.

"Mr. Richardson will see you now." The receptionist accompanies her to his office.

After introductions, they are seated and the interview begins. Mr. Richardson asks some of the questions Fran has anticipated, but a few really catch her unprepared. At one point her heart starts pounding and she is sure he can hear it. But the voice of Jesus says calmly to her, ***"Just take your time. Think about your answer. Don't rush."***

So, after a short pause, Fran replies as best she can, explaining that she wasn't sure how to answer the question. The interview lasts almost an hour, and he seems interested. But, as it ends, Mr. Richardson says to her, "Well, Fran, you certainly have a great deal to offer, but I'm a little concerned that you've been out of the marketplace for eight years or so. Some other candidates I'm interviewing have more recent experience, and—"

"Well, I can understand your concern. I'm sure I'd feel the same way in your shoes." Fran hears herself responding but is amazed at what she hears. "You may wonder if my skills have gotten rusty, but I'd like to point out that during those eight years I've learned better time-management skills than I was ever forced to learn on the job. And, as my résumé points out, I've managed several important functions and held responsible positions of leadership in my community and my church throughout those years, in addition to devoting myself to my most important career, raising my children. I just think it's important to realize that the same skills I used in those assignments will be very beneficial to my employer."

Mr. Richardson seems impressed with her reply and looks at her intently. "You know, my wife would stand up and applaud if she were here. I'm sure you're right, Fran," he says with a smile.

"Thanks, Lord," Fran whispers to Jesus. "That was straight from you."

After assuring her she will receive strong consideration, he advises that they'll be back in touch shortly.

Walking to the car, Fran feels like the world has been taken off her shoulders. "It's over, Lord," she says to Jesus. "And I think it went pretty well. I don't think I handled that question about why I thought I would be best suited for this job very well, but actually it went better than I thought it would. Thanks, Jesus."

She calls Lynn when she gets home and shares the experience, thanking her for her prayers. Throughout the afternoon, as she thinks about it, her hopes begin to rise. It looked like a nice place to work, and she begins to get excited.

Every time the phone rings her heart stops beating. "Oh, come on, Fran," she says to herself, "he's not going to call you back today." Nevertheless, she can't keep from hoping.

However, not only does she not receive a call that day, but three more days pass without a word from the agency. With each day, Fran gets more and more worried. She talks to Jesus about it and finds it difficult to not be fearful. Uncle George advises her to keep looking, not to put all her eggs in one basket, so she spends most of her days on the phone, trying to drum up another interview.

She does manage to set up an interview for next week, but it's not a job she really wants. However, she knows she can't be too choosy in this job market. On Friday the call comes, not from Mr. Richardson but from his secretary. Could Fran come back for a second interview with Marilyn Brown? Marilyn, she learns, is the manager for whom she would be working. They agree on 9:00 Monday morning. All weekend Fran thinks about the interview, and naturally her hopes rise. A second interview has to be a good sign. She asks several friends and family members to pray for her.

On Monday morning, however, she sleeps a little too long and has to rush to get to the interview on time. She's not accustomed to getting the kids off while getting herself ready, too. This will be a new life-style for her, once she starts back to work. In the rush, Fran just doesn't have that quiet time with Jesus. Of course he understands, but she knows that she is the loser. That time alone with Jesus at the beginning of the day makes a huge difference in how her days go. What was it Pastor Gates said? "The day is often won or lost in the morning hours."

As soon as she arrives, right on the button at 9:00, Ms. Brown is ready to see her. She's a tough interviewer. Fran seemed to get along with Bob Richardson better, and she can feel herself squirming a bit and sounding nervous.

After more than an hour, Marilyn says, "Well, I've narrowed the selection to three people, Fran, so you are competing with two others. Frankly, their experience is more recent than yours, but I haven't made a decision yet."

Fran tries the response that seemed to work with Bob, but somehow Marilyn doesn't seem impressed. "Well, I'm sure that's true, Fran, but there's a big difference between the business world and volunteer work, church work, and running a house." Fran can hear her condescending tone. This interview was not a pleasant, encouraging experience.

On the way home, tears start to flow down Fran's face. "Lord, that was just awful. Now I know I don't have that job. I didn't impress Marilyn at all. She thinks I'm just a dumb housewife."

"Fran, are you depending on me or on your ability and experience?" Jesus asks in his direct but gentle way.

"Well, I'm depending on you to take care of me, but I have to do my job right too, don't I?" Fran struggles with this issue a lot. Where does trust take up and effort leave off? Don't we have to do the best we can before God can bless us? Can we expect God to take care of us even when we don't perform the way we should?

"Oh, Fran," Jesus replies, "it's so important for you to understand that I'm going to be here for you regardless of your performance. I don't love you more or less, depending on how well you do."

"Well, if that's the case, I can just sit down, forget job hunting, and wait for you to drop one in my lap, right?" Fran says, with some sarcasm and frustration. "I don't understand what trust means, I guess."

"Well, let's look at it this way," Jesus says. ***"If you do get this job, who will get the credit for it?"***

"Oh, if I get this job, it will be a major miracle. . . ." She quietly continues: "If I get this job, it will be a miracle right from you to me, Lord, because you know I didn't do well on that interview."

"If you had done well on that interview, who would get the credit?" Jesus asks again.

"I . . . I don't know . . . ," Fran stammers as she grapples with the principle Jesus is teaching her. "Lord, it wouldn't matter whether I had them eating out of my hands at that job interview, or whether I made a fool of myself. My life is in your hands, you are sovereign, and you are in control, whichever way it goes, no matter what happens."

"You see," Jesus says, ***"you tend to take credit for yourself when you think you've performed well, but when you haven't, you're willing to give the credit to me. But, either way, it is my power in you that enables you to do anything. Sometimes I show myself to you most powerfully through your weakness."***

On Thursday Marilyn calls Fran, telling her that she has extended a job offer to one of the other candidates and he has accepted. Marilyn says that Fran ran a close second, but his recent experience tilted the scales in his favor.

Naturally, Fran is disappointed. But the lesson she learned on Monday is still with her, and she's been praying a lot in these four days, learning to trust Jesus no matter what the outcome is. So, even in the midst of the disappointment, Fran turns to Jesus and says, "Lord, I would like to have had a nice, happy ending to this story, but I accept this from you, and I know you have something better for me."

Throughout the weekend, as she has to tell friends and family that she didn't get the job, her pride takes a bit of a beating, but her faith is strengthened. She knows she's learned some good lessons. Besides, there's an inner peace, that unreasonable peace, that peace that passes understanding. She would have to say this has been a good experience.

Trying to put it behind her, she continues to look for jobs, running down every lead. On Tuesday she answers her phone, and it's Marilyn Brown. "Fran, I'm sure you didn't expect to hear from me again, but a curious thing has happened. The man I offered the job to changed his mind and decided to stay where he is. His company offered him a better deal, so, if you're still interested, we'd like to make you a job offer." She describes some of the details, including the salary.

Fran can't believe her ears. After she'd given up hope, the job comes through. It's a bit of an ego crusher to realize she's not their first choice, but she sees that as a humbling experience. It also clearly indicates that God was in control, making the maneuvers she could never make in order to open this job for her.

"Thank you, Lord! What do you think? Should I take it? The salary is not as much as I had hoped—"

"Yes, but you know that the work is interesting and that the benefit package is excellent."

Marilyn interjects, "Hello, Fran, are you still there?"

"Oh, yes. I'd be pleased to accept the offer." She agrees to start in two weeks. She feels certain that Marilyn offered her a lower salary, knowing Fran was desperate. But that's okay. She now has a chance to prove her value to the company, and Fran enters the workday world again. Many lessons lie ahead, but Fran feels confident that, with Jesus beside her every day, she'll be able to handle it. After all, he got the job for her, didn't he?

THINK ABOUT IT!

1. What difference did Lynn make in Fran's life during this job-hunting episode? How did Lynn help Fran? Think of how God has used friends in your life to support and encourage you. Are there some friends in your life now who need a helping hand or a kind word of encouragement? Are you open to being used by God in the lives of your friends?

2. What can we learn from Fran's experience about someone who is grieving? What do they need from friends during this time?

3. Notice that Fran was angry over Jim's death. Was that wrong?

4. Fran feels guilty because she kept Jim from buying mortgage insurance. Should she?

5. Jesus continually reminds Fran of the importance of keeping her thoughts and words in line with Philippians 4:8. Do you tend to allow your thoughts to be negative and discouraging? What can you do to stop that bad habit?

6. Jesus used Uncle George as his instrument to help Fran. Think of someone in your life whom God has used to impart his wisdom to you.

7. Fran prayed about her interview, but she also prepared and did everything she could to be ready. Do you think it was necessary for her to do all that preparation, or should she have just prayed and trusted God?

8. What did Fran do when she was nervously waiting for the first interview to start? Have you done any significant Scripture memorization lately? Can you see how God can use the Word we have hidden in our hearts and minds?

9. Did you ever hear yourself saying something wise and articulate and wonder where it was coming from? How was Fran able to express herself so well to Bob Richardson even though she was nervous? Why, then, did the interview with Marilyn Brown not go so well?

10. Fran saw the job rejection as a way to learn to be humble. Can you think of some similar disappointing experience you've had that taught you humility?

2
Fighting the Superwoman Syndrome

"Alice, you can do it yourself if you'll just try," Fran says as her six-year-old begins her usual morning whining about getting dressed. "Honey, you know how to tie your shoes; why have you become so helpless lately?"

"I don't like getting up so early," Alice whines on. "I don't like you going to work. I liked it better before Daddy died."

Oh, great, Fran thinks, *she knows how to hit my guilt buttons.* She stops, takes Alice in her arms, and says to her, "Listen, sweetheart, it's not all that bad. All you have to do is get up fifteen minutes earlier than you used to, so I can take you to school and still get to work on time. Now, you know Mommy has to work, and Jesus gave me this good job. Come on, now, help me out. I need your cooperation."

"Yeah, Alice," her eight-year-old son chimes in, "you're just a crybaby. Come on; hurry up."

"Now, Drew, it doesn't help for you to pick on her. Please, you two, be kind to each other. All we have is each other. Now your shoes are tied, Alice. What kind of cereal do you want for breakfast?"

Trying not to hurry them, but ever watching the clock, Fran puts breakfast on the table and they start to eat. "Wait a minute," Fran says, "we haven't said our prayers. Whose turn is it to pray this morning?"

Fran has tried to establish this morning time

together, but it is really difficult. The time is always short, the kids are fussy and at each other's throats, and it hasn't proven to be the sweet early moments she had envisioned.

"I prayed yesterday," Alice says.

"You did not," Drew replies. "I did. It's your turn, Alice."

"Listen, kids," Fran says, "I just can't take this constant bickering in the mornings. We've got to do something about it. Both of you be quiet; I'll pray."

They all bow their heads in an uneasy silence, and Fran prays, though, quite frankly, she's not sure it gets above the ceiling. "Lord, we're having some problems here, just getting going in the mornings. Will you please help us? And please protect Alice and Andrew today; help them to do well in school. I pray in Jesus' name. Amen."

Fran hopes the prayer will have a quieting effect, but no such luck. "Mom, Alice didn't do her chores this morning like you told her to. Her bed is not made up, and her clothes are all over the bathroom floor."

"Listen, Drew, I'll handle those things. You just take care of yourself," Fran says. "Alice, we all have to pitch in to make this work. I explained that to you when I went back to work. If we all do our part, it won't be hard on anyone."

"Yes, it will." Alice starts to cry. "It's hard on me. I don't like it. I don't want to go to school today. I want my daddy." With that, Alice runs away from the breakfast table and heads for her room.

"There she goes again, the crybaby," Drew's words follow Fran as she goes to Alice's room. This scene has been played out many times in the last three weeks since Fran started back to work. Alice pulls the "I miss

Daddy" routine, Fran feels guilty, Drew gets his two bits in, and the day is off to a rough start.

"Oh, Lord," Fran says to Jesus, who is there through it all, "what am I doing wrong? It's not my fault I have to work; what are you doing to me?" It seems as if Fran often releases her frustrations on Jesus and then feels badly about it later.

"Fran," Jesus says, ***"I'm right here. Don't panic."***

"But, Lord, what do I do? I'm afraid Alice is going to be really harmed by all she's gone through—Jim's death, the disruption of our family routine, etc. She seems to get worse and worse about it."

"Fran," Jesus says quietly to her, ***"how was Alice doing before you went back to work?"***

"Well, I thought she was adjusting very well. I saw no problems, but now . . . ," Fran replies.

"Now, she's making a scene almost every morning, getting you upset as well as Drew, and causing your days to be pretty miserable, right?"

"You pegged it absolutely right, Lord. Since I started working . . . ," Fran pauses. "Hmm, what's the connection here? Alice resents me working—but why? She knows I have to work."

"Children know things but they can't always assimilate them into their feelings. What do you think Alice's behavior is really about—missing her father or selfishly reacting to a change in her life-style?" Jesus helps Fran to think it through.

"You mean she may be using this just to get her way? Kids are good at that kind of thing, aren't they, Lord?"

"Yes, they are, and it's also Alice's way of coping with change. Change is hard, you know, even for adults, and it's especially hard on kids. She just doesn't

know how to adjust, and it's frightening to her, so she whines and cries for her daddy. Not really hard to understand, is it?"

"No, I feel like doing the same thing many days," Fran says. Because Jesus is there to give her counsel, Fran is composed as she reaches her daughter and is able to calm her down, help her get herself ready for school, and even put a smile on her face. One truth about Jesus that Fran is learning, particularly now that she's a workplace woman, is to go to him for counsel. His name is, after all, Wonderful Counselor, and Fran is amazed to discover how wise he is.

Not only has Jesus helped Fran to understand herself and the children, but he's also given her great comfort at work. He goes with her every day, and his presence is so important to her, especially as she adjusts to this new life-style. The first three weeks on the job have been exhausting, as well as interesting and frightening. There's so much to learn, and Fran feels overwhelmed.

At night she is so tired, it's all she can do to get supper and put the kids in bed. She tries to keep the house in good shape, like she always did before, but that's not easy either. Getting a routine in place has proven much more difficult than Fran imagined. She just never thought about the fatigue factor.

As she arrives at work today, she says to Jesus as they walk in from the parking lot, "Well, this is my first time to meet this client, Lord. Sure hope I don't say something wrong."

"Just remember, Fran," Jesus replies, ***"I will be there. You can call on me for help anytime you need it."***

"Thanks, Lord, but . . . ," Fran starts to respond.

"But what?" Jesus asks.

"Well, I just mean, I really don't expect—eh, I mean, I really wouldn't ask you . . . ," she stumbles around as she tries to explain that she doesn't expect Jesus to help her with business counsel. After all, he doesn't have business experience, but somehow she finds it difficult to verbalize that.

"You wouldn't ask me to help you in your job, Fran?" Jesus responds. ***"Why not?"***

"Oh, I just didn't think you'd know . . . or be interested in . . . I mean, these are just job things." Fran begins to see how poor her rationale is. "Come to think of it, I don't know why I don't turn to you with my job problems. You would certainly understand them better than I do," Fran says, with a sheepish look on her face.

"Do you remember," Jesus says, ***"when Peter was having trouble catching fish? I gave him some fishing advice, and what happened?"***

"Uh, well . . . , he caught more fish than he could haul in," Fran remembers.

"Right," Jesus says, ***"and I was not a fisherman; I was a carpenter."***

"I get the point, Lord." Fran smiles at Jesus. "I can turn to you with my business dilemmas and decisions because you are Lord and you know everything. Then, please, do help me today to choose my words well and to think very clearly with this client. It's important that I make a good impression on Marilyn, my boss."

"Well, true," Jesus responds, ***"that is important. But is that the best motivation you can come up with?"***

"What do you mean? I just want to make a good impression on my boss. Nothing wrong with that, is there?" Fran asks, with a little irritation at having to defend herself.

"Just stop and think," Jesus says calmly, ignoring

her irritation. ***"What are you here to do? Impress your boss or help your client?"***

"Well, help my client, of course, but . . . ," Fran's voice trails off. "You mean I should focus on doing a good job and not on trying to make myself look good, is that right, Lord?"

"Motivation is all-important, Fran. If you're working just to make yourself look good, your client won't be your highest priority. If you're working to give your client the best possible product, you don't have to worry about how you look.

"That," he continues, ***"is part of what it means to be a servant. It gets your mind off yourself and focuses your energies on others. Believe me, you will do your best work when you are truly trying to help others, not trying to advance yourself. And, by the way, it will reduce a lot of your stress and tension when you're not self-focused."***

As they enter the building together, Fran thinks over what Jesus has just said to her. She begins to see what an enormous difference it makes in her attitude to make that change in her motivation. Funny how the way you think makes all the difference in the world. What was that verse in Proverbs she read recently? Oh, yes, chapter 23, verse 7: "As he thinks in his heart, so is he" (NKJV). Lately Jesus has been driving home how critical it is for Fran to think correctly and biblically.

The meeting with her new client is set for 10:00 A.M. Marilyn has lectured Fran several times about this client—what to say, what not to say. Fran will be the account assistant, working under Ed Rowland, but eventually Fran will take it over completely. Obviously, it's important for Fran to impress this client favorably.

She gets all her paperwork together and begins to

review what she has learned. As ten o' clock draws nearer, the butterflies start acting up. "Oh, dear, I hope I don't mess this up, Lord," Fran says to Jesus as he sits by her side.

"Just stop and pray about it, Fran," Jesus urges her.

"You mean, pray here in the office?" Fran asks, a little startled. "What will people think?"

"Well, you're not going to use the PA system," he says with a smile. ***"Just pray before you go into that meeting. It will help you greatly to be aware of my presence and not to be too self-conscious."***

Fran's desk is in the middle of a room with many desks, and she has virtually no privacy. She has been told she'll get an office when she advances to account rep, but now she's just a lowly assistant. So she's a little confused about how to pray at her desk, with all the noise and commotion going on around her.

"Why not go get a drink of water?" Jesus suggests.

As she does, she notices that the employee break room is empty. Quickly she walks to a quiet corner and spends a quick three minutes in prayer. "Lord, I need your calm spirit within me; I need your clear mind to think for me; I need your wise counsel to give me good answers and ideas. I rely on you, totally, for this business meeting. Thank you for going there with me and for caring about all these aspects of my life."

Fran finishes her brief prayer before anyone interrupts her and goes back to her desk with a much calmer spirit and an eagerness to take this first big plunge in her new career. As she walks into the conference room, she thinks, *Hey, Fran, you can do this. Remember, when you worked before, you did a great job with clients. Everybody thought you were terrific. You've got lots of people skills, so just do it like you've always done it. You'll be great.*

Her self-confidence takes an upward leap as she thinks about all her past success, and she feels good about herself. Marilyn introduces her, and the meeting begins. Still feeling very sure of herself, she decides to offer a suggestion at one point. It sure sounded like a good idea to her, but Marilyn quickly puts it down and gives her a look that could kill!

"Oh, no," Fran whispers to Jesus, "I really blew it. How could Marilyn put me down like that in front of the client? What did I do wrong?"

"You were relying on yourself, not on me," Jesus quietly responds.

"What? But I prayed before coming in here," Fran replies.

"Yes, but what were you thinking as you walked in the door?" Jesus asks.

Fran remembers her self-confident pep talk that she was going through, pumping herself up with all the good things she had done. "You mean," she says, "I relinquished my reliance on you and started to think I could do it myself. You're right; I should have kept my mouth shut."

Fran is feeling like she's totally blown it, when one of the clients turns to her and asks, "Fran, what do you think about this ad idea? Do you think the average housewife will go for it?"

Fran sees Marilyn roll her eyes and nervously turn in her chair, obviously uncomfortable with this situation but unable to do anything about it. The knots in Fran's stomach double, and fear starts to grip her. Quickly, instantaneously, she turns to Jesus. "Lord, help." It's all she has time to say, but he hears and answers.

"Well, though I'm very new on the job, as a homemaker for the last eight years I can speak with some certainty. I've thought a lot about that, and I think it would work, but I'd make one change in your approach. . . ." Fran shares her honest reactions to the ad campaign, which she had wanted to say earlier but was afraid to.

The client listens closely and seems impressed by Fran's contribution. In fact, her suggested change is agreed on, and the meeting breaks up at about eleven-thirty. As the client leaves, Marilyn says to Fran, "Well, you lucked out on that one, Fran, but be careful what you say to a client. You almost blew it at the beginning, if I hadn't bailed you out."

"Sorry, I was just trying to be helpful. Guess I was a little nervous."

"Well, I can't afford to let your nerves lose us a good client, Fran. Just be careful," Marilyn says over her shoulder as she walks away. Her words are stinging in Fran's ears because she had felt so good about the client's reaction. She sits at her desk and fights to keep the tears back. "Lord," she says, "I'm obviously off to a bad start with Marilyn. What do I do?"

"Pray for her," Jesus says.

"Pray for her?"

"Just pray for her," Jesus repeats.

It's the only answer Fran can get from Jesus, and it's not the answer she wants to hear. But before she has time to think about it any further, her phone is ringing.

"Oh, hi, Joan," Fran recognizes the voice of her good friend from church. "Yeah, things are going pretty well, but it's not easy. How about you?"

Fran listens while Joan tells her that she needs to

talk to her. Joan and her husband have been having some difficulty lately, and Joan needs a friend to talk with. She and Fran were very good friends before Jim died but haven't been quite as close since. However, Joan has been calling more lately, and Fran senses that she really needs to talk.

"This afternoon?" Fran says. "Oh, Joan, I'm sorry. I'd love to, but I have to get home to the kids. You know how that is." Fran pauses. "Well, I suppose I could try to meet you right at 5:30 for an hour or so. Yeah, okay, I'll do my best. See you at 5:30 at the donut shop in the mall."

Wow, Fran thinks, *poor Joan needs a friend to talk to, and I know I should be that friend, but I have so much to do tonight. Well, I hope Aunt Ginny won't mind if I'm an hour late today.* Jim's aunt has been watching the kids in the afternoons, and Fran picks them up on the way home. Ginny has agreed to do this until Fran can find a suitable arrangement, but Fran feels like she's imposing. More guilt!

With all there is to do for this new client, Fran decides to work through lunch and calls Louise, a co-worker, to explain she won't be meeting her today. She gobbles down some potato chips and a soft drink from the vending machine as she works on the new project.

Midway through the afternoon the phone rings. "Hi, Mom." Fran hears Drew's voice on the other end.

"Oh, hi, Drew. How was your day today?" Fran is always glad to hear from her kids but feels a little self-conscious about talking to them at work, especially since it's so easy to be overheard in their office. Drew explains that he has lots of homework and doesn't know how to do his book report.

"Don't worry, Son, I'll help you tonight. Get everything else done that you possibly can, and I'll help you with the report after dinner." But he still seems worried.

"Listen, Drew, I said I would help you. I know it's due tomorrow." She pauses while he continues to talk. "Son, you're not listening. I'll help you tonight, okay?" After inquiring about Alice and telling Ginny she'll be a little late tonight, she hangs up and discovers that Marilyn is standing behind her, waiting to talk to her.

"Oh," Fran says, a little flustered, "I didn't see you there, Marilyn. Sorry."

The look on Marilyn's face communicates that she is not happy with having to wait for Fran to finish a personal conversation. More guilt.

Marilyn gives Fran some directions and tells her to have the report on her desk before she leaves. As she walks off, Fran feels like screaming. It's three o' clock; how can she get this done by five?

"Oh, brother," Fran says to herself, "Marilyn is really out to get me, and I don't know why. What have I done to her? How can I ever get this ready in time? And I'm supposed to meet Joan at 5:30! I'll have to call her back."

As she turns to use the phone, she remembers that Jesus is there. "Lord," she says, dialing Joan's number, "this day is turning into a disaster. I need to be three people to do everything I have to do today."

"Hi, Joan. Listen, I'm so sorry, but my boss just handed me an assignment to be done before I leave today. I'm not going to be able to make our date; I'm going to have to work late instead." When Joan replies, the disappointment in her voice is evident.

"Yeah, I promise, as soon as possible. I'll call you tomorrow." Fran hangs up the phone, and the guilt sets in on her again. She is trying to please everyone, but it appears that no one is happy with her. Marilyn is upset, Drew is complaining, Joan is disappointed—and where does that leave Fran? In guilt!

Fran works frantically to finish as quickly as possible. She's never done this assignment before, so it takes longer than she anticipated. Finally she prints it out and is ready to take it to Marilyn's office. Looking up, she notices that it's 6:15 already. "Oh, dear, I'm going to be late," Fran says, as she cleans off her desk to make a quick exit.

Marilyn is not in her office, so Fran leaves the report on her desk, with a note to call her at home if she has any questions. The traffic is worse than usual. She needs to get milk and cereal for breakfast tomorrow but decides to pick up the kids first. At nearly 6:45 she arrives at Ginny's house.

Drew comes rushing out the door. "Mom, where have you been? You're late! I told you I had this report to do tonight. We'll never get it done." He throws his books in the car, while Fran gives Alice a hug and straps her in. She thanks Aunt Ginny, apologizing for being late, trying to explain. Ginny didn't seem as understanding as usual—or is it Fran's imagination? GUILT! Everywhere she turns, Fran is confronted with it.

After stopping at the store and refereeing a fight between Drew and Alice, they finally arrive home. What a day! Fran is exhausted, and she still has tons of things to do. Frozen pizza is the featured entrée tonight, for she's too tired to cook. But she's starving because she never ate lunch. *What a diet,* Fran thinks, *potato chips and pizza. I used to cook hot vegetable meals for my kids; now it's pizza.*

As the evening progresses, the frustration and exhaustion get to Fran, but mostly she is overwhelmed with guilt. Her thoughts are totally occupied with what she sees as her failures in all areas: she can't do her job to suit Marilyn, Drew thinks she's a terrible mom, Aunt Ginny doesn't like having to keep the kids, Alice wants her daddy back, Joan thinks she's a lousy friend—and she can't even put a good meal on the table anymore. Her mind is full of all this guilt, and the tears start to flow.

"Fran," the voice of Jesus startles her. She had forgotten he was there. ***"Fran,"*** he calls again.

"Jesus," she cries, "I'm just a mess. I can't do anything right." She sits down in her bedroom and lets the tears flow.

His still, small voice keeps speaking to her. ***"Why don't you get your Bible and read it?"***

"I don't have time, Lord. I've still got to help Drew with that book report. . . ." But, even as she says it, she realizes that she must find some strength and comfort from the Word of God. She'll never get through this evening without it. So she takes her Bible and turns, as she often does, to the Psalms. David is so open and real in how he talks to the Lord, and it helps Fran a lot when she's struggling. She finds the passage she read a few days ago, Psalm 46:

> *God is our refuge and strength, an ever-present help in trouble.*
> *Therefore we will not fear, though the earth give way and the mountains fall into the heart of the sea,*
> *though its waters roar and foam and the mountains quake with their surging. . . .*
> *The LORD Almighty is with us; the God of Jacob is our fortress. . . .*

"Be still, and know that I am God; I will be
exalted among the nations,
I will be exalted in the earth."
The Lord Almighty is with us; the God of
Jacob is our fortress.

"Lord," she says quietly to Jesus, "I feel as though all I do is run to you for strength and refuge. I'm always in need of your help."

"It's okay, Fran, that's what I want you to do—run into me for refuge! I am your fortress! I understand you; I created you; I was with you all day long. I know how you feel, and I care. I'm your Wonderful Counselor."

"Lord," Fran continues as the tears flow even more, "You will have to be my strength. I just can't do this on my own. I'm never going to make it as a single working mom; it's too much for me. Lord, listen to my cry, for I am in desperate need!"

She reads the psalm again, aloud, to the Lord, and knows that he does hear, that he does understand, and that he will be her refuge and her strength. When there is no one else to run to, Jesus is always there, never leaving her or forsaking her. When no one else understands or has time to listen or care, Jesus is there, ready to comfort, seeing the tears, feeling all that she feels. Right there, all the time. Incredible!

As Fran starts to think of her Wonderful Counselor, the tears turn to tears of thanksgiving and joy. His quiet voice gives her some needed guidance.

"You know, Fran," Jesus says, ***"I'm not asking you to be all things to all people. Most of your problem tonight is that you feel so guilty because you think you haven't pleased everyone. Remember, the one you have to please is me."***

"But how can you be pleased with me today, Lord?" Fran asks. "I've been in panic mode most of the day, lost my patience with the children, had a pity party, felt angry toward Marilyn. I mean, this is not how a Christian is supposed to act, is it?"

Jesus smiles at her. ***"I love you, regardless of how you perform. I will never love you more or less depending on whether you've been a good performer or not. That's not the way I love, Fran."***

"Oh, Lord, how I wish I could get that through my head." The tears start again, as she learns once more a little bit about the love of Jesus. It overwhelms her to realize how unconditional his love is.

"What do I do with all this guilt? I feel guilty because I'm not the perfect—you know—perfect everything," Fran says to Jesus.

"You are going to have to learn," Jesus responds, ***"that just because you feel guilty doesn't mean you are. There is true guilt and false guilt. True guilt is what you feel when you are deliberately disobeying me and you know it. False guilt is what you feel when you are trying to jump through everyone else's hoops, when your self-image is dependent on what others think of you, and when you're trying to be all things to all people."***

This is a whole new train of thought for Fran for, until she started working, she had not really struggled with the superwoman issue much. Somehow, with her high energy level and natural talents, she had managed to be a "superwoman" most of the time. People used to say things like, "Oh, Fran, where do you find time to do all this?" She had been on every committee at church and in the middle of all kinds of school functions for the kids, kept the house perfect, made great meals, and so forth. But now, with the demands of work, she just can't live up to her former image. This new lesson doesn't come easily or overnight. She liked being superwoman.

In the midst of her thoughts, Drew calls her to help, and she walks, with calmness, to his room, where they get the report ready for tomorrow. He puts his arms around her neck as she starts to leave. "Thanks, Mom. I think my teacher will be happy with this, don't you?"

"Yes, Drew, you did a good job. I'm proud of you. But the important thing is whether you and God are proud of it." She hugs him a little longer. "You better get ready for bed; it's getting late."

The phone rings, and she answers and hears Marilyn's voice on the other end. "Well, I looked for you before I left, but couldn't find you, so I hope the report was what you wanted," Fran explains. But she finds that Marilyn wants to make a few changes in it.

"Okay, no problem," Fran replies, "I'll get to it first thing in the morning." She pauses to hear Marilyn's cryptic response. "Yeah, I can be there a little early. Okay, see you then."

Fran hangs up the phone, shaking her head. "Lord, this woman doesn't like me. She is nitpicking everything I'm doing. Now she wants me there early in the morning." Fran can feel the panic and anger start to rise, but then that still, small voice calms her down.

"Fran, just keep trusting Marilyn to my care. Remember, pray for her."

"Right, Lord," Fran says with a weary smile. "I'm not going to worry about Marilyn tonight."

Somehow she got the kids up a little earlier the next day and managed to make the changes Marilyn requested in time. The rest of the week went better; Fran kept turning to Jesus more and more for help, for strength, and for wisdom—and as her refuge she could run to when there was no other place to go.

At church on Sunday, Pastor Gates was preaching from Mark 1:35-39. The disciples thought Jesus should come and preach to a town full of people who had gathered to hear him, but Jesus said, "Let us go somewhere else. . . ."

Jesus didn't try to do what everyone else said he should do; he even disappointed people at times. But he knew what the Father had called him to do, and he never disappointed the Father. For the first time, Fran is learning that it's okay to disappoint people, for you can't make everyone happy. But she has to keep her focus on pleasing Jesus.

"Lord," she says as they drive home from church, "this is a new thing for me. I'm accustomed to pleasing people and getting lots of good feedback because I'm a superwoman type. Now, I'm learning that I have to choose how I spend my time and energy, because I can't do everything there is to do. I can't even do everything I want to do."

"But," Jesus reminds her, ***"you can still do what I want you to do. Remember, at the end of my life on this earth, I said, 'I have finished the work the Father sent me to do.' Yet I had not healed everyone, or preached to everyone, or made a disciple of everyone. Work to please me, Fran, and that will help greatly with the guilt problem and all the frustration you've been experiencing."***

Fran smiles and thanks Jesus for his constant counsel and help. "I promise to stop trying to be superwoman, Lord; I promise."

THINK ABOUT IT!

1. If you're a parent, do you find yourself, like Fran, easily taking on guilt whenever you think your kids are not well adjusted or are having difficulty coping in some way or another? Why is it so easy for working moms to feel guilty all the time? Was Fran's guilt true or false? Do you know how to distinguish false guilt from true guilt?

2. Fran had to learn that Jesus was totally capable of helping her with any type of problem, including business decisions. Have you learned to take all your cares to him and look to him for guidance in every area of your life?

3. Jesus pointed out Fran's wrong motivation and attitude in trying to impress her boss. Why was her motivation not appropriate? How can you keep the right motivation? (See Colossians 3:23-24.)

4. Fran learned how important it is to have a moment of prayer before heading into an important meeting. If that was the only time Fran took to pray, do you think it would have been effective?

5. What could be behind Marilyn's attitude toward Fran? Has someone ever treated you badly or given you a hard time for no apparent reason? Why do you suppose that Jesus told Fran to pray for her?

6. Do you think Fran should have met her friend Joan after work, even though she needed to get home to the kids? Why did Fran feel guilty about that?

7. Fran still struggles with trying to please God through performance and continually has to learn that God loves her unconditionally. Can you think of a time recently when you tried to earn God's favor by

doing something good for him? Why is it important to understand that we do not earn God's blessings by striving to be better and better?

8. Fran finds she can no longer be "super-woman." Why is that hard for her to accept? How did she find her worth and her identity in being a "super-woman"? Do you ever do the same thing?

3
Learning How to Witness

Four months have passed since Fran began her job as account assistant, and the routine is becoming more manageable. She finally seems to have the kids on a fairly good schedule. Alice has stopped whining every morning, and Fran has found a widow—Miss Polly, the kids call her—who lives close by and comes to stay at the house with the kids until Fran can get home. It takes a chunk out of her household funds to pay her for those three-plus hours each day, but it helps a great deal that the kids are home when Fran gets there.

Through all the everyday trials of a working mom, Fran is learning to turn to Jesus for help, wisdom, and comfort. She is aware of his presence on a daily basis more and more, and the days that she continually communicates with him are much easier.

She's been working really hard on her job, trying to learn quickly and do the best she can. While she feels the clients are pleased with her work, she hasn't gotten much good feedback from her boss. Marilyn seems to resent any success she has, as though Fran is in competition with her. But she's been following Jesus' direction to pray, and every day she asks that Jesus will help her see Marilyn through his eyes and love her as he loves her.

Being a witness on the job has proven to be much tougher than Fran ever imagined. She had dreams of sharing the gospel over lunch, inviting coworkers to church, and seeing several come to a saving knowledge of Jesus because of her witness. But she has found lots of closed ears—and few opportunities to share what it means to be a Christian.

As she and Jesus walk into the office this Friday morning, Fran says, "You know, Lord, I feel like I'm not doing a very good job as a witness here. Yesterday I tried to share the gospel with Pat at lunch, but she got very nervous and, frankly, I did, too. I hope you're not too disappointed that I haven't led anybody to you yet."

Jesus smiles at her warmly. ***"Fran, think about how I witnessed to individuals when I was here on earth."***

"How you witnessed?" Fran asks with a puzzled look. "You didn't have to worry about it, did you, Lord? After all, you were in the world to be a witness."

"And so are you, Fran. Remember what I said just before I ascended back into glory with my Father: 'But you will receive power when the Holy Spirit comes on you; and you will be my witnesses in Jerusalem, and in all Judea and Samaria, and to the ends of the earth.'"

"Yeah, I remember that verse in Acts, and I know I'm supposed to be a witness, but there's not much witnessing you can do on a job, Lord," Fran replies. "You see, I don't have time to do much except my work, and somehow it just doesn't seem appropriate to start talking about the Four Spiritual Laws in a business setting."

"Remember how I witnessed to individuals when I was here on earth," Jesus repeats, but by this time they're in the office, and Fran doesn't have time to pursue it with him any further. She's still puzzled, but now she faces a busy day with ringing phones, interrupting coworkers, demanding clients, and lots of paperwork to do.

The first thing on the agenda today is a meeting with the art and production people to decide how to proceed on an advertising campaign for her client. Fran is currently assisting Ed Rowland, a senior account rep, but she hopes to make this account all her own before too long.

"Well, Lord," Fran says as she gathers her papers for the meeting, "it's time to face the lion's den. These meetings can be so unpleasant, especially when you ask people to do something a little extra for the client. They seem to forget that the customer pays their salary."

"Yes," Jesus responds, ***"but put yourself in their shoes. They get demands from everyone, and their staff has been cut back lately. They don't have it easy either."***

She stops in her tracks to think about what Jesus said. "I hadn't thought about it that way, Lord. I'm sure I would be frustrated if I had their job. Please help me, Lord, during this meeting to be sensitive to the others and not to be judgmental. I need the right words that will enlist their cooperation. Help me to remember that sweetness of speech increases persuasiveness."

Fran has learned that a short time of prayer before these meetings really helps her. As she starts to rush to the meeting, she remembers something else. "And, oh, Lord, please help me with Bud. He drives me crazy with his dirty language and his off-color jokes. Please keep him from sitting next to me again, and help him to clean up his act."

She heads for the conference room. Bud is head of operations, but he is very crude, and Fran has lots of difficulty being around him because of his language.

She's been very confused as to how best to let him know that she doesn't approve of the way he talks, but so far all she has done is used a lot of body language and facial expressions to indicate her objection. It hasn't been lost on Bud; he knows Fran doesn't care for him.

As she and Jesus enter the meeting room, Bud and his assistant are the only ones there. *Great,* Fran thinks, *just what I wanted—to be alone with Bud.* Instead she greets him, "Hi, Bud, how're you doing?"

"Fran, come right in," Bud replies in his loud-mouthed way, "just the person I wanted to see. I was telling Mike here a new joke; I think you'll like this one. Did ya hear about the traveling salesman who can't find a hotel, so he knocks on a farmer's door—"

"Wait," Fran says, "I don't think I want to hear it, if you don't mind. You can save it for someone else."

"Ah, come on, Fran, you interrupted a good joke. Let me finish. . . . so he knocks on this farmer's door and—"

"Bud, I'll wait outside," Fran says angrily. "When you're through with your jokes, let me know." With that she leaves the room.

"Lord, I don't care what he thinks. I'm not going to listen to that kind of talk," Fran says to Jesus. "I'm sure you agree that I did the right thing."

Jesus seems rather quiet, and that bothers Fran. "Well, I did do the right thing, didn't I? You didn't want me to sit there and listen to that garbage, did you?" Fran is starting to feel rather defensive.

"No, I didn't want you to listen to his offensive jokes," Jesus replies, ***"but I wonder if you could have found a better way to defuse the situation and turn it***

in another direction, rather than make that kind of scene."

"I didn't make a scene," Fran reacts, "Bud did. If he had just behaved appropriately, this would never have happened." Fran is not ready to hear what Jesus has to say. About that time, Andy from the Art Department walks up, and they go into the meeting together.

"Oh," Bud says as Fran reenters the room, "you decided to come back, did you, Fran? Sorry if I offended you," he says with a laugh and without any sincerity.

"What are you talking about?" Andy asks.

"Oh, just Fran here. She has a problem with some of my jokes," Bud says cynically.

"Well, I don't think she's the first one to have a problem with some of your jokes, Bud," Andy replies. "But let's get on with this meeting."

Fran is relieved to have someone else there, and she appreciates Andy's coming to her defense. But throughout the meeting it seems that Bud is intent on offending her if he possibly can.

"Lord," Fran whispers to Jesus, "this is really intolerable. He keeps using your name in vain; he knows how that bothers me."

"Next time he does that, why don't you quietly ask him if he knows me?" Jesus suggests.

Fran had never thought of that approach before. Not five minutes pass before Bud again curses with the precious name of Jesus.

"Do you know him?" Fran looks at Bud and asks quietly.

"What?" Bud replies, taken aback.

"Do you know the person whose name you use so often?" she repeats.

"Oh, Fran, get off my case. That's just the way people talk," Bud says.

"Well, it's true, I talk about Jesus myself, but not in curses and swear words. That's because I know him, and I figured if you knew him, you wouldn't want to use his name as a curse word either," Fran says, hardly believing her own boldness.

The room gets rather quiet, as everyone waits to see how Bud will react. Bud has been with the company a long time, and people have just come to accept him, rude and crude as he can be. Actually, he does his job well and knows everything about the business. But he doesn't spare anyone when it comes to a foul mouth, and it seems even management is reluctant to say anything to him, probably because they use similar language themselves at times.

"Yeah, well, I know you're religious," Bud responds, uneasily. "I'll try not to use . . . not to talk like . . . well, I'll try to remember when you're around to lay off. Don't want to upset you, Fran." He throws some sarcasm in, but still it's obvious that Fran has made him think.

"Thanks, Bud, I appreciate that," Fran replies, and the subject is dropped.

Fran feels very shaky after that interaction with Bud. She can't get her mind back on track. "Lord, did I do the right thing?"

"I think what you said was just fine, Fran," Jesus says. ***"But I also hope that someday you'll be able to see Bud the way I see him."***

Before she has time to respond to Jesus, the meeting is concluding, and she's heading back to her office. Thinking over all that happened, she realizes that her initial reaction of walking out of the room was probably not the best way to handle the situation. She says to Jesus, "I know you weren't happy with the way I handled Bud's dirty joke, but please tell me what I should have done."

"Perhaps just quietly walking out, rather than announcing it, would have been better," Jesus responds. ***"You see, Fran, Bud has a problem much bigger than his foul mouth. Bud doesn't have any life or any hope because he doesn't know me. His foul mouth is a symptom, but it's not the root cause. And while it's not necessary for you to have to listen to his dirty jokes or foul language, it's also important that you see beyond the facade and know that underneath is a hurting man."***

"But he doesn't have a right to talk that way in front of other people. I'm not the only one who gets tired of it," Fran replies, thinking of Andy's comment.

"Please, Fran," Jesus says, ***"don't get defensive. You're simply learning how to deal with these situations. You can't learn until you're in them, and I just want you to learn from every experience."***

"Okay, I see what you mean," Fran replies, but she still can't decide whether she should feel guilty or not. She stood up for the Lord, but did she do it the right way? Not an easy question, but she has to give her full concentration now to her job for the rest of the day.

Throughout the weekend Fran thinks back over her encounters with Bud. She talks a lot about it with Jesus, and at church she has an opportunity to talk with Greg, the pastor of evangelism, with whom she's always been able to talk candidly.

"Greg," she says, "I'm struggling with how to be a witness on my job. This past week I took a stand with a guy who is always telling dirty jokes and using foul language, but I don't think the Lord was really pleased with the way I handled it. It came off in an offensive way and made him look bad—you know what I mean?"

"Yeah," Greg replies, "those are not easy ones to answer, Fran. You certainly want to take your stand without being afraid, but to do that without alienating people—that's the hard part. Remember how Jesus witnessed, Fran. He waited for people to ask questions and then he answered."

"Funny you should say that, Greg. 'Remember how Jesus witnessed'—I've been thinking about that myself."

"If you'll look at many of his one-on-one encounters, you'll see that he led people to ask questions, and then he gave them the gospel. Just think about the woman in Samaria at the well, how he kept leading her toward asking him what he wanted to tell her about," he explains. "I always think of the passage in 1 Peter where we're told to be ready to give an answer for the hope that is in us, with reverence and gentleness."

"Where is that verse?" she asks. "I need to memorize it."

Greg reaches for his Bible. "Let's see, 1 Peter 3—yep, here it is, verses 15 and 16."

"Thanks," Fran says as she makes a note of it. She reads the whole chapter and thinks a lot about being ready to give an answer. That night she spends some time in prayer before going to bed.

On Monday morning, as she and Jesus head back to the office, she remembers that the first thing on the agenda is another meeting with the production group to try and get a job accelerated. She needs their help but dreads another confrontation with Bud. As they enter the meeting, it seems the only chair available is right next to him. Fran thought that by coming a couple of minutes late to the meeting she could avoid a one-on-one confrontation, but she didn't count on having to sit next to him.

"Oh, Fran, don't tell me you're going to sit next to me," Bud says. "Be careful, you might catch something."

She whispers to Jesus, "Why does this guy always get to me, Lord? He does everything he can to offend me. Why?"

"Don't you remember the passage in Corinthians," Jesus reminds her, ***"where Paul wrote that my disciples have a special aroma—the fragrance of Jesus Christ? To some it is the aroma of life, to others of death."***

"Yeah, but why does he have to humiliate me in front of the whole department?"

"As you allow me to live my life through you," Jesus says, ***"you have to expect some people to be offended. People were offended by my life and my principles. Not everyone will love you, Fran, but as long as you are not trying to be offensive, you really have to learn not to take these insults personally. There are people who don't like the light to shine in their darkness."***

"But Bud is so—oh, I don't know—so obnoxious and arrogant."

"But," Jesus interrupts her, ***"remember that underneath that tough exterior could be a man really hungry to know me and a person who is really hurting."***

"Oh, not Bud," Fran says, as she takes her seat next to him. "I just hope he leaves me alone today."

But no such luck. As soon as she sits down, Bud starts in again. "Oh, my, she is going to sit next to me. I don't believe it. Didn't know they let you religious people sit next to sinners like me," Bud says loudly with a big laugh. "Aren't you afraid I'll offend your born-again ears?"

Fran starts to seethe inside. "Lord, do I have to take this?"

"Stay calm, remember he's upset with your aroma," Jesus reminds Fran. ***"Measure your words carefully."***

Fran was going to tell him that it's not necessary to make fun of her just because she has some principles and advise him to clean up his act. But, thanks to the reminder from Jesus, she says instead, "Well, Bud, since you're a sinner, we at least have that in common. I am, too."

"You are?" Bud laughs uneasily. "No, not you, Fran."

"Yeah, just a sinner like everybody else," she says.

"I don't get it," Bud is obviously taken aback by her response. "You go to church all the time, don't you?"

"Yeah, I do, Bud, because I'm a sinner." She is evasive on purpose, trying to make him curious.

"Boy, you got me there," Bud responds. "I don't understand, Fran."

Fran can feel this quiet nudging from Jesus. ***"Why don't you invite him to lunch, Fran? This is not the best place to get into this discussion."***

"Are you kidding? He'd never go to lunch with me." But even as she says that to Jesus, she finds herself saying to Bud, "Well, it's true. So no reason I can't sit next to you, Bud. In fact, no reason we can't have lunch. How about it?"

Bud looks shocked. "Lunch? You mean, me and you? You sure you could put up with me that long?"

"Yeah," Fran says, "I'll even pick up the tab."

"You're on," Bud replies.

Fran notices that the room has gotten rather quiet, and everyone has been listening to this exchange.

"Wow," Fran whispers to Jesus, "I'm glad I didn't say what I started to say. I was ready to take Bud on and stand up for my rights, Lord. Thanks for stopping me."

"It seems you're getting better at letting go of your rights, Fran," Jesus says.

"Well, I know I'm a slow learner, but I'm learning that when I give my rights over to you, you always give me something better." She feels the glow of his approving smile.

After the meeting, the morning goes by quickly and Fran's phone rings about twelve-fifteen. It's Bud. "Hey, if you were just joking about lunch, Fran, I'll let you off the hook." His voice is so much softer, Fran hardly recognizes it.

"Are you kidding? I'll meet you in the cafeteria in ten minutes."

As she starts to get ready to leave, she checks her purse to make sure she has enough money. "You know, I told Bud this was my treat, but I'm running low on cash and payday is not for another week. Let's see," Fran says, "I only have fifteen dollars. Well, I'll have to brown-bag it for the rest of the week, I guess."

"The money you're spending on lunch with Bud," Jesus says quietly, ***"is an eternal investment. It may make your budget a little tight this week, but you've just sent a deposit on to heaven."***

Before leaving for lunch, Fran stops to pray quickly. "Please give me wisdom and discernment as I talk with Bud. Help me to see him the way you see him. And Lord, give me your love for him."

As they sit down with their trays, Bud says, "Man, I couldn't believe you were serious about lunch. I thought you hated my guts."

"Well," Fran responds, "to tell you the truth, I haven't been overly fond of you, Bud. But I figured it wouldn't hurt us to just get to know each other better. Maybe we'd find something to like about each other." She looks at him with a grin.

"Yeah, well, I know you don't like the way I talk, but that's just the way I am, Fran. I've always had a foul mouth." Bud forces a nervous laugh. "That's the way my old man talked, so I guess it runs in the family."

"Talk about his family," Jesus whispers to Fran. ***"He just gave you an open door."***

So, following his leading, Fran asks, "Does your family live around here?"

"Yeah, but I don't see them too much. My old man—well, he's an alcoholic and mean as the devil when he's drunk. So, I just stay out of his way," Bud says rather quietly.

"Sounds like you had it kinda rough growing up," Fran says.

"Yeah, my dad used to beat all three of us kids when he'd get drunk, if we got in his way. Beat my Mom, too. . . ." Bud stops abruptly. "Hey, you didn't want to hear this, Fran." He seems embarrassed that he allowed himself to talk about his problems.

"You know, Bud," Fran says, "I've discovered that often behind our exteriors we all have problems and hurts that people never see."

"You look like you got it all together," Bud says.

Fran laughs. "Well, my life has had its share of pain. You know my husband was killed in an accident almost a year and a half ago. So, I know something about trouble, but God has stayed close to me, and Jesus is truly my best friend. He comforts me and gets me through the rough times."

"My wife lost her father last year, and she's still having a rough time," Bud says. The conversation continues as they begin to get to know each other and find out what's underneath the surface.

"Oh, my goodness, we've been talking for an hour, Bud. I can't believe the time flew so fast. We better get back, but listen, I'd really love to have lunch again sometime. I've enjoyed getting to know you."

"Yeah, well it's okay with me," Bud replies. "You're a lot nicer to talk to than those guys I usually eat with. And frankly, I don't really enjoy all that men-talk stuff like you think I do, Fran."

"Well, you did great at lunch today, Bud. Not one word was inappropriate," Fran says with a laugh.

"Next time it's on me, Fran—how about next week, that okay with you?" Bud asks.

"You bet; give me a call," and with that Fran and Bud part ways to go back to their jobs. As they walk back to her office, Fran says to Jesus, "You know, I actually like Bud. No wonder he puts up such a front, with the home life he had as a kid."

"Well, I wanted you to get to know Bud, because, believe it or not, he has a searching heart. He's open to truth, and you will have some opportunities to share with him the truth about your relationship with me," Jesus tells her.

Fran is learning that effective witnessing has to begin with a heart of love and caring. We have to see people the way God sees them, through his eyes. She's also learning that you can't tell from the exterior what's underneath. Over the months she had thought some people would listen, and they wouldn't. She had thought Bud was impossible, and now she sees that he is hurting with a lot of hidden heartaches, and he is much more open.

Not long after her first lunch with Bud, Fran is under pressure to get a proposal finished for an early meeting with a new client the next day. She says to Jesus, "I'll be glad when this is finished; Marilyn made a few more changes. Now I've got to get Joyce to make the changes and reprint it. You know, I just dread even approaching Joyce. She has such a rotten attitude. When you ask her to do anything, she's as sour as a lemon, she's lazy, and her work is poor."

"Yes," Jesus replies, ***"I've noticed. She presents a challenge for you, doesn't she?"***

"Well, challenge is a nice way to put it. She drives me crazy! After all, she is the administrative assistant for the department. It's her job to help us with these projects. But she acts like she's doing you a favor when she does her job. I just can't stand people with lazy attitudes."

"Fran," Jesus quietly responds, ***"don't forget that no one is in your life by accident."***

Fran stops in her tracks and gives Jesus a puzzled look. "No one is in my life by accident? Yeah, but . . . ," Fran pauses. "You mean, you have purposely allowed Joyce into my life? You want to cause me grief and frustration? What good does Joyce do me?"

Jesus smiles at her self-centeredness and says, ***"You may not think Joyce is doing you any good, but have you forgotten that often I work in you through other people? Besides, Joyce needs you in her life."***

Fran really doesn't want to hear that. She knows that Jesus means she should be compassionate and caring toward Joyce, but that's just asking too much. "Look, Lord, all Joyce has to do is what she's paid to do. I'm not supposed to baby her when she's so lazy, am I?"

"No, not baby her, but love her," Jesus responds. ***"You know, I love her—just as much as I love you."***

Fran wrinkles her nose. "Frankly, Lord," she responds, "I thought you had better taste." She says it with a chuckle, but she knows it reveals her inward feelings. "Besides, how can I love someone I don't even like?"

Expecting a negative reaction from Joyce, Fran heaves a sigh and heads to her desk. "Joyce, here are the last changes to the Walton proposal. Please make them and reprint it for me. I'll need it before you leave today, if you don't mind," Fran says, trying to sound pleasant.

"If I don't mind?" Joyce replies. "Well, I do mind. It's 4:00 and I leave here at 4:30. Why'd you wait till so late to give it to me?" Joyce snatches it from Fran's hand as she slowly puts down the magazine she was reading.

"Joyce, I just got the changes from Marilyn. You know it has to be done today. Sorry, but that's the way it is," Fran says with irritation in her voice.

Jesus nudges Fran's arm. ***"Remember, sweetness of speech increases persuasiveness."*** Jesus quotes the verse from Proverbs that he often brings to her mind.

"But, Lord," she replies, "all I'm asking is for her to do her job. If she'd get busy, she could have it done in less than an hour. I just don't feel like babying her; she doesn't deserve it."

"If you run on your feelings, Fran," Jesus reminds her, ***"you'll never be able to love people you don't like. Love is an action. Do the right thing, whether you feel it or not."***

Fran turns to Joyce again and with great effort says, "Look, Joyce, I know it's late; I wish I could have gotten it to you sooner. But I really would appreciate your help. I don't think you'll have to work much past 4:30. I'll be in my office if you have any questions."

"Much better," Jesus whispers to Fran.

She looks at him and says, "Well, I said it through clenched teeth."

"That's okay, you acted the way love should act, not the way you felt."

"Well," she whispers back, "I would never have done it if you hadn't been here."

"That's the whole idea, Fran," Jesus smiles at her. ***"That's why I'm with you all the time—to give you the power to do what you could never do by yourself."***

Fran's heart is touched. "Thanks, Lord. Please don't give up on me. I know I'm a slow learner in this area, but help me to learn how to love like you do."

Joyce's voice almost startles Fran. "Okay, well, yeah—okay, I'll try to get it done." Fran can see a slight change in her attitude. "Thanks, Joyce," she says.

On the way home from work this day, Fran says to Jesus, "Lord, I could see a slight change in Joyce after I tried to find the right words to motivate her. Thanks for bringing that verse from Proverbs to my mind about choosing my words carefully. But really, I shouldn't have to baby her just to get her to do her work. Nobody babies me."

"Well, nobody babies you, that's true, but you do have someone to help you," Jesus looks at her with that knowing smile. ***"You see, Fran, you have to keep remembering that Joyce doesn't have my presence with her like you do. Have you ever thought about what her life must be like? Do you know her at all?"***

"Know her? Well, all I know is she's divorced, has a two-year-old boy, I think, and, from what I hear, I guess she has a lot of financial problems." Fran tries to piece together what she does know about Joyce. "Someone told me she's in the bars a lot, looking for guys and getting drunk."

"You know, Fran, you have some things in common with Joyce. Why don't you get to know her better?"

"You mean because I'm a single mom, too? Yeah, but beyond that we certainly don't have anything in common. She's not my type, Jesus; I don't think so."

"She's my type, and she's not in your life by accident," Jesus repeats what he told her earlier, but this time with more conviction.

"Okay, okay—so what do you want me to do?" Fran asks.

"First, I want you to pray for her every day. Then I suggest you invite her to lunch and just get to know her better," Jesus replies.

"Pray for her and invite her to lunch. Yeah, I guess I can do that," Fran agrees. "Can't say I want to, but since you suggested it, I will." She smiles at Jesus.

"You know, Fran, my kind of love is an action, not a feeling. If you'll obey me, you're going to learn some interesting and important lessons about loving people you don't like."

"Well, okay, I'll see if she will have lunch with me tomorrow. I'll do my best, but you know I'll need your help because I don't feel like doing it," Fran confesses.

"I'll be right there with you. You can count on me," Jesus assures her.

With that they pull in her driveway, and Fran puts on her "mother hat" to begin her second and most important job.

The next morning Fran prays for Joyce before she leaves home, asking Jesus to help her see Joyce the way he sees her. As Fran arrives at the office, she looks for Joyce to invite her to lunch. She finds her arriving at her desk, late as usual. Joyce gives Fran a sour look.

"You got more changes to that proposal?" she says with irritation.

"No," Fran replies with a chuckle, "I just wanted to know if you're available for lunch—my treat?"

The look on Joyce's face is a mixture of surprise and suspicion. "What's this all about?"

"Not about anything—just lunch," Fran responds. Joyce agrees, reluctantly, and they set up a time.

After her morning meeting, Fran walks out to Joyce's desk and finds her talking on the phone to a friend. She hangs up, and they head down the street to the coffee shop.

Fran turns to Jesus and says with tongue in cheek, "You're coming, too, Lord. You got me into this, so you gotta get me out."

So, the three of them sit down for lunch. Joyce looks at Fran nervously and says, "You've had me worried all morning. I figure you're gonna chew me out about something."

Fran looks in her eyes and for the first time sees the fear and loneliness there. "No, Joyce, honestly, no hidden agenda here. I just realized on the way home yesterday that you and I have worked together for six months, but I really don't know you. I've found that it helps to get to know the people you work with, and we have something in common. I'm a single mom, like you."

Joyce is still a little suspicious, but she starts to

relax. "Yeah, I know. It's tough, isn't it? How do you manage with two kids? I can barely make it with one."

Fran replies, "Well, I guess you do what you have to do, but my kids are a little older. I remember the terrible twos—your son is two, right? What's his name?"

"Toby." Joyce's face lights up as she starts to talk about her son. "Yeah, he's a handful, but he's so cute." She shows Fran a picture. "Wish I had more time with him. Who keeps your kids, Fran?"

"A lady in the neighborhood keeps them after school. How about you?" Fran gets out her kids' latest school pictures to show Joyce.

"Day care center—very expensive. In fact, they've been threatening to refuse to keep Toby because I'm behind in paying them. My ex hasn't paid any support in months." Joyce pours out her story to Fran. "I don't know what I'm going to do, Fran." Tears start down her cheeks, and she quickly tries to hide them.

Fran looks at Jesus. "You're right, Lord, this woman needs a friend. She's not in my life by accident." The smile on Jesus' face tells Fran he's pleased.

"Oh, Joyce, I truly understand how you feel. There's nothing more important than your son and his care while you work. How much money do you owe the day care center?"

"I'm one month behind—four hundred dollars. And Fran, I just don't have any money," Joyce replies.

"What about your family? Can they help you?"

"Family? Are you kiddin'? My family . . . ," her voice trails off. It's obviously too painful for her to even talk about.

Jesus whispers to Fran, ***"What about your church's emergency fund to help people?"***

"What a good idea, Lord," Fran says and turns to

Joyce. "Look, Joyce, I have a suggestion. Our church has a fund to help people who are in financial trouble. As a member, I can request help for you. Would it be okay if I submit a request that they help you pay what you owe the day care center?"

Joyce looks at Fran in bewilderment. "You'd do that for me? But why?"

"Why? Just because you need help, and I want to help you. Everybody needs a helping hand some time or other. I'd pay it myself if I could, but my funds are a little tight, too. Now, I can't guarantee they'll do it, but at least I can ask. Okay?"

"Yeah, okay. . . ." Joyce puts her head in her hands and can no longer hold back the tears. She sobs quietly.

Jesus nudges Fran, and she reaches across the table and takes her hand. "You know, Joyce, I don't believe that anyone is in our lives by accident. And I'm sure it's not an accident that I decided to invite you to lunch today. I believe it's God's way of showing you he loves you and is going to take care of you."

Joyce looks up. "I'm not sure I even believe there is a God, Fran, but I appreciate your help. Sorry I'm so emotional; it's just that—well, I've been so worried about Toby. I was ready to run away—but where would I go? You've at least given me some hope."

Back at the office, Fran makes a call to the church and gets the ball rolling. She says to Jesus, "Lord, I can't believe how my feelings about Joyce have changed in a short twenty-four hours. Thank you so much for helping me see her the way you do. I hope I can help her."

Jesus smiles back at Fran. ***"You have already. And I think you've learned some valuable lessons about loving people you don't like, right?"***

"Right, Lord," she answers.

In a couple of days the committee chairperson calls to say Fran's request has been approved, but they can only give Joyce $300. Fran is very thankful and makes arrangements to pick up the check tomorrow.

But now she has to figure out how to get the remaining $100. Looking at her checkbook, she feels discouraged. She has about $120 to cover expenses until payday, and she has to buy groceries, pay Miss Polly, and keep her household running for about two weeks. She knows she can't give the whole $100, but maybe $50.

Well, where would she get the other $50? She bows her head at her desk to pray about it and ask God to send that $50. She has no idea where it will come from, but believes with all her heart that God will supply it by tomorrow.

That evening Lynn calls to see how she's doing, just a friendly check-up call. They don't get together as often as they used to, but they try to stay in touch by phone and pray for each other faithfully. Fran shares with Lynn what happened with Joyce and tells her that the church has agreed to donate $300 to help her out.

Fran is about to tell Lynn she still needs another $50, but decides not to, for some unexplainable reason. But Lynn asks her out of the blue, "Is that enough money to pay for Joyce's overdue child-care bill?"

"No, not quite, but I'm sure God's going to supply her need," Fran replies.

"How much more do you need, Fran?" Lynn asks.

"Well, I'm going to put in $50, and then all I need is another $50," Fran answers.

After a short silence, Lynn says, "I'd love to give you that other $50, Fran. Will you let me do that?"

"Will I let you? Of course, but I hope you don't feel

pressured or anything. I wasn't trying to get a donation out of you."

"Oh, I know that. I called you, remember," Lynn says. "It's my joy to help her out. In fact, I'd like to invite her over with you sometime and get to know her. Maybe we can really help her out, not just physically but spiritually, too."

"Lynn, what a great idea," Fran says. "You have such a warm and giving heart. God bless you."

"I'll bring the check over in the morning before you leave," Lynn says, and they say good-night.

Fran hangs up the phone and finds tears streaming down her cheeks. She is overwhelmed with God's provision for Joyce and so thankful he allowed her to be a part of this blessing. "It truly is more blessed to give than to receive, isn't it, Jesus?" Fran says.

The next day Fran has the incredible joy of telling Joyce the good news, though she never tells her that she contributed part of the money. She doesn't want Joyce to feel obligated to her personally. Joyce can't believe her ears. "I just don't understand why you would do this for me, Fran. I'm not your family or friend, and I haven't even been a good assistant for you." She can't keep the tears back.

They go into an empty conference room, where they can close the door for some privacy, and Fran puts her arm around Joyce, feeling a genuine love for her. She tells her about Lynn and her invitation to come to her home. Joyce shakes her head in disbelief, thanking Fran profusely. "I just don't understand why you would do this for me," she keeps saying.

"Well, there's only one reason, Joyce. Jesus has done so much for me that he gives me the desire to do something for others. Believe me, this is my joy and pleasure."

THINK ABOUT IT!

1. Fran is finding that sharing her faith in Jesus on her job is not as easy as she had imagined it would be. What difficulties have you discovered in this area? Have you had anyone ask you a question that opened a door for a witness to your faith in Jesus?

2. Fran was very uncomfortable when Bud told off-color jokes. What do you do when you're in that situation?

3. What do you think about Fran's response to Bud concerning his profane use of the name of Jesus? What other ways could she have handled that situation? What can we do to be prepared for dealing with profanity and off-color jokes?

4. Jesus refers Fran to 2 Corinthians 2:15-16, concerning the fragrance that a Christian gives off. Have you ever been in a situation where you knew that your "Christian smell" offended someone? How did you feel? How did you react?

5. Was it smart for Fran to invite Bud and Joyce to lunch? Are there any people in your life you might need to invite to lunch?

6. Fran finds it a little distasteful to think that Jesus loves Joyce as much as he loves her. Can you relate to those feelings? What good news does Jesus have for us concerning this?

7. Amazingly, after a private conversation with Joyce, Fran sees her totally differently. Is there some-

one in your life right now that you just find it difficult to tolerate? Would you be willing to simply get to know them better and try to see them through Jesus' eyes?

8. Fran gave money to Joyce, even though money is very tight for her. Do you think it was a burden for Fran? Can you remember a time when you gave something sacrificially, only to discover that you gained far more than you gave?

9. Would you say that Fran has a jewel of a friend in Lynn? Why is it important for us to have these kind of friendships and "support people" in our lives?

4
Facing a Tough Ethical Decision

The alarm clock rings. Fran gropes for the off button and crawls deeper under the covers. *If only I could sleep in just one day, just one day . . .*, she thinks. The last thing she wants to do is get up, but she's learned that the only way to do it is to do it! So she fixes that cup of tea and, while the house is still quiet, sits down to read her Bible and pray.

At first Fran really isn't emotionally motivated to get up early like this. Her body would rather have another half-hour of sleep. But she's learned that this early time with Jesus makes all the difference in the world in how her day goes. As she starts to read and pray, her heart warms up and her emotions come along, too. She quietly sings a chorus to herself as she finishes: "God is so good, God is so good, God is so good, He's so good to me!"

So, with her heart and mind tuned in to things of the Lord, she faces the day ahead. Her highest priority is her children. *I wish I had more time with them,* she thinks, but she's thankful they're doing well in school.

"Come on, kids, let's go. Let's not be late today. Come on, Drew. Alice, let's go." The day starts. *Why are the kids so slow and cranky in the mornings?* she thinks to herself, as she does almost every morning. *"Mom, I don't want to wear this." "Mom, where's my homework paper?" "Mom, Drew got into my stuff again. Tell him to stay out of my room."*

Calmly she handles all their miniature disasters, fixes some breakfast, reads their verse for the week at the table, prays with them, and gives them a big hug and kiss as she drops them off at school.

As she and Jesus pull into the parking lot at her office, she says to him, "Lord, my greatest worry is that I'm shortchanging my kids because I have to work. I mean, are they going to grow up with emotional problems because every morning we have to rush off like this?"

Jesus smiles and says, ***"Your kids are doing fine, Fran. You know, even when you're not with them, I am. I love them very much, and they are constantly in my care."***

"Oh, Lord, thank you so much. I can't tell you how comforting that is to me. What would I do without you?" Fran asks, as she walks to her desk.

"What's on your agenda today?" he asks, as Fran hangs up her coat.

"Well, I have a meeting with a very important new prospect tomorrow, so I have to get ready for that. It's the first prospect that I've handled on my own. After six months, I'm finally getting this opportunity, and I think that if I do well I'll get promoted to account rep rather than just assistant. That would mean more money, and I could use it!"

As Fran begins to work, her boss comes over. "Fran, about this presentation tomorrow, I was looking over your proposal, and I think you need to make the numbers look more attractive."

"Oh, are we willing to cut our prices?" Fran asks, hoping she will say yes.

"No, no, that's not what I mean. I just think you have to make that number look better."

"Gee, Marilyn, we went over that carefully. I think that's a very realistic estimate of the time we'll need for this project," Fran responds.

"Yeah, well, we can always go back to the client after we've gotten the business and make up some reason for needing more hours. I think we've got to have a lower number here in order to get the business. I want you to cut that number in half." She walks back into her office.

Yeah, Fran thinks, *she's probably right. Our competition does this all the time; I guess everybody does it.* As she starts to adjust the figures, she feels Jesus right there beside her. In fact, he's leaning on her desk, watching every number she s changing.

She's a bit nervous. "Well, Lord, what am I supposed to do? She's my boss and I'm just following instructions." But she knows that won't work with Jesus.

"Do you remember when I told the Pharisees that we are to render to Caesar what is Caesar's and to God what is God's?" Jesus asks her.

"Yes," she answers, "but what's that got to do with these figures?"

"It's a principle, Fran, and you need to apply it here. What do you owe your boss? Honesty, hard work, a submissive attitude—yes. But not compromising your standards and integrity."

"You mean, Lord, that if I put figures in here which I know are not honest, I will be displeasing you?" Her head drops on her desk, and she thinks, *Being a Christian sure makes it hard sometimes. How in the world am I going to handle this?* She feels trapped and alone.

After a few minutes, Jesus shuffles in his chair a bit

and clears his throat. She had almost forgotten he was there. "Jesus," she says, "what am I going to do?"

"I thought you'd never ask. Think about what happened when you landed that new account last month, the one you worked on with Ed. Remember what the client told you?"

Her mind starts recalling the experience. The client had explicitly requested that the proposal be very conservative, because they had just had a most unpleasant experience with a competitor who gave a low bid and turned in a much higher invoice, making excuses all along. The client had said to them, "I don't want any surprises. Give me honest estimates."

"I'll explain to her how we can use this to our advantage by telling the client up front that we know they want a realistic proposal, and they won't get any surprises at the end of the project. Yeah, thanks, Lord. I think I can make that work."

So, she finishes the proposal and gets ready to take it in for Marilyn's approval. Then she thinks, *What if she insists I do it her way? What if it offends her that I suggest something different?* Fear starts to grip her mind; her knees get weak. She looks at Jesus, who seems to know exactly what she's thinking.

"It's a little scary, isn't it?" he asks.

"Not just a little, Lord. I'm putting myself out on a limb here."

"Yes, I know that. But you're rendering to God what belongs to God; you're doing the right thing. I'm going in there with you. You're not alone."

That helps a little, but she still doesn't know what she'll say if this backfires. Again, reading her thoughts, Jesus says, ***"You know, sometimes discipleship is costly. You're doing what's right because I want you to, and***

you're taking a risk. It could be detrimental to your job. Remember, nothing can separate you and me, so as long as we're together your future is secure. Just do what you know is right to do; I'll take care of you."

"Okay, Jesus, but please give me the right words to say," Fran says. He promises to do that, and she takes a deep breath and walks into her boss's office.

"Marilyn, I believe it would be to our advantage to go in with a very realistic estimate and promise the client no surprises at invoice time. Instead of doing us harm, I believe we can build lots of credibility and gain a competitive edge with this approach." She relates the experience she and Ed had with the other client and holds her breath to see what Marilyn's reaction will be.

She looks at Fran's figures and hands the proposal back to her. "Fran, I've been around this business longer than you. Change the figures; that's your best shot at getting the business." She expects Fran to leave but looks up to find her still standing there. "You got a problem with that?" she asks.

Fran's heart is beating a mile a minute. *Lord,* she thinks, *where are you? What do I do now?* She turns slightly to make sure Jesus is still there beside her, and he gives her an assuring look and whispers, ***"Don't be afraid. I'm with you. If God is for you, who can be against you?"***

Fran remembers the pastor's message on that verse last Sunday. It gives her strength and courage, and quietly she turns to Marilyn and says, "Yeah, Marilyn, I do. I have a problem with submitting a low bid when we know we can't come in at those numbers."

"Well, if you can't do it the way I want it done, I'll have to turn this prospect over to someone else who can follow orders." She stares at Fran.

Fran has worked hard on this account, and Marilyn knows she doesn't want to lose it. A promotion hinges on it, and Fran needs the money. She feels the anger starting to rise and the blood rushing to her face. Then, she feels the presence of Jesus. He whispers, ***"Don't let your anger take over. Hold your tongue, and stand by your convictions."***

She gulps, and says to Marilyn, "Obviously I don't want to lose this account; I've built a lot of rapport with the client. I think they like me and trust me; but if you feel someone else should have the account, that's your call." She turns to go.

"You mean you'd give up the account before you'd change those figures?" Marilyn asks incredulously.

"Yeah, Marilyn, it's hard, but I would. Otherwise I'd have a hard time looking at myself in the mirror each morning," she says to her with a slight smile. "Besides," she continues as she reaches the door, "if I would be dishonest with a client, how could you ever be sure I wouldn't be dishonest with you, too?"

She walks out quietly, hoping to hear Marilyn stop her and change her mind. But she doesn't. With her head hung down, she goes back to her desk, and Jesus pulls up beside her again.

"Lord, that's not fair. I deserve that business, and I could get it honestly. Now, I've made her mad; my job is probably up for grabs." Fran starts feeling sorry for herself.

Jesus responds to her very quietly, ***"I understand how it feels to be mistreated; I've been there."***

She looks in his eyes and sees the love and understanding he has for her. She recalls the verse in Hebrews that says he is touched with the feelings of our weaknesses. She remembers Calvary and feels ashamed of herself for having a pity party.

"I'm sorry, Lord . . . ," but as she starts to apologize he interrupts.

"Please, Fran, I understand. It hurts to be treated wrong. But you did the right thing, and I will honor you for that. Can you trust me?"

Fran chuckles. "Do I have any other options?"

Jesus smiles at her. ***"Sure, you can capitulate and change the numbers. That would be easy to do."***

"But it would break your heart, wouldn't it, Lord? No, I'll do it your way. I trust you."

As she sits at her desk, pondering what will happen next, Tom, a new account assistant in the office, comes up to her desk. "Uh, Fran, uh . . ." He stammers around a bit, then proceeds. "Marilyn told me you're giving up the Ross account and that I should get the background from you so I can make the presentation to them tomorrow."

The words hit Fran like a two-ton truck. She can't believe Marilyn is doing this. She's worked so hard for this business, and now she has to turn it over—to Tom, of all people. He's brand new and thinks he knows everything. Talk about rubbing salt in the wound! Again, anger starts to rage inside her.

But as she turns to get the file from her credenza, she sees Jesus sitting right there. "Lord," she whispers, "I can't stand this guy. This is so unfair."

Jesus looks in her eyes and reminds her, ***"Fran, you did the right thing. I will vindicate you. Now, don't take it out on Tom. Remember, I'm here to help you."***

Fran is amazed at the instant calm and peace she feels. She turns to Tom and, without any anger or bitterness, explains the status of the Ross proposal as she hands him the file. He grins like a Cheshire cat. "Wow, this could be a big account, Fran. Why'd you want to give it up?"

Everything in her wants to dump it all on Tom and tell him how unfair this is to her. Obviously, Marilyn hasn't given him the exact straight scoop. As she opens her mouth to vent her anger, the presence of Jesus causes her to change her mind. Instead she says, "Well, it's kind of a long story. It is a good account; good luck, Tom."

As Tom walks out, she remembers the verse in Proverbs 12 that she read just a couple of days ago: "A fool shows his annoyance at once, but a prudent man overlooks an insult." And in the next chapter: "He who guards his lips guards his life, but he who speaks rashly will come to ruin."

"You know, Lord," Fran says, "I can't believe I didn't dump on Tom. I wanted to, you know. But somehow . . ." She smiles. "It was because you were here, listening to everything I was saying."

"Well, Fran, you're learning a wonderful principle, to practice my presence with you all day long. It's true—if you had done what your old nature wanted to do, you would have lashed out at Tom and Marilyn. But because I'm here to give you strength, you behaved just beautifully—just the way I would have done it, Fran."

Jesus' words bring tears to her eyes. "Thanks, Lord. Well, I'd better try to find another prospect to take the place of that one. You know, Lord, that cost me a good bit of money."

Jesus puts his arm on her shoulder. ***"Discipleship is often costly, but doing it your way costs you a lot more, Fran. Do you believe that?"***

"Yes, when I remember to look at it through Forever Eyes, Lord. You'll have to help me keep doing that, though, because I often forget to put on my eternal eyeglasses."

"I'll be glad to keep helping you, as long as you invite me to join you every day. If I'm not here, obviously I can't help you."

"You have an open invitation. Every day, Lord!" Fran smiles at Jesus and turns back to her work. "Well, Lord, help me with this new prospect. You know how hard it is to get through to this person." She picks up the phone and, amazingly, is able to get through to him. Even more amazing, he's willing to listen. As a result she has an appointment with him tomorrow afternoon.

"Great," she says as she hangs up the phone. "I've been trying for two months to get through to that man. Thanks, Lord." He smiles at her.

Even though the day has been a disaster, she feels a lightness of spirit and an underlying joy that she can't describe. It sure makes a difference to have Jesus there all day. So, with enthusiasm she gets into her work, and before she realizes it, it's time for lunch.

"Well, Lord, let's take a break."

"Sounds good," he replies, and they head off to the cafeteria. They pass Marilyn's office and see that Tom is there, discussing the Ross presentation. The anger and resentment start to rise up again in Fran's heart.

"Oh, Lord, there I go again. I thought I had taken care of all that anger, but everything in me wants to see Tom fall flat on his face tomorrow and lose that account. I hate to admit it, but that's the way I feel," she confesses to Jesus.

"Well, it's good that you tell me how you feel. Even though I know it anyway, you need to say it. Fran, the

feelings aren't sin; those are natural human reactions to unfair treatment and injustice. It's only if you harbor and nurture those feelings that they become sin. Don't feel bad that you feel angry again; just confess it, ask me to help, and I'll do it for you all over again."

"Okay, Lord, but it'll serve Marilyn right if Tom blows it tomorrow." As soon as she says the words, she sees Jesus shake his head a bit. "I know, I shouldn't say that."

"No, Fran, because what you are expressing is malice. Malice toward Marilyn and Tom. You want to see some harm come to them because they have harmed you. Colossians 3 says to put off malice."

"Malice? Wow, that sounds terrible." Fran had never thought of herself as a malicious person before.

"It is terrible. You need to watch out for it. It's especially easy to harbor malice in your heart when someone has done you wrong. Do you remember what I said about the people who crucified me?" Jesus asks her.

Fran thinks for a moment. "'Forgive them, for they know not what they do.' Is that what you mean, Lord?"

"Uh-huh, that's it. Can you forgive Marilyn and Tom since they don't know what they're doing? They don't have me in their lives, you know. What can you expect from anyone who doesn't have my power to help them? They're just behaving the way their human natures tell them to behave. Just think of how you would have behaved if I hadn't been there."

Fran is always amazed at how Jesus puts everything into perspective. As soon as she thinks about it that way, Fran is able to feel sorry for Marilyn and Tom, and the malice goes away. "Thanks, Lord, I needed that reminder."

As they approach the cafeteria, Jesus gives her one

more quick word of advice. ***"A good idea is to pray for them, Fran. Pray for their well-being, pray they'll become believers, pray for your attitude toward them. When you pray for them, you'll think about them correctly, and that malice will go."***

"Okay, Lord, I promise to pray for them every day." Fran smiles at Jesus as she gets her lunch tray.

She selects a table near the window, and halfway through her salad, a friend joins her. "Hi, Fran," Debbie says as she pulls up a chair. "Haven't seen you today. May I join you?"

"Hi, Debbie. Sure, sit down. Guess I've been holed up at my desk. How're things?" Fran asks.

"How're things with you?" Debbie replies to Fran with a knowing look.

"Okay." Fran lets it lie there.

After a couple of seconds, Debbie asks, "You mean you're not going to tell me about it? Everyone in the office is talking about it."

"About what?"

"The Ross account. Tom's going all over the office, gloating over getting the business, telling everybody it's going to be the biggest sale this month. Something happen, Fran? That was your account." Debbie's questions give Fran the perfect opening to set the record straight and get things off her chest, but just as she starts to talk, Jesus shuffles in his chair, and she remembers that he is there.

Fran changes her mind, and the words that come out of her mouth are much different than first intended. "Well, it just became necessary for me to relinquish the account, so Marilyn assigned it to Tom. Not much else to tell, Debbie."

Fran whispers to Jesus, "Thanks, Lord. That wasn't what I first intended to say."

Jesus whispers back, ***"Well, you prayed this morning that I would set a guard over your lips and help you to say the right thing. So, I simply answered your prayer."*** Fran shakes her head in amazement. It works; it really works. The power of Jesus Christ can operate in her life when she prays it in and is continually conscious of his presence with her.

Debbie's puzzled look causes Fran to smile. "Well, I don't think you're telling me the whole story," she says, but Fran just keeps on eating.

"By the way, Debbie, how's your mother? Any progress with the chemotherapy treatments? Is her prognosis improved at all?" Fran has been praying for Debbie and her mother, who was recently operated on for breast cancer.

Debbie's face drops. "Oh, Fran, we don't know much yet. But Mom is so sick with those treatments. I don't know . . . ," and her voice chokes up. Fran puts an arm around her.

"I'm so sorry, Debbie. I can imagine how tough it is. I'm still praying for her and for you." Debbie looks at Fran again with some puzzlement and says, "Thanks, Fran, it helps to know you care."

Throughout the afternoon, Fran goes about her job, talking with Jesus on and off, asking for his help and advice at various points, sharing a thought or laugh with him. Having him there makes so much difference. When her kids call after school, she gives them some words of encouragement, promises to be home on time, and thanks the Lord for his protection and care for her children.

At quitting time, as Fran is putting on her coat,

Marilyn walks in. "You know, you have one more chance to change your mind. We've redone the proposal the way I wanted it done. If you'll go with that, I'll tell Tom the account is yours."

Fran smiles at Marilyn and finds it isn't even difficult to say, "Thanks, Marilyn. I appreciate that offer, but my answer's still the same. Good luck tomorrow. Hope Tom gets the business." She's absolutely amazed that she can say that with honesty.

Marilyn shakes her head. "I'll never understand you, Fran. You're strange."

Fran chuckles. "Oh, by the way, I have an appointment tomorrow with John Warton. Been trying to get through to him for weeks. Maybe that'll turn into something big," she says to Marilyn.

"Yeah, if you don't blow it again." Marilyn is obviously upset that Fran won't back down and walks away without another word.

"Lord, I may have really damaged my career here. Marilyn doesn't admire my stand; it just makes her angry," Fran says to Jesus.

"I know. Some people are attracted by the aroma of Christ and some find it very uncomfortable. Never mind, Fran. You do what's right; I'll take care of you."

And with those words of comfort, they leave together.

A couple of months have passed since the episode with the Ross account. Fran kept thinking that there would be a fairy-tale ending to the story, that she'd be vindicated for doing the right thing—that Marilyn would apologize to her, or Tom would insist she take the Ross account back—or something dramatic.

But in fact, none of that happened. Actually, the

presentation to Ross didn't go very well, as Fran heard the story, and the account was lost to their competition. It might have worked out that way anyhow, but Fran would like to think that she could have made the sale. Marilyn has been rather cool and aloof since then, undoubtedly dealing with her own guilt. She blames Fran for the lost account, since Fran wasn't willing to follow orders. She's made several digs at her one way or another and has been very sarcastic and nonsupportive.

Today, as Fran arrives at work with Jesus at her side, she's a little nervous because it's the day of her six-month appraisal. She's actually been there a little over seven months, but Marilyn kept postponing the appointment. It's an important appraisal because it could mean that Fran gets promoted to account rep.

She says to Jesus, "I'll be glad when this is over. I hate appraisals. But I hope it goes well because I need the extra money that would come with the promotion."

Jesus replies, ***"Fran, I'll go right into that appraisal with you, so take a deep breath and know that whatever happens, I'm in this with you."***

"Thanks, Lord." She smiles at Jesus' words of encouragement. It really helps her to keep her perspective. After all, she works for Jesus, not for Marilyn, and as long as he is pleased with her work, she has the approval that is important. "You know, Lord, my track record is good for a rookie, I think. Ed's client has said lots of nice things about the way I've handled their business, and I got that big order from John Warton last week—nobody's been able to break that account before. So I think I'm in good shape."

"Do you think Marilyn will have anything to say about the Ross account?" Jesus asks.

"Well, who knows, Lord, but with my good record, I don't see how she can refuse to give me a good rating on my appraisal. After all, I didn't lose that account; Tom did! Well, it's about time to go." Fran starts to rush out.

"Why don't you have a quiet moment of prayer before you go in there? Do you have time?" Jesus asks.

Fran smiles. "Of course I do, Lord. I can't afford not to take time for prayer, can I?" She sits down beside Jesus and prays quietly, "Dear Father, give me your strength, your perspective, your calmness, and your wisdom as I go into this appraisal. I ask you to put the right words in my mouth. I pray for a favorable appraisal, if that is your will. Thanks for giving me Jesus to be right here beside me during this. That helps a lot. I pray this in his name. Amen."

Together they head toward Marilyn's office.

"Come on in, Fran," Marilyn says in a rather rigid voice, as she closes the door behind her. "I've already completed your appraisal, and what I'd like you to do is look it over and then we'll discuss it." She hands her the appraisal form.

Fran's eyes begin to focus on the appraisal, and slowly she realizes she has been given a very poor rating. Marilyn has given her the grade of "Does not meet the requirements of the job," which means that Fran will be put on notice. By being put on notice, she is given three months to improve, and if she does not, she will be fired. She gulps hard and looks at Jesus.

"Lord, do you see this? Can you believe it? There's no way she can justify this poor rating. It means I not only don't get the promotion, I may get fired. Lord!"

"Yes, Fran, I see it." Jesus responds. ***"The important thing now is to stay calm. Remember, you prayed***

about your words, so be very careful what you say. Measure your words carefully."

With her heart beating like crazy, Fran looks up at Marilyn. "I guess you can see that this appraisal is very shocking to me. I really don't understand how you can honestly appraise my work as not meeting the requirements. I've had excellent sales success and gotten some new accounts. I just don't understand," Fran says to Marilyn, as she hands her the sales figures.

"Listen, Fran, numbers don't tell the whole story. You demonstrated a total unwillingness to obey orders, you were insubordinate, and as a result, we lost the Ross business. I could fire you for that, Fran, but I'm giving you a break. You have three months to shape up and decide if you're a team player or not. Otherwise, you'll be looking for another job."

Fran can't believe her ears. "Jesus," she says, "are you going to let her get by with this? You know how unfair this is; after all, I was doing what you told me to do, I was doing the right thing, and now I'm about to lose my job. Jesus, where are you?"

"I'm right here, Fran; I haven't moved an inch," he says comfortingly to her, as he looks in her eyes. ***"Please look at me. Have I ever failed you? Have I ever left you or forsaken you?"***

"No," Fran replies, "but this is different. I'm really in trouble. What do I do?"

"I thought you'd never ask," says Jesus, and he quietly begins to put into her mind what she should now say to Marilyn. Fran can feel a quiet calm come over her—what's that verse—the peace which "passes understanding"? That's what it is—unreasonable peace.

The words she had prayed for form in her mind, and Fran turns to Marilyn and says, "Well, Marilyn, I think the procedures give me the right to voice my objection to this appraisal, isn't that right? I'd like to exercise that right. I believe I'm supposed to put it in writing and submit it to Bob Richardson of Human Resources, so I'll be glad to do that."

Marilyn's face gets red, and she gets up and stands over Fran intimidatingly. "You can do whatever you like, but it won't get you anywhere. I've reviewed all this with Bob, and he's in total agreement with what I've done. Insubordination is an offense for which any employee can be fired. You'll find it in the personnel handbook, if you don't believe me."

"Oh, I believe you, Marilyn," Fran replies, "but I don't feel I've been insubordinate, and I'd like to follow the procedures for expressing my nonconcurrence." All of a sudden Fran feels very fearful. *What am I saying?* she thinks. "I'm in trouble, and I'm making Marilyn very angry. Jesus, this is escalating, and I don't know what to do. I've never seen Marilyn so out of control and hateful. Jesus!" Fran feels a sudden panic attack.

Jesus whispers in her ear, ***"Please remember that Marilyn is angry because you did the right thing. You were a light shining in her darkness, and she didn't like it. Don't take it personally; I'm going to get you through this, Fran, I promise."***

Just hearing his voice assures Fran, and the peace that passes understanding sweeps over her again. But somehow, the more peaceful she feels, the more upset and out of control Marilyn seems to be. After pacing in front of Fran for what seems like an eternity, Marilyn turns and says, "There's a place on page three of the appraisal for your comments, if you insist on getting yourself in further trouble. After you write them, return the appraisal to me. I'll take it to Bob."

"Marilyn," Fran says, "if I remember correctly, I believe the procedures indicate I'm to take it directly to Bob's office, and then an interview will be scheduled. Isn't that right?" Again, the calmness of her own voice amazes Fran.

But when she sees how angry this makes Marilyn, she says to Jesus, "Oops, I think I said the wrong thing. Guess I shouldn't have brought that up, eh?"

"No," Jesus responds, ***"it's okay, Fran. Marilyn is uncomfortable because she knows you could get her in a bunch of trouble if you go talk to Bob."***

"Get her in trouble? Why, of course," Fran replies. Suddenly it's all so clear to Fran. Marilyn is bluffing about Bob, trying to frighten Fran. Marilyn never dreamed Fran would think of talking to Bob. This is simply her way of getting back at Fran.

"You know, Lord, I just hadn't stopped to put it all together. I heard that Marilyn's manager was very upset with her for turning the Ross account over to Tom at the last minute. He blamed her for losing that business. So she's just looking to get even with me, I think."

"Right," says Jesus, ***"but, you know, you now have the advantage over Marilyn. She knows that if you escalate the issue, she'll be in further trouble."***

Fran turns her attention back to Marilyn, who is staring at her with a look of fear and hatred, and, beginning with some words of profanity, she says to Fran, "If you think you can get me in trouble, you're wrong, Fran. My job is secure; they'll believe what I tell them, not what you write on that form or say to Bob."

For the first time, Fran sees that Marilyn is an insecure, desperate woman. The facade of being in charge and together has fallen off her like a coat. Fran had always seen her as competent and in control, but now the scales have dropped from her eyes, and she sees a different woman. Suddenly Fran can feel nothing but pity for Marilyn. "Lord," she says to Jesus, "look at her. She's pitiful."

Jesus nods his head in agreement. Fran asks, "Well, Lord, how do I respond to her now? Do I keep insisting on my right to talk with Bob? I feel so sorry for her."

Jesus smiles. ***"You feel sorry for her. Isn't that interesting? A few minutes ago you were frightened, and Marilyn was a huge problem in your life. Now you feel sorry for her."***

Fran sees the humor and smiles back at Jesus. "Well, you know, Lord, that's because you allow me to see people through your eyes. If you weren't here beside me, I wouldn't feel sorry for Marilyn."

"Yes, Fran, you're looking through my eyes now, and you see Marilyn to be what she is: a very insecure and frightened woman. All that intimidation is just her way of covering up."

All at once Fran knows what she should do. She turns to Marilyn and says, "You know, maybe it's not really necessary for me to talk to Bob at this time. If you'll just tell me exactly what I have to do to improve my performance and put that in writing for me, I'll do everything I can honestly do to improve. I believe another appraisal will be due in three months, and perhaps by then you will be able to change it. That could solve the whole issue, couldn't it?"

Fran turns to Jesus with a funny look on her face. "I didn't intend to say that. Where did that come from?"

Jesus smiles at her. ***"From me. You prayed for wisdom, so I put that idea in your mind. That's an answer to prayer, Fran."***

Fran shakes her head in amazement and looks at Marilyn, who has rather quietly sat down and seems much calmer, almost sheepish. "Fran," she says, "I, uh, I'm sure, uh . . . well, yeah, I think that's a possibility. You could possibly pull your appraisal up in three months. Do you still want to talk to Bob?" Marilyn asks very hesitatingly.

"No," Fran replies, "as long as I have in writing exactly what I'm supposed to do, and as long as it's something I can realistically achieve, I'm willing to give it a three-month trial before talking to Bob."

Marilyn is obviously relieved and looks at Fran in bewilderment. "You mean you aren't going to do anything at this time, is that right?"

"Yes, Marilyn, I would prefer to work this out between us if possible. I don't like confrontations like this, and since I know I'll work hard and do the best job I can, I think I should have a good shot at dramatically improving that appraisal, don't you? Provided, of course, we don't run into anymore 'Ross' experiences." Fran looks to see how Marilyn responds to her reference to Ross. She wants to make certain Marilyn understands that she is still unwilling to compromise her integrity, even to keep her job.

"Well," Marilyn replies, "that's one of those unfortunate occurrences, Fran. Let's hope it won't happen again."

"Then we'll have another appraisal in three months, is that right?" Fran asks.

"Well, I have the flexibility of scheduling it sooner if I like, but at least in three months, yes," Marilyn answers. "If I've covered all your questions, I guess that's all we need to talk about now." Marilyn looks at Fran with what could almost be described as a smile.

As Fran and Jesus leave her office, the atmosphere is totally different. Fran says to Jesus, "Sounded like Marilyn just heaved a big sigh of relief, Lord. Did you hear that?"

"Yes," Jesus answers, ***"I think Marilyn realizes you could have hung a noose around her neck today, but you chose not to. Do you remember the passage in Matthew 16 that you read this morning about taking up your cross daily and following me?"***

"Now that you bring that up, I have to tell you that I'm not sure I know what it means to take up a cross daily and follow you. I mean, who would voluntarily want to take up some hardship or sorrow? Guess I don't understand what you mean, Lord," she replies.

"Well, what you've just done, Fran, is what it means. Your own natural will has today been placed at a crossroad with what I wanted you to do. You chose to do it my way instead of doing it your way. You were willing to let Marilyn off the hook, not knowing what the outcome would be. You faced a cross today and decided you would take it up. That's what it means."

"You mean, that was my daily cross?" she asks, rather puzzled.

"Any time you relinquish your will and choose mine, you've taken up your cross to follow me. That's what discipleship is." Jesus smiles at her.

"Jesus, if I'd been on my own, I would have kept pushing her and insisted on talking with Bob. But now I see that by backing off, I've saved Marilyn's neck, and her whole attitude changed toward me—right in front of my eyes. Your way was a lot better than mine."

"Well," Jesus replies with a grin, ***"I always lead you in paths that are good for you. You know, my plans for you are good ones, not plans to harm you, Fran."***

"Thank you, Jesus. Thank you for being so patient with me and leading me step by step, day by day. I can't imagine facing this unfair, unjust world without you by my side. But then, nobody could understand cruel treatment better than you." Fran's heart is stirred again to realize how much she loves Jesus for what he has done for her.

"By the way," Jesus says, ***"did you realize that Marilyn read 1 Corinthians 13 today?"***

"She did?" Fran replies. "I didn't see a Bible on her desk. I don't think she's ever read it, Lord."

"No, not in the Bible. She read it in you, Fran. You are the living edition of God's Word. Now, you can wait and see what will happen because you chose to be merciful." Jesus looks at Fran with that wonderful look of love. ***"Well done, good and faithful servant."***

Tears come to Fran's eyes. Just to know that the Lord is pleased with her is all she needs to know. "You know, Lord, even if I'd been fired on the spot, I could make it just hearing you say those words to me. I guess I don't really need Marilyn's good appraisal; all I need is yours."

THINK ABOUT IT

1. Have you ever had to choose between your loyalty to your job or employer and your loyalty to Christ?

2. List the things you feel you will never compromise, no matter what the cost. Are you truly committed to these standards?

3. Have you ever felt malice in your heart toward anyone? What can you do to make certain you do not harbor malice?

4. Evidently Marilyn was not impressed by Fran's willingness to stand up for what she believed. Have you found that people sometimes don't seem to respect your ethical stand?

5. Fran resisted the strong temptation to unload her frustration on Debbie. What do you think would likely have happened if she had told Debbie all she wanted to about her unfair treatment? How was she able to keep her mouth shut?

6. Have you ever been in a situation where your discipleship to Jesus Christ cost you something, as it did Fran? How did you feel as you stood firm in your commitment to Jesus?

7. How was Fran able to stay calm when confronted with the shock of Marilyn's appraisal? When have you experienced that "peace that passes understanding"—feeling peaceful in the midst of a troubling situation?

8. What did you think about Fran's method of handling the situation? Would you call it a "threat" or a way of letting Marilyn off the hook?

9. What do you imagine Marilyn thought about Fran when she left her office after that appraisal?

10. Do you pray regularly for God's wisdom? Describe some situations in which you have been conscious of that prayer being answered, such as having a good idea or making a good decision on the spot.

5
Struggling with Singleness

Four months have passed now since the appraisal with Marilyn. Marilyn's attitude toward Fran has changed significantly. The antagonism seems to have gone away, as well as the sarcastic remarks.

About a month ago, Marilyn told her that she was giving her a new appraisal to replace the negative one. She rated her above average in most every category, actually gave her a few compliments, and put through her promotion to account rep. Now Fran has her own little office. You could hardly call it spacious, but at least she has tall partitions around her desk and a door, which gives a sense of privacy.

The two-hundred-dollar-a-month raise that came with the promotion is very helpful, although by the time Uncle Sam gets his cut, she isn't left with much. She's still hoping she can manage to keep the house, but she recognizes that that may not be feasible. Things go pretty well as long as there are no unusual expenses, but there's no extra money to take care of the unexpected.

Fran has learned to love the book of Proverbs and finds it a very practical source of help in all kinds of situations. Since there are thirty-one chapters, she reads one each day, coordinating the chapter number with the day of the month.

Since Jim's untimely death, Fran finds that her life

is consumed with just keeping her family going. For the first year after his death, she had to learn to do so many things she'd never done before—and all that in the midst of terrible grief. Now, as a working mom, her time and energy are needed to do her job and be the mother she wants to be. She's learning how much sacrifice it takes to try to wear both of those hats.

But since almost two years have now passed since she became a widow, Fran is beginning to feel the desire and the need for male companionship. She finds herself looking at attractive men, quickly checking their ring finger to see if they're married, and daydreaming about whether she'll ever find someone to take Jim's place.

Fran's social life revolves primarily around her church. It always has, and she certainly intends for her children to have the firm and solid foundation of biblical teaching and good friends that they find in their church. But now that she's single, Fran isn't quite sure where she fits in at church anymore. She never realized how everything in church is so geared toward couples and families. Of course, she has a family, and she wants her kids to take part in those family activities. But somehow, as a single woman, she feels awkward.

Her church does have an active program for singles, and several have invited her to become a part of it. Although Fran is finding it difficult to view herself as single, she doesn't fit in with the married group either. On this Tuesday evening, a new friend, Patsy, has urged her to come to church for a special singles event.

As she and Jesus head to the church, she says, "You know, Lord, I never thought I'd be part of this singles scene again. And here I am, going to a dinner for singles. I'm not real comfortable with it, but at least I don't feel like a square peg in a round hole when I'm with the singles."

"It's been a difficult transition for you, Fran," Jesus replies. ***"No doubt about that."***

"The hardest part is just not fitting in, especially at church. At first I went back to the couples' class that Jim and I attended, but people didn't seem to know what to do with me. I seemed to make them nervous, but just because I'm single doesn't change who I am. I couldn't understand why they treated me differently."

"Well, Fran, it seems that people are good at building walls of all kinds—walls between marrieds and singles, young and old, career and traditional moms, divorced and never-marrieds, professional and blue-collar people—all kinds of walls. You know, I came to tear down those walls, but Christians still keep putting them back up. It breaks my heart."

"I guess I've done my share of building walls," Fran replies, "but now that I know how it feels from the other side, I'm going to do my best never to do that again and just accept everyone as they are—an individual loved by God and very special."

"The church should be the one place where the walls come down," Jesus says.

"Well," Fran replies, "I'm so glad you never build a wall between me and you, Lord. It doesn't matter who I am or what I do, you still love me and accept me, and I know sometimes I'm very hard to love."

Jesus smiles at Fran. As they pull into the parking lot, Patsy pulls in beside her. "Hi, Fran, glad you came tonight," Patsy calls as they get out of their cars.

"Yeah, well, I decided it couldn't hurt, but I'm a little uncomfortable," Fran says. "Guess I still don't think of myself as a single."

"You'll meet lots of nice people here—who knows, Fran, maybe even a man," Patsy replies.

"Yeah, right, what man wants a woman with two kids to raise?" Fran asks with a laugh, but inwardly she hopes that there might be some man here tonight who would find her interesting.

She and Patsy decide to sit together at an empty table, and as they chat away, the table begins to fill up with other singles. A man sits across from Fran and introduces himself as David; he's new to the city and the church. He looks about thirty-five, not too tall but nice looking and clean-cut, and Fran enjoys their conversation.

"You know, Lord," she whispers to Jesus, "he really seems to be interested in talking to me. And I've already told him I have two kids. Didn't seem to scare him off." Fran is a little excited.

"Fran," Jesus responds, ***"you don't have to worry about your kids. They're great kids, and the right kind of man will not find them a problem."***

"Do you think David might be that kind of man?" Fran asks.

"Oh, please, Fran, don't let your thoughts and imagination run away with you. You've just met him. Just talk to him like any other person, be interested in him because he's a person, and don't start projecting about a possible relationship. It's much too soon," Jesus warns Fran.

"Okay, okay—I'm sorry. But he is paying a lot of attention to me."

After the dinner and program, David continues talking with Fran. He asks if she can have a cup of coffee with him at the diner down the street. She looks at her watch and knows she should get on home because she promised the sitter to be home by 10:30—but she can't resist.

"Well, sure, David, I can talk for a few minutes," Fran replies. David suggests they go in his car. All the time Jesus is tugging at Fran's sleeve trying to get a word in edgewise, but Fran ignores his tugs.

As they get out of the car at the restaurant, Jesus says hurriedly to Fran, ***"Fran, you're not listening to me. This is not a smart thing for you to do; you promised the sitter, and you don't even know this man."***

"But Lord, it's a public place, and I met him at church. What harm could there be?" Fran says and brushes past Jesus to walk with David into the restaurant.

The next hour flies by, as Fran and David talk. She learns that he is an architect, just transferred to the city, and is divorced. He explains that he was married for only a few years before they both knew it was a huge mistake, but they stayed together twelve years. He has two sons, ages eleven and thirteen, who live with their mom. He became a Christian after his wife divorced him five years ago.

Suddenly Fran looks at her watch. "Oh, my goodness, it's almost 11:30. I must go; the sitter is expecting me." David drives her back to the church parking lot, and, as she rushes to her car, he asks if he can call her. She gives him her number.

In the car on the way home, her heart is flying high. "He liked me; he really liked me. And he was so easy to talk to. Got a good job, obviously the divorce wasn't his fault, and besides, he wasn't a Christian then. Nice guy." As Fran thinks about David, she suddenly realizes that Jesus is there, reading her thoughts, as always. There are times she wishes Jesus didn't know every thought she had.

She says to him, "Well, there was no harm in that, Jesus, right? It felt good to have some male attention. It's been a long time."

"No, nothing wrong except you were somewhat inconsiderate of your sitter, since you promised to be home by 10:30," Jesus says. ***"Would you have done that if Patsy had asked you to go to the diner?"***

"Well, no, I'm sure I would have insisted I had to go home—but don't I deserve some fun once in a while? Good grief! Do I have to always be the responsible mother?"

"Maybe a phone call to the sitter would have been considerate," Jesus responds. ***"At any rate, just think about how quickly you were willing to neglect your responsibility because of a man you have just met."***

"Yeah, you're right, Lord," Fran replies. "That is out of character for me. But it felt so good to be with a man."

Jesus looks at Fran very intently. ***"Please remember how vulnerable you are right now, Fran. You've been by yourself for quite a while, and any male attention is going to start the chemistry going. Don't be fooled by feelings. And please, don't let your need for male attention cause you to abandon all your common sense. Do you remember the advice you gave Louise?"***

Louise, Fran's friend from the office, is also single, and she fell hard and fast for a new man she met. Fran warned her not to move too fast, but Louise didn't listen and ended up with a broken heart.

"But this is different, Lord. . . ." Fran's voice trails off.

"Yes, it's always different when it happens to you, isn't it, Fran?" Jesus laughs.

"But the man Louise met was not even a Christian. David is a believer. This is different," Fran defends herself.

"Well, that certainly is a significant difference, but it doesn't mean you can let all your heartstrings go wild and not be cautious. Being a Christian is not the only important qualification for a potential relationship, Fran. That's just the beginning. There are many other very important issues to consider," Jesus says.

By now they've reached home, and Fran hurries into the house, apologizing to the sitter, who is obviously worried and upset. She pays her a little extra and watches as she walks home across the street, feeling a little guilty at her thoughtlessness tonight.

She crawls into bed but can't sleep. She goes over in her mind the entire evening, recalling the conversation with David, how he looked at her, what he said. In her imagination, the importance of the occasion grows. The next morning, as soon as she shuts the alarm off, she's thinking about the night before and how nice it was to talk to David.

She sits down with her Bible to spend some time with Jesus but finds her mind is totally uncontrollable. She's reading words on the page but not comprehending anything. She tries to pray, but her mind wanders. Finally, she just gives up and rushes to get off to work on time.

Jesus is with her all day, as usual, but Fran is too preoccupied to talk with him much. In fact, she has trouble keeping her mind on her work, and the day seems to drag on and on. Several times she finds herself staring at some papers while daydreaming about

David. *Wonder if he'll call tonight? Wonder if he really likes me?* Frequently Jesus hems and haws to get her attention, but she doesn't want to talk to him today. She's enjoying her fantasies.

She leaves right at 5:00, rushing to her car, again ignoring the presence of Jesus. She decides to pick up hamburgers for the kids rather than cook tonight. Tonight she is going to pamper herself with a bubble bath and a manicure. She just noticed her dishpan hands.

The kids seem more demanding than usual this evening, and she hurries them to finish their homework, do their chores, get their baths, and get ready for bed. Alice cries because she can't wear her new Sunday dress to school tomorrow, and Fran loses patience with her. "Alice, stop your crying. You're not wearing that dress to school." Fran raises her voice.

As she's putting a load of laundry in, the phone rings, and Fran's heart stops. Maybe it's David! She rushes to the phone, waits until it rings one more time, then tries to answer casually, only to discover it's Patsy.

"Hey, Fran, I saw you leave with that new guy—what's his name?" Patsy asks.

"David," Fran replies. "Well, we just went to the diner for a cup of coffee. Just talking, you know."

"Fran," Patsy says, "men don't ask you for a cup of coffee just to talk. He obviously is interested in you. He seemed like such a nice man; lucky you."

As they hang up, Fran is feeling even more encouraged that David will call tonight. She decides to postpone the bubble bath, in case he calls while she's in the tub, and sits down to work on her nails. With one eye on the television and the other on the phone, the evening wears on, but no call from David. Her mother calls and wants to chat, but Fran pretends to be busy in order to get her off the phone.

Finally at 11:00 she drags herself to bed, feeling disappointed. For the first time the whole evening, she's aware of Jesus there beside her. She begins to talk to him.

"Lord, I was really hoping David would call," Fran admits. "If he really was interested, don't you think he'd call tonight?"

"Fran," Jesus says, ***"I want you to think about what you've done since meeting David last night. What did you think about all day?"***

"David," Fran says, rather embarrassed.

"And what kind of thoughts did you have? Were they true?" Jesus asks.

"What do you mean? There was nothing wrong with my thoughts; I was just kinda daydreaming, I guess—thinking he would call, what I'd say, where we'd go, what I'd wear. Just daydreaming; no harm done," Fran answers.

"That kind of daydreaming does some harm, Fran," Jesus teaches her. ***"You see, you were allowing yourself to imagine all kinds of things based on one very short, very casual conversation. Frankly, Fran, I wouldn't call that thinking things that are true."***

Fran remembers Philippians 4:8. "So what you're telling me, Jesus, is that I'm beginning to make a fool out of myself over this man."

"Well, you're not at that stage yet, but you're headed in that direction. You've let your imagination read a lot into one brief conversation with a man you really don't know, Fran."

"But it felt so good to have that male attention," Fran says, brushing away a couple of tears.

"I know," Jesus responds. ***"I understand your need for male attention, but you can trust me to meet your needs in other ways, if necessary. And even if there isn't another man in your future, I am capable of fulfilling you and making your life very meaningful. Can you trust me?"***

"Yes," Fran says, with the tears freely flowing now, "I can trust you, but I can't imagine living the rest of my life without a husband. I'm lonely; it's not fun being a single in a married world."

"Well, you don't have to live the rest of your life, Fran," Jesus says very kindly, ***"just today. I've gotten you through the last couple of years; I can get you through today."***

"But, Lord, I want to know—are you saying I may have to be single forever?" Fran asks, with fear in her voice.

"I'm saying you can trust me, whether single or married."

"But Lord, if I just knew there would be a nice man for me down the road somewhere, I could be happy waiting, even for lots of years—if I just knew," Fran says.

"And if you knew, you would never have to walk by faith, would you? Besides, you don't need to know the future. You just need to know that I'm going to be with you through all your futures, and I've promised to take care of you. Furthermore, I've told you that I have good plans for you; you can trust me."

"But what if your plans are for me to be single?" Fran repeats.

"Then being single will make you happy, you'll find contentment, and your desires will be met," Jesus answers, ***"if you can trust me. You see, Fran, if you live in fear of what might or might not be, you'll be misera-***

ble. I would never give you a spirit of fear, and right now you're fearful of being single forever. Can you realize how that makes me feel to see that you can't trust me for your future?"

"How you feel?" Fran is stunned. "You mean, it hurts you when I get upset about being single?"

"It hurts me to realize you don't really trust me with all your life," Jesus responds. ***"Have I ever failed you?"***

"No, never. I guess I never realized that this fear of being single is really a lack of trust in you, Lord. And I guess I never thought about how awful it is not to trust you, because you are totally trustworthy. Can you please forgive me?"

"Done," Jesus says. ***"You know, this is the same issue you faced when Jim was alive. Remember when you felt your marriage was rocky and you were worried that Jim had found someone else?"***

Jesus reminds Fran of that terrible time early in their marriage. "Oh, yeah, I'd almost forgotten. Because Jim was working lots of overtime, I got to imagining he was in love with someone at work—imagining, letting my thoughts run away with me," Fran muses. "Guess I'm pretty good at that, huh?"

"Well, you lived in a lot of fear for a couple of weeks, remember?" Jesus says. ***"And what was it you finally had to learn?"***

"I remember talking to you about it, and you told me I wasn't trusting you. Trust is really important, isn't it, Lord?" Fran remarks.

"Yes, because without faith it's impossible to please me. I want to see that you have faith in me no matter what the circumstances are. Sometimes I allow those circumstances into your life to teach you to trust

me," Jesus explains. ***"And it's also good for you to remember that you have issues of fear, whether you're married or single. Single people aren't living some second-class life, Fran. After all, I was single while here on earth. And married people don't have it all easy. Don't forget that."***

"You're right, Lord; you always are." And with that conversation, her eyes close and she gets some much-needed sleep.

As the week progresses, Fran finds herself still thinking about David, but with more perspective. But she is still hoping he will call, and every time the phone rings, her heart skips a couple of beats. But Thursday and Friday evening come and go without a call from him.

Lynn drops by on Saturday morning for a cup of coffee. As they catch up on what's been happening, Lynn says, "You know, I miss these quiet moments we used to spend together, Fran. I know how busy you are, and I always hesitate to impose on your time. But it sure was nice when you were home during the day and we could get together occasionally."

"Oh, Lynn, I miss those times, too, but please, don't stop coming by and calling. I appreciate your friendship more than I can say, and it doesn't matter how busy I am, I need you and I want our friendship to stay strong," Fran insists. "Please don't ever hesitate to drop in just like always."

"You said you were going to that singles dinner at church," Lynn remarks. "How was it?"

"Well," Fran replies, "I guess *interesting* would be the right word." And with that, Fran relates her experience with David on Tuesday evening. "I've got a lot to learn about this single stuff, Lynn, but I thought when he said he'd call, that meant he'd call right away. I don't think he'll ever call."

The two of them discuss the difficulty of getting back into the "single life-style" and the traumas of dating and relationships. Just as Lynn is starting to leave, the phone rings. "Just a minute," Fran says, "let me get this call."

"Hi, Fran, this is David," she hears from the other end of the phone. She truly did not expect it to be David, and it catches her by surprise.

"Oh, David, hi," she finally manages to say. "No, sure I remember you, of course. I just wasn't expecting . . ."

Lynn turns around with a look in her eye, interested in what's happening. She gives Fran the thumbs-up sign and motions that she's going to leave. Fran continues talking to David. "Yes, I enjoyed our conversation, David. What? Tonight? Well, it would be nice to have dinner with you, but, you see, I have two kids and to find a baby-sitter this late—well, I don't see how I could."

After a pause, Fran says, "Well, sure, I guess I could try and find a sitter. Yeah, okay, call me back in an hour or so. I'll let you know."

As she hangs up the phone, her heart is beating a mile a minute. Dinner tonight! Then I wasn't making it all up in my head. David did like me; he is interested. Oh, wow, where will I find a sitter tonight? She calls a couple of her teenage sitters, but they're busy. Her Aunt Ginny—maybe she could do it—or Miss Polly, but Fran doesn't have the nerve to call either of them so late.

Half an hour has passed and Fran has not come up with an idea. She could ask her mother, but they live way across town, and getting the kids there or asking them to come over—well, again, she hates to dump things on them late. And her folks have done a lot for her since Jim died.

The phone rings, and Fran says, "Oh, great, David already. Well, I just can't make it tonight, that's all." But she answers the phone to discover it's her mom. "Hi, Mom, how are you?" After a few minutes of conversation, Fran gets up her nerve and asks, "Mom, are you and Dad busy tonight?"

"No," she replies, "why?"

"Well, I just got an invitation to go out to dinner tonight, but I can't find a sitter this late. I was just wondering—maybe I could bring the kids over and pick them up in the morning on the way to church. Would that be too much trouble?"

"Well," her mom pauses, "I'm always glad to have my grandchildren, you know that. Who are you going out to dinner with?"

"David, a man I met at church Tuesday night—you know, at the singles' dinner," Fran says, hoping her mom won't ask too many questions.

"You say he just called. Kind of late for an invitation, don't you think?" Mom says.

"Well, I guess things are different these days. Anyway, I'd like to go, if you don't mind keeping the kids," Fran says again.

"No, I don't mind. But I'm not sure I like you accepting this invitation so quickly. Doesn't sound right to me, Fran," her mom says.

Fran starts to get upset. Moms have a way of interfering, and, after all, this is none of her business. "Well, I met him at church, Mom. You know he's a nice man if I met him at church. I haven't been out to dinner without the kids in months. I think it would do me good,"

Fran tries to sound nonchalant. They agree to six o' clock and say good-bye.

David calls in a few minutes, Fran confirms she can have dinner with him, and then she looks at the clock. Almost noon. Wow, she's going to have to get busy to get everything done and be ready for dinner. Hurriedly she dives into some housecleaning chores. She calls the kids in from playing and lectures them about not picking up their clothes and not helping her enough.

"Alice, just look at your room. You know you're supposed to clean it before going out to play. And Drew, your books are all over the family room. Would you two please do your chores like you're supposed to!" she says emphatically.

She dashes off to the grocery store to do her weekly shopping. Trying to make the money stretch each week is still a major challenge, so Fran has to shop very carefully. She cuts out coupons and goes where the bargains are, to save money, so it takes a little extra time. She remembers the good ol' days before Jim died, when she didn't have to pinch every penny so hard!

Finally she gets the house in decent order and starts to think about her hair, what's she going to wear, and so forth. The adrenaline is really flowing, and Fran is excited about this evening. She'd forgotten what pre-date trauma was like—a combination of excitement and nausea. It feels like high school all over again.

Lynn calls about four-thirty to ask what happened. "Oh, Lynn, I'm going to dinner with him tonight. He called to invite me out," Fran tells her.

"You mean, he waited until Saturday morning to invite you out for Saturday night," Lynn says almost as a reflex. Hearing Fran's silence, she realizes it's a touchy point. "Well, maybe he didn't know what his schedule would be until this morning, who knows," she tries to cover up. "I hope you have a great time, Fran."

"Thanks, I'll give you all the details," Fran says, but as she hangs up the phone, she gets that same sick feeling she had after talking with her mom. Fran knows that asking and agreeing to a date at the last moment doesn't look really good. Why didn't David call her earlier in the week?

She also knows that her willingness to accept on such short notice sends a certain message to David, but she doesn't want to think about that. She's enjoying the feeling, the excitement, too much and doesn't want the spell broken.

As she sits down to give her nails a quick going over, she remembers for the first time since David's call that Jesus is there. "Well, Jesus, I guess you're not happy with my date with David, either," she says, trying to make light of it.

"I've been watching you all afternoon, Fran. You're really excited about this date, aren't you?" Jesus asks, ignoring her other remark.

"Surely there's nothing wrong with that, is there? Don't I have a right to some fun?"

"A right?" Jesus asks. ***"You're still superconcerned about your rights, Fran."***

"Well, I just used the wrong word. I mean, don't I have—uh, don't I deserve—I mean, what's wrong with a date? You made men and women for each other, and David and I are attracted to each other. It's just that simple," Fran responds.

"Oh, you don't have to convince me of the value of male/female relationships or marriage. I created the two sexes, as you say, for each other. I instituted mar-

riage. I understand your feelings," Jesus responds slowly. ***"But what I'm not happy with is your overreaction to this invitation—to this man. You've shown very little caution or discernment, and you really don't know him."***

"Well, I met him at church," Fran defends herself.

"Yes, but you don't even know anyone who knows him. He's new to the church, and you're taking a risk to be alone with a man who is an unknown," Jesus responds.

Fran feels guilty about it, but she really thinks it's being blown out of proportion. She's simply going to have dinner with a nice man. "After all, Lord," she says to Jesus, "I'm having dinner with him so I can get to know him."

"Might have been better to meet him at church tomorrow," Jesus suggests.

The air is rather heavy between them, and Fran just leaves it at that point. It's time to take her shower, fix her hair, and find the right thing to wear. Then she hastily gets the kids ready, puts them in the car, and heads out to her mother's house. They had offered to pick up the kids, but Fran felt too guilty to let them do that. So now she has to rush them over and then rush back to meet David.

Finally, with all that behind her, Fran feels free. She checks her hair one more time and sits down to wait for David. She turns on the television but doesn't really watch it. The clock keeps ticking away, and already David is twenty minutes late. *Well, maybe he's having trouble finding the house,* she thinks, while another ten minutes pass.

Finally the front doorbell rings. David makes no mention of being late, and they head out to the restaurant. The conversation goes along smoothly, picking up where they left off Tuesday evening. Fran tells David more about her family and her job. Then David starts talking about his marriage.

"My ex-wife tried to take me for everything I'm worth when we divorced. I've taken her to court twice to get the payments reduced, but it doesn't work. She tells lies and they always believe what the woman says," David says, with bitterness in his voice.

Fran is very uncomfortable with the conversation and feels an uneasiness in her spirit about his attitude toward his ex-wife. Trying to change the subject, she says, "How about your sons? Do you get to see them often?"

"Well, before I moved here I saw them once or twice a month. Now, it'll be a little harder," David says, "but they're busy teenagers. They don't have a lot of time for anything but soccer and girls!"

Again, a bell goes off in Fran's head. *Only saw his sons once or twice a month? Wow, doesn't say a lot for his role as a father.* But David continues, "Besides, I support them well. I give their mother enough money to keep them up first class, so they have everything they need."

"Fran," Jesus says quietly, ***"I hope you're listening."***

Fran squirms in her seat. Being reminded that Jesus is there makes her a bit uncomfortable, but there's no denying that David is not making the best impression. However, she changes the subject, and the evening continues nicely.

In the romantic setting, with the music and the good food, Fran thinks, *He really is a nice-looking man.* He smiles at her warmly and reaches for her hand.

"I'm so glad I met you, Fran," David says, as the

waiter is pouring their coffee. "You don't know how lonely it's been to move to a city where you don't know anybody. I'm glad you could be with me tonight."

The touch of his hand feels good. It's been a long time and Fran enjoys the feeling. "Well, I'm glad we met, too, David. Church is a good place to meet nice people. I understand loneliness. Since Jim's death I've been terribly lonely, but I've also learned that Jesus can fill up some of the lonely places. He's become more of a friend to me than ever before."

"Yeah, right," David responds. It's the first reference to anything spiritual all evening and David doesn't seem too comfortable. He changes the subject, as the dinner comes to a close.

After paying the bill, they head out to his car. David takes Fran's hand as they walk out, and again it feels good. As he opens the door to the car for her, before she realizes it, he puts his arm around her and kisses her firmly. She tries to pull away without being obvious, but it catches her by surprise.

"Sorry if I surprised you, Fran," David says, with his arm still around her, "but you're a beautiful woman, and I've been wanting to do that all evening."

"Well," Fran stammers, "yeah, well—we better get on home, David." And she quickly gets in the car.

All the way home, while keeping up some small talk, Fran feels that kiss. It's a combination of guilt and excitement. The chemistry starts fast, and, from David's rather nervous chatter, she gets the feeling that he's thinking about it, too.

As they get to her door, she starts to say goodnight. It's an awkward moment. She doesn't intend for him to kiss her again, but in a way she hopes he'll try. Fishing for her keys, she says, "Well, I hope to see you in church tomorrow. And thanks again, David. It was a really lovely evening."

"Your kids aren't here, are they?" David asks, as he holds the screen door.

"No, they're at my mom's for the night," Fran replies.

"Well, then, no reason I have to rush off, is there? Can we drum up another cup of coffee?" he asks with a disarming smile.

Fran feels obligated. After all, he bought her such a nice dinner, but she knows it's not smart to be alone with him. "Well, it's kinda late; maybe another time," she says.

"Oh, come on, Fran, we're both adults," David says, moving closer to her. "And the house is empty. You have needs, so do I; why don't we enjoy the evening."

Seven hundred alarms now go off in Fran's head. "David," she says, "I don't know what you have in mind, but the answer is no."

He actually starts to push the door open as Fran unlocks it. "David," she repeats, "I said good-night."

"Fran, I didn't take you out just to have someone to eat with," he looks her in the eyes, and the charm has vanished. "Now, come on. You got rid of the kids tonight so we could be alone—admit it."

"David," Fran says with alarm, "what are you saying? I didn't get rid of my kids; they're just sleeping at my mom's. And I certainly had no intention of anything more than dinner." She opens her purse and finds a twenty-dollar bill. Pushing it into his hand, she says, "There, I've paid for my meal; now, please leave."

"Fran, this is ridiculous. I don't want your money," he says, "let's just have some fun. You're single, I'm single—what difference does it make?"

"David, I thought you were a Christian," Fran says with shock.

"I am, but that doesn't mean I'm a monk! I am a man, after all."

At this point, he starts to push the door open again, and Fran remembers to call for help. "Lord, help, please help!"

"Pull the door shut again, Fran. It will then automatically lock. And stay on the porch until he drives off," Jesus whispers in her ear.

Quickly, before David realizes what she's doing, Fran pulls the door shut. "David, I will stand here on this porch until you drive off. Good-night," she says, and the finality in her voice finally gets the message across. David leaves, tucking the twenty dollars in his pocket as he goes.

"Fran, I'm sorry I wasted your time. I thought you were a woman who knows the score. Obviously I was wrong," he said over his shoulder as he got into the car.

Watching him drive away, her heart is beating so hard she thinks it will jump out of her chest. She leans against the door as her knees start to buckle. "Oh, Lord, thank you, thank you, thank you. If you hadn't given me that idea, who knows what would have happened."

Fran goes into the house and sinks down on the sofa. The tears start rushing down her cheeks as she realizes what happened. "Oh no, oh no, how could I have been so stupid? Oh, Lord, I think he would have raped me if I hadn't gotten that door closed. Did you see the look in his eye?"

"I saw his heart, Fran; that's why I wanted you to get to know him better before you were alone with him," Jesus says to her gently.

"I'm sorry, Lord. I didn't listen to you or Mom or

Lynn—or anybody," Fran says sobbing. "I just wanted to be with a man so badly that I lost all reasoning and all my sensibilities. Oh, I'm sorry."

"Don't cry anymore. You're safe. I know you never intended for the evening to go like this. You've learned some good lessons you won't forget," Jesus says.

"I sure learned them the hard way, didn't I?" Fran says, as she finds a tissue to wipe her eyes. "Wow, what a night."

She fixes a cup of warm milk to calm her down and takes a hot bath before going to bed, all the time thanking the Lord for his protection over her. "Even when I'm stupid, you still protect me. Thank you, Jesus."

As she crawls in bed, she surveys her room and thinks about her kids. "Oh, I love those kids. And I hardly gave them any time today. I just fussed at them for not doing their chores." The tears start to trickle again.

"Now, Fran," Jesus says quietly, ***"don't start wallowing in guilt. You made some basic mistakes; you went ahead and did what you wanted to do without listening to me, but no harm has been done. So, learn from it, grow from it, and let it go."***

She tries to do what Jesus has said—put it behind her—but as she lays her head on the pillow the guilt and remorse sweep over her. How could she be so stupid? How could she make such a fool out of herself? She wants to crawl under the covers and never come out again. In the loneliness of an empty house, self-pity crowds in around her. She wonders, *Am I doomed to sleep in an empty bed for the rest of my life?* The tears start to flow. She finally cries herself to sleep, only to wake up in the middle of the night and start the same guilt and self-pity thought patterns all over again.

What was supposed to be a wonderful evening turned into a nightmare, and Fran struggles with the aftermath.

THINK ABOUT IT!

1. Jesus warns Fran that she is now very vulnerable and can make poor decisions and judgments because of that. What makes Fran so vulnerable? Do you recognize when you are vulnerable? What are some of your typical behavior patterns during these vulnerable times?

2. What could Fran have done to keep from fantasizing about a relationship with David? Why didn't she do it? Can you relate?

3. Have you ever found yourself daydreaming too much? What harm can that do to you?

4. Fran chooses to ignore good advice given to her by Lynn and her Mom, not to mention what Jesus says to her. Why is Fran so willing to abandon her common sense and be less responsible? Is this normal behavior for Fran? Can you think of a time when you were willing to do the same kind of thing?

5. At dinner with David, Fran saw lots of danger signals. What were some of them? If she had been very smart, what could she have done at that point to avoid the problem she had with David at her home?

6. David's moral standards are not what Fran expected. Do you think he could really be a Christian and feel the way he does about sexual relationships?

7. Jesus doesn't promise Fran that she'll be married someday. What does he promise her? Why do single people have the tendency to think that life without marriage would be miserable? Is it wrong to want to be married? When does the desire for marriage become a problem?

6
Recovering from Failure

This Monday morning, as she wakes to face another day, Fran is totally unmotivated. Given her experience the past weekend with David, she feels like a spiritual disaster, a terrible mother, and an overall failure. Jesus told her to put it behind her, but it keeps cropping up in her mind.

Lying in bed, the guilt and despondency build, and nothing in her wants to get up and get going. Her mind keeps dwelling on all the bad things, and in addition she feels sorry for herself.

"You know," she thinks, "I do the best I can, work hard, try to be careful, and then David comes along. What was so wrong about having dinner with him? How could I have ever known he would turn out the way he did? I'm sure I'll never find another man to marry, and the rest of my life I'll be working hard, pinching pennies, trying to raise the kids by myself. It's just not fair."

Tears start down her cheeks as she remembers some conversations from yesterday. Her mother wanted to know about her date, and, though she tried to be very evasive and casual, eventually her mother dragged most of the story out of her.

"Well," her mother had said, "I'm just thankful you're safe. But Fran, I told you not to rush into anything. You just wouldn't listen."

"Mom, you don't have a right to run my life. I'm a grown woman."

Her mom, with a very hurt look, had responded, "I'm not trying to run your life, Fran; I believe your father and I have stood by you these past months and helped you a great deal."

So, feeling even more guilty, Fran had abruptly gathered up the kids and left the house with those harsh words hanging between her and her mother. Then Lynn called in the afternoon, wanting to hear the details. Fran needed a sympathetic ear, so she poured out the whole story, but Lynn wasn't as sympathetic as she hoped she would be.

"Well, Fran, I was praying God would keep you safe, and I'm glad to know he answered my prayer. But I never dreamed you'd find yourself in such a situation. Guess you'll have to be more careful from now on," were her words of advice, and advice was not what Fran was looking for. She knew she had to be more careful. Couldn't anyone just feel sorry for her?

Reviewing all this in her mind this Monday morning, the world looks pretty bleak to her. Pity parties, she discovered, are lonely affairs; no one comes! Yet self-pity seems to have a strange attraction for Fran, and once she gets into such a mind-set, she has difficulty abandoning it.

So she waits until the last minute, then gets up in a rush. Getting her two kids ready to go to school turns out to be a bigger chore than usual, and she ends up raising her voice and arguing with them as she hurries them. "Alice, I think you are the slowest seven-year-old in the country. Will you please hurry up!"

"I'm not slow, Mommy; I'm not the slowest seven-year-old, Mommy, I'm not," Alice starts to cry, as Fran's words have hurt her.

"Okay, honey, you're not the slowest. But will you just hurry?" Fran tries to brush off her remark and dry Alice's tears. But as she lets them off at school, Alice looks like a wounded kitten and Drew is sulking, refusing to give her a kiss as he leaves. It's not a good start for her week.

As she pulls her car onto the expressway for the bumper-to-bumper commute, she remembers that Jesus is there beside her, going to work with her again.

"Good morning," he says cheerily.

Fran is truly in no mood for a conversation with him. She got up too late for her morning time with him, but it wouldn't have done any good anyway, she figured. Not with the mood she was in. "Morning," she quietly mumbles, hoping he will not pursue the conversation.

"Not a great Monday start, huh?" Jesus asks in his calm manner.

She forces a smile back at him but still keeps quiet.

"You seem a little angry this morning, Fran." Jesus comments. ***"Do you know why?"***

Fran responds nervously, "No, I'm not angry; just tired. Guess I'm not in the mood to talk much."

Jesus asks, ***"Could it be the argument you had with your mother yesterday? There were some pretty strong words between you."***

Now visibly angry, Fran says, "Well, we just don't see eye-to-eye on everything, and sometimes Mom tries to tell me what to do. I'm a grown woman, and I don't like to be told what to do." As she says the words, she knows how bad they sound.

"Do you think you treated her with respect, since she is your mother?" Jesus continues, quietly but firmly.

Fran doesn't like it when Jesus starts asking these kinds of questions. She squirms a little as she weaves in and out through traffic, trying to be preoccupied with her driving and ignore Jesus. But he won't let her do that.

"I'm sure you don't always agree, but were those harsh words necessary, Fran?" Jesus asks.

"Okay, okay, Jesus," Fran responds, "I'll call her today and apologize. It's my fault; it's always my fault!"

"I don't think an apology will do you much good with that attitude."

They turn into the parking lot at the office. Fran is relieved they are there because she really doesn't want to talk about this anymore. She said she'd apologize; what more does Jesus want?

As they walk into the office, Fran finds a notice on her desk of a phone call from a prospect who is cancelling an appointment with her today.

"Oh, good grief, I've waited two weeks for this appointment, got everything ready, and now he cancels," she says, as she slams her attaché on her desk and turns to take off her coat, almost knocking Jesus over in the process. "Oh, I'm sorry, Lord, I forgot—"

"You forgot I was here? That's okay, Fran. But I am here, even when you forget."

Fran feels very ashamed, but what can she say? She's just not in a good mood. She begins to think about what she said to her mother yesterday.

She turns to Jesus, "You know, Lord, I didn't mean to be disrespectful to her, but she keeps treating me like a little kid and laying guilt trips on me all the time."

Jesus answers, ***"Would you admit that you have***

drastically overstated the case, Fran? Does she truly treat you like a kid and lay guilt trips on you all the time, as you say? Or did she just hit the nail on the head yesterday, and that got to you?"

His incisive question catches her off guard, and she realizes Jesus won't let her take a superficial, selfish approach. He peels off the layers and gets to the real core. He always does.

Tears start to trickle down Fran's face. "Well, I've just been so lonely since Jim died, and David seemed like such a nice guy. Was it really my fault? Besides, what I do with my social life is none of her business." Fran looks at Jesus to see if she has his sympathy.

He calmly replies, ***"Do you really think it's none of her business? She has two grandchildren and a daughter to think about. She loves you very much. She has earned her right to state her opinion, don't you think?"***

Jesus' question reminds Fran of all that her mother and dad have done since Jim's accident to help her and the kids. Of course, Jesus is right; her mother has a right to inquire and be concerned.

"Well, she thinks I shouldn't do anything except take care of the kids. She doesn't want me to go out with anyone. I don't think she'll ever like another man for me; she was crazy about Jim. She wants me to be single forever," Fran says, and again a few tears start trickling down her cheek.

"Did you ever think," Jesus says, ***"that your mother may have a perspective that is clearer than yours, since your emotions are understandably involved? Maybe she just wants you to take things very slowly, Fran."***

"It's more than that. She thinks because I'm not married now that she can take Jim's place and run my life for me. And she's just got to learn that I'm not her little girl anymore," Fran responds, with the anger starting to build again.

"I think you've got some things to work out there, don't you?" Jesus asks, as he looks directly into her eyes.

Fran is struggling for an answer when the phone rings. "Good morning, this is Fran, can I help you?" She is relieved to have the interruption. But as she listens, what she hears doesn't go down well.

She replies, "What do you mean, you're not going to make that deadline? Andy, we had a meeting the other day on this very issue. You said it was no problem. I've made a commitment to the client. What's the matter with you people over there in the Art Department? This is the second time this month you've blown a deadline for me. You know, I work like crazy to get this business, and then you people sit on your duffs and goof off and lose it for me. Do I have to come over there myself and get the job done? What is it with you guys?"

The air is full of electricity as Fran pauses. "Yeah, well, you haven't heard the last on this one, Andy," she says, as she hangs up the phone with emphasis. Looking up she sees Jesus looking at her with wounded eyes.

"You seem to have angry words for a lot of people lately, Fran," he comments.

But she defends herself: "Listen, Lord, those guys need somebody to tell them off. They don't care about the client; they don't care about commitments. You can't pussyfoot around and be effective in this business. It's my job to see that my clients are served well, and I was just doing my job."

She opens her attaché, and lying on top is her Bible, which she carries with her each day. As she moves it out on her desk, the guilt moves in.

"Oh, Lord, I can't believe me. Listen to me. All I've done is hurt people with words lately, and you know what book I've been reading in the Bible, of course. James! 'Behold, what a great flame a little fire kindles!'" Fran sits at her desk with her head in her hands.

"You really have blown it a good deal in the last few days, Fran," Jesus says. ***"You've had some angry words for the children as well as your mother. You weren't very kind to Lynn yesterday, when she called. . . ."***

"Well, she started in with the 'you'll-have-to-be-more-careful' stuff. That's not what I needed from a good friend; I just needed someone to listen."

"And that justifies your abruptness with her?"

"I'm sorry, Lord," Fran says, as she gets up to close her door. The tears start to come, and she tells Jesus, "I'm really sorry. I've been rotten lately. Haven't spent any time with you, I've been angry at everyone. Oh, I wish I could just fall into a hole somewhere. I'm really ashamed of myself. Will you please forgive me?"

"Of course. You're forgiven," he responds as he touches her hand.

Fran looks at him and shakes her head. "You always forgive me so readily, and it seems I have to ask for forgiveness a lot. I've hurt you; I could see it in your eyes. I really am sorry. Please forgive me."

"No need to ask again," Jesus responds, ***"you're forgiven. But Fran, think about how you got to this place. What has been the series of events that led you to the angry outbursts, the despondency, the failures?"***

"Well, I guess it all happened when I met David and I really wanted him to ask me out. I just seemed to focus on nothing else, and that led me to some poor decisions."

"Good thinking, Fran," Jesus assures her.

"But I still don't know what was wrong with wanting to go out with a man and enjoying male attention," Fran replies, shaking her head.

"Oh, Fran, don't get things confused here. Your normal desire to want male attention and to enjoy those social occasions is not wrong. Wanting to be married again is not wrong," Jesus replies. ***"The problem is not with your desire but with the priority you were beginning to give to it."***

"The priority . . . ?" Fran has to think about this. "You mean, I was becoming obsessed. Wow, you're right, Lord, and look how fast it happened!"

"It sure doesn't take long to lose your focus and find yourself thinking wrongly, does it?" Jesus asks. ***"You remember when you first got some tugs from me and from others that you were rushing into this relationship? You remember some of the danger signals that you ignored? Those are the places where you walked away from the path that was straight in front of you, Fran."***

"Just a few days ago I was marking that passage in Proverbs—I think it's Proverbs chapter 4," Fran says, as she reaches for her Bible. "Yes, here it is. Proverbs 4:23-27: 'Above all else, guard your heart, for it is the wellspring of life. Put away perversity from your mouth; keep corrupt talk far from your lips. Let your eyes look straight ahead, fix your gaze directly before you. Make level paths for your feet and take only ways that are firm. Do not swerve to the right or the left; keep your foot from evil.' "

"Guard your heart, Fran," Jesus repeats, ***"for that is the seat of your emotions. If you let your emotions***

run the show, you'll find yourself making poor decisions frequently."

"'Take only ways that are firm,'" she quotes. "I guess I took some ways that were shaky. I wanted to make them seem okay in my mind, but they weren't. Going out with a man I do not know and no one I know does either; accepting such a late invitation; jumping through hoops to make it happen. Sure was foolish of me, Lord. I feel stupid."

"No, Fran," Jesus says comfortingly, ***"don't beat up on yourself. The important thing is you have learned from this. It will strengthen you greatly the next time you face any kind of temptation. Remember, you've been forgiven."*** Jesus touches her hand for reassurance.

"I know you forgive me," Fran says, "but how do I undo all this damage I've done to others? I've really blown it. I mean, the way I talked to Andy just now—and just last week I was sharing something about the Lord with him. He'll never listen to me again. I've ruined my testimony."

Jesus replies, ***"Well, you can't unspeak the words you spoke, but you can try to heal the wounds."***

"You mean apologize? But what will I say? I feel so stupid!"

"I know, but it's very important for you to apologize. Why don't you begin with your mother."

"Okay, I'll call her," Fran agrees and reaches for her phone. "Hello, Mom, this is Fran. Listen, I can't talk long now because I'm at work, but I just wanted to tell you how sorry I am for yelling at you yesterday. That was wrong of me, and I really am sorry."

Her mother immediately accepts her apology, and tries to apologize herself. "No, Mom, I think you did have a right to say what you did. After all, you are my mother, and you were right about David. I should not have gone out with him, and I won't anymore. But I'm really sorry about how I talked to you. Will you forgive me?"

With her mother's reassurance of forgiveness, Fran says, "Thanks, Mom. I'll talk to you tonight. Have a good day."

As she puts down the phone, it feels like one mountain was taken off of one shoulder. "Thanks, Lord, for helping me get to this point," Fran says to Jesus. "I know I've been stubborn, but thanks for being patient with me."

Jesus nods and smiles at her, but before he can say anything, the phone is ringing.

"Oh, David." Fran is shocked to hear his voice on the phone. "How'd you get my number?"

"You told me where you worked, Fran; wasn't hard to figure out," he replies. "Listen, I'm sorry about Saturday night. That wasn't very smooth of me. I was hoping you'd give me a chance to redeem myself."

"Well, I appreciate the apology, but I don't believe we'll be seeing each other on a personal basis any longer," Fran says. "I hope you'll keep coming to church, and I'll be praying for you."

He tries again to convince her to see him, but she resolutely refuses. As she hangs up the phone, she says to Jesus, "Isn't that crazy? I can't believe he would call me, but he truly sounded apologetic. Was I too hard on him?"

"Take only ways that are firm, Fran," Jesus quotes the verse again. ***"Above all else, guard your heart."***

"You're right, Lord. That was the right thing to do," Fran agrees. I must remember to call Lynn tonight and apologize to her, but right now, I'm going down to Andy's office to apologize. Will you go with me, Lord?"

Together they walk to Andy's office and find he's in a conference with one of his people, talking about Fran's job. He looks up at her and says, "Look, Fran, I'm doing the best I can do. Don't start buggin' me again; we're gonna' work overtime tonight. . . ."

"Andy, please, I didn't come to bug you, I came to apologize. I was way out of line talking to you like I did. I know they've cut back your head count and you're under tight budget restraints. It's not your fault. I just took my frustrations out on you. I'm really sorry, Andy."

Andy's mouth is hanging open. He dismisses his employee and invites her to take a seat.

"Well, at least you apologized," he says, with relief in his voice. "Everyone else is jumping down my throat, but you're the only one to apologize. Thanks, Fran."

"Well, I just couldn't let it go that way, Andy," she says. "I knew I was wrong. You know, last week I was telling you about my relationship with Jesus. Frankly, it was Jesus that caused me to see how badly I behaved, and it's because of him that I came to apologize. One of the great things about being a Christian is that when we blow it badly, as I did with you, Jesus gives us the strength to see ourselves, forgives us when we ask, and then helps us to make restitution."

Andy is not quite sure how to respond. "Well, whatever, I appreciate it. I will try to meet the deadline. I promise you, I'll try."

"That's all I ask," Fran smiles at him. "Keep me informed and I'll stay in touch with the client."

Andy looks at her with a puzzled expression. "You're different, Fran, even when you yell at me." She smiles back, and she and Jesus head back to her office.

"Jesus, you even use failure to bring glory to your name, don't you? There you've gone and turned my ashes into beauty again," Fran notes, shaking her head. "Thank you, Lord."

"That's my specialty, Fran, taking brokenness and failure and turning it around. I've been doing it for a long time, you know."

"Yes, and I'm sure you'll have to do it again for me someday. But I hope I can get better at not causing you grief like this. I don't want to be a perpetual problem for you," Fran says. "But I still have to apologize to Drew and Alice. I can't wait to see them tonight and tell them I'm sorry for the way I treated them this weekend."

"They'll understand, and they'll learn from your example."

"They'll learn from my bad example?" she asks with surprise.

"Yes, they'll learn that when they blow it, when they have failed, it's not the end of the road. They'll learn, as you are, that if they'll just keep bringing the failure to me, not running away from me, their failures can become new beginnings," Jesus explains.

"Failures can become new beginnings. That's really good to know, Jesus. Thank you."

1. Do you find that it's hard to stop feeling sorry for yourself once you get into a self-pity mode? Why do we often wallow in self-pity?

2. Fran is "not in a good mood" on this Monday. You've had days like that. What can we do to avoid doing a great deal of harm when we're "not in a good mood"?

3. Do you think it was important for Fran to apologize to her mom, Lynn, Andy, and her children? Is it hard for you to apologize when you need to? How do you feel after you've finally made that apology?

4. Do you think Fran had a right to resent her mother's interference in her life? Was her mother interfering? How do we know when we're getting good advice or interference? Even if someone is interfering, could it be possible they are giving us good advice that we should heed?

5. How did Fran let her imagination run away with her when she talked about her mother? Do you find that you can easily blow things way out of proportion when you are "not in a good mood"?

6. Fran wanted Lynn just to listen to her, not to give advice. Do you think Lynn should have been more sympathetic with Fran?

7. How do you interpret the verse in Proverbs that says, "Above all else, guard your heart"?

8. Has God ever used a failure in your life as a means of bringing glory to him?

7
Battling Burnout and Stress

Fran looks at the clock. "Ten o'clock, and I still haven't done the ironing," she says to herself, wearily. But knowing the kids don't have anything ready to wear for tomorrow, she sets up the ironing board in front of the television and prepares to iron while watching the late news.

Alice's dresses require extra time, but she likes to dress her up and feels it's important to teach her good dressing habits. Drew's clothes are much easier, but a pair of jeans every day still creates a heavy ironing load. Slowly she presses her silk blouse; she loves this blouse, but it does take extra care. She had to hand wash it and hang it carefully, then iron it very slowly. It takes about ten minutes just to iron that blouse.

The news goes off, but Fran is still ironing. At eleven o' clock she says "Well, I'll finish this ironing tomorrow morning. I'll have to get up early. Right now I've got to get that bathroom clean." She invited some friends from work over for a light dinner tomorrow evening—something she's been wanting to do, so she just finally did it. She spent the entire evening making some salads and trying to get the house looking decent.

She tackles the bathroom with fervor, scrubbing and scouring to make it sparkle. "It's amazing how two kids can mess up one bathroom so badly," Fran thinks to herself. Finally she puts away all the cleaning stuff and looks at the bathroom. It looks pretty and she is pleased, but her body is very fatigued.

Slowly she undresses for bed. "I'm not going to even bother taking off my makeup," Fran decides, as she sets the alarm a half-hour earlier and crawls into bed. "Oh, Lord," she starts to pray as she lays her head on the pillow, "I need your strength. Help me to get up in the morning and get everything done before tomorrow night. And please bless our time together tomorrow; I want my home to be a testimony, and I want to share you with the people at work. Thank you. . . ." But before she can complete the sentence, she falls asleep, exhausted.

The next morning when the alarm goes off at five, Fran jumps like she was shot. "What—what is it?" She starts to reach for the phone and gradually realizes it is the alarm clock. "Oh my goodness," she says out loud, "what time is it?" Turning on the light, she remembers she had set the clock early today in order to get everything done before leaving home.

"Oh, I just can't get up yet," Fran says and crawls back under the covers, pulling them over her head. She stays there for twenty minutes, feeling guilty because she knows she needs to get up, but everything in her resists putting her feet on the floor. Finally, she manages to sit up in bed.

"I am so tired," she says. "I don't know how I'm going to make it today. I think every bone in my body is aching."

Stumbling downstairs into the kitchen, she puts a cup of water in the microwave for tea. *Gotta get a cup of tea before I can do anything,* she thinks. "Come on, hurry up," she mumbles to the microwave. Those three minutes to boil water seem like an eternity to Fran.

Finally, with tea in hand, she looks into the family room and notices the ironing board still standing where she left it last night. "Oh, no," she says out loud, "I forgot about that ironing." Wearily she turns on the iron and sits down to wait. She senses a rustle nearby and realizes Jesus is there. "Oh, good morning, Lord," she says.

"Good morning, Fran," he replies. ***"You look a little harassed today."***

"Yeah, well I'm just tired. But I hope to have some quiet time to spend with you before I get off today—soon as I get this ironing done," she quickly adds, with an apologetic tone.

"Fran, I understand your need for more sleep, and I know that you're tired. I'm here with you all the time, just remember that," he says to her. ***"Remember, I'm here to give you strength."***

And with those words of comfort, Fran heaves a sigh and relaxes her shoulders. She then realizes how uptight she was, with all of her muscles flexed and her teeth clenched. "I guess I'm a little stressed out, Lord," she quietly admits to him.

"Yes, and it's understandable, isn't it?" Jesus responds, as Fran gulps down the last of her tea and begins to iron.

"What do you mean?"

"I mean, you've been going at quite a pace lately. It's understandable that your body is rebelling against it," Jesus replies. ***"Do you remember that when I was here on earth in a body like yours, I took rest periods?"***

"Sure, but you had twelve disciples who did all the little stuff," Fran responds defensively. "If I had someone to clean and cook and do the little stuff, I could rest once in a while, too." Hearing her words, Fran feels very ashamed, but as she looks at Jesus, he is smiling at her.

"Sorry, Lord, I know that wasn't true or nice. I'm sorry," she says as she looks into his eyes. "But honestly, as a woman and a mother, I'm responsible for so many little things, and if I don't do them, the place would shut down. I don't think men understand that sometimes."

"You mean, like ironing?" Jesus asks.

"Yes," Fran replies, as she starts on the third pair of Drew's jeans. "Who would iron these jeans if I didn't?"

"Maybe they don't need ironing," Jesus responds quietly.

"You mean let my son go to school in wrinkled jeans? Oh, no, I'm not letting down my standards. My kids are going to look good," Fran says, very self-righteously.

"Well, why do you have to iron them this morning?" Jesus asks.

"Because I'm having some friends over tonight from work, and I've got to get this all done before they get here," Fran answers.

"Why?" Jesus asks.

"Why? Well, because . . . well, what would they think . . . well . . . ," Fran pauses as she tries to come up with a logical explanation. "I guess, Lord, it really wouldn't matter whether the ironing was done or not." This is a totally new thought for Fran, that she could leave something undone.

"Why am I so obsessed with being the perfect housekeeper? Why do I focus so much time and energy on these things?" she asks, stopping to think about it for the first time.

"Perhaps," Jesus responds gently, ***"you've taken some pride in being perfect. Perhaps you iron those jeans for you, not for Drew. Perhaps your own self-image is tied up in your performance. Perhaps it's time for some serious reevaluation of your priorities."***

Fran feels so overwhelmed by what Jesus has just said to her that she turns off the iron and sits down on the sofa. It's almost more than she can comprehend. But she begins to get a glimpse of what he's saying to her.

"Lord, I've had pride in my heart about my ability to cope, to handle everything, to have perfect children and a perfect house. I never realized it before," Fran admits to Jesus. "I want to show off my kids and my house tonight; that's what I've been thinking. My motives are all wrong."

Seeing herself in this way upsets her, but Jesus says, ***"No, no, Fran, all your motives aren't wrong. You have good motives, too. You want those people from work to know me; you want to be a good friend; you want to share what I've given you. It's just that intermixed with the good motives are usually some others that need to be swept out."***

Fran looks at Jesus. "You aren't condemning me, are you? You know my heart; you know how proud I am; you know how self-serving my motives tend to be, but you are not condemning me."

"There is no condemnation for you because you are in me, Fran," Jesus reminds her.

"Yeah, Romans 8:1—I know that verse; I've memorized it. But it just dawns on me that you don't look for ways to condemn me. You aren't trying to place guilt on me, even when I deserve it."

"No, my desire for you is that you will be con-

formed to my image, and that's a growing process, Fran," Jesus reminds her.

"So," Fran replies, "you let me see things little by little, as I can handle them, in order to help me become more and more molded in your image. And now, you want me to take a serious look at my priorities as a working mom and make some choices. Is that right, Lord?"

"Absolutely right, Fran," Jesus looks at her with a broad smile. ***"Don't you remember? You've been praying Romans 12:1-2 every day for quite a while now, and I'm answering your prayer."***

"You mean offering my body as a living sacrifice and asking you to help me not to be conformed to this world but to transform me by renewing my mind? Yes, I have been praying that and I meant it," Fran says excitedly, "but I just didn't realize my prayers were being answered."

"When you ask anything in my name, I will hear and answer."

"I shouldn't be shocked to see that you are working in my life, should I? I'm ashamed to see how much of my motivation for working hard and trying to do things right has really been for selfish reasons, but I appreciate knowing it. Please help me, Lord, to clean up my motives," she asks with sincerity.

"I will continue to do so," he assures her. ***"And as you see this more clearly, you're going to be able to make better and better priority decisions, which means you'll know when to put the ironing board away and let Drew wear jeans right out of the dryer."***

Fran laughs. "Okay, no more ironing today. Away with this board. Whoopee!" she says as she puts it up.

"Hey, Mom, what's the matter?" A sleepy-eyed

Drew walks into the family room just as Fran is celebrating.

"Oh, honey, did I wake you up? I'm sorry. I was just talking to myself—and talking to Jesus, too." She gives him a big hug. "I guess it's almost time you were up anyway. Is Alice awake yet?"

"Nope, she's still a sleepyhead," Drew replies. "You were talking to Jesus? What do you mean?"

"Well, I just mean that since Jesus is with us all the time, we can talk to him wherever we are."

"But you were ironing. You can't talk to Jesus when you're ironing, Mom. You have to have your Bible and bow your head and close your eyes. In fact, it's best if you're in church!"

"Oh, Drew, let me tell you something wonderful," Fran says, as she takes his hand and sits on the sofa with him. "Jesus is not only our Savior and our God, but he is also our best friend. And he has told us we can talk to him anytime, anywhere. And that means, even when I'm ironing, I can talk to Jesus."

"Are you serious, Mom? That doesn't sound right."

"But it is right. The Bible tells us he will never leave us or forsake us, and he promised before he went back to heaven that he would be with us all the time, even to the end of the world," she explains. "That means, Drew, that when you're at school, you can talk to Jesus. When something happens that makes you mad, you can talk to Jesus about it—right then and there. When you have a problem and you can't talk to me because I'm at work or something, guess what?"

"I can talk to Jesus," her son answers.

"You got it," Fran says as she squeezes his hand. "I can't be with you all the time, but Jesus can. Nobody else can promise you they will never leave you, but

Jesus can. You know, Drew, I talk to Jesus at work all the time."

"You do? But what does everybody else think when they hear you talking to Jesus?"

"Well, they can't see Jesus or hear him talk to me, but I can still talk to him," Fran explains. "And even though they can't see or hear me talk to Jesus, I'm sure they can tell the difference in me when I talk to him and when I don't."

As they're talking, Alice walks in, rubbing her eyes. "How come nobody woke me up? What's going on?" she asks.

"Oh, come here, sweetheart." Fran gathers her onto the sofa with Drew. "We were just having a little conversation about talking to Jesus."

"Yeah, Alice," Drew jumps in, "guess what. Mom says I can talk to Jesus when I'm at school. I don't even have to have my eyes closed."

"Me, too? Me, too, Mommy? I want to talk to Jesus at school." Alice looks at Fran with those big wide eyes.

"Yes, darling, you too. When Jesus is our Savior, we can talk to him all the time," Fran replies.

The three of them spend a few more precious, memorable moments together on the sofa before they start their busy day. Fran tucks that morning away into her file of unforgettable experiences and thanks Jesus over and over for this incredible opportunity to share something so important with her children.

Because of the time spent with the kids, the rest of the morning is a bit off-schedule. Fran doesn't have time to polish the silver, as she had planned to do this morning. There wasn't time to put the finishing touches on the meal that she had planned to do. Drew wears a shirt that didn't get ironed, but Fran is amazed to see that once he has it on, you can't tell the difference. Certainly it didn't matter to Drew that it wasn't ironed.

After dropping the kids at school, Fran talks to Jesus while fighting traffic. "Lord, I just have a feeling that this morning was the beginning of an important change in my life. I feel like I've turned a corner," Fran says.

"Well, Fran," Jesus responds, ***"you had a wonderful lesson in priorities today. You had your morning totally planned with busywork, things you thought had to be done this morning. Instead, I had a divine appointment for you, a heavenly interruption, and you did something far more important than getting the ironing done or polishing silver."***

"We do need to have Forever Eyes," Fran says. "Guess I need better eyesight in order to have better priorities, huh?"

"Well, staying focused on what's eternally important will help you know when to let something go and when it truly needs to be done now," Jesus says.

"Oops," Fran suddenly exclaims, as she slams on the brakes to avoid hitting the car in front. "What's the matter with you, driving like an idiot? I can't believe how some people drive." Looking at her watch, she realizes she's running late. "Oh, come on you guys; move your cars. I don't want to be late for work."

Sitting in traffic, Fran starts to tighten up again. "You know, fighting this traffic every morning is just a major pain in the neck, Lord," Fran says. "By the time I get to the office, I'm already stressed out."

Finally they pull into the parking lot and Fran rushes out of the car, grabbing her attaché and purse, making a mad dash for the door. "Oh, good grief, I don't want to be late," she fumes to herself as she walks rapidly.

"Why don't you sing?" Jesus asks her.

"Sing?" Fran looks at him incredulously.

"Yes, instead of fuming all the way to the door, why not sing or hum?" he suggests. ***"Remember David; he sang when things got tough. Try it. It won't slow you down, and, while you're rushing, you'll also be releasing some of that stress."***

"Okay, here goes," Fran says, and she begins to sing under her breath her favorite chorus. "He is Lord, He is Lord, He is risen from the dead and He is Lord. Every knee shall bow, every tongue confess that Jesus Christ is Lord." By the time she has sung it twice, she's in the door and, amazingly, her shoulders have relaxed and some of the stress has gone away.

"Hey, that's a good idea, Lord," she says to Jesus as they walk to her desk. "I'll try that again."

"Sure, even when you're rushing around the office, if you'll hum or sing while you rush, rather than worry or think negatively, you'll discover it helps reduce your stress," Jesus says.

About ten o' clock Fran gets a hunger pang and gets herself a cup of tea and a doughnut from the cart. Taking a brief break, she sits back to enjoy her tea at her desk, but in the process hits her elbow and spills tea all the way down her blouse.

"Oh, good grief, my good silk blouse. Oh, no, I doubt I can get this tea stain out," Fran fusses as she tries to repair the damage. "Oh, this is my favorite blouse, and it wasn't cheap. Oh, no!"

"It's just a blouse," Jesus says quietly to her.

"What do you mean, it's just a blouse? I don't have

money to throw away, and this is a good blouse," Fran says as her blood pressure rises.

"Fran, it's just a blouse. When you allow the things you own to cause you undue stress, something's wrong."

"Lord, I'll probably have to take this to the cleaners to get the tea stain out. Do you know what they charge to clean a silk blouse? It's ridiculous," she replies, with even more stress and strain in her voice.

"Then give it away," Jesus says to her.

"Give away my blouse? What for? I love this blouse."

"You don't own that blouse; it owns you. If it continues to cause you stress, give it away. You spend a lot of time washing and ironing it and, when you wear it, you worry all the time about damaging it. Is it worth it?"

"I hadn't thought about it that way. I guess I do get stressed out over things that are of my own doing, don't I?"

"You know, Fran, the more you can get rid of the little stresses in your life, the easier it will be on you. I haven't called you to live in burn-out mode, and I don't want you to be frayed around the edges all the time," Jesus says to her.

"But Lord, my life is so busy, and so many people have demands on my time. It just seems impossible not to be stressed out," Fran says.

"Certainly there's a lot of stress in your life that is unavoidable. That's why it's very important to get rid of the stress that isn't necessary," he says.

"And this blouse is one of those, huh?"

"Well, get rid of it or change your attitude toward it," Jesus advises.

As the day progresses, Fran frequently mulls over

the lessons she's been learning in the last few hours. Gradually, with those Forever Eyes, she sees how she brings much stress on herself and how it is her responsibility to keep her body and her mind as stress-free as possible.

On the way home, Fran thinks about some of the problems she worked on at the office today. *I really have got to find a better way to handle the paperwork on my job. It just seems to eat up so much time and keep me from more important things.* She keeps thinking about the problems of the day and, as she does, her shoulders get tighter and tighter, and the knots grow in her stomach. *I'm also worried about coming in on budget for this latest campaign. The costs are mounting, and I didn't count on that extra photography that we're doing.*

"Why don't you dump them in the river?" Jesus says to her.

His voice startles her; she often forgets that he's there listening to her words and thoughts. "Dump them in the river? What are you talking about?"

"You'll be crossing the river in a few minutes. I suggest you dump all the problems from work in the river so you can enjoy your evening without all that unnecessary stress. You need to learn to leave the job behind you and not bring home problems that can't be solved at home."

Fran laughs as she thinks about Jesus' idea. "Well, I guess it's not a bad way to remind myself that I need a break from the problems of the day."

"Yes," Jesus replies, ***"and gimmicks like that can help you remember. As you dump them in the river, you can also quote a verse, like Psalm 62:5: 'Find rest, O my soul, in God alone; my hope comes from him.' Or Isaiah***

32:18: 'My people will live in peaceful dwelling places, in secure homes, in undisturbed places of rest.' Remember that you're headed to a peaceful home where you need some undisturbed rest. You need a break from the cares of the job. Dump them in the river and watch your stress levels go down."

As she crosses the Fox River, she says out loud, "Okay, all you problems from the day, here you go into the river. Now you just stay there till I come back on Monday. I'll see you then." She giggles as she says it, feeling rather foolish, but her shoulders do start to relax, and a smile breaks out on her face. Quietly she thinks about how often she brings home problems from work and realizes how they only add stress to her life.

With those things off her mind, she begins to think about the evening ahead. She says to Jesus, "I'm really excited about having some of the women from the office over tonight. I think it's a good opportunity to get to know them and build some relationships. And I've noticed all day today that, instead of worrying about how the house looks or if they'll think I'm a good cook, I've been more focused on them and wanting to get to know them."

"That's much more healthy, isn't it?" Jesus asks. ***"Certainly you want to have a lovely home and you want it to be clean. But what you're doing in having these women over is a wonderful ministry, and the details about the food and the house are not nearly as important as the fellowship and the building of relationships."***

"I've been putting this off for months because I wanted to have everything just right," Fran says. "Maybe if I didn't worry so much about everything being just right, I'd have more opportunities to build relationships."

"Fran, if those women are comfortable here tonight, and if the fellowship is good, it will be because you show them love and attention," Jesus says. ***"They won't notice dust on the furniture as much as you think they will."***

"Well, Lord, I guess many women just have these ideas about housekeeping," Fran explains. "We tend to associate our image as women with our cleaning and cooking skills. Truth is, I love to cook and entertain, and I enjoy a clean house."

"Nothing wrong with that. I've given you those things to enjoy. Just keep your priorities in line, and remember that your ministry to these women does not depend on your perfection as a cook or housekeeper."

As she walks in the door, Drew runs up to her. "Mom, guess what I did today. I talked to Jesus at school, just like you said. You remember Brian—that kid who made fun of me last week? Well, he started doing the same thing again. Said my ears were big and all kinds of stuff like that. I was starting to get real mad at him, and I remembered what you said. So, when I went back to my desk, I just asked Jesus to help me not be mad at Brian. I didn't bow my head or close my eyes or anything, and nobody knew I was talking to Jesus. But I did, and it worked. I didn't say anything mean back to Brian, but just told him God gave me my ears and that's the way they are. He shut up after that."

His mother listens with a huge grin on her face and gives Drew a big hug. "Oh, Drew, that's so good. I want you to remember to tell that to Grandma and Grandpa when they are here on Sunday. What a good idea!"

Alice runs in with her story for the day, and Fran stops to listen. Somehow all that she has to do doesn't seem as important as these conversations with her children. Already Fran can see how she's wearing her Forever Eyes better.

So, with calm in her spirit, she feeds the kids and does the things needed to be ready when her friends arrive at seven o' clock. Actually, Louise arrives a little early, before everything is ready, but Fran just asks her to help and she's glad to join in.

"You know," Louise says, "I've learned a little secret. I never go shopping on the way home from work anymore."

"You don't?" Fran asks. "Why not? That's when I do most of my grocery shopping."

"Because that is the highest traffic time. It takes longer, and it's far more frustrating," her friend replies. "This morning I stopped at the store on the way to work, and the store was practically empty. I breezed through, got what I needed, and checked out without standing in line, and the clerk even had a smile on her face. Saved me lots of time and aggravation."

"Hmm," Fran says, "I hadn't thought about that, but the truth is, by the time I get out of the grocery store in the afternoons, my stress levels have gone up quite a bit! Good suggestion, Louise. I'll try to remember that—shop when there are no crowds."

When the others arrive, they somehow all end up in the kitchen, talking, munching on some cheese and crackers, and helping Fran as needed. She smiles as she sees them enjoying the conversation and doesn't worry about the fact that the kitchen is a little messy. No one seems to notice.

The evening progresses, and the women seem to

love being there. They give Drew and Alice lots of special attention, which makes them feel very good. As Fran sends them off to bed around nine o' clock, Alice says, "I hope you'll come back again. It was fun having you here."

"What a nice thing to say, Alice," Fran says, as she walks them upstairs. "I was very proud of you and Drew tonight." The smile on Alice's face says it all; she loves to please her mommy.

Since it's Friday night, no one seems to be in a rush to leave, and Fran keeps pouring coffee and tea while they linger. At one point, Jerri says to her, "Fran, how long have you been a widow?"

"Almost three years," she replies.

"I've been looking at your pictures here. Jim looks like a terrific guy. I'm sure you miss him," Jerri adds.

With that opening, Fran very comfortably tells her friends how Jesus has been her strength and enabled her to face Jim's death. She hadn't planned to give her testimony, but it was a natural opening, and they all listen attentively.

Finally, one of them says, "You know, it's almost eleven-thirty. I really have to go, but this has been a lovely evening. Thank you, Fran. I can't remember when I've had such a relaxing time."

"Yeah, me too," Phyllis adds. "And I love your house. The meal was delicious, but next time let us bring the food."

"Great idea," Fran responds. "Let's do it again soon." Everyone agrees, and finally the house is empty.

Fran walks through, looking at all the dirty dishes and realizing that the house is just a tool to use, not a possession to show off. God used it tonight for his glory, and she is very pleased at how it turned out.

As she walks into the downstairs bathroom, she notices that Drew had left the towel on the tub with his telltale fingerprints all over it. Fran picks up the towel and smiles. "Lord, before today I would have had a fit because Drew didn't follow the rules about the towels and keeping the bathroom tidy. But who cares?"

"Yes, it isn't worth getting upset about, is it?"

"In fact, these dishes can sit here till tomorrow. I'm tired and I'm going to bed," Fran says. "Furthermore, I'm not setting my alarm tomorrow. I need some rest."

"Yes, you do," Jesus agrees.

THINK ABOUT IT!

1. For the first time Fran realizes that her motivation for keeping a perfect house and having perfectly dressed children is suspect. Why is she so driven in these areas? Is it wrong for her to want her house to be clean and shiny and her kids to look good? When does motivation change from valid to obsessive?

2. Fran has memorized Romans 8:1 but is just now understanding the full implications of "no condemnation." What does Romans 8:1 mean to you? Do you live in the joy of "no condemnation"?

3. Fran is surprised to discover that her prayer to be transformed by a renewed mind is being answered. Romans 12:1-2 is a wonderful daily prayer for all of us to use. Have you tried it? Can you see how God is transforming your mind?

4. Fran discovers that her "divine interruption" is a treasured moment. Can you think of any "divine interruptions" that have turned out to be special, memorable times for you?

5. What things do you own that cause you a great deal of worry and bother? Are they worth it?

6. Do you have the tendency, like Fran, to try to win approval from others by your good housekeeping or cooking? Does this keep you from having people in for fellowship as much as you would like to? Which is more important?

7. Fran is learning to put on Forever Eyes and finding it makes a big difference in her life. How can you learn to wear Forever Eyes more and more? What differences would it make in your life?

8. Do you tend to bring your problems from the job home with you or take your home problems to work with you? Separating the two worlds as much as possible can reduce stress. Think of some gimmick you could use to remind you to leave the job behind when you walk out each evening.

8
Fretting over Finances

After Fran gets the kids in bed this Tuesday evening, she says to herself, "It's the first of the month. I've got to write checks tonight."

One of the toughest aspects of being single for Fran is the total responsibility for the finances that now rests on her shoulders. Although she and Jim had talked about how their money was spent before he died, Jim was the one who took care of the day-to-day financial decisions, including paying the bills. But since his death that job has become Fran's, and she doesn't enjoy it at all.

Of course, it's particularly difficult because there's hardly ever enough money to pay all the bills. She and Jim had moved into their home three years before he died, when Alice was just a toddler, and it was a bit of a stretch for them. But they loved it and felt it was worth it to have the space and live in such a good neighborhood with good schools.

However, the mortgage payment was pretty steep—almost eight hundred dollars a month plus taxes and insurance. Time after time Fran has thought about how much better off she would be had she allowed Jim to buy mortgage insurance. He wanted to buy it, but Fran thought it was foolish. She couldn't imagine Jim would ever die—certainly not before her and not anytime soon—so she didn't want to spend the forty dollars a month for the premiums. Now, if she had let Jim buy it, the house would be paid off.

But it's not, and she has to accept that fact. As she starts to write checks, she says to herself, "Well, what bills will I pull out of the hat this month?" She adds up all the bills on her calculator.

"Mortgage $800, escrow for taxes and insurance $100, utilities, good grief, that phone bill is ridiculous," Fran says as she examines the bill to see if it is accurate. "And this doctor bill for Alice. All she had was an infected ear; you'd think from this bill she had major surgery. . . .

"Oh, great," she exclaims, "I'm $200 short of paying my bills this month. If the kids just didn't have to eat, I guess we could get by!"

"But don't forget," Jesus says to her, catching her by surprise, ***"I've promised to take care of you. You will not be brought to shame, or go hungry, or miss anything you need."***

Fran wasn't aware of his presence until he spoke to her, and then she felt a little annoyed. "Yeah, but I still have to pay these bills, and I can't go to my folks again for more money. They've done so much already; I have to get us to a place where we're self-sufficient, Lord. That's the only right thing to do."

"Well, Fran, take a look at your bills. Which ones can be eliminated or reduced?" Jesus asks in his calm and logical manner.

"Well, this cable-TV bill—I guess that could be eliminated. But the kids really enjoy the family-oriented channels," Fran rationalizes. "They're about the only decent channels for them to watch, especially when I'm not here."

"Yes, but they have a lot of good Disney videos,

and your mom has bought them several Bible videos," Jesus reminds her. ***"Don't you think that's enough?"***

"Yeah, you're right. They don't need to watch so much TV; they need to do more creative things with their time. It's just easy for me to plop them down in front of the television when I'm tired or busy," Fran candidly admits. "But I'll cancel the cable tomorrow."

"You do need to find ways to reduce your expenses," Jesus agrees. ***"Even little things can help, like the money you spend on lunch."***

"What do you mean, the money I spend on lunch?" she replies, defensively.

"Well, even in the cafeteria your lunch usually costs five or six dollars per day. If you brought it from home, you could probably cut it to one or two dollars per day. I've noticed that lots of other people bring their lunches."

Fran calms down and thinks about it. "I guess you're right. Louise often brings her lunch. Since I have to make the kids' lunches every day, it wouldn't be that much more trouble to make my own." She thinks a minute. "Guess I just really enjoyed the luxury of not having to worry about it—but I could probably save twenty dollars a week, and that adds up."

Looking through the rest of the bills, she says, "There's really not much else here I can do away with. This credit-card bill is too high; I bought that new dress last month, but I have to have nice clothes to work in. And these real-estate taxes went up again this year. I don't believe it."

"Yes, your housing costs are extremely high for the salary you make," Jesus comments. ***"That's your largest expense."***

"Well, I know I could sell the house and live somewhere cheaper, but . . ." That's the one thing Fran doesn't want to think about. She loves her home, and she's been hanging on by her fingernails to keep it. But the upkeep is not easy. She kills herself in the yard on summer weekends, trying to keep the grass mowed and the flowers blooming.

"But I love my home, Lord," Fran says. "Every woman wants her own home, and the children are comfortable here; it's home to them. I don't think it would be wise to change schools."

"Fran, it's time for you to seek counsel," Jesus says to her. ***"Remember Proverbs 19:20: 'Listen to advice and accept instruction, and in the end you will be wise.' And Proverbs 20:18: 'Make plans by seeking advice; if you wage war, obtain guidance.' You need to wage war against these financial woes. They're causing you a great deal of stress and it's getting worse, not better. So seek some counsel."***

Fran thinks about that as she finishes writing checks. "Wonder who I should talk to?" she asks herself. "Guess I need to get some advice about what my house is worth and then start looking at town houses or something." The thought depresses her. This house has become a part of her, and she doesn't want to give it up. She feels anger start to rise up in her, just thinking about it.

It's just not fair, she thinks, as tears start down her cheeks. Looking at her wedding picture on the desk beside her, she remembers life with Jim. *It's just not fair. Why did Jim die? Why did God take him from me? It's just not fair!*

Fran puts her head down on the desk, and the sobs shake her body as the pain and loneliness flood her memory. The early days after Jim's death were full of pain and questions and anger at God. But she thought she had gotten past all that. Now here it was again, seemingly as strong as ever.

Suddenly she sits up and says out loud, "Lord, it's just not fair. I didn't do anything to deserve this life. I was doing what you wanted me to do and so was Jim. Seems to me your promise to take care of me just didn't hold true," and all the anger she feels comes pouring out.

"I understand," Jesus replies, quietly.

"How could you understand? You've never had to raise two kids by yourself." The words come out of her mouth before Fran can stop them.

"I understand loneliness; I was rejected by my closest friends," Jesus reminds her. ***"Even my Father turned his back on me as I hung on the cross. I understand because I've experienced every kind of pain that you have, Fran."***

The room gets very quiet, as Fran's sobs subside. She thinks again of how much Jesus suffered for her and feels very ashamed at her outbursts. "Lord, I'm so sorry . . . ," she begins, but Jesus interrupts her.

"No, Fran, no need to apologize. You're complaining to the right person," Jesus says as he touches her shoulder and gives her a warm smile. ***"Remember David—Psalm 142. Why don't you read that psalm right now?"***

Fran reaches for Jim's Bible, which she keeps on the desk, opens it to Psalm 142, and begins reading:

> *I cry aloud to the Lord; I lift up my voice to the Lord for mercy. I pour out my complaint before him; before him I tell my trouble.*

> *When my spirit grows faint within me, it is you who know my way. In the path where I walk men have hidden a snare for me. Look to my right and see; no one is concerned for me. I have no refuge; no one cares for my life.*
>
> *I cry to you, O Lord; I say, "You are my refuge, my portion in the land of the living." Listen to my cry, for I am in desperate need; rescue me from those who pursue me, for they are too strong for me. Set me free from my prison, that I may praise your name.*
>
> *Then the righteous will gather about me because of your goodness to me.*

Fran's spirit is at peace as she finishes the psalm. "I guess David felt the same way I do, and he said just what he felt to you, didn't he, Lord?"

"Yes, Fran," Jesus replies. ***"I know there are times when you have these feelings; since I know what you think anyway, you might as well say it out loud. Then at least we can deal with it."***

"I know I was wrong to be angry with you and to feel sorry for myself. I truly am sorry."

"I accept your apology and you are forgiven," Jesus says. ***"But take a couple of minutes and let that psalm minister to you, Fran. It will help you the next time you feel like you've been deserted."***

"It seems to me that David had mixed feelings. In one sentence he says, 'it is you who know my way,' and in the next sentence he says 'no one is concerned for me,'" Fran says. "Sometimes in these human bodies we have such limited eyesight and understanding, Lord.

David couldn't understand what was happening to him, just like I can't understand what's happening to me."

"That's right, Fran, but I took care of David, didn't I?" Jesus asks.

"Yes, and you'll take care of me, too, right? It's interesting that David says 'set me free from my prison,' because I feel like I'm in a prison, too. A money prison. Because of the lack of money, I've got to sell my house, uproot my kids, change my life—if I just had more money all that wouldn't be necessary."

"Fran," Jesus says to her, ***"money is not the answer to your problems. Money is not your security blanket. You keep thinking that money will meet your needs. That is truly placing your hope in the wrong place."***

"But my problems would go away if I had more money—wouldn't they?" Fran asks. "Are you saying you can solve my problems without money? But how?"

"Fran, I have many creative ways to meet your needs, but first you have to trust me," Jesus says.

"Oh, Lord, I do trust you, you know that," Fran says defensively. "But how am I going to pay these bills without money?"

"Do you remember what I taught the disciples in my Sermon on the Mount? You cannot serve both God and Money. Money is a powerful thing, and it can cause you to be its slave."

"Well, my parents raised me to be very careful about paying bills on time and to save money. They lived through the depression, so they were always frightened about not having enough money," Fran remembers. "Maybe that's why I want more money, to feel more secure."

"Fran, being a good steward and spending your

money wisely are certainly good things. But you must watch that you don't look to money as the answer for your needs."

As Fran seals the last envelope and licks the stamps to mail her bills, she thinks again about seeking help and advice. She recognizes that she must take some drastic steps to bring her costs in line with her income. Well, she would talk to her mom tomorrow. That was a good place to start.

The next day as she arrives at work, she dials her mom before getting the day started. "Hi, Mom, it's me," she says cheerily. After a little chitchat she says, "You know, Mom, I guess I'm going to have to sell the house to make ends meet. I didn't have enough money this month to pay all the bills."

There is a silence on the phone as Fran waits for her mom's reaction. "Well, honey, your father and I were talking about that last week. It's probably a wise thing for you to do. I know you hate to sell your house, but frankly, we're not in a position to help you out a great deal, and—"

"Well, no one was asking you to help, Mom," Fran replies, with anger in her voice. "I was just telling you, that's all."

"Oh, I know, honey, but . . . ," her mom pauses. "Well, anyway, your father and I agree that it might be a wise move for you to find a less expensive place to live."

This is not how Fran wanted the conversation to go, so she abruptly changes the subject. "Well, I gotta go, Mom; got lots to do. I always have lots to do!" And with that she rather suddenly says good-bye.

As she hangs up the phone, anger and frustration start to rise. "Easy for her to say: 'Sell your home.' Wonder how she'd feel if she had to sell her home," Fran mumbles out loud.

"What's the problem, Fran?" Jesus asks.

His voice startles her. Many times she says and thinks things she wishes she hadn't when she is reminded that Jesus is there, and this is one of those times. "Problem? Who, me? No problem, Lord," she says with a touch of sarcasm.

"Why did you have such a negative reaction when your mother confirmed your decision to sell your house?" Jesus probes.

"I didn't have a negative reaction, but it just seems that no one really understands or cares. . . ." Fran starts to complain but decides not to say any more.

"Is this a pity party?" Jesus asks quietly, with a slight smile.

Fran is in no mood for this conversation. "I've got to go talk to Andy about this project," she replies as she grabs a file and marches out of her office. Fuming as she walks up the stairs to the third floor, she says to herself, "I'm not going to talk to anyone else about this; no one cares anyway. I'll figure it out myself. Mother and Dad are tired of taking care of me, she says. Well, fine, I won't ask them for one thing more."

"Fran, you're letting your thoughts get way out of bounds," Jesus says as he walks beside her. But she doesn't want to talk to him and pretends she doesn't hear.

Later in the day, her phone rings. "Mrs. Langley?" the voice asks.

"Yes," Fran replies.

"Mrs. Langley, I'm calling for Dr. Hughes. I'm sorry to bother you, but I was just calling to inquire about the bill for Drew's dental work. It's a little past due, and we were wondering when you might be able to pay it."

Fran is stunned as she realizes what this is—a collection call. "Uh," she mutters, very embarrassed, "well, I know it's a little late, but I'll try to pay right away. I'm sorry, it's just that so many bills have come due this month—I'm sorry."

"Are you saying then that you'll get a check off to us soon? When can we expect it, Mrs. Langley?" the cold voice asks on the other end of the phone. Fran can't believe how pushy he is.

"Uh, well," Fran tries to think, "I'll try to get a check off this week."

"Then we can expect full payment this week, is that right, Mrs. Langley?" he continues.

Fran is starting to get irritated. "Listen, I'm doing the best I can. We've been Dr. Hughes's patients for several years, and we pay our bills. So, believe me, I'll get you a check as soon as I can, hopefully this week."

"Well," the voice continues, "I'm sure you realize this is already sixty days late, so we'll expect your check in the next few days."

"By the way," Fran replies, "you shouldn't be calling me here at work. Don't call me here anymore, please."

"Well, Mrs. Langley, if you pay your bills on time, we won't have to call you again at all," he says with emphasis.

Fran slams the phone down. "I don't believe that guy. I'm going to call Dr. Hughes and give her a piece of my mind."

She dials the doctor's number and gets the receptionist. "Is Dr. Hughes in?" Fran asks.

"She's with a patient. Can I help you?" the young voice asks.

"Well, I just received a call from someone about Drew's dental bill, and he was very rude and very pushy. I'm just calling to tell Dr. Hughes that I don't appreciate the way he treated me."

"I see. Well, Mrs. Langley, I imagine it was from our collection agent. We turn past-due bills over to them for collection. I'll take your message and give it to the doctor," she says.

Fran hangs up. "Is that all she can say: 'I'll give your message to the doctor?' No 'I'm sorry;' no apology? I tell you, that's the last time we'll go to that dentist."

Fran has never been so humiliated in her life. People calling her at work to collect money. That doesn't happen to nice, law-abiding people like her, but here it's happened. She just can't believe it. The rest of the day is pretty much a wipeout, because Fran can't think of anything else. As the day progresses she gets angrier and angrier.

Several times during the day, Jesus tries to get her attention, but Fran chooses to ignore him. She knows what he'll say: "Fran, you're feeling sorry for yourself." "Fran, you're letting your imagination run away with you." "Fran, I'll take care of you." She's in no mood for his pep talks this afternoon, so she ignores him, pretending to stay busy.

Fran stops at the neighborhood station to fill the tank up on the way home. Johnny, who has been servicing their car since they moved there, says to her, "Mrs. Langley, do you realize your tires are real thin? I was just noticing them. Those two on the back, well, there's hardly any tread left. You oughta get some new tires soon, I think."

Fran looks at Johnny and then looks at the tires. She can't believe her ears. How dare he suggest that she buy new tires, today of all days. She's so upset she can't even respond. She pays him for the gas and drives off quickly.

As she arrives home, Drew rushes up to her. "Mom, what happened? We can't get the Disney channel anymore!"

"Oh, Drew, I cancelled the cable service today," Fran replies.

"You cancelled cable? But why?"

"Because we can't afford it, that's why," Fran replies, her volume rising.

"Mom, you gotta be kidding! That's our favorite channel. What do you mean, we can't afford it? We've always afforded it before," Drew says.

"Drew, we don't have money like we did before your father died. You kids have to realize that," Fran replies.

"Oh, we realize it all the time. That's all you talk about," Drew shouts back at her with anger.

"Now, listen to me, Son." Fran grabs him by the shoulders. "I'm doing the best I can for you kids, working all the time. It's not my fault your father died. I have to cut our costs, and we can do without cable television, that's all there is to it. Furthermore, we're probably going to have to sell the house and move to a cheaper place."

As soon as she says it, she knows she said the wrong thing. "Move to another house? Mom, we can't leave this house. Mom . . . ," Drew looks at her with fear in his eyes, and tears start to roll down his cheeks. Fran is ashamed at how she has upset him unnecessarily. This was no way to tell him such bad news.

She releases her grip on his shoulders, takes his hand, and leads him to the sofa. "Oh, Drew, I'm sorry I yelled at you," she says, as she takes him in her arms. He cries freely.

"Mom, I don't want to move. I want to stay right in this house. This is our home. Mom, where are we going to move?" Drew's fears and anxiety pour out at once.

Hugging him close, Fran says, "Drew, I don't know where we'll move. But without your father's salary, we just can't afford this house. I don't make as much money as your dad did."

"But Grandma and Grandpa will help us. They have before." Drew looks up with hopeful eyes.

"Yes, they've been very helpful, but we can't keep asking them to bail us out. They're not rich, and that's not fair to them," Fran explains. "But listen, Drew, we'll figure something out. And whatever happens, we'll be together and Jesus will get us through." Fran has a little difficulty getting those last words out, after her behavior today. Still, she knows Jesus is close beside her and does care about her and Drew.

"Now, I need to ask you a big favor," Fran says. "I want this to be our secret for a while. Please don't tell Alice yet, okay?"

"Why not?" Drew asks.

"Because she'll be upset, and I want to wait until I know what we're going to do before I tell her," Fran says. "But you're my man now, and I can share these things with you. You're older and you can handle things better, right, Drew?"

"Yeah, okay, but please, Mom, please, let's not sell the house. I don't mind doing without cable, but please don't sell the house," Drew begs, as tears start to flow again. Fran holds him, unable to answer because of the tears in her own eyes.

Later in the evening she calls to apologize to her mom for her behavior on the phone today. As always, her mom pretends nothing happened. She says, "By the way, Ellen down the street had a big garage sale last Saturday. Do you know how much she got for her stuff? Two hundred and fifty dollars! I couldn't believe it."

"A garage sale?" Fran asks. "She got that much? Yeah, well, once Jim and I had one, when we wanted to get rid of all the baby stuff, and we got even more than that. I wonder. . . ." She begins to think. "If I could get enough to pay off the dentist and buy the new tires I need, that would be a great help. If I have a garage sale, will you come help me, Mom?"

"Of course, honey, I'd love to," her mom replies. "That would be fun. You know, Fran, you ought to talk with George before you do anything. He's got good business sense, working in the bank and all. Why don't you call him?"

"Good suggestion, Mom," Fran replies, as they finish their conversation.

She dials Uncle George's number, and he answers in his usual cheerful manner. She says, "Uncle George, I need some help and advice, and I wondered if you could just talk with me. This house is getting to be too expensive for me to keep. The mortgage payments and the taxes are really more than I can afford on my salary, so I guess I'm going to have to sell it and move to a cheaper place. But Mom suggested I talk to you first."

"Oh, Fran, I'll be glad to talk with you," George says. "Tell you what, why don't you come by the bank on your lunch hour tomorrow?"

"Great, I'll see you then," Fran says, with a feeling

of relief as she hangs up. Somehow it helps just to have someone to talk to who knows about finances.

"I'm glad you called George," Jesus says to her quietly.

"Oh, Jesus," Fran says rather sheepishly. "Well, yeah, it was my mom's suggestion. . . ." She pauses. "Actually, it was your suggestion, wasn't it? Yesterday you told me to seek advice. Well, I'm going to talk to Uncle George tomorrow."

"Good," Jesus responds.

"Did you see what I did to poor Drew tonight? I really dumped all my frustration on that kid," Fran confesses.

"Yes, I was hoping you would talk with me about it first," Jesus answers. ***"If you had talked to me, I don't think you would have dumped on Drew."***

"I'm sure you're right, Lord. I'm sorry. Seems all I do is apologize to you lately."

"Well, Fran, money has power. And it is one of the most difficult areas for my children to learn to trust me," Jesus says.

"I certainly haven't been trusting you in that area, Lord," she admits. "But when I look at the checkbook and look at the bills, I just go into panic mode. And then that collection call today—that was terribly embarrassing. And tires for the car—I just don't know how I'll ever pull us out of this."

"It sure does call for some trust and faith on your part, doesn't it?" Jesus comments. ***"Remember this, Fran: Money problems are either going to cause you to be worried and frantic, or they are going to cause you to learn to trust me more. It's your choice."***

Fran mulls that over. "It's my choice, you say? Either I can continue to act and react like I've done today, or I can refuse to get upset and pray more about it and trust you. But I feel that panic set in, and I just can't avoid it."

"Feeling the panic doesn't mean you're not trusting me," Jesus says. *"But at that point of panic, you must make a choice either to continue in panic mode or to trust me. Remember, if you go by your feelings, you'll often be in trouble. In spite of the panic feelings, you can trust me, even in the midst of them."*

"It brings to mind that verse I learned when I was a kid in Sunday school: 'What time I am afraid, I will trust in Thee.'"

"Yes, David wrote that," Jesus says.

"Seems like David and I have a lot in common," Fran says as she reaches for her Bible to locate the verse. "Here it is, Psalm 56. 'When I am afraid, I will trust in you. In God, whose word I praise, in God I trust; I will not be afraid. What can mortal man do to me?'"

Fran meditates on those verses. "David says, 'I will trust in you.' Guess that's what you mean when you say I have to make a choice, huh?"

"Yes, Fran, regardless of your feelings, if you will set your will to trust in me, you'll discover that the fears subside. And when the fears subside, then you can think correctly and hear my voice and know what to do. But when fear takes over, trust goes out the window, and you're going to find yourself doing and saying all kinds of things you wish you hadn't."

"Wow, that sure happened to me today," Fran says, as she rethinks her day. "I blew up at Mom, I was abrupt with a few people at work, I gave Johnny at the service station a rude reaction, and then I let poor Drew have it. I was out of control."

"Actually, you were controlled by fear and by your

own incorrect thinking. Remember when I said to you early in the day that you were letting your thoughts get way out of bounds," Jesus reminds her.

"Yes, but I wasn't in any mood to hear you. I can't believe how quickly I was in such a terrible frame of mind. Just last night you had assured me of your help and given me that wonderful psalm. Sure doesn't take long to get off the right path, does it?"

"No, when you let your thoughts get out of control, you can find yourself in enemy territory pretty quickly," Jesus says.

Fran spends a little more time reading her Bible and talking with Jesus and then goes to bed with a quiet spirit.

The next day her talk with Uncle George was encouraging. He explained some options she'd never thought about. Interest rates for mortgages are almost three points lower now than when she and Jim bought their house. She could refinance her home at a lower interest rate and cut her payments by almost one hundred fifty dollars a month. And several banks were offering these mortgages with greatly reduced closing costs. He showed her how she could recover all her closing costs in six months and then be ahead of the game.

He also pointed out that she could claim another deduction on her income tax and have an extra forty to fifty dollars in her paycheck. She ends up getting money back each year from the Internal Revenue Service, so she could lower her deductible if she wanted more monthly cash flow.

He also gave her the name of a friend in real estate who could give her some good advice on selling her house. "By the way," Uncle George said, "have you seen those new town houses on Maple Street? They're nice, and the price looks reasonable. Wouldn't that be the same school district for your kids if you moved there?"

She hadn't known about them because she never drives down Maple, but on the way home she made a point to do it. They were nice; two and three bedrooms, and it looked like they would be thirty to forty thousand dollars cheaper than her house. Well, that would certainly lower her costs and wouldn't cause a great deal of disruption in the kids' lives, since they'd be in the same schools.

As Fran drove on home, she said to Jesus, "I do have some options, don't I, Lord? Thanks for putting Uncle George in my life to help me. Now I just need to know what is the best thing to do."

"Well, Fran, keep praying for wisdom and seeking good advice," Jesus reminds her.

"And keep cutting back on costs." Fran smiles.

THINK ABOUT IT!

1. Money problems get to Fran quickly, destroy her peace, and cause her to say things she regrets. Do you find that is true in your life, too? Why is it that money gets to us so easily? Why is it so hard for us to trust Jesus when it comes to money matters?

2. Fran decided to cut costs as much as possible. Does that mean she can never spend money on herself, or must always feel guilty about expenditures that are not totally necessary?

3. Can you think of some people in your life that God has used to give you good financial advice? Do

you seek that advice when you should? And are you willing to take the advice when it means you have to implement some new financial disciplines?

4. Is it wrong for Fran to want to keep her home? Do you think she should sell it?

5. Jesus explains to Fran that when she needs to complain, he is the best person to complain to. How often do you complain to Jesus instead of to everybody else? Why is it better to complain to him?

6. Notice how Scripture has a calming effect on Fran. Do you run to the Word of God for comfort and help when you're feeling stressed and worried, or do you just worry and fret more?

7. Why do you think her mother's reaction angered Fran?

8. Why did the collection call upset her so much?

9. Fran is still learning how to bring her thoughts in line and not overreact or get mired down in self-pity. It's good to remember that we don't learn these lessons once, but throughout our lives. However, we should also be able to see progress and not be making the same mistakes forever. What progress can you see in your ability to trust God about financial matters?

10. What impression do you think Drew is left with after this experience? Can this be used for good in his life, even though Fran didn't handle it well?

9
Helping a Married Friend

Why, Fran asks herself as she fixes breakfast for the kids, *are Monday mornings so hard? Just seems like getting ready for work and starting another week gets tougher every Monday.*

"Mondays do seem to be your worst day, don't they?" Jesus comments, startling Fran for a moment. She looks at Jesus with surprise and then remembers that he can read her thoughts even when she doesn't speak them out loud. Everything is known to him. Sometimes that's a great comfort; at other times it bugs Fran a little because there are certain thoughts she'd like to keep to herself!

"Well," she responds, "they are tough. But I think Sundays are in a way even worse. Do you know what I mean, Lord?"

"Because you're alone, you mean."

"Yeah. When I'm at church it seems everybody else is married with husbands and family and a normal life. And I sit in church with the kids by myself. . . . Well, it makes me lonely and reminds me that I'm different," Fran tries to explain.

"There are other single moms at your church, Fran," Jesus reminds her. ***"You're not the only one."***

"You're right, Lord, but just a few of us. Most of my friends are married. Take Elinor, for example. I saw her in church yesterday. You know, we used to be real close when Jim was alive—spent lots of time together as couples. She and Rick, her husband, well . . . , he's got a good job, they have a nice house, Elinor seems to really like her teaching job, she dresses real pretty—she's got everything. And sometimes—"

"I understand," Jesus says. ***"Sometimes you compare yourself and feel like you got the short end of the stick. Why should you be left alone to raise your kids by yourself and worry about money and have all the responsibility—right?"***

"Right." Jesus always understands how Fran feels. She doesn't have to go into lots of detail with him. He knows her better than she knows herself.

"Comparing yourself to others is a dangerous habit, Fran," Jesus says. ***"It always leads you to wrong thinking. You either think you're better than others or end up jealous and envious. I strongly recommend that you break this wrong thinking pattern and not compare yourself to others."***

Tears start down Fran's face. "I know, you've told me that before. But it's hard when I see Elinor and wonder why she has it so easy."

"Remember this," Jesus says, ***"things are not always the way they look on the outside."***

At that moment, the kids rush into the kitchen for their breakfast, and Fran is busily occupied getting them ready for school.

Later, as she and Jesus drive to work, Fran is still feeling sorry for herself and dreading the upcoming week. She's thinking about how easy Elinor has it compared to her when Jesus says, ***"Why don't you phone Elinor and get together?"***

"Well, she could call me," Fran replies. "She's got more time than I do."

"Why don't you call her?" Jesus repeats, without addressing the self-pity he hears.

"Okay, I will," she says. Later Fran leaves a message at Elinor's school and, just before it's time to leave, she gets a return call.

"Elinor," she says, "I was just thinking about you today and how long it's been since we got together and talked, like we used to. We're both so busy and everything, but I was hoping we could find a time for dinner or something—just to catch up."

Elinor seems eager to get together, and they set up a date for Thursday evening. Thursday arrives and Fran gets to the restaurant on time but has to wait almost thirty minutes before Elinor joins her.

"I'm so sorry I'm late," she says as she rushes in, out of breath. "I tried to get out of the house, but I had to get Rick's dinner and the kids, . . . well, I'm sorry."

"Don't worry about it," Fran replies. "I've got a sitter, and it's a rare night out for me. So I'm in no rush."

They are seated and, after ordering, Fran starts the conversation. "How's everything with the family, Elinor? Your kids are so big now. Rick's job still going well?"

"Yeah, okay. . . ." Elinor drops her eyes but looks up with a forced smile. "Everything's fine, Fran. How about you?"

Jesus whispers in Fran's ear, ***"Isn't it amazing how often people say 'Everything's fine' when it isn't?"***

And that prompts Fran to say, "Are you sure everything's fine? You don't look so good tonight, Elinor. What's wrong?"

"Oh, Fran, I shouldn't complain to you—I mean, you've got it much worse than I do, being alone without Jim. No—really—I'm okay," Elinor tries to brush it off, but Fran insists.

"Just because I'm a widow doesn't mean I can't listen to my friends. Come on, talk to me."

"Well," Elinor slowly responds, "it's just Rick's attitude toward me and all the household responsibilities. He refuses to do anything to help around the house. When I went back to teaching this year, I thought he'd pitch in and help with the kids and all the housework. But he just leaves it all up to me, and we end up in lots of fights about it. That's why I was late tonight. I asked him to fix the kids' dinner—all he had to do was warm it up—and see that they did their homework. But he said no, he was tired."

And for the next half-hour Fran listens as Elinor tells of the marital problems she and Rick are having over this issue. Rick had encouraged Elinor to go back to teaching to help with increasing household expenses. And Elinor really enjoys teaching. But she expected him to be willing to carry his load of home responsibilities, only to discover that he sees that as women's work.

"You say you fight a lot about this, Elinor, but do you ever have some nonemotional discussions about it?" Fran asks.

"Oh, I've tried a hundred times, Fran, but as soon as I start, Rick gets angry. 'There you go again, griping and complaining all the time,' he says. And from that point on it's emotional," Elinor explains.

"What do I say to her, Jesus?" Fran asks. "I never had this problem because I didn't work until after Jim died."

"Well, encourage her to do with Rick what you did with the kids when you went back to work," Jesus suggests.

"Elinor, I have a suggestion," Fran says. "Why

don't you draw up a responsibility chart for the household? Just make a list of all the chores that need doing daily and weekly, then have a family conference. Explain that things have to change since you're teaching again and everyone has to carry his or her share. Show them your chart, ask for suggestions for sharing the responsibilities, and see what happens. I did that with the kids when I started to work and then posted the chart on the kitchen bulletin board. It seemed to make a difference for us; maybe it'll help you."

"You mean, put it all down in writing? Who takes out the trash, washes dishes, vacuums, does the laundry, etc.?" Elinor asks.

"Yeah, seems to me that it's a lot clearer to everybody that this is just a logical and fair way of sharing the work load. When I did that it changed their attitudes from 'Mom begging for help and nagging them all the time' to 'everybody carrying their load and doing their own chores,'" Fran explains.

"You mean, the kids do their chores now without you nagging?" Elinor asks.

"Oh, nothing's quite that simple. I still have to remind and encourage and occasionally threaten. But that chart is very visible, and they get to mark off when they've finished a job, so they take it much more seriously and actually have some pride in their accomplishments.

"But," she continues, "I'm also letting some things go. I don't keep house like I did before going back to work. Here's a good secret, Elinor. Write it down and don't forget it: A thin coat of dust protects the finish on your furniture."

"A thin coat of dust . . . ," Elinor fumbles in her

purse for a pen until she realizes the humor and laughs. “That’s good, Fran. I’ll remember that.”

“It is good to remember that we aren’t going to be held accountable to God for keeping a perfect house all the time,” Fran reminds her friend. “It takes a lot of stress off you and the family when you can simply let some things that are not terribly urgent go for another day. And remember, when it comes to household chores, you can spend time and energy or you can spend money.”

“What do you mean?” Elinor asks.

Fran replies, “Well, perhaps you could budget money for such things as a cleaning service every two weeks, using a laundry service for Rick’s shirts instead of ironing them yourself, and hiring some teenagers for yard work.”

“Well, your ideas sound like they’re worth a try. But what if Rick doesn’t agree to the budget changes or to the job chart?” Elinor asks.

“Then, in private, I’d explain that without this kind of cooperation, you’re not going to be able to continue teaching. You can’t keep trying to be superwoman; it’s too hard on you and the family. Without some changes in the sharing of the responsibility, do you really want to teach next year?”

“You mean, just tell Rick it’s either help or I quit?” Elinor seems frightened. “He won’t like that. He doesn’t like me telling him what to do.”

“Wait a minute, Elinor. You’re not telling him what to do. You’re suggesting a way to solve the inequity of the work load so that your marriage and your home life can be greatly improved.”

“Seems reasonable the way you say it, Fran, but you don’t know Rick. He’ll go into his speech about wives being submissive to their husbands and that if he thinks I should teach, I'll teach," Elinor says shaking her head.

"If that is his response, I'd look for a mediator—a couple or one of our pastors who can help the two of you talk it out without anger. Someone has to help Rick understand the real meaning of biblical submission. It is not a license for dictatorship," Fran adds.

"Well, that's the way Rick interprets it."

"You know, Jim and I had this same discussion about a year after we were married. He was ordering me around—do this and do that—and never seeking my advice or listening to me. Finally, I blew up and threatened to leave—you know how you do when you're first married! But, as a result, we agreed to get some help, and we talked with Pastor Gates. He helped Jim a lot, gave us a couple of good books to read on the true biblical meaning of submission, and it really helped," Fran shares with Elinor.

After a couple of hours of talking and lingering over their meal, they part with a hug and a promise to pray for each other. On the way home, Fran says to Jesus, "Poor Elinor, that's a tough spot. I mean, I get tired of having all the responsibility at my house, but at least I don't have to deal with all the anger that's inside Elinor because of Rick's attitude. In a way, I have it easier than she does," Fran says.

Jesus smiles back at her. ***"See how your perspective changed in one evening? I told you things were not always the way they appeared on the outside."***

"Well, do you think I gave her good advice tonight, Lord? Hope I didn't come on too strong," Fran says.

"No, you didn't. I liked what you said to her. Elinor made the mistake of going back into teaching without

having a clear understanding with Rick. She assumed he would be willing to help her with the work load, but she never talked with him about it beforehand. And instead of assigning jobs and responsibilities to the kids, she just complains all the time to them and feels sorry for herself. That demotivates the family even more, so it becomes a catch-22. If she'll take your advice, it might break the cycle and help," Jesus says.

"Do you think she should threaten to quit if Rick doesn't change?" Fran asks.

"Well, threaten is a strong approach. I'd suggest she use words that don't challenge Rick's manhood or authority unnecessarily. But she surely should let him know that it is an option she may exercise if necessary," Jesus says.

"You mean, she has to handle his male ego carefully?" Fran asks with a sarcastic tone.

"Fran, remember, 'Sweetness of speech increases persuasiveness.' Choosing the right words often makes a huge difference in whether people want to do what we want them to do or not. Elinor should be focused on solving the problem, not proving something to Rick or standing up for her rights," Jesus replies.

"That's the same thing you told me when I was dealing with my boss when she was giving me trouble." Fran looks at Jesus with a grin.

"Fran, people are people. Whether it's wives dealing with husbands, employees with managers, coworkers with each other, or employees with customers, the same principles of communication still apply and still work. When Elinor learns how to communicate better with Rick and the kids, she will also communicate better with everyone else in her life," Jesus explains.

As they get near the house, Fran says, "Well, that

was an interesting night. Not what I thought it would be—but interesting."

"Funny," Jesus says, ***"you didn't talk about yourself at all tonight, Fran. It was all about Elinor, did you realize that?"***

"No, I hadn't thought about it. Oh, well, that's okay. If I ever need a listening ear, Elinor will be there for me, I'm sure. I just hope it was helpful to her. In a way, it was very helpful to me. Doesn't make my situation look so bad after all, right, Jesus?"

And with that they pull into her driveway.

THINK ABOUT IT!

1. Jesus tries to teach Fran the dangers of comparing herself to others. Can you remember times when you've compared yourself to others? How does it usually make you feel?

2. Elinor finds herself in a communication deadlock with her husband and children. She can't understand why they don't help her more. What was her first mistake that led to this dilemma?

3. Do you like Fran's idea about assigning responsibilities? Do you think it might work for Elinor?

4. Do you think Elinor needs to reassess her priorities about what's important to be done and what isn't? Have you had some difficulty with that, too? What are some things you stew over in the house that really aren't worth it?

5. Does Elinor have the right to tell Rick she can't continue working if the household chores aren't

shared? Do you think this is her best approach? How else might she handle it?

6. Rick seems to have a very one-sided interpretation of biblical submission. How do you interpret Ephesians 5:21-28?

7. By getting involved with someone else's problem, Fran sees her own situation as much easier, another reason to be others-focused, not self-focused. Can you remember when you had a similar experience?

10
Dealing with a Possible Job Loss

A few weeks have passed since Fran talked to Uncle George. She had her house appraised for selling but was also advised that the market is bad right now, and selling a house is not easy. It's a buyer's market so, after talking further with Uncle George as well as her parents, she decided to refinance, cut costs, and try to stay where she is. Uncle George helped her with all that, and the paperwork was finalized last week.

This is all frightening to Fran because the numbers are so big to her. The economy is certainly not in good shape, which is frightening as well. But repeatedly Jesus kept assuring her that she was making good, well-thought-out decisions and that he would not forsake her.

As she arrives at work today, Jesus is again right beside her. As they settle into her office, Louise rushes in and shuts the door behind her. "Fran, sit down. You're not going to believe what I heard. We just lost two key accounts, our largest. They took their business somewhere else. That's about 25 percent of our division's business. Do you realize what that means?"

Fran sits down; she does indeed realize what it means. "You're kidding, Louise. We lost both those accounts? Why?"

"Money. Simpson and Elliott came in with incredibly low bids when our clients' contracts were up for renewal, and they went for it. Fran, there will be some drastic cuts around here, you can be sure of that. And you know who gets cut first—those of us with less than five years' service. That's me and you. Fran, we could be out of a job in a week."

Louise's words hit Fran like a ton of bricks. "They wouldn't do that. We have good records; we bring in business. We do our jobs well."

"Don't kid yourself," Louise replies. "When it comes to laying people off, it's last in, first out, regardless of your contribution to the company. I gotta go to a meeting; let's have lunch and talk more."

"Yeah, sure," Fran replies as Louise rushes out of her office.

"Lord, did you hear that? If Louise is right, I could be in serious trouble. I guess I'd have to collect unemployment, but unemployment won't pay my bills, and I have no money saved away. You know I'm just barely able to make ends meet. And jobs are hard to find. Lord, what should I do?" Fran looks at Jesus with panic in her eyes.

Jesus answers, ***"First, you need to remember that I am still in control of your life and nothing takes me by surprise. Can you remember some promises I've given you in the past? What about that psalm you memorized recently?"***

"Oh, yeah," Fran says, "Psalm 56."

"Why don't you recite some of those verses again. You know, it wasn't an accident that you've been memorizing that psalm." Jesus touches her arm for reassurance and smiles at her.

His calming voice and words start to have an effect on Fran. She begins to quote: "'When I am afraid, I will trust in you. In God, whose word I praise, in God I trust; I will not be afraid. What can mortal man do to me?' Well, quite honestly, Lord, right now it feels like mortal man—my employer—has the power to do something pretty dreadful to me—take my job away."

"Yes, I know," Jesus replies, ***"but even if that happens, they can't separate you and me, can they?"***

"No, of course not."

"Then that means I'll keep all my promises to you, right? Recite out loud some of my commitments to you."

"Well, you've promised never to leave me or forsake me."

"Right," Jesus responds, ***"and what else?"***

"And you've promised to supply all of my needs according to your riches," Fran replies.

"Do you think I have the riches and resources to meet your needs and those of your children, even if you lose your job, Fran?" Jesus pins her down.

"Yes, I believe you can meet my needs," she responds, a little shaky.

"Well, believing I **can** ***meet your needs is one thing; but do you believe I*** **will** ***meet your needs, Fran? You're facing possible financial hardships, lack of income, loss of a job. Now you need to search your heart and see whom you trust. Do you trust your employer more than me?"*** Jesus asks.

"Oh, no, Lord, of course not. I trust you more than anyone. You know that," Fran strongly assures him.

"Okay, if you really believe I will keep my promises to you, then you don't have to panic, do you?" Jesus looks at her with a smile. ***"You can relax. This company does not hold your future in their hands; I do."***

Fran can't keep back the tears. "It's so easy to forget that, Lord. Thanks for reminding me. I can trust you with my future. But I have a feeling you're going to have to remind me of that quite often in the next few days as this all starts to play out. I'm sure the fear and panic will raise their ugly heads again."

"Well, then, I suggest you type those two verses from Psalm 56 on a card and prop it up right there on your desk so you have to see it all the time. You need to remember that, when you are afraid, I'm here for you and no earthly person or organization can get to you except through me. Nothing happens to you by accident. I filter everything that touches your life. You are my responsibility, and I'm capable of taking care of you quite well. Will you keep trusting me?" Jesus asks.

"I will, Lord," Fran replies, as she takes his hand. "I'm okay now. I'd better get to work. Got lots to do today."

With that, Fran's mind is at rest, and she begins her day's work. Lunchtime rolls around, and Louise sticks her head into Fran's office. "Hey, it's time for lunch; let's go."

"Okay, I'll meet you in the cafeteria in five minutes," Fran answers as she finishes up some figures on which she's working. Just as she's starting to leave for lunch, her manager walks into her office.

"Fran, we need to find some time to talk this afternoon. How's your schedule?" Marilyn asks in a rather subdued manner.

Fran can feel her heart beating faster. "Any time's okay with me, Marilyn. What's up?"

"Oh, I'll give you all the details later. Why don't you come to my office about three o' clock," Marilyn replies.

"Sure, okay—see you at three, Marilyn." Fran turns to Jesus as Marilyn leaves. "Well, Lord, looks like Louise was right. This will probably be it—the big news. I wonder how much notice they'll give me. I wonder if they'll give us any severance pay, and what about our vacation that's due to us?" Fran starts thinking about all the possibilities.

"You know, Fran," Jesus says, ***"I wouldn't start borrowing trouble from tomorrow. It's not profitable to come to conclusions before you know the facts. That's not truthful thinking."*** He reminds her of her study in Philippians 4, where Paul describes what to think about and what not to think about. ***"Imagining future events and speculating on what you will do if certain things happen often gets you into untruthful thinking and unnecessary stress."***

"Okay, Lord, I'll just wait and see what she says. Now, I better go meet Louise. She'll be in panic mode, and I'll need you there to help me stay calm."

"Remember, Louise tends to be excitable and, while she is a believer, her faith is not very strong. She hasn't grown a lot lately. So don't allow her to destroy your trust in me."

"Thanks, Lord, I'll remember," Fran assures Jesus.

As they settle down at a secluded table, Louise starts in right away. "So, have you heard anything else, Fran? Do you believe what I told you? I'm telling you, I got it straight from Tim over in accounting."

"Well, frankly, I've been stuck in my office all morning finishing up a proposal, so I haven't talked with anyone else. However, Marilyn did ask me to see her this afternoon at three, and she seemed kinda somber," Fran reports to Louise.

"See, what did I tell you? I bet you anything she'll drop the shoe on you then. She'll probably see me today, too. I'm sure I'll get the axe; I've been here less time than you," Louise laments, while picking at her food. "You know, I'm not so hungry. If I lose my job, what will I do?" She pushes her tray away and puts her head in her hands.

"Louise, I went through a panic attack after you left my office, but I remembered a verse from Psalm 56. It says that, whenever we are afraid, we must trust in the Lord, and it asks, 'What can mortal man do to me?' All this company can do to you is let you go. That's all, Louise, and that's not the end of the world. Jesus has promised to take care of you."

"I knew you would say something like that, Fran, and I know your faith is strong, but I'm sorry. I just can't dismiss it so easily. This is serious. Jobs are almost impossible to find these days. And unemployment runs out fast." Louise turns her head so Fran can't see the tears.

"I know it's serious, Louise, but do you think Jesus just helps us when it's easy? Either we can trust him or we can't, and this is where the rubber meets the road. It's easy to say we trust him when everything is going well and we have other resources to meet our needs. But now, you and I face the distinct possibility that our trusted resource—our job—may not be so trustworthy after all. We should have known that all along, Louise. Only Jesus is totally trustworthy, and I'm just going to keep putting my trust in him to take care of me and my kids. He'll take care of you, too. You belong to him."

Fran's words seem to have little effect on Louise. "Lord," Fran says quietly to Jesus, "she's not listening to me. She needs to hear it from you, I think."

"Yes," Jesus answers, ***"and she will hear it from me as soon as she comes to me for help. She hasn't done that yet."***

Fran turns to Louise, "You know, Louise, why don't you take the rest of the lunch hour and go out to your car to be alone. Just spend some time in prayer. I think that will help you a great deal. You need to hear it straight from Jesus to you—he's not going to fail you now, Louise. He will keep his promises." Fran puts her arm around Louise.

"Okay, Fran. I think you're right. I'll see you later," Louise says as she walks off with her food untouched. Jesus and Fran get up to leave as well.

They return to her office, and she completes her project with peace in her heart that really amazes her. At one point she says to Jesus, "You know, Lord, with this meeting coming up with Marilyn, I would expect myself to be useless. But here I am calmly working away. That's not like me, you know."

"I know, Fran, it's like me," Jesus responds. ***"You're becoming more and more like me. That's what you're supposed to do—that's what every Christian should be doing. And you're experiencing that peace that passes understanding."***

"I sure am, Lord. That unexplainable peace. That's because of you—you are my peace, and you're here with me all the time. That's why I have peace," Fran smiles at Jesus as she goes back to work.

Time passes quickly, and Fran looks at her watch. "Wow, it's 3:00. Time to go see Marilyn. Let's go, Jesus; I wouldn't think of going to this without you."

"Why don't you pray before you head into that meeting?" Jesus suggests.

"Good idea," she agrees and closes her door for a moment of privacy. "Dear Father, I want to tell you again that I trust you, and I know you will take care of me. I don't know what's going to happen in this meeting, but please make your presence very real to me, give me your peace, your wisdom, and your protection.

I pray in Jesus' name—and oh, by the way, thanks again that Jesus is here with me, so I don't have to face this all by myself. Amen."

Then together she and Jesus head down the hall.

Marilyn shuts the door behind Fran as she sits down. "Well, you've probably been hearing some rumors going around today, Fran. Everybody else has. What I'm trying to do is stop the rumors and give you some facts so you can know what's happening. Frankly, this all just came to me this morning in a management meeting. It's been very sudden for all of us, but, as you've probably heard, we lost two huge accounts."

"Yeah, that's what I heard," Fran responds. "And I heard that a bunch of us would have to be laid off."

"Well," Marilyn says, nodding her head, "unfortunately, that's the case. They are telling me I have to let five of my fifteen account reps go. And the rules are that the newest employees go unless there are some extenuating circumstances. I've been looking at the records, Fran, and you're number eleven."

"So, that means I'm out of here, I guess." Fran looks at Marilyn.

"Well, I don't know for sure yet," Marilyn responds. "You see, John, who is number ten, has been here only six months longer than you, and John has had an unsatisfactory performance rating for almost a year now. This is just between you and me, Fran, but I had started the process of putting John on notice. Would you believe I filled out the forms yesterday but didn't sign them or turn them in. If I had just moved on that sooner, it would make things simpler. But I'm hoping I can let John go and keep you. You're one of my best performers; we've been through a lot together. I respect you, and I want to keep you if I can."

Fran smiles at Marilyn, remembering the tough experience they had early in their working relationship. It reassures Fran to see that the Lord brought her through that one and will take her through this tough spot as well.

"Well, Marilyn, I appreciate those words of confidence more than I can say. That means a lot to me, regardless of what happens. And I feel sorry for John. He has a family, too, doesn't he?"

"Yes, and that's been part of his problem lately. He's been going through a nasty divorce, and it has really affected his work. I've tried to hang in there with him until he could get everything settled, but it just drags on and on, and his performance gets worse and worse. At any rate, I have to do what's right for the company."

"Wow, Marilyn, you're really in a tough spot. I don't envy you," Fran replies.

Marilyn looks at Fran with amazement in her eyes. "I'm in a tough spot? But my job's not threatened, and yours is."

"Yeah, but what I do won't affect other people's lives, and you have to make choices that affect others. I think that must be especially tough. Marilyn, I just want you to know that I will be praying for you in this—I'll be praying for all of us."

"You'll be praying for me? Well, I guess it can't hurt. I don't want to give you any false hope; I may not be able to save your job. Technically, John should stay and not you," Marilyn says as she struggles to understand Fran's serenity.

"I understand, Marilyn. You know, I need a job, too; I have two kids to support. But if you decide to keep John, it'll be okay because I know I'd worry a lot about him out of work. It might be harder for him to find a job than me, and, with this divorce, he might break under the strain."

"I have to tell you the truth, Fran. If I didn't know you as well as I do, I wouldn't believe you could be so calm and say what you did. You're different. What makes you different? I know you're religious, but it's something else," Marilyn asks with a puzzled look.

Fran chuckles. "I don't know, Marilyn. I don't think of myself as religious, but I do have a personal relationship with Jesus Christ, and I rely on him to meet my needs and give me strength. If you see a difference in me, I figure it has to be Jesus that makes the difference." Fran nudges Jesus on the elbow while Marilyn's not looking.

"Well, I don't understand that. I never thought I'd like one of you 'Jesus freaks,' but I have to admit, you're different. Someday let's talk about it more," Marilyn suggests.

"Love to, Marilyn. I guess I am a 'Jesus freak,' as you put it, and I'd love to tell you why. Let's have dinner soon," Fran replies with a smile.

"Okay, soon as I get all this terrible ordeal over with. Well, there's not much more I can tell you now. I'm meeting with the human resources people late today and tonight, so maybe I'll have an answer for you tomorrow. Meanwhile, I wanted you to know the status. Remember, this must stay between us. I wouldn't share this with anyone but you, Fran. I trust you to keep it confidential."

"Not to worry. I'll talk with you tomorrow." Fran gets up to leave. "Oh, by the way, how about Louise?"

"I'm afraid she'll have to go. She's number thirteen. But I haven't talked with her yet, so keep that to yourself."

Driving home that evening, Fran says to Jesus, "That was pretty incredible what Marilyn said to me today, Lord. She wants to keep me, and several months ago she was trying to fire me!"

"Yes, and I was very pleased at how you responded to her today. I hope you will make it a point to follow up on that dinner invitation. Marilyn has some open ears to hear," Jesus reminds Fran.

"Well, I know I have to be ready to give answers for the hope that is within me, and it looks like she wants to ask some questions. It's just hard to believe the relationship has changed so drastically. Thanks, Lord, that's your doing."

Her evening with the kids is normal—helping with homework, having some fun, reading to them as they go to bed. Afterwards, she plops in her favorite chair, feeling rather bushed. "This day has been exhausting. I feel pretty wiped out," she says to Jesus.

"You know," she continues, "I really worry about John. If he gets laid off and not me, it could be devastating for him. And with all his expenses now—he's got it worse than me, Lord. Should I suggest to Marilyn that she should keep him and not me?"

"Well, I think it would be better to let this work itself out and just keep your hands off of it, Fran. As long as you're willing to accept it either way and you know I'll take care of it either way, you're in a win-win situation. But I will certainly remember your concern for John," Jesus assures her.

"And Louise, too, Lord. If I stay and she goes, that would be hard for both of us."

"I haven't forgotten," Jesus replies.

They are interrupted by the telephone. "Hello, Louise," Fran says. "Yes, Marilyn talked with me."

"Well, I looked all over for you before I left today, but couldn't find you. What did she say, Fran?" Louise asks impatiently.

Fran had hoped to avoid Louise because of the confidentiality of the information Marilyn had given her. Now she had to tiptoe through this. "Well, she confirmed that we lost those accounts and that there would probably be changes, but she didn't want any wild rumors going around. She had a meeting late today and tonight; maybe she'll know more tomorrow."

Louise keeps probing for more information, but Fran is careful to avoid betraying Marilyn's confidence. She doesn't like to keep things from Louise, but it's not her place to tell her the bad news.

Finally, they hang up after Fran tries to comfort and reassure Louise again. But Louise is finding it difficult to see God's hand in this situation.

"Louise will need you in the days ahead to help her learn to trust me. She's not in your life by accident, you know," Jesus says to her with a smile. ***"But you need some rest, so I'll say good-night for now."*** Fran heads for bed.

The next day Marilyn caught Fran first thing and told her she had decided to fight the decision to lay off five people and had convinced them to cut that to four. After all, if you don't have account reps, how can you replace the business you lost? Marilyn made a strong argument and won her case. So, both Fran and John would stay, but Louise would be laid off.

Fran left Marilyn's office more worried about Louise than anything else. "Oh, Lord, how can I help her? She'll be upset that I'm staying and she's going."

"Now you can't assume that," Jesus says. ***"Remember what I told you last night. Louise will need your help now, so be prepared to encourage her."***

Later in the morning Fran sees Louise leaving Marilyn's office. "Oh no, I can tell by the look on her face, she got the bad news. I'd better go see her." Fran really hates to have to face her, but she knows she has to.

"Louise," she says as she approaches her desk, "you talked to Marilyn?"

"Yeah," Louise says, looking pretty rejected. "I hear you made the cut."

"Just barely," Fran replied. "Listen, Louise, I'm so sorry. I wish there was something I could say or do. I really am sorry."

The tears start down Louise's cheeks. "I appreciate that, Fran. I'm glad you didn't get laid off; I know that would have been very hard on you with the kids and everything."

Fran's heart rejoices at Louise's ability to be happy for her even in the midst of her pain. It shows real spiritual maturity. "Louise, that's so kind of you to say. I was afraid to even talk to you because I know how I'd feel if I were in your shoes."

They walk toward the ladies' room. Safely inside where no one can see them, the tears come more freely for Louise. "Oh, no, Fran, I'm glad you don't have to go through this. But it sure is scary," she says, wiping away some tears.

"It sure is," Fran replies as she puts her arms around her, and tears start to roll down her cheeks as well. "I'll do anything I can for you, Louise. I'm here for you anytime you need me."

"Thanks, Fran; I'm sure I'll need you. But I was

thinking about what you said yesterday. This is a time to learn to trust God in new ways, and I want to come through shining like gold."

"You will, Louise, because you already are," Fran assures her.

After a few more words of comfort, they head back to their jobs.

On the way home that afternoon, Fran talks to Jesus about Louise. "She really handled it very well," Fran says.

"Yes, she did, Fran, and so did you," he replies.

"So did I? I didn't get laid off."

"I meant you were very compassionate and helpful to her."

"But I didn't have anything to say to her or any great suggestions. All I could say was I'm sorry," Fran says.

"And that's exactly what she needed to hear," Jesus says. ***"She didn't need Romans 8:28 thrown at her at the time, nor did she need a pep talk. She needed someone to weep with her as she was weeping. She needed a sympathetic, caring friend, and that's what you were."***

She looks at Jesus with amazement in her eyes. "I never even thought about it. That had to be you, Jesus, giving me that discernment, because it was instinctive."

"No, not instinctive, Fran; it was my Spirit within you giving you the right instincts," he says as he smiles at her.

The thought really astounds her, and she quietly ponders the wonder of her actions and reactions being controlled by the Holy Spirit. It's just beginning to dawn on her that she has an incredible power within her. *This is the way I want to live my life,* she thinks to herself. *Not in my power but in his. It's the only way to go.*

THINK ABOUT IT!

1. Jesus asks Fran if she believes he *will* meet her needs rather than if he *can* meet her needs. What is the difference between those two questions?

2. Fran went into panic mode at the thought of losing her job. How did she get out of it? Can you remember the last time you were panic-stricken over some situation? How did you deal with it?

3. Is it wrong for a Christian to go into panic mode? Is that a sign that we don't trust God? What's the difference between "going" into panic mode and "staying" in panic mode?

4. In Matthew 6:25-34 Jesus gives some clear teaching on worrying. Verse 34 points out that we shouldn't borrow trouble from tomorrow. Fran starts to do that by imagining all the bad things that could happen to her if she gets laid off. When was the last time you borrowed trouble from tomorrow? What did it do to you?

5. Jesus warns Fran not to let Louise's lack of faith destroy her own faith. Have you ever allowed someone else to destroy your faith because you kept listening to them instead of listening to Jesus? Describe what happened.

6. Louise seems a little irritated at lunch when Fran reminds her of Scripture. Do you think it was wrong for Fran to quote Scripture to Louise at that time? Why did Louise have that reaction?

7. Marilyn is amazed to see that Fran is able to think of her supervisor's predicament when she could be laid off. What gives Fran the capability of being compassionate at a moment like this?

8. When Louise gets the bad news, Fran comforts her and sympathizes with her, but she doesn't quote any Scripture to her. Do you think she should have? Notice what Louise says about learning to trust God. Do you think she heard what Fran said yesterday?

9. Fran really came shining through in this experience. Does this guarantee a victory every time she faces a problem in the future? Why do we have to keep learning and relearning these basic truths again and again?

11
Failing at Success

Things have quieted down a bit at the office since the layoff. Fran misses her friend Louise, who is still looking for another job. However, they've just landed a new large account at the agency, and Fran is hopeful that before Louise finds another job they may rehire her.

She meets with Louise one evening a week for prayer and encouragement, and it's obvious to Fran that Louise is growing in her faith by leaps and bounds. "Funny," Fran says to Jesus, "Louise is probably a great deal stronger in her faith because she was laid off and is out of job than she would be otherwise."

"Yes," Jesus replies, ***"it is true that many of your most important lessons are learned through trials. Louise spends a lot of time studying the Bible now, and every day she finds time for quiet prayer. She's learning how important that is to her spiritual growth, and she's learning to walk by faith. Don't worry about her, Fran, she's going to be all right."*** Jesus looks at her with a smile.

"Well, I never was really worried about her, Jesus, because she belongs to you, but I just hated to see her suffer through all that pain and fear of being unemployed. But there was nothing I could do for her."

"Oh, you're wrong, Fran. You have done a great deal for Louise. Your love and concern and your listening ear have been very important ingredients in Lou-

ise's ability to cope with this period of unemployment," Jesus reassures Fran.

"Really? But what have I done for her?"

"You've been there for her. That's what. And, of course, you keep telling me all about her. I don't think a day has gone by that you haven't asked me to take care of Louise." Jesus smiles warmly at Fran.

"Have I been a pest? I didn't mean to be," Fran asks.

"Oh no, not a pest. That's exactly what you should do. Do you remember the parable I taught about the woman who pestered the judge to death until he gave her what she wanted? What I was showing through that parable is that I honor persistent prayer. It shows faith and compassion and trust," Jesus explains.

"Well, I'd better get dressed for work or I'm going to be late. Thanks for these quiet moments alone with you each morning," Fran says as she closes her Bible.

"Before you go, Fran, why don't you just make a few notes in your journal about what you learned from your Bible reading today. That helps you remember, don't you think?" She briefly writes down what truth or encouragement she received for herself from the Bible. It has proven to be a great spiritual help to Fran.

As she arrives at the office, there is a note on her desk from Marilyn. Fran reads out loud to Jesus, "'Please see me as soon as you arrive.' Hmm, wonder what this is all about," Fran ponders. "Guess I better find out. Come on, Jesus, I don't know what I'll have to face, and you'd better be there with me." Fran grins at Jesus as she takes his arm.

They head toward Marilyn's office. Peeking her head inside, Fran says, "You wanted to see me?"

"Oh, yes, Fran, come on in. Have a seat. I think I

have some exciting news for you, for a change. It's nice to have something positive to tell you. There's been enough bad news lately to carry us for a while." She walks around from behind her desk and takes the chair next to Fran's.

"Well, I can't wait to hear it. You've got my curiosity up," Fran replies.

"Well, here's the deal. We've got a shot at a new client—a big one, Mitchell's Sandwich Shops."

Fran's eyes double in size. "Mitchell's Sandwich Shops? Why, they're one of the fastest-growing franchises in the country. I didn't know we were even talking to them."

"We've had to keep it quiet. In fact, it's still not for public consumption, but the secret is out that they're looking for a new agency, and we're one of the three they are considering. So, top management has assigned a vice president from headquarters to oversee this bid, and we will be assisting him. I met with him yesterday at headquarters, and he asked me to describe my three best sales people, and you were one of those three. After showing him personnel jackets and answering lots of questions, he has picked you to assist him in trying to land Mitchell's."

Fran's mouth is hanging open. She looks at Jesus and whispers, "Did I hear correctly, Jesus? Oh, me!"

She turns to Marilyn, "I don't know what to say. Obviously I'm honored, but I have to admit, I'm also scared. Do you think I can handle it, Marilyn?" Fran asks.

"Do you think I'd take a chance on this account, Fran? I wouldn't even think of putting you in there if I weren't sure you could handle it. You know how to put a proposal together, you're good on your feet, and I think you'll get along well with Hank. That's whom you'll be working with—Hank Clark, VP of marketing."

Marilyn's words of encouragement mean a lot to Fran, but the mention of Hank Clark strikes a note of fear. "Hank Clark—wow. I've heard all kinds of stories about how tough he is. He used to work in this office years ago, didn't he?"

"Yes, and he is tough. But he's good and fair, and if you perform the way I know you can, you won't have any problems with him," Marilyn assures Fran. "Now, he'll be here tomorrow and wants to spend the day with you and me setting the strategy for this proposal. Your first meeting with Mitchell's is next week, so there's no time to waste."

"Okay, Marilyn, I'll clear the calendar for tomorrow."

"Just be prepared for a long, hard day. You might want to spend some time today reading all you can about Mitchell's. Do your homework," Marilyn advises Fran.

As they head back to her office, Fran can feel her hands shaking. "Look at me, Jesus, I'm shaking like a schoolgirl. This is really a big deal; I can't believe Marilyn has given me this opportunity. If I can do a good job and we land this client . . . well, I'm set. That's the kind of break that only comes once. Wow, just think, Hank chose me above the other two. I wonder who they were. That's pretty neat, isn't it, Jesus?" Fran looks at Jesus with excitement, but notices a different reaction from him.

"Why don't you close your door and let's talk about this," Jesus suggests.

As Fran obeys, she senses a feeling of disappointment in Jesus. "What's wrong, Lord? Aren't you happy for me? This is a big deal—I've got a great opportunity."

"Oh, Fran, I'm pleased you have an opportunity like this, but I see it differently from the way you do. First, let me ask you, how do you think you got this break?"

Fran shrugs and replies, "Well, I guess it's because of my sales record last year, and I did a good job cracking some new accounts. Also, I think I'm pretty good at making presentations. Seems they go over well, so that's probably why Hank chose me. . . ." Fran's words trail off as she starts to hear what she's saying.

"So, you think you earned this opportunity all by yourself—hard work, intelligence, performance?" Jesus asks Fran, and she is convicted by her own words.

"No, Lord, I didn't do it all by myself. You have been my help and my partner through all of this. I don't have any ability that is not a gift from you to me. I apologize for the pride and arrogance of my reaction," Fran says quietly to Jesus.

"It's okay to feel happy about this. Certainly you should feel good to be chosen, and that is an honor. But I simply want you to learn to be humble and not fall into the trap of thinking you've achieved some great success on your own. Besides, I don't measure success by promotions or incomes or sales awards. I measure success by obedience."

"I'm ashamed of my reaction, Lord, but please forgive me and please help me. I couldn't have gotten this opportunity without you, and I certainly can't do a good job with it unless you help me," Fran says.

"Now you're on the right track, Fran," Jesus says to her.

"Okay, I better start doing my homework on Mitchell's. I think I'll go to the library and read everything I can on this company," Fran says as she puts her coat on. "They've got a good business section; it should give me lots of help," and with great enthusiasm she sets out to start the process of preparing for her meeting with Hank.

Fran brings a stack of books and magazine articles home with her from the library that night and, after a brief time with her kids, curls up in her favorite chair for a night of study and reading. She has already made lots of notes about Mitchell's Sandwich Shops and is beginning to analyze the financial statements from their last annual report.

Several times during the evening, she stops to ask Jesus to help her understand all the material and remember what she should. Jesus suggests, ***"Why don't you think about the kind of questions Hank is likely to ask about Mitchell's and make sure you've got those answers ready."***

"What a good idea, Lord," and Fran gets busy with that assignment. She goes to bed late but feels good about her preparation. As she wearily crawls under the covers, she thanks the Lord for his help and is asleep before the "Amen" gets out of her mouth.

But waking up the next morning is not difficult; in fact, she's awake before the alarm goes off, with the adrenaline pumping. She feels too excited to sit still but knows that she needs some quiet time to center herself and her thoughts before this day begins.

"You know," Jesus says to her, ***"the busier I was on earth, the more I spent time in prayer with my Father. And I just had to get away from everyone and everything for some quiet time. It wasn't always easy to do, but I made it a priority."***

"It wasn't easy for you to spend time with the Father?" Fran asks. That thought had never entered her head before.

"Well, I mean, I was tired, too. I needed sleep and food, just like you do. And I had to make time for my Father sometimes at the expense of sleep, so in that sense, it wasn't easy. It took discipline. Remember, I was fully the Son of Man, and I experienced all the trials and weaknesses of a human body, just as you do, Fran," Jesus tries to explain.

"I know, Lord, but I have to admit that my mind tends to blow a fuse when I try to figure all that out. How you could be fully God and fully man—it's beyond my finite mind, but I believe it. And it's a great comfort to know you've been here before me and you understand what I face. I'm so thankful you're going to be with me today, Lord. Will I ever need you!" Fran starts to get up and get the day started.

But Jesus puts his hand on hers. ***"Before you leave, just reread that verse I gave you today from Isaiah 50. You may need it."***

"Oh, thanks for reminding me," Fran says as she finds verse 7 in her Bible. "'Because the Sovereign Lord helps me, I will not be disgraced. Therefore have I set my face like flint, and I know I will not be put to shame.' I'll keep that verse in mind all day, Lord," Fran says, as she hurriedly and excitedly starts to get ready.

She's warned the kids to be ready to leave early today, and they are. "Mommy, do a good job," Alice says to her, as she jumps out of the car at school. "Yeah, Mom, don't blow it," replies her son in his underhanded way of encouraging her. Fran smiles as they leave, thinking how blessed she is to have two such lovely children.

She arrives at the office a half-hour earlier than usual, and the place is quiet. She reviews all the notes she took in preparation and reminds herself of some important facts about Mitchell's Sandwich Shops. Her coworker, John, sticks his head in the door.

"I hear you're having a meeting with Big Bad Hank from headquarters," he says to her in a lighthearted way.

"Big Bad Hank? You mean Hank Clark?" she replies.

"Yeah, didn't you know he's called Big Bad Hank? Supposed to be one tough critter, Fran, but don't worry, you can handle him."

"Thanks a lot, John—you're a great encouragement," she says with some sarcasm. "What have you heard about him?"

"Only that he'll ask you lots of questions and you better do your homework. But I've heard that, if he likes you, he'll do right by you. This could be your big chance," John says with a smile as he walks away.

Fran looks at Jesus. "Just what I needed to hear. Now I am nervous. What if I can't answer his questions, Lord?"

"Fran, can you think of anything you should have done that you didn't do? Given the short time you had to prepare, do you think you did your best?" Jesus asks her calmly.

"Yeah, I think so, but . . . ," Fran stammers.

"No buts, then. Just trust me. Can you trust me?" Jesus asks as he looks into her eyes.

"Lord, you know I trust you," Fran replies almost impatiently. "But please just bring back to my mind what I know and help me choose the right words, will you please?"

"Of course. Now remember this: the outcome of

this meeting is not the most important thing in your life, right? You have me, you have two terrific kids, you have a supportive family, you have a meaningful life full of good things. Your future does not rest on this job or on this new prospect or on this meeting with Hank. Your future is in my hands, not his. Keep that clearly in your mind all day long, and you'll be calm no matter what happens." Jesus' words really help Fran get her eternal focus, and she feels very prepared and ready.

She's the first one in the conference room, but shortly thereafter Marilyn comes in with Hank. He doesn't look like Fran imagined he would. He's about six feet tall and quite good looking—maybe ten years older than Fran. She had imagined him in his sixties, ready to retire, balding, with glasses and a sour look on his face. It takes her a minute to adjust.

As she shakes hands with Hank, he looks straight into her eyes and gives her a disarming smile. All of a sudden she is self-conscious. *I wonder if I wore the right suit today. Maybe I should have been more conservative. Probably should have gotten a haircut yesterday. Hope there are no runs in my hose.* All these stray thoughts ramble through her mind as she's being introduced.

They sit at the conference table, and Fran gets her notes out of her file. As she does, she sees Jesus, sitting right there beside her. ***"Don't be nervous, and don't worry about how you look. The subject is Mitchell's Sandwich Shops, so stay calm and focused,"*** he whispers to her, and it really helps a lot.

Hank starts the discussion, "Tell me, Fran, what do you know about the management of Mitchell's?" So begins a long morning of questions and answers. Fran feels as though she's in school again, being drilled to see if she did her homework. At times she thinks Hank is doing everything he can to catch her in a mistake or make her answer look stupid. But for the most part she feels confident about her answers, and only two or three times does she have to say, "I don't know, but I can find out."

After lunch, Marilyn explains she has another appointment and leaves Fran and Hank to complete the plans for the presentation to Mitchell's. As the afternoon progresses, she and Hank start to put their strategy together for the pitch next week. He says, "I want you to make this presentation, and I'll play the role of consultant. We need to establish your leadership here so I can eventually work out of the picture."

Fran gulps. "Well, Hank, I'll do whatever you say, but—"

"But what?" Hank replies. "You're scared? Well, that's good, Fran. A little fear helps you perform better. But I'm not scared of putting you up there in front of this prospect. You've obviously got the skills and ability to communicate, you make a good first impression, you look good. . . ." He pauses as he looks at her with another one of those smiles.

Fran is uncomfortable. "Thanks—well, I appreciate your confidence. I'll do my best."

"I'm not worried," he replies. "I think we've done enough for today. I'm flying out tomorrow afternoon, so that gives us tomorrow morning to practice the presentation. Put together a rough outline and work on the presentation tonight. Be prepared to pitch it to me in the morning."

Fran feels like she's been hit by a truck. "Okay," she replies mechanically, but she's absolutely overwhelmed with the assignment Hank just gave her.

"Good," he says, as he packs up his briefcase. "I'll see you here bright and early in the morning. Unless . . ." He pauses. "Unless you'd like to spend some time working on it together tonight. We could have dinner and come back and work—or work at the hotel where I'm staying."

Bells go off in Fran's head. Instinctively she says, "Well, if you want me to give a presentation to you tomorrow morning, I think I'd better spend this evening working on it by myself."

Hank smiles at her. "Good enough. See you tomorrow."

As he walks out, Fran sinks down into her chair beside Jesus. "Oh, my goodness," she says to herself. "I don't believe what I heard. He expects me to have a presentation ready for him tomorrow. I'll be up all night."

"Yes, that is quite an assignment," Jesus says quietly.

She had forgotten he was there. "Oh, Lord," she says, "please help me. I don't know how I'm going to get this done."

Jesus starts to respond, but Fran interrupts. "The kids! I'll have to get someone to keep the kids tonight because I won't be home before midnight, I'm sure." She heads back to her office and dials her house.

"Hi, Mom," Drew's voice comes over the phone. "When you coming home? I got this big spelling test to do tomorrow, and I need you to help me. And Roy Benson, well, he invited me to sleep over Friday night. Can I, Mom? Can I?"

Somehow at this moment Fran is not prepared to be a mother. She tries to switch hats quickly but finds it rather difficult. All she can think of is getting the presentation done by tomorrow.

"Listen, Drew," she says, "I'm not going to be able to help you tonight because I've got to work late. Let me talk to Miss Polly."

"You're going to work late? Mom, you worked late last night and couldn't help me with my math," he responds in his agitated way.

"Drew, please don't be difficult today. Just let me speak with Polly," Fran insists.

"Well, if I flunk that spelling test it's all your fault," Drew says. "And can I sleep over at Roy's? Huh, Mom, can I?"

"I don't know about that, Drew. We'll talk about it later," she says. Fran is not at all pleased with Drew's friendship with Roy. His language and attitude are not the kind that she likes to see in Drew's friends.

"Mom, I have to know tonight. Roy's going to call me later. All you have to say is yes," Drew replies.

"I'm not saying yes right now. Let me talk with Polly," Fran says more loudly.

"Do you mean I can't? Is that what you're saying? You never let me do anything with Roy."

"I've told you, Son, that I don't think Roy has the best manners or language. Why don't you and Alice and I do something special Friday night? How's that? Now please let me talk to Polly," she says.

He doesn't want to give up but reluctantly hands the phone to Polly. "Polly," Fran says, "can you stay with the kids tonight? I know it's late, but I've just learned I have to have a presentation ready by tomorrow morning, and I'll never make it unless I work very late. You could sleep in the guest room. I'm sorry to ask but . . ."

Polly is obviously not pleased. "I was supposed to go out to dinner with a friend tonight," she says.

"Oh," Fran replies, "well, I'll call my mom and see if she can come over."

Polly agrees that if Fran's mother can't come she'll stay, but it's obvious she doesn't want to. As Fran dials her mother's phone, the feelings of guilt start to move in on her. *You're a lousy mother,* she thinks to herself. *And you're a lousy daughter—imposing on your mom like this.*

"Well, what choice do I have?" she says out loud, as she waits for her mother to answer. At that moment she senses the presence of Jesus. She's been too busy all afternoon to even think about him. And now his presence makes her defensive.

"Well, Lord," she says, "what am I supposed to do? I'm only one person, and I can't be home and do this presentation for tomorrow. Something has to give."

"I understand," Jesus says, as Fran slams the phone down because her Mom's line is busy. ***"I know you don't want to work late but you have to tonight. I understand, Fran, and it's not going to ruin your kids."*** Fran is once again reminded that Jesus is not in the business of condemning her. He understands better than anyone, and it helps a great deal.

"Being a working mom is really being pulled in two directions all the time, Lord," Fran says, with her head in her hands. "Drew was so upset, and I didn't have time to talk with him. And they'll be in bed when I get home. . . . I don't know, Lord. It just seems like mission impossible to be a good mother and a good employee."

"Fran, please remember, when you didn't work and you stayed home with your kids all the time, Drew still got upset because you didn't do everything he wanted you to do. And they both knew how to lay guilt

trips on you then. This is not just a working mom's issue," Jesus says to her quietly.

Fran thinks back over those years when Jim was alive and she didn't have to work. It was true; the kids had problems then. She lost her patience with them then. They often demanded what she wasn't willing or able to deliver. It is so easy for a working mom and a single mom to see every conflict with her children as a result of her circumstances. Fran had to be reminded often that kids are kids and raising them isn't easy, no matter what your circumstances.

She breathes a sigh of relief, thanks Jesus for his comfort, and dials her Mom's number again. With lots of apologies, she asks if her mom can stay with the kids tonight. Recognizing her dilemma, she agrees and tries to cheer Fran up. "And don't worry, Fran," she says, "I'll help Drew with his spelling."

"Well, you got me through a lot of spelling tests, I'm sure you can help him, too," Fran says. "Mom, thank you so much. You've bailed me out again."

"That's what mothers are for, Fran," she replies. "You'll do the same thing for Drew and Alice when they get older."

With that crisis settled, Fran clears her desk for the long night of work ahead of her. She turns on the computer on her desk and starts writing. Two hours later she realizes she's hungry and sends out for a pizza. About ten o' clock the cleaning people come by. She takes a break while they clean her office and then gets right back at it. She puts some proposed flip charts together, wishing her drawing and printing skills were better, but does the best she can.

Finally at 12:30 she says, "That's it. I think that's the best I can do." Wearily she grabs her purse and heads for her car. The security guard walks her to the parking lot and watches as she drives off. When she arrives home, everything is quiet. Drew and Alice left her a note, telling her they missed her and loved her. Fran smiles as she reads it, recognizing her mother's hand in it. But it is such a nice touch at the end of this terribly long day. It helps with some of the guilt!

She drops into bed without brushing her teeth or taking off her makeup and sets the alarm clock for fifteen minutes later than usual. The next morning her mom is up before her, getting the kids' breakfast ready and packing their lunches. Fran stumbles into the kitchen for a cup of tea.

Giving her a big hug, she says, "Oh, Mom, you're an angel. What would I do without you? Thank you so much."

"Fran, you know I don't mind doing this for you once in a while. It gives me a good time with the kids, too," she says. "You know, I'm a little concerned about Drew's friendship with this Roy."

"Yeah, me too," Fran says. "Why? What happened?"

"Well, they talked on the phone for a few minutes and Drew's attitude changed when he was talking to Roy. I didn't like the way he talked about you and his sister. I made him hang up pretty quickly, and he didn't like that," her Mom reports.

"Oh, boy. I can see I've got some work cut out for me there. I've got to break off that relationship, but you know how hard that is to do," Fran says.

"Yes, I know," her mom answers. "I'll pray with you about it."

Her mom rounds up the kids and takes them to school, saving Fran some needed time. She dresses in what she calls her "power suit"—navy blue with a blue striped blouse. Very conservative, nice fit; all business. "Well, even with the bags under your eyes, you look pretty good. Now go get 'em!" she says to her reflection in the mirror.

Driving to work, she begins rehearsing the presentation in her mind, forgetting that Jesus is there beside her. She hasn't had time to talk to him this morning, but he finally gets her attention.

"You really want to do a good job today, don't you, Fran?" he asks very simply.

"You bet, Lord," she replies. "This is a big chance for me. If I can land this account and Hank assigns it to me—wow, I will have moved up in this company at record pace."

"Makes you feel good to think about that, doesn't it?" Jesus asks.

"Sure it makes me feel good. Why not? I like to succeed. It's more fun than failing."

Jesus keeps trying to engage her in a conversation, but the traffic and the presentation have her mind pretty well occupied. She parks the car quickly and rushes into the office.

She stops at Joyce's desk and asks her to help. Since Fran has gotten to know Joyce and helped her out, her attitude has changed dramatically. She works harder and really seems to enjoy helping Fran. In fact, she's agreed to come to a singles' meeting at church with Fran next week.

The two of them get the conference room set up. Joyce offers to bring in some coffee and sweet rolls while Fran sets up the flip charts and gets her notes together. At 9:00 Hank arrives and, along with Marilyn, takes his place in the conference room to critique Fran's presentation.

Fran dives in with all her natural enthusiasm and, as the morning goes along, she senses things are going well. As Hank starts to get ready to leave for the airport, he turns to Fran. "I have to tell you, I'm very impressed. I've never seen a better draft presentation since—well, since I did them myself," he says with a smile. "You've done an excellent job. Polish up the few things we talked about, get the Art Department to make you some first-class charts and slides, and be ready to go next Tuesday. I'll review it that morning, and the client will be here at 1:00."

As he leaves, Marilyn turns to Fran. "Good job, Fran," she says. "I'd like to review the presentation Monday morning, but you're in good shape."

Fran walks to her office on clouds—her feet hardly touch the floor. She immediately picks up the phone and calls her mom. "Guess what," Fran says, "I did it! Hank thought my presentation was great. Said it was the best he'd seen. Oh, Mom, it went really well," Fran reports.

"Great, Fran," her mom rejoices with her. "I'm glad to hear it."

Fran tries to think of who else she can call. Her mom doesn't really understand how big these things are, never having been a businesswoman herself. She starts to dial Louise's number but then thinks better of it.

She thinks of calling Lynn, but Lynn also might not be able to see why she's so excited about this. So she drops into Andy's office. They've gotten to be pretty good friends since they had that run-in a few months ago. "Well," she interrupts his train of thought, "I'm going to need your help again."

"Hi, Fran." He looks up. "Going to need my help again, huh? What are you up to this time?"

"I just finished my preliminary presentation for Mitchell's with Hank, and now we go to final form. I make the presentation next Tuesday, so I'm going to need lots of charts and slides. Hank says no expense spared; do it right."

"Oh, great. We'll be glad to help with Mitchell's. We need the business. Things are a little slow around here since we lost those two big accounts, and if I can't keep everybody busy, I'll have to let some more people go," Andy says. "How'd it go with Big Bad Hank?"

"No problem," Fran says. "He liked my presentation. Said it was just what he wanted."

"Good job, Fran," Andy says with a smile. "We'll be glad to help any way we can."

"Thanks, Andy," she says, and walks back to her office with a big grin on her face. All afternoon, as the word spreads around the office, people drop in to congratulate her and wish her good luck next week. By the end of the day, Fran's head circumference has grown by a couple of notches.

As she drives home, she thinks, *Wow, Fran, you did it! You really did it! It sure feels good to hear someone like Hank say such complimentary things. Guess you're just good at this stuff, no two ways about it.*

Jesus shuffles in the seat next to her, and, for the first time all day, she thinks about him. "Oh, Lord, thanks for your help today. It went really well," Fran says, a little sheepishly.

The silence hangs between them for a few minutes. ***"You did do a good job, Fran,"*** Jesus replies. ***"You used your gifts well."***

"Thanks, Lord," Fran says, but not a lot of conversation ensues. Fran is still so excited about her success and so keyed up about getting ready for next week that she doesn't really want to think about anything else.

All week long she works like crazy on the presentation. She and Andy design some dynamite slides; she practices the presentation several times. Even on the weekend, she drops the kids off at a friend's house and spends a few hours at the office, getting everything ready for Monday, when she'll present it to Marilyn.

At church on Sunday, her mind wanders during the sermon, and she keeps thinking about those compliments from Hank. She daydreams about what he'll say when she lands the Mitchell account and how impressed everyone will be. She can hear their words and feel the handshakes of congratulations. And she can see the numbers on her paycheck getting larger and larger because of Mitchell's.

She almost wishes the weekend would hurry up and end, and Monday she heads off to work earlier than usual. The kids fuss about having to get up early, but she tells them—again—how important this presentation is. "Mom, we get the point," Drew says. "We're tired of hearing about that presentation."

"Drew, that is not a kind thing to say." Fran reprimands him but realizes that she has talked of little else all weekend.

"Mommy, when is it going to be over so you can spend some time with us?" Alice asks.

"I've spent time with you, Alice," Fran responds defensively.

"Yeah, but you promised us a fun night Friday night, and then you said you were too tired," Drew reminds her.

"Listen, things come up. This Friday we'll go see

that new movie we've been talking about, go out to dinner, and have a great time. I promise," Fran says.

By the time she drops them off at school, her mind is once again focused on the presentation. The trial run goes well with Marilyn. She only has one suggestion to make. Fran puts the last-minute touches on it and gets ready for Tuesday.

Sleep is hard to come by Monday night, for Fran is really pumped up. The next day she greets Hank enthusiastically, they review the presentation, and he is very pleased. He coaches her further on areas not to get into, points out some typical objections she can expect, and advises her on how to deal with them.

He offers to take her to lunch, but she's too nervous to eat, she says. Finally 1:00 arrives. As she heads for the conference room, she says quickly, "Lord, please help me."

"I didn't know you knew I was here," Jesus answers, without sarcasm, but with obvious pain.

"Well, of course I know you're there, Jesus," Fran answers. "I always know you're there."

"No, Fran," he replies quietly, ***"not always."***

There's no time for the conversation to go any further, as the people from Mitchell's are at the receptionist's desk. Fran, Marilyn, and Hank walk down to greet them and the session begins.

All that preparation pays off. Fran is ready for Mitchell's. A few times Hank jumps in to bail her out of a tough question, but most of the time she handles everything very smoothly. It's obvious that the clients are impressed. After three intense hours, they announce that their decision will be made by Friday, since they are very anxious to move forward and get a new advertising campaign going.

As the Mitchell people leave, Hank again has words of praise for Fran and Marilyn. "You've done a super job," he says. "If my experienced instincts are correct, I think we've got it. We'll know soon."

As he leaves, Marilyn says, "I've never heard Hank give so many compliments, Fran. I'd better be careful or you'll have my job." She smiles as she says it, but Fran feels a little uneasy about the comment.

"Good grief, Marilyn, I'd never have done it except for your help and Andy's," she says, trying to sound humble and share the praise.

Fran rushes to Andy's office and thanks him again. "Andy, it went great. Hank thinks we'll get the business. Your slides and charts were very impressive. Thanks again for all the work you put into this for me."

"It's nice to work with someone who's so organized and professional," Andy says.

Fran's head is swimming with all the compliments she's gotten today. She floats out of the office, enjoying the heady sensations immensely. "We're going to celebrate tonight," Fran says. "I'm taking the kids out for dinner."

"Yes, that's a good idea," Jesus says, as he gets in the car with her.

"Oh, Jesus, thanks again," Fran says. She knows there's something wrong between her and Jesus, but she doesn't want to confront it tonight. She wants to enjoy this success.

The kids are delighted to go out to eat, and they make a little party out of it. The next morning, Fran is tempted to sleep in. "After all," she thinks, "I deserve it." So she shuts the alarm off and sleeps another thirty minutes. That means she doesn't have time to spend with Jesus, as she usually does. The day starts at a hectic pace.

By the end of the day, she's exhausted and heads home, intending to go to bed early. After helping the kids with homework and getting them to bed, she decides to leave the dishes in the sink. *They don't have to be done tonight,* she thinks, and she grabs a book to read for a few minutes. Fran loves to get lost in a book and finds it gives her a needed break. It also puts her to sleep; after reading for a half hour, she makes her way to bed and falls in.

The next morning she gets up when the alarm goes off, grabs a cup of tea, and sits down with her Bible. Even though she really doesn't feel like she needs time with Jesus today, she does it out of discipline—and probably because she feels guilty about neglecting him and the Word for the last few days.

It's the sixteenth day of the month, so Fran opens her Bible to Proverbs 16. Verse 3 makes her a little uncomfortable: "Commit to the Lord whatever you do, and your plans will succeed." She thinks about that for a minute. *Did I commit all of this to the Lord?*

As she reads on, verse 5 catches her attention: "The Lord detests all the proud of heart. . . ." Wow, that's strong language. But verses 18-20 stop Fran dead in her tracks:

> *Pride goes before destruction, a haughty spirit before a fall.*
> *Better to be lowly in spirit and among the oppressed*
> *than to share plunder with the proud.*
> *Whoever gives heed to instruction prospers,*

and blessed is he
who trusts in the Lord.

Pride! Jesus starts talking to her about pride. ***"You know, Fran, one of the greatest challenges you will ever face is success. Remember how you acted when you thought Marilyn was going to fire you?"***

"Yes," she replies, "I ran to you for help."

"And remember what you did when you thought you had blown your witness at work?"

"I came and humbly asked you to forgive me and help me," Fran says quietly.

"And remember what you did when you thought you might lose your job?"

"Yes, Lord, I remember," she says meekly. "I ran to you immediately. I knew I needed you."

"But look at what you've done over the last week, dealing with this big success," Jesus points out. ***"As soon as things start coming easy and going your way, you forget about me. You start taking credit for yourself, instead of giving me the glory."***

Jesus does not condemn but rather says it in a loving and caring way. He wants her to learn a valuable lesson. ***"Success is very dangerous, Fran. Not many of my children handle it very well. You're in more trouble dealing with success than you are dealing with failure."***

"Wow, I'd never thought about that," Fran says. She reads the verses again. "'Pride goes before destruction, a haughty spirit before a fall.' I'm setting myself up for lots of trouble with my proud spirit, Lord," and the tears start down her cheeks. "Lord, I'm so sorry. I'm so sorry for my haughty attitude. Not once did I thank you properly. Not once did I use this opportunity to give you the credit. And the credit is all yours. I can't believe how quickly I get back into the world's mold and start behaving just like everyone else." Her heart is truly broken as she realizes how she has disappointed Jesus throughout the past week.

She thinks of the times when she refused to give him the credit. She thinks of how proud she felt about herself and how quickly she was willing to accept all the praise. She realizes how she was deriving her self-worth from what other people thought of her, rather than going back to Jesus and building her confidence on him. All of this comes rushing into her mind, almost overwhelming her, and she sobs as she sees herself.

"Lord, how in the world can I ever learn not to be proud? How can I ever be successful without being proud?" Fran asks.

Jesus, as always, has wonderful words of wisdom for her. ***"Oh, my dear, success is not wrong. I want to give you success, but all I ask is that you give all the glory back to me. If you had just recognized each day where the success came from and been aware of how easy it is to get proud, I would have kept you from that prideful attitude. But it's not too late."***

"It's not?" Fran asks. "Really? It's not too late?"

"No, never," Jesus says. ***"It's never too late to humble yourself and seek my face and turn from your wicked ways. Then I can hear you and answer your prayer and save you."*** Those familiar words from 2 Chronicles 7:14 come to Fran's mind.

"But how do I humble myself?" Fran asks.

"Mostly it's in your attitude, Fran, and in your thoughts," Jesus says. ***"When people start praising you, just turn the praise right over to me—pass it along. And don't go looking for praise. Don't talk about your***

successes all the time—even to the kids. Don't allow yourself to build it up in your mind."

"That reminds me of that passage in 1 Corinthians," Fran says and flips the pages to that book. "Here it is—chapter 4 starting at verse 7: 'For who makes you different from anyone else? What do you have that you did not receive? And if you did receive it, why do you boast as though you did not?'"

"I've been boasting as though this success was mine. For that I'm truly sorry. Lord, I give you all the credit, as I should have done long ago, and I tell you this: If I cannot handle success, please don't let it come my way. If landing the Mitchell account would cause harm to my relationship with you, then I pray that the account would go to someone else," Fran prays.

Her whole mind-set has dramatically changed. She sees this success through the eyes of Jesus and eternity, realizing that she is headed for trouble and destruction if she continues to take the credit and let pride take over her heart. Mostly she feels so bad that she has treated Jesus so poorly—after all he's done for her. Success can be a gift from God, but if we don't give him the credit it can cause our spiritual destruction.

On Friday Hank calls Fran to say that he has just heard from Mitchell's and the account is indeed theirs. He congratulates her again, but this time Fran says, "Thanks Hank, but I wasn't in this by myself. I could never have done it without the Lord's help—and a lot of people here, too."

She doesn't even think about saying it. There is nothing else she can say; that is the truth. Hank seems a little awkward, at a loss for words, but he assures her she has done a good job, and next week they'll start to work on this account. It is hers.

She hangs up the phone, and Marilyn walks in. "I just heard; congratulations," she says, and shakes her hand.

"Thanks, Marilyn, but you know how much help I got. This was a team effort. I'm just grateful we landed the account. Maybe we can rehire some of those people who've been laid off," Fran says.

"Actually, that may be the case," Marilyn says. "You'll be tied up almost exclusively with Mitchell's, and I'll need someone to take your regular work load. I'm asking for permission to rehire Louise, if she's interested. But don't say anything yet; I haven't gotten the sign-off."

"Oh, that would be great," Fran says. "I won't say anything to Louise, but I sure will pray about it." Marilyn gives her a puzzled look and walks out.

Fran shuts the door and prays, "Oh, Lord, to you goes the glory and the honor." She opens her Bible to one of her favorite psalms—number 103. She reads it out loud as a prayer to Jesus:

> *Praise the Lord, O my soul; all my inmost being, praise his holy name. Praise the Lord, O my soul, and forget not all his benefits. . . . He does not treat us as our sins deserve or repay us according to our iniquities.*

She has to stop at this point and find some tissues. God has honored and blessed her even though she was proud and boastful. She is overwhelmed again with God's goodness and pours out her heart in praise to Jesus.

THINK ABOUT IT!

1. In Luke 18:1-8 Jesus tells the parable of the persistent widow who refuses to quit asking the judge for justice. Why do you think Jesus wants us to keep praying and not give up? What have you been persistently praying for that is still unanswered? Don't give up!

2. At first, Fran attributes being selected by Hank for the Mitchell's account to her good performance and abilities. Is it wrong for us to recognize our own gifts and strengths? What was the problem with Fran's initial reaction?

3. Do you know what your special gifts and abilities are? Have you recognized them and thanked God for them? What are you doing to develop them as best you can?

4. When do you find it is most difficult to sit still and spend time in meditation and prayer with Jesus? Do you think we should discipline ourselves to do so, or is it just wasted time when you are not emotionally into it?

5. What if Fran hadn't done her homework on Mitchell's? Could she still ask Jesus to help her? Would he? Have you ever asked Jesus to bail you out when you knew you didn't hold up your end of the bargain? What happened?

6. Fran feels guilty because of the effects of her working late on her children and her mother. Was that true guilt or false guilt? Did Jesus condemn her for having to work late for this special project? Were her kids harmed because of it?

7. What was Fran's first reaction when she real-

ized that Hank was pleased with her presentation? What should have been her first reaction?

8. Do you think it's easier for most people to handle failure or success? Which comes hardest for you?

9. Fran enjoys her success very much. Was that wrong? When do we cross the line between being thankful and joyful over a God-given success and being proud? When have you struggled with this issue?

10. Fran prays that if she can't handle success, Jesus will not give it to her. Do you think that is a good prayer? Have you ever said that to Jesus?

12
Turning from Temptation

Fran's life at work takes a significant change with the acquisition of the Mitchell account. Marilyn was able to rehire Louise, which of course was cause for great celebration. Fran had her over for dinner and had a big cake decorated just for her that read: "Congratulations, Louise! God is faithful!" The kids helped her decorate it, and Louise was very touched.

Marilyn assigned most of Fran's former accounts and prospects to Louise, and Fran is now working exclusively with Hank on Mitchell's. Two weeks have passed since they landed the account, and Hank has been out once for a preliminary meeting with the client. Fran is frantically putting together their first proposal for the advertising campaign. It includes print, television, and radio, and Fran has been working night and day with the creative people to come up with some dynamic suggestions.

She has spent lots of time praying about her performance and asking God for wisdom and creativity. She feels very inadequate for the job but is convinced that it is a gift from the Lord to her, and therefore he'll give her the help she needs to do it well. Daily she reminds herself that this success is not of Fran but because of Jesus, and she gives him back all the credit that has been given to her.

But along with the honors comes the responsibility. Fran feels it very heavily and knows that a lot rides on how well she manages this account. She also knows she'll be watched very carefully, and, if she's not up to the task, they'll take it away from her at once. They're not going to let her risk losing this client.

As she works at her desk this morning, the phone rings and it's Hank calling from headquarters. "Fran," he says, "I'll be out there first thing in the morning to review the campaign you've come up with for Mitchell's. Then we'll be meeting with them on Thursday—is that right?"

"Yes, Hank," she replies, "we'll present the campaign on Thursday at their offices at 10:00."

"Good. I'll see you tomorrow."

Another long night, Fran thinks to herself, but she can take it home with her and work on it after the kids go to bed. Fran is trying very hard not to let the pressures of the job take away her time with her children. Also, she tries not to let it occupy every thought so that when she is with them, she can focus on them and give them the attention they need from her. It's not easy, but she prays daily for balance.

"Lord," she says as she hangs up the phone, "please help me to keep this job in perspective. You know me. I want to do the very best job I can, and I tend to be obsessive when it comes to working on a project. Help me, please, to keep my priorities straight and not neglect my children."

"Fran," Jesus responds, ***"I hear your prayer and I definitely will do just that. Just keep reminding yourself that no matter how critical and important all of this seems, it is not eternally significant compared to your relationship with me and your relationship with your children."***

"I understand that, Jesus," Fran says, "but it's very easy to lose my perspective in the midst of all the hustle and deadlines and daily crises that occur here. And, quite frankly, I can see that heading up Mitchell's is going to be a crisis-mode kind of job. They are very demanding—and not terribly organized. They ask for a lot at the last minute."

"Certainly you want to do the best job you can," Jesus says, ***"and I'll help you with creative ideas and good use of your time. But please, don't be swept away by the world's viewpoint. Don't forget who and what is truly important."***

Fran puts in a long night and heads out early on Wednesday for the office, to be ready when Hank arrives. They meet all morning with Marilyn, and just before lunch Marilyn explains that she must leave the discussion because of a prior commitment with another client. Hank assures her they can carry on without her. As Marilyn leaves, he turns to Fran, "Well, where do we go for lunch?"

"Lunch?" Fran responds. That's one thing she hadn't thought about. "Tell you the truth, that wasn't high on my priority list today, Hank," she says with a laugh. "I suggest we have something sent up here from the cafeteria so we get the most out of our time today."

"Well, I think we need to get away for lunch. You know the territory better than I do; you choose," Hank insists.

Fran feels uncomfortable. She looks at Jesus and says under her breath, "What do I do?" An idea immediately comes to mind.

"You know, Hank, I think it would be very helpful if Andy joins us for lunch. He really needs to be in on these discussions about Mitchell's. I'll call him and see if he's available." She starts toward the telephone.

"Uh, Fran, let's hold off on meeting with Andy till later today. I think you and I need some more time to discuss our strategy. I have some ideas to bounce off you at lunch, but we need to get out of here. Let's go."

Thankfully Fran can choose the restaurant, and she chooses one close to the office, with good food but not heavy on atmosphere. Fran has this uncomfortable knot in her stomach about being alone with Hank in a nonbusiness setting.

Many times she's caught him looking at her as a man looks at a woman and has felt very uncomfortable. He's made several comments about how she looks and what she's wearing, and, while that's very nice for the ego, somehow it seems a little too personal. He's asked some questions about her and suggested they have dinner. Fran had a good reason to say no, but there is definitely some electricity in the air between them.

As they are seated at their table, Fran says to Jesus, "Lord, stay close by. I may need some help before this luncheon is over."

He whispers back, ***"Remember, your first allegiance is to me. Don't be intimidated by his position."***

"Okay," Fran replies with a questioning look, wondering what in the world Jesus said that for. It sounded ominous.

After ordering, Hank turns to Fran. "So, you say you're single, Fran. A widow, right? Your husband died not long ago, I believe."

"Yes, three years ago, Hank, and I have two children. But I have lots of wonderful friends and family who help me out a lot, so, while it's been a difficult three years in many ways, I know how blessed I am to have a great support team. And the job has certainly helped to keep my mind occupied, if nothing else," she looks at Hank with a nervous smile.

He hasn't taken his eyes off her. "Well, you certainly have a promising future. You've done an outstanding job so far with Mitchell's, and I would say that if all goes well you can expect to be moving up fast and making lots more money. Your income ought to increase by ten thousand dollars this year—easy, maybe more." Hank drops the figure and waits to see Fran's reaction.

She gulps hard and says, "Well, there's no denying that the money would be helpful."

"And you're getting top-level exposure in the company. I'll be assigned to this account at least for the first year, and you and I will be working *very* closely together," Hank says.

Fran wiggles in her chair and looks toward Jesus, who is quietly taking it all in. ***"Change the subject,"*** he whispers to her.

"Well, I know Marilyn plans to put a lot of time in on this account, too. I'm sure lots of us will have to work hard on this one, and I'm just thankful to have the opportunity."

"Fran, the key is you and me—not Marilyn. She's got lots of other balls to keep in the air; she's not going to have time to put in on Mitchell's. The president has assigned me to this client because he doesn't want us to blow it; we need this account for lots of reasons—dollars, morale, Wall Street confidence, stock prices, etc. But basically, it's me and you, babe," Hank replies as he leans closer to Fran.

"Well, that certainly puts the fear of failure into

me, Hank. All I can tell you is I'll give it my best shot," she replies, trying to move away inconspicuously.

"When I'm out here, just wipe your calendar clear, day and night. We'll be spending lots of hours together," Hank says to her, and the tone of his voice is definitely bothersome to Fran.

She turns to Jesus, "What have I gotten myself into?"

"Take your stand right now, Fran, before it goes any further," Jesus instructs her.

"Take my stand? What do you mean?" she asks.

"I mean, let him know you will not spend nights with him, and your children take priority over your job."

"Oh, great Lord. That will do me in for good . . . ," Fran replies, but instantly she knows he's right. She remembers what happened when she waffled with David.

"Do what's right, Fran," Jesus says, ***"and I'll take care of you."***

Fran turns to Hank, who is smiling at her in a very non-businesslike way. "Hank, this whole thing has happened so quickly that perhaps I didn't ask enough questions at the beginning. But you should know that, as a single mom, my first priority is my children. I spend my evenings with them, almost without exception. I can take work home, I can put in extra hours, but I can't stay at the office late, night after night."

Hank pulls back a little. "Hey, Fran, this account is very important, and you have to be willing to put in the hours."

She responds, "My experience is that after nine or ten hours at the office, not much is really accomplished. I believe in applying all my energy for eight or nine strong hours, and then picking up where I left off the next day. Sometimes a deadline requires some late-night work, but most of the time it's just poor planning or use of time. I believe I can work with you on this account and still be home with my kids, but if that's a problem for you, it's good we got it out now, so you can decide if you want to switch reps."

"You mean you'd give up this opportunity? I thought you were a smarter businesswoman than that. These kind of deals don't come along every day," Hank warns.

"I know, Hank, and I've been very excited about the possibility. But if you need someone who can work with you late-night hours at the office on a regular basis, I'm not the right person. That would be too much of a hardship on my children." Fran can't believe how calm she feels as she says it.

"Look, Fran," Hank says with a changed tone, "there are other—eh—side benefits that come with us working together, too. It's not all hard work, you know. After all, you're single and I'm separated from my wife. . . . No reason we can't enjoy each other's—eh—company, right?" There's no denying that Hank has great charm when he chooses to turn it on. He's good looking, and when he looks her in the eye, she feels pretty helpless. Fran can see how he could sell you anything.

The danger signals go off in Fran's head, but at the same time she is flattered and a little nonplussed by Hank's veiled suggestions. She doesn't want to do anything to harm her chances with Mitchell's or upset her relationship with Hank. So she shuffles in her seat and smiles back without saying anything.

"Fran," Jesus whispers, ***"are you willing for him to think those suggestions are okay with you?"***

"No, Lord, but I didn't tell him I would see him. I won't," Fran says.

"Don't play around with temptation," Jesus says, but his words are drowned out as Hank continues.

"I've been trying to find out if there is a man in your life. Maybe you're living with someone or something," Hank says, "but it's hard to get that kind of information discreetly. So, I'll just ask you: are you taken?"

"No," Fran starts to reply "but—"

"Great," Hank says. "That's what I was hoping to hear. Listen, why don't we have dinner tonight, and then tomorrow, after we've finished with the presentation at Mitchell's, we ought to have some time together before I leave. I can catch a late flight out tomorrow night."

"Uh," Fran stammers, "sorry, but tonight I can't, Hank. I have kids, remember; we were just talking about that."

"Fran," Jesus persistently whispers in her ear, ***"tell him where you stand on this."***

But instead, Fran comes up with the children excuse and gets the subject changed as quickly as possible. Finally they head back to the office and finish their planning session for tomorrow. At about five-thirty Fran says, "I really need to get going. I don't think there's anything else to do here, Hank. I will rehearse tonight, and we can meet here in the morning for a final run-through. Andy says he'll have the revised slides by 8:00 in the morning."

"Yeah, I want you to be fresh as a daisy tomorrow," Hank smiles at Fran. "But let me give you one more chance for dinner tonight. Go home, see your kids, get a sitter, and meet me at Victorio's at 8:00. Great Italian food. How's that for an offer you can't refuse?"

"I love Italian food, but tonight I'll have to resist," Fran tries to be nonchalant, but she's sweating underneath. "A late night is exactly what I don't need."

"Fran, you can't take this too seriously," Hank says. "You need to relax and enjoy yourself. Tell me, have you dated anyone since your husband died?"

Fran is very uncomfortable with the personal questions. ***"Get out of here fast,"*** Jesus says to her. ***"You don't have to answer his questions. This is no longer business."***

Fran knows Jesus is right, but that's not easy to do. He is, after all, a vice president with a lot of power over her and her position, not to mention her earning ability. And she has to admit that he is good looking and charming.

"Well, as a mother of two young kids, I don't have a lot of time for socializing," Fran says.

"I can see that," Hank replies, "and that's even more reason you ought to have dinner tonight. But I won't push you. However, tomorrow when this proposal is completed, you and I will celebrate somewhere before I go to the airport."

"Yeah, well, I'll probably celebrate by coming to the office and getting busy. I have to do all that work, remember," she says, trying to ignore his suggestion.

"All work and no play is going to ruin you, Fran. The matter is settled," Hank says. "You have a rain check for dinner for tomorrow."

Fran gives him a lame smile, shaking her head in a frustrated way, but she doesn't think he gets the point. She just wants to get out of there, and she does quickly.

On the way to the car Jesus says, ***"Fran, weren't you listening to me?"***

"Lord, I didn't go out to dinner with him. What else can I do?" Fran asks defensively.

"You should have made it clear to him that you don't go out with married men—for one thing," Jesus answers with emphasis. ***"You're playing with fire. Remember what I taught my disciples. If your right eye causes you to sin, gouge it out and throw it away. If your right hand causes you to sin, cut it off and throw it away. It is better for you to lose one part of your body than for your whole body to go into hell."***

"Lord, what's that got to do with my conversation with Hank?" Fran asks incredulously. "I don't get it. Do you mean I should quit my job or tell Hank to go fly a kite—or what? I'm not working because I want to, you know."

"Fran, I want you to be honest with yourself. What are your feelings toward Hank?"

"He's my boss—three levels removed. I want to do a good job and get a good raise," Fran replies, as they get into the car.

Jesus replies, ***"Dig deeper, Fran. You might as well be honest with me because I know what you're thinking anyway."***

Fran is quiet as she pulls out in traffic and then looks at Jesus. "Well, you mean, do I find him attractive? Yes, of course I do. I can't help that. He's good looking, very masculine, and very charming when he wants to be. But that doesn't mean I'm going to start a relationship with him."

"No, but it certainly doesn't hurt, does it?" Jesus says.

"Lord, I'm a strong Christian. I know what's right and what's wrong," Fran defends herself. "I'm not going to be fooled by Hank's flattery and invitations. But that doesn't mean I have to deny that he's attractive to me."

"No, it's best you don't deny it, Fran," Jesus agrees. ***"In fact, you ought to be extremely aware of it and very much concerned about it. You are vulnerable, Fran, very vulnerable. Remember that important passage in 1 Corinthians 10: 'So, if you think you are standing firm, be careful that you don't fall! No temptation has seized you except what is common to man. And God is faithful; he will not let you be tempted beyond what you can bear. But when you are tempted, he will also provide a way out so that you can stand up under it.'"***

"Are you saying this is a temptation, Lord?" Fran asks, slightly stunned.

"What would you call it? You're attracted to a good-looking man who is charming and who wants to have a relationship with you that is not right. If that's not temptation, what is?"

"But you know I would never get involved with an illicit relationship, Lord," Fran replies. "You know that! Besides, I didn't go looking for him. He's the one who started all this."

"That's right, Fran. The temptation is not a sin. But how you handle it is the key issue. I know that you're made out of flesh like everyone else, and you are even more vulnerable because you don't see how vulnerable you are. You think you're standing straight and nothing can topple you over in this area. But Fran," Jesus says emphatically, ***"listen to me. You are on the verge of falling."***

"Lord, please, have more faith in me than that," Fran insists. "Even if I had dinner with Hank, I would never let him get to first base with me, you know that."

"He just got to first base with you," Jesus replies very quietly.

"What do you mean?" she asks.

"Listen to what you said, 'Even if I had dinner with Hank. . . .' You're already contemplating the possibility."

"Are you saying it would be yielding to temptation for me to have dinner with Hank, even if I did nothing wrong?" Fran asks.

"Absolutely," Jesus responds, ***"because you know his intentions are not upright, you know the relationship is out of bounds for you, and you know what an intimate quiet dinner implies. You'd better look for your way of escape, Fran, before it's too late."***

"My way of escape?" she asks.

"Yes, every temptation has a way out, if you look for it. But if you go much further with this temptation, you're going to be beyond the escape hatch," he says.

"Well, Lord, it seems to me my only way of escape is to give up the Mitchell account, and that would mean I'd lose my job," Fran says with tons of self-pity in her voice.

"Frankly, Fran, if that was your only way of escape, it would be absolutely the right thing to do," he says. ***"And it may come down to that. Are you willing to pay that price in order to keep from falling into sin?"***

Fran thinks about what Jesus has said. Tears start down her cheek. "Oh, Lord, this is a hard question. I don't want to give up my job; I like it, and I'm just breaking into some good money. It seems so cruel that I would have to give up this job; you gave it to me to begin with. That's not fair."

Jesus ignores her and refocuses on his original question: ***"Are you willing to pay the price of giving up***

this job if you have to in order to keep your life pure and clean for me?" He doesn't beat around the bush. He doesn't offer alternatives. He doesn't show any pity. He gives it to Fran straight. Discipleship can be costly; are you willing to pay the price?

Fran is crying now and can't answer him. It just seems so overwhelming and so unfair. She pulls into the driveway and leans on the steering wheel as the tears continue to flow. Fishing around for some tissues, she tries to dry her eyes so she can go into the house. Drew peeks out the window, sees the car, and heads out the front door to greet her.

"Oh, great," Fran says, "here comes Drew," and she frantically tries to dry her eyes so he won't know she's been crying.

"Hi, Mom," he says, as he opens the door. She turns her face to avoid looking at him.

"Hi, Drew. I'm on my way in now, son. Go ahead; I'm right behind you," Fran tries to avoid his look.

"You okay, Mom?" he asks.

"Oh, sure, I'm fine. How was your day?" She starts a conversation with him and regains control.

Throughout the evening her mind is on what Jesus said to her. She helps the kids, reads them a story, and lets them watch a new videotape her mother gave them on Daniel in the lion's den. They talk about the story, and then it's time to tuck them into bed.

Thinking about that story, she opens her Bible to Daniel 3 and begins reading the story of Shadrach, Meshach, and Abednego. They refused to bow their knees to the graven image of Nebuchadnezzar, and he was furious. He heated up the furnace seven times hotter than ever, but they didn't budge. They stood up to that king and said, "If we are thrown into the blazing furnace, the God we serve is able to save us from it, and he will rescue us from your hand, O king. But even if he does not, we want you to know, O king, that we will not serve your gods or worship the image of gold you have set up."

"Even if he doesn't," Fran says out loud to herself. "This is my fiery furnace, and I'm about ready to bow to the golden image of success and money—and who knows what else—maybe even sex. Yes, Lord, it could happen to me."

She contemplates the passage for a few quiet minutes and thinks about what could happen to her if she keeps playing around with Hank's suggestions. "Even if he doesn't," Fran repeats to herself. "Even if I lose this job, I will not bow to the graven images of this world."

She looks at Jesus, who sits quietly while she is meditating. "Lord, here is my pledge to you," she says with determination. "I will take your way of escape; I will let Hank know tomorrow that an intimate relationship is impossible and that, even if it means my job, I will pay that price. I promise you, Lord, to cut off my hand if I have to. But like those three guys in front of that pagan king, I believe that the God I serve is able to save me and will rescue me from this problem. I'm taking the way of escape, Lord. It's up to you to get me through it, if that means another job or whatever."

The look on Jesus' face is all she needs. ***"Well done,"*** he says to her. ***"You are a good and faithful servant. You have made a wise choice, and I will never leave you or forsake you. Remember this: you have made a hard choice, but it is the easy way out."***

"It is?" Fran says. "Seems like the easy way would be to go along with Hank. It's going to be awfully hard to tell him to take a hike."

"Yes," Jesus agrees, ***"but just think of what it would cost you if you don't choose the right way. First, it would cost you the sweet fellowship we have. Then, if you did it your way, it would cost you your purity of life, your clean conscience, your reputation, and your testimony. And, in the end, having a relationship with a man in Hank's position could still cost you your job. You have no idea how much grief you've just saved yourself."***

That overwhelming, incredible peace that Jesus gives floods Fran's mind and soul. *Oh, what joy it is when you do it his way,* Fran thinks again. Dying to self is so hard at the point of death, but Jesus was right. It is the way to life. The burden is off her shoulders. She knows what she has to do, she's willing to do it, and she is confident that God will make it right for her.

The next morning she spends extra time in prayer and meditation before leaving home to face what may be a very difficult day. She calls Lynn and asks her to pray for her, giving her a brief explanation. She also catches Louise at the office and asks her to pray, without giving her too many details. Louise too promises to pray for her.

The day progresses normally, and they head over to Mitchell's office for the presentation. It goes better than expected, and Fran is obviously doing a terrific job with this client. They like her, they respect her, and they trust her. And they buy her creative approach for the ad campaign. Many hours are spent in discussing it, followed by a long lunch at a nice restaurant.

At about four o' clock the meeting ends, and she and Hank head out the door, with Andy and Marilyn alongside. Fran hopes she can just leave with them and nothing more will be said, but Andy and Marilyn head for Andy's car, and Hank insists that Fran ride with him back to the office so they can discuss a few final items.

She sends up an emergency prayer and trusts that her friends are praying for her now, too. As they get in the car, Hank turns to talk to her without starting the engine. "Fran, I was very proud of the job you did today. You've got this account well under control. We've made a good choice, and you're headed for the top."

"Thanks," Fran says. "I appreciate your confidence, but, believe me, behind it is lots of hard work and lots of prayer."

"Prayer," Hank says, with a chuckle. "I've heard of lots of sales tactics, but that's the first time I've heard of anyone using prayer." It is obvious that he is not impressed.

"Well, I know that prayer makes a difference," she replies calmly. "I pray about everything."

"Good," he says, trying to turn the conversation in another direction. "Whatever works. Now, my flight doesn't leave until 9:00, and we've got four or five quiet hours to celebrate. Where would you like to eat?"

She whispers to the Lord, "You will have to take over for me. Please, Lord, come to my aid."

"I'd like to eat at home with my kids," she says quietly.

"Oh, don't tell me you're giving me that line again," Hank says with some irritation. "What's wrong with me, Fran? I don't have a disease, you know. Any reason we can't enjoy some time together while we're working our heads off on Mitchell's?"

"Please give me courage, Lord," Fran prays quickly. Then she is amazed at the words that come out of her mouth.

"Hank, I recognize that in our society being single

to most people means you're available for any and all kinds of relationships. It's as though nothing is wrong as long as you're single. But I have to tell you that I don't see it that way. Yes, I'm single, but I'm not available for a relationship with you beyond our professional and business association. You're a smart man, and I want to work with you on this account because I know I can learn a lot from you that would help me improve in my job. But one thing I will never do is compromise my personal standards of conduct."

Fran continues, as Hank becomes very uncomfortable. "There is not even the remotest possibility that you and I could have any kind of a personal relationship. You're still married, and I'm praying that your marriage will be restored. Marriage is precious—take it from one who has lost her husband. If you think I'm the best sales rep for this job, fine. But for any other services, you're barking up the wrong tree." Fran looks Hank straight in the eye.

Her words hang heavy between them. "Lord," she said, "where did you get that speech? Are you sure that's what you wanted me to say?"

"Just be still, don't say a word. You've done the right thing, and I will not allow you to be disgraced," Jesus responds.

It seems like an eternity before Hank says anything, and when he does she sees that his face is red. It seems to be a combination of anger and embarrassment. "Fran, I don't know what you think I was implying, but let me tell you that you have chosen to read it all wrong. Never did I even breathe the idea that you and I could have anything but a professional relationship. I'm telling you, you women have your feelings on your sleeves these days, after the Anita Hill affair, I guess. Well, you can just get off your high horse, Fran. I was not in any way suggesting anything other than working on this account."

Gradually, Fran realizes what Hank is doing—protecting himself from any possible allegations, worrying about what she might say or do. She says, "Hank, if I've misinterpreted your words, I apologize. But, quite frankly, I'm not a naive, stupid woman, and I don't think they could be interpreted any other way. However, you can relax; none of this goes beyond this car." Again she looks him in the eye and speaks with confidence.

He seems to relax. "Well," he stammers a bit, "I think it's all just a misunderstanding. Let's forget it and get back to the office. I want to see if I can catch the 6:00 flight."

THINK ABOUT IT!

1. Fran recognizes her tendency to be obsessed with whatever project she is working on, and she keeps asking Jesus to give her a balanced perspective on this job. Where do you tend to be obsessive and lose balance in your life? Do you pray regularly for Forever Eyes so that you aren't one-sided?

2. Fran tried to avoid being alone with Hank for lunch but didn't succeed. Was there a better way to handle it? Should she have refused to go with him alone?

3. Jesus reminds Fran not to be intimidated by Hank. What are the things about Hank that could indeed be very overwhelming to Fran (or any woman) in this situation?

4. Fran is quick to let Hank know that she cannot be expected to work late hours at the office on a regular basis. Was that a smart thing for her to do? Do you think she handled it in the best way?

5. Fran finds she's fairly calm when she tells Hank that he might have to choose someone else for this account. What has made her stronger and more confident since her early days at the agency?

6. At lunch Fran continues to dodge the question of having a relationship with Hank by using her children as an excuse. Why did she have difficulty being more direct? Have you ever been in a similar predicament?

7. Most people wouldn't see anything wrong with Fran dating a man who is separated from his wife. What does God think? How does God feel about marriage? On learning of Hank's marital status, Fran's first thought should be to do everything possible to encourage his marriage, not to be another nail in the coffin. What might have happened had she stated her principles when he told her he was separated?

8. Jesus points out to Fran that she is very vulnerable to this temptation, mostly because she doesn't see how vulnerable she is. To what temptations are you most vulnerable? What can you do to prepare so that you don't succumb?

9. Jesus forces Fran to answer his question: Would you give up your job if you had to in order to escape this temptation? What choices have you faced where you knew that the purity of your life and your commitment to Jesus hung in the balance?

10. Jesus points out that taking his way of escape

is the easy way out for Fran. You and I have an enemy who lies to us all the time and tries to convince us that doing it God's way is the hard way out. What can we do to choose correctly when faced with temptation?

13
Encountering Dishonesty and Cheating

"Fran, you got time for lunch today?" Louise asks as she pokes her head around Fran's door. Louise and Fran have become good friends, and it's great to have a fellow believer to talk to on the job. Since Louise was rehired, she and Fran have continued to meet at lunch once a week to pray for the company and for the people with whom they work. It has been a wonderful time of fellowship, and they've seen lots of answers to prayer.

But this is not their prayer day and Fran is, as always, swamped with work. She usually works through lunch, eating a sandwich at her desk. "Something wrong?" she asks Louise, who has a worried look on her face.

"Well, kinda," Louise replies. "I just need some advice, but I know how busy you are so—"

"No, let's do it," Fran answers. "I should take a break anyway. I'm getting into a bad habit of working through lunch." They agree to meet in the cafeteria at 12:15.

Sitting down in a quiet corner with their trays, Fran says to Louise, "You looked worried. I have a feeling something is bothering you."

"Yeah, you're right," Louise agrees. "Do you want to ask the blessing?"

"Sure," Fran replies, and they bow their heads together for a moment of prayer before eating. "Lord, we thank you again for bringing Louise and me together here; we know that is no accident. Whatever the problem is today, please give us wisdom and strength. And thanks for the food. In Jesus' name, Amen."

After the prayer, Louise says, "Fran, you know how Marilyn made such a point in the staff meeting last week about charging expenses to the clients for billing purposes. And how she was emphatic about long-distance phone calls being charged to the right account—no personal calls, and all that."

"Yeah," Fran replies. "She told me that telephone and copy costs are out of sight and they're trying to get a handle on them. It's a nuisance having to go through that phone bill each month and identify the calls, but I can see why they want to do it."

"Well," Louise says, lowering her voice, "that's what I'm upset about. Jerry is—well, he's lying about those expenses, charging personal calls to the company and stuff like that, and today we had some words about it." Jerry is the senior account manager with whom Louise works. While she reports to Marilyn, she is assigned to work with Jerry, who has been with the agency for several years and has some large key accounts.

"What kind of words?" Fran asks.

"Well, I got the telephone report and marked all the client calls, like I'm supposed to do now. There were about twenty to twenty-five other long-distance calls on his phone that were not client numbers. So, I tallied them up and attached a note that he owed fifty-two dollars and some change for his personal calls and put it on his desk," Louise explains. "Then he calls me in his office, shuts the door, and says 'Since when are you telling me to pay for calls?' "

Louise lowers her voice further and waits for a couple of people to pass by before she continues. "I told him these were the new instructions I had received from Marilyn and reminded him of what was said at the staff meeting. He said, 'Well, I've been working for this company for twelve years, and I'm not having someone checking my calls and telling me what I owe. You just forget this, Louise,' he said. 'I'll take care of it.' "

Louise looks at Fran and shakes her head. "What did you say?" Fran asks.

"I didn't know what to say," Louise responds, "but I know what Marilyn expects me to do. So, I said something like 'Well, Jerry, I'm just following instructions. Marilyn told all of us account reps to be responsible for these phone bills. She'll expect me to give this report back to her. What do you want me to tell her?' I asked him."

Louise takes a deep breath. "Well, he threw the report at me and said, 'You just note that those calls are client calls. Divide them up between three or four of the clients. That's what you do.' "

"So I said, 'Gee, Jerry, I didn't realize these were client numbers. Just tell me which numbers go with which clients, and I'll be glad to do that.' He stared at me with a look that could kill and said, 'You're supposed to do as I direct you to do, so just do it, Louise. Don't make a big deal out of it.' "

"Oh, great," Fran says, "he really put you in a tough spot. What happened then?"

"Oh, Fran, I'm ashamed to tell you, but I didn't have the guts to stand up to him. He is so intimidating, and you know how much trouble he can cause when he wants to," Louise replies. "So, I just took the report and said I'd see what I could do, or something like that. I just walked out, and I should have stood up to him."

She is obviously very upset with herself for not standing up to Jerry. "Louise, don't be so hard on yourself," Fran comforts her. "I can certainly understand why you did what you did. I probably would have done the same thing."

"But Fran, I didn't do the right thing," Louise says. "You know, I just kept thinking about how much I need this job, and that I didn't want to rock the boat, and I know Jerry can turn anything around for his own benefit. He is politically connected, and I would never win in a fight against him. So I just capitulated. I should have told him I would not falsify a report." Louise puts her fork down and pushes back from the table, very agitated.

"Louise, you were caught totally off guard, and that's understandable. Besides, you haven't falsified the report yet, have you?" Fran asks.

"No, it's still sitting on my desk, but it's due tomorrow. Marilyn's secretary will be bugging me for it soon. Now, what am I going to do?"

"Well, what are your options?" Fran asks.

"My options are to charge the calls to clients, who'll never know the difference, and be done with it. Or, to turn the report in with those calls unaccounted for, which means it will be returned to me to complete the report. Or, to go back and tell Jerry that I can't verify the calls when I know they are not client calls," Louise explains.

"Well, let's consider those options," Fran says, as she finishes her salad. "If you charge the calls as Jerry wants you to, you will be lying, right?"

"Well, I don't know," Louise replies. "Is it really lying when I'm simply following directions? I tried to do it by the book, but Jerry is forcing me to falsify the report. Therefore, can I really be held accountable?"

"Would you be doing something that you know to be inaccurate and wrong?" Fran asks.

"Yes," Louise answers, "but only because I've been told to. Besides, Fran, it's fifty-two dollars, which is a drop in the bucket. It's not a big deal."

"Not a big deal, Louise? Not a big deal to Jesus if we do something that we know is wrong?" Fran asks.

"I know, I know," Louise says, putting her head in her hands. "I'm just trying to find a way out, but you're right, Fran. If I falsify that report, I'm just as guilty as Jerry."

"And furthermore, if you do it once, you'll have to keep doing it every month, right?" Fran continues. "So, the first option is neither right nor smart since you will then be a part of the deception, and Jerry can always trap you with the fact that you did it once. I think of those verses in Proverbs 4 that warn us not to even swerve off the path. Even little compromises—or what we call little compromises—can lead to major disasters. I think this is one example of how taking the easy way out could get you in deeper and deeper."

"But Fran," Louise says with fear in her eyes, "if I refuse to do what Jerry told me to do—well, you know Jerry. He will find a way to take it out on me somewhere, somehow. That's just the way he is."

Fran touches her arm for assurance. "When we allow the consequences to determine our actions, then we are really heading for trouble. We have to base our actions on biblical principle and then trust God for the consequences."

"Yeah, but wow," Louise says, "when it's your job on the line—I don't know, Fran. It's tough. I've been laid off once, and I'm still trying to catch up financially. I'd be in a big mess if I lost this job."

Fran says, "Look, Louise, we need to pray about this, don't we? You're beginning to let your imagination run away with you—you've got yourself fired already. Let's take a walk outside and pray about it."

Louise agrees, and they take their trays back and head outside. Fran says to Louise, "I'll pray first. Lord, we're in a mess here. What do we do? You know the situation and you know Louise is trying to do the right thing. But you also know her job could be on the line if Jerry decides to take it out on her. So, what we need is some divine wisdom. Lord, please give Louise or me an idea of the best way to handle this, so she's not putting Jerry on the spot, but she's also not a part of this deception."

Louise then prays, "Lord, I desperately need your strength. I'm scared to death of losing my job again, and I realize that I'm depending on my job for security instead of depending on you. I confirm what I know to be true, that you will take care of me, and you can do that with or without this job. I also confirm that I trust you with the consequences, and I promise to do the right thing and not to compromise my standards or ethics. I claim the promise you gave me when I was unemployed: 'Cast your cares on the Lord and he will sustain you; he will never let the righteous fall.' And since I have the righteousness of Jesus Christ, I claim this promise again—you will never let me fall. I'm in your hands. Now, please give me wisdom."

The quiet peace of Jesus seems to fall on Fran and Louise like a blanket as they finish praying. Sitting on a bench outside, Louise says, "Isn't it amazing how Jesus gives us peace when we finally turn to him!"

"Yes," Fran replies, "it is. But sometimes we're so silly and wait so long to turn to him, don't we?"

"Yeah, I could have done this as soon as I walked out of Jerry's office and had the peace of Jesus flooding my mind at once. But instead I chose to fret about it all morning. Thanks so much for helping me get focused again on Jesus," Louise says, taking her hand.

"You know, Louise," Fran replies, "this is what the body of Christ is all about. You encourage and support me when I need it, and I do that for you when you need it. How many times have I run to you in panic mode?" she asks with a laugh.

"We really do need each other, don't we?" Louise agrees. "Well, now to decide what to do."

"I have an idea," Fran says. "Want to hear it?"

"Are you kidding? Shoot," Louise replies with anticipation.

"I'm not saying it's the right thing to do. It's just another option to consider," Fran warns. "But here it is. Take the form back in to Jerry and explain that this presents a dilemma for you. Tell him that you cannot in good conscience charge those calls to clients' accounts since you cannot personally verify those calls. However, what you can do is verify the ones you are sure of and then he can decide about the others. He can either determine which clients get charged or, if the calls are personal, pay the company. But he must complete that report—in his handwriting—with notations as to how those calls are to be charged."

"Hmm," Louise says, "so what I'll be saying to him is, 'I won't lie for you, but if you want to lie for yourself, I'll give you that opportunity.' "

"Yes, in a sense that's it," Fran answers. "But you will make it clear to him that *you* cannot do it, and it is his decision. You can even cover yourself with a memo to him, asking him to indicate who the calls are to be charged to, if you think you need to do that."

"But, Fran, I know those calls are personal. They are all calls to California, where his girlfriend lives. You know, he's getting divorced, and this woman, Gail, calls him about four times a day at least. She lives out there, and I know these calls are her home and her office numbers because I've taken messages from her many times," Louise explains. "So, I can't claim to be ignorant."

"I understand," Fran says, "but you aren't claiming to be ignorant. You're just refusing to verify the calls, one way or the other."

"Am I just dodging the issue then?" Louise asks. "I mean, as a Christian, should I not report these calls as personal since I know they are?"

"Wow," Fran says. "This is a tough question. We need to dig into the Word and pray about it some more. But we've got to get back to work. Why don't you come over to the house tonight—after the kids get in bed—and we'll see what we can come up with."

"Oh, that's so kind of you, Fran, but I know how much you have to do, and I've been to your house so often. I hate to do that to you."

"Do what to me? Come on," Fran insists, "this is an issue we both need to consider. I'm sure I'll come face to face with something similar one of these days. Come on over."

With that they agree that Louise will come over to Fran's house for further prayer and consideration. All through the afternoon, Fran's mind keeps going back to the dilemma, and she talks with Jesus about it several times.

"Lord," she says, "I can't think of any specific verse in the Bible that gives clear guidance on what Louise should do. Are we, as Christians, to be the police watch-dogs, so to speak? Are we supposed to report people when we know they're wrong, or is it enough just to keep from being a part of their wrongdoing?"

"Fran," Jesus assures her, ***"you're asking good questions. You're thinking about it carefully, and I'm glad you asked Louise to come over for prayer. This will get both of you into some good Bible discussion."***

"Well, how will she ever know the right thing to do, Lord?" Fran asks. "Just seems like there are some questions that fall in that gray area and don't have any right or wrong answers."

"Well, my principles are clearly defined in the Bible, and they will always give you general guidance. In addition, you have the Holy Spirit within you to guide your thinking. And you ask for wisdom, which I gladly will impart to you and to Louise. You can trust me to guide you, even in areas that look murky and confusing."

"Wonder what Pastor Gates would say. Do you think we should call him for help?" she asks Jesus.

"Seeking advice and counsel from trusted fellow believers is certainly a good idea many times," Jesus replies. ***"After all, that's what Louise has done—she's seeking your help."***

"Yes, and it's a little scary," Fran adds. "I don't like to think that she will be taking my advice. Suppose she gets in trouble; she'll blame it on me. I don't want to be responsible for what she does."

"Fran, caring and helping always have a cost

attached to them," Jesus tells her. ***"But it is not your job to tell Louise what to do but simply to help her work her way through to the right answer. You just do the best you can to keep her focused on biblical principles and let her discover the answers for herself."***

"Okay, Lord," Fran sighs. "You know, sometimes being a Christian really makes life more difficult. I mean, a non-Christian would probably have no problem with this, do what Jerry said, and let it go."

"That's true, but it's also true that there are people with strong principles even though they're not born-again believers. And, you know, when those people live by my principles, it works out for their good too, because my principles are there to help people."

"That's an interesting thought," Fran says. "Even if people don't know you personally, they can benefit by living good, moral lives. But they can't get to heaven by living a good moral life, and that's the problem."

"Yes, you're right, Fran," Jesus agrees. ***"Many times they live good lives—sometimes more moral than even some of my children. And they think that qualifies them to be eligible for heaven. But, of course, no one can ever live up to my Father's standards."***

"No one except you," Fran interjects. "You lived a perfect life and totally fulfilled God's law, and that's why you were able to die for all the sins of the world. You know, Lord, it must be terribly difficult for those people who are trying to live good enough lives to please you and win their way to heaven. I'd hate to be in their shoes."

"It's very frustrating for them. They are living in a performance-driven mode, and it's never enough. Remember what Louise said about how she was before she accepted me as her Savior?"

"Yes, I remember," Fran replies. "She would try so hard to be better than everyone else and would constantly condemn others, pointing out how much better she was than they were. She thought that would win her favor with you. She has often told me what a great relief it is to know that you love her just as she is, and she doesn't have to perform for your approval."

At the end of the day, Fran reminds Louise she'll be looking for her around eight o' clock. She heads out the door for her other—and most important—career, being a mother. Just as she finishes helping Alice with her arithmetic and gets her and Drew ready for bed, the doorbell rings. Louise has brought a new video for the kids—the story of Samson and Delilah, which she got at the Christian bookstore.

"Oh, Mom," Alice begs, "please let us watch it tonight—please." Louise has been so good to the kids, and they think of her as another aunt. Fran can't resist Alice's big blue eyes.

"Okay, you can watch it, and then off to bed. What do you say to Louise?" Fran prompts her.

"Thank you, thank you!" Alice says with a big hug and kiss. Drew, more reserved, thanks her also, but without the kiss. They all watch the video, and then it's off to bed.

"Whew," Fran says to Louise. "As much as I love them, it's always nice to have the peace and quiet that comes once they're in bed."

"But they're so nice, Fran," Louise says. "They really are nice."

"Thanks, Louise. But you're spoiling them. You don't have to bring a gift each time you come."

"I know, but that's the kind of gift I love to give,"

she adds. "Well, have you given the problem any more thought?"

"Off and on all afternoon. I couldn't come up with a specific verse that I thought gave a specific answer, could you?"

"Well, not exactly," Louise says. "But I know it would be wrong for me to falsify the report. That much I know."

"Right, I agree," Fran says. "So now we just have to consider your other options."

"Let's start with prayer," Louise suggests, and they spend considerable time praying together. Both pray for wisdom from above, and Louise again confirms to the Lord that she is willing to do his will no matter what the cost will be to her. Fran prays that their minds will be renewed by God's Spirit so they won't think incorrectly and will know God's good and perfect will.

"Louise," Fran says, "I suggest we start by listing all the options you have."

"Good idea," Louise agrees, and they get a pad to write on. After some discussion, they come up with three options:

1. Turn the report in incomplete and see what happens.
2. Return the report to Jerry and ask him to complete it, as Fran suggested.
3. Turn the report in with the notation of what Jerry owes, as Louise first intended to do.

"Now that we've listed these three options, let's think about what will happen in each case," Fran suggests. So she and Louise write down everything they can think of. Option one, they decide, is simply postponing the inevitable. The report would come back to Louise for completion, and she'd still be faced with the dilemma. Option three would be a direct confrontation with Jerry and would undoubtedly cause him to be very upset with Louise, even though he would be forced to pay for his personal calls. Obviously, if that can be avoided, it would be best for Louise.

"You know," Louise says, "it's not like Jerry would even miss the fifty-two dollars, Fran. He makes plenty of money. You'd think I was talking about fifty-two thousand dollars, the way he acts about this."

"Remember," Fran responds, "money makes people do crazy things—even small amounts of money. That's why Jesus said you can't serve God and Money, with a capital *M*. It has power over people to cause them to do all kinds of dishonest things, often totally out of proportion to the amount."

"You know, you're right," Louise says. "I remember last week I was filling out an expense account for the trip I made to a client's office in Michigan. I had dinner that evening at my cousin's house, so it didn't cost me anything. But I was really tempted to put down a meal cost, since the company would never know. I had to force myself not to turn in a meal cost because I wanted to pick up the extra fifteen dollars."

"Oh, it's happened to me many times," Fran says, "and I haven't always done the right thing. But now I stop and ask myself, 'Fran, are you willing to interrupt your relationship with Jesus for fifteen dollars—or whatever measly amount it is?' And I think of Judas Iscariot—his price was thirty pieces of silver. But, you know, the minute he got the money, he knew it would never buy him a clean conscience. It's not hard for me to understand why Judas killed himself."

"I guess I can't be too hard on poor Jerry," Louise says. "After all, if it weren't for Jesus, I'm sure I'd do the same thing. And even with Jesus, I'm tempted to cheat for a few measly dollars."

"Yeah, you're right," Fran agrees. "I just realized we didn't pray for Jerry. We should."

They stop where they are to pray for Jerry, for his salvation, for his family, for Gail, and for a change of his heart to be willing to do the right thing. "I hadn't thought about praying for him," Louise says as they finish. "I guess I saw him as my enemy."

"Well, he is in a way," Fran says, "but Jesus says to do good to your enemies and pray for them."

"Where is that passage?" Louise asks.

"Matthew, I'm pretty sure," Fran says, and begins to look through her Bible. "Yeah, here in the Sermon on the Mount—Matthew 5," and together she and Louise consider verses 38 through 48.

"Do you think turning the other cheek and going the extra mile means I should do what Jerry wants me to do?" Louise asks.

"Well, we always compare Scripture with Scripture to make sure we're interpreting correctly," Fran says, "and we know from many other passages that it's never right to do wrong, even when you think you're doing wrong to do right."

"Oops, you lost me there," Louise chuckles. "It's never right to do wrong, no matter what good intentions I may have, is that what you're saying?"

"Yes, and you said it a lot better than I did," Fran laughs. "But we have prayed for Jerry, which is what Jesus taught us to do, and we should continue to pray for him every day."

"Certainly," Louise agrees. "But back to option

two. Should I put it back in Jerry's lap? Or is it my responsibility, as a Christian, to report Jerry's personal calls against his wishes?"

"Well, let me just ask you a few questions," Fran says. "You did exactly what you were supposed to do the first time—right?"

"Right," Louise says. "I fully intended to follow company instructions. But Jerry didn't want me to."

"So, up to this point, you've done exactly right. Now, since Jerry does not report to you, and you are not responsible for his behavior, do you think it would be either right or necessary for you to forward your report without his permission?" Fran poses the question to Louise.

They discuss it at length, and Louise finally concludes that she is not called to be the policewoman of the office—not even of Jerry. She is called to do her job with total honesty and not to be a part of any deception. If Jerry chooses to cheat, that is his decision. But she has to be certain that he understands she will not be in any way connected with his deception.

Fran refers Louise to 1 Peter, and they read chapter 3. "Look at this passage," Fran says, "starting in verse 13: 'Who is going to harm you if you are eager to do good? But even if you should suffer for what is right, you are blessed. "Do not fear what they fear; do not be frightened." But in your hearts set apart Christ as Lord. Always be prepared to give an answer to everyone who asks you to give the reason for the hope that you have. But do this with gentleness and respect, keeping a clear conscience, so that those who speak maliciously against your good behavior in Christ may be ashamed of their slander. It is better, if it is God's will, to suffer for doing good than for doing evil.'"

"I think Peter wrote this passage for me." Louise smiles at Fran. "Sure gives me good advice, doesn't it?"

"Yes, it does, Louise," Fran agrees. "You may suffer for doing what is right, but you will be blessed. Remember that, if you don't do it right, you'll suffer, too. Much better to suffer for doing right."

"I think I need to be prepared to give Jerry an answer as to why I refuse to do what he has asked me to do, don't you?" Louise asks, and they talk about how Louise can explain her actions without sounding preachy or dumping condemnation on Jerry. After some further discussion, Louise says, "Wow, it's almost 11:00. I've overstayed my welcome. Fran, how can I ever thank you?"

"Thank me? Louise, we've had a wonderful Bible study and time of prayer. I've learned a lot tonight, and I'm sure I'll have to face something later on where I'll need all this support," Fran insists. They hug each other and say good-night.

As Fran wearily prepares for bed, she says to Jesus, "I'm tired, but that was time well spent, Lord."

"Yes, Fran," Jesus assures her, ***"it was, for both of you. Do you think Louise feels fortified now for whatever she faces tomorrow?"***

"I think so, but of course the fears and doubts will attack her again tomorrow," Fran says. "Our enemy won't give up this easily."

"Right, but greater is he that is in you than he that is in the world." As she sets her clock to get up, Jesus says to her, ***"Set it twenty minutes later tomorrow."***

"But that means I'll have less time with you," Fran says.

"You've had quality time tonight with me, Fran," Jesus responds. ***"You need the twenty minutes' sleep."***

"Thanks, Lord," and with that she puts her head on the pillow and is instantly asleep.

The next morning Fran arrives at the office before Louise and puts some homemade cookies on her desk, along with a note from Drew and Alice thanking her for the video. Fran writes on a card, "When I am afraid, I will trust in you. In God, whose word I praise, in God I trust; I will not be afraid. What can mortal man do to me? Psalm 56:3-4," and props it on her desk near the cookies.

Fran's morning is completely taken with a meeting, so she doesn't even see Louise until lunchtime. When Fran returns to her office, she finds a note on her desk from Louise saying, "Call me ASAP," and she does. They agree to meet for a quick lunch because Louise wants to tell her what happened.

"Well," Louise says as they get seated at the table, "I told him, Fran. And he didn't like it. He said I was making a big deal out of this and being silly about it. But I told him I just saw it differently from the way he did, and, while I wanted to cooperate with him, this was a matter of conscience."

"What did he say?" Fran asks.

"He said he didn't have time to bother with that report, so just turn it in as I originally had planned, and he wrote a check for the $52.40. I know he wasn't happy about it, but I also know I did the right thing. I sure am glad we talked about it last night because I know I handled it a lot better than I would have otherwise. I don't know, Fran, but I don't think he'll take it out on me. I could be mistaken, but I really think I saw a renewed respect for me, just the way he acted."

Fran pats her arm. "I'm so proud of you, Louise; you're a great encouragement to me. And the good news is, even if you should suffer for what is right, you are blessed. You can't lose, no matter what happens."

"I truly feel that way," Louise says. "But my heart was in my throat. It was not easy."

"But a lot easier than doing it the wrong way," Fran says, and Louise agrees.

As she gets back in her office, Fran says to Jesus, "Lord, aren't you proud of Louise? Didn't she handle that well?"

"Yes, indeed," Jesus says. ***"That was a growing experience for her, and she'll be much stronger from now on. And for you, too, I think."***

"I agree," Fran says. "Even though it was Louise's problem, I learned a lot from it."

She gets busy working on a brochure due to the printer tomorrow. About an hour before it is time to go home, Bud walks into her office. "Hey, Fran, we need to make a decision about who is going to print this brochure for us. I've got three bids on the job, and here's the one I recommend," he says as he plops a proposal on her desk.

Fran looks it over and says, "Where are the other two bids?"

"Oh, they're back in my office, but this is the best one," Bud replies.

"You mean, this is the lowest price?" Fran asks.

"Naw, it's not the lowest price, but you get what you pay for, you know, Fran," Bud says with a laugh.

"Well, I'd like to see the other two bids to see what the difference is," Fran says.

"Hey, Fran, don't worry your head about it. This is my department; take my advice—this is your best printer," Bud says to her.

"Yeah, but I'm the one who has to explain the

expenses to the client, and I need to know why we would select a higher bid. There has to be a good reason to do that," Fran insists.

Bud shuts her door and sits down in her office. "Look, I've been in this business a long time and one hand washes the other, you know what I mean? This guy's been trying to get his foot in the door here for months, and I keep telling him his prices are high. But he does good work, and I think we ought to give him a shot."

"Why, Bud?" Fran asks. "What will he give us that the others won't, and what is the price differential?"

"Well, he'll give better service, I think—and we're only looking at a couple thousand bucks, no big deal," he says.

"It's a big deal to my client," Fran argues. "Please, Bud, I want to see the other bids, okay?"

"Hey, will you just do me a favor this time, and take my word for it?" Bud insists, getting a little irritated with her.

"Not unless you give me a better explanation than the one you've given me," Fran says, as she pushes back in her chair and looks Bud straight in the eyes. She and Bud have become pretty good friends since the episode when she confronted him with his foul language. She's gotten to know him as a hurting man, one who has had little love or acceptance in his life. But she's not about to let their friendship cloud her business decisions.

"Okay, if you have to know, this guy's got tickets to Sunday's football game, and he gave 'em to me," Bud says. "That is the hottest ticket in town—do you know what they're going for? And all he wants is a chance to get his foot in the door."

"You mean," she says, "he bribed you."

"It's not a bribe, it's just the way things are done, Fran," he says. "There you go with your 'holier-than-thou' attitude."

"You can call it whatever you like, Bud," Fran says quietly, "but it's a bribe. Now, I want to see all three bids before I give approval for the printer. If he gives us the best deal for my client, then he'll get the business. Maybe he should deduct the cost of the football tickets from the quote." She hands the proposal back to Bud.

"You know, I was just getting to like you, and now you pull this on me," Bud says. "I thought we were buddies."

"We are friends, and this doesn't change that. But that friendship doesn't mean I'll compromise my standards or do the wrong thing for my client. I have a responsibility, and I take it seriously."

"Come on, Fran . . . ," Bud starts to say. "Oh, it's no good arguing with you. I'll bring you the other bids—and I'll call to see if this guy can lower his price any further."

"Besides," she says, "doesn't company policy prohibit you from taking those tickets from a vendor?"

"This is the way things are done—to hell with the policies!" Bud yells as he storms out the door.

Fran sits in stunned silence as he leaves, rethinking what has just happened. She says to Jesus, "Lord, did I do the right thing? It happened so fast."

"Yes, you did," Jesus assures her. ***"You see, Fran, many times you're confronted suddenly with ethical decisions, and you have to make fast choices. But when you fortify your mind with biblical principles, as you and Louise did last night, then making those choices becomes easier and easier. You didn't need to ask me***

what to do at that moment. You knew, and you did it right."

"Well, I didn't make Bud happy," Fran says.

"If you were trying to win a popularity contest, you wouldn't be my disciple."

"You mean I have to have enemies in order to follow you?" Fran asks with some consternation.

"No, I mean that, when you follow me, you will often find that you have to take a stand for my principles, which means inevitably you'll have to stand against some others. That's why I told my disciples to count the cost before following me," Jesus reminds her. ***"But remember what you told Louise this morning: 'If you suffer for what is right, you are blessed.'"***

THINK ABOUT IT!

1. Louise and Fran meet once a week at lunch to pray for their company. Do you have any coworkers who are believers? What steps can you take together to make your job your mission field?

2. Fran says, "When we allow the consequences to determine our actions, we are really headed for trouble." Cite some examples in your own life where you found yourself in bigger trouble because you were fearful of the outcome if you did it God's way.

3. Louise and Fran recognize their need for each other. Who in your life gives you that kind of support and encouragement? Are you that kind of friend to others?

4. Do you think Louise was obligated to blow the whistle on Jerry since she knew the calls were personal ones? Are we called to police others and report

when we know their behavior is unethical? Is there only one clear-cut answer?

5. Fran fears that if she gives Louise advice that she follows, and the advice gets Louise in trouble, Louise will blame it on her. How legitimate a concern is this when we offer advice?

6. Is Fran right—being a Christian sometimes makes life more difficult? Can you think of a time when you felt that way? How can Forever Eyes help us in those situations?

7. Fran suggests that Louise sit down and map out her strategy for dealing with this problem with Jerry. She urges her to list her alternatives and carefully consider the consequences of each. Have you ever done that when facing a dilemma? How can that be helpful?

8. When have you suffered for doing right? In what ways did God bless you as a result?

14
Combating Sexual Harassment

"Fran, could you come to my office, please?" Marilyn asks, catching Fran in the middle of an extremely busy afternoon. But Marilyn is her boss, so Fran drops everything and walks to her office.

"Well, Jesus," she says to him as they walk down the hall, "wonder what it is this time. These meetings in Marilyn's office usually turn out to be pretty significant. Please stay close and give me wisdom."

As they walk into her office, Marilyn introduces Fran to John Sims, new vice president of operations for their division. His is a new name to her, and she wonders why she has received this special introduction.

But Marilyn quickly explains. "We're having a departmental meeting tomorrow so that John can meet everyone. He's being reassigned to our division after many years with the company in other locations. But he wanted to meet you today. Hank has told him about the good work you're doing with Mitchell's, and John thought—"

John interrupts Marilyn, "Actually, I need some orientation, Fran. I want to spend the first couple of weeks becoming better acquainted with this office—your clients, the people, and so forth. I've found the best way to do that is just to spend a few days with individuals in different areas and departments and learn the ropes by watching. So I asked Marilyn if I could be assigned to observe and work with you for a few days. I hope I won't be in your way."

Marilyn shifts in her seat, obviously not happy with the way John took over. She says, "Actually, Fran, I wanted to ask you if you have time. I know how busy you are, and you've got some critical deadlines with Mitchell's, so if this is not a good time for you, well—"

John interrupts again, "Oh, Fran, don't worry about that. I promise to be a quiet mouse in the corner. I just want to watch. Hank has told me how good you are, and I want to observe the best. If I can help in any way, certainly I will, but I promise not to slow you down." He looks at Fran with a warm smile.

Fran is trying to catch her breath and figure out which way to go here. "Jesus," she whispers, "my spirit tells me this is not going well. What should I say?"

"Tell the truth; follow Marilyn's lead," Jesus responds quickly.

"Well, welcome to our office, John. Certainly we want to do everything we can to help you get up to speed quickly, but Marilyn is right. I've got some tight deadlines facing me this week, and I honestly won't have time to even tell you what I'm doing. You'd probably be better off with someone whose schedule is a little more flexible."

"I think you're right," Marilyn agrees. "John, why don't we—"

"Please, I'm not going to be a problem," John insists. "And if at any point you find I'm slowing you down, well, just tell me and I'll move on. You can kick me out at any time." John gives Marilyn a look that could kill and refuses to be denied.

Great, Fran thinks, *I can kick you out. Sure. I'd like*

to see me try. But she says, "Well, as long as you understand the situation."

"I totally understand," he replies. "So it's settled. I'll spend time with you starting tomorrow."

"Okay, see you then," Fran says and walks back to her office. "Lord, why do I think this is trouble? Why was John so insistent on spending time with me? He could learn more from someone else who'll have time to talk to him. He made a point to tell me that Hank had recommended me—I wonder what all that is about."

"Remember this," Jesus says. ***"There are often hidden agendas that don't show on the surface. This is one of those times to be shrewd as a snake and innocent as a dove."***

"You know, Lord," Fran says, "I was just reading that passage last week and meditating on exactly what it meant. And I made some notes on it in my journal. I need to look at that again."

"Good idea, Fran; that study will be very helpful to you," Jesus replies.

As she walks into her office, she looks and discovers she did indeed put her journal in her attaché today. Fran likes to use her lunch break—when she has one—to meditate on Scripture, and often she writes in her journal then.

"Matthew 10:16—that's where I read that passage. In fact, Jesus, you were the one who said it to your disciples when you were sending them out to combat the evil spirits," Fran says. "I guess I related to it because I feel as though I'm pretty innocent sometimes. You know, just a little naive perhaps, from a protected environment. Then I noted some verses in Proverbs that spoke to me, too. In chapter 8, verse 5, it says, 'You who are simple, gain prudence.' I looked that up, and *prudence* means 'good judgment or wise caution in practical affairs.' And in chapter 14 it says, 'A simple man believes anything, but a prudent man gives thought to his steps.' And then, this verse in chapter 22 really caught my attention: 'A prudent man sees danger and takes refuge, but the simple keep going and suffer for it.'"

As Fran continues to read her notes and meditate on these verses, Jesus says to her, ***"It's no accident that you've been studying this theme lately. I want you to be fortified and prepared—to be prudent and shrewd, while at the same time retaining the purity of an innocent dove."***

"'To be prudent and shrewd,'" Fran repeats. "So that means I shouldn't believe just anything, but give everything careful thought, and when I see danger, I should recognize it and not just keep going as though nothing has happened."

"That's a good way to sum it up," Jesus says with a smile.

"But what has all this got to do with John Sims?" Fran asks. "Is there a connection here?"

"How often have you discovered that what you were reading or studying in my Word was exactly what you needed for a situation you faced?" Jesus asks. ***"My Word is a lamp unto your feet and a light unto your path, so that you don't take wrong steps or fall—so that you act with prudence."***

"There's a connection—I get the message," Fran says. "Well, I'll have to study those passages again tonight and see what else I can get out of it. But now, I've got some work here that's demanding my attention."

That night Fran did take time to go through those passages again and write down all the verses that had to do with being wise and shrewd. The strong message she received from her study was that God expects us to be cautious and knowledgeable so that we are not harmed by our own naive and unsuspecting attitudes. On the other hand, Fran had some questions about that because she didn't want to become a suspicious person and imagine problems where they didn't exist. So, she prayed about it and asked Jesus to give her discernment.

The next day as she's getting a cup of coffee, Marilyn finds her and asks her to come into her office for a minute. "Fran, I want to apologize to you about John spending these few days with you. I did everything I could to get him off your back, but, as you heard, he was going to do it his way. I know you don't have time to mess with him, so just do what he said. Ignore him, don't waste time on him, but above all else, don't miss your deadlines for Mitchell's. That's your priority."

"I appreciate your guidance, Marilyn, and I'll do my best," Fran says. "I just can't figure out why he insisted it had to be me."

"Oh, I can figure it out," Marilyn responds, with a disgusted look on her face, but says nothing further.

"Well," Fran says after a few seconds of anticipation, "please share your insight with me."

"I don't want to prejudice your mind against him," Marilyn says, putting on her manager demeanor again. "I'm sure you'll have no problems. Just don't miss your deadlines, and let me know if you have any difficulty."

As Fran walks back to her office, she reviews the whole conversation in her mind. "Lord," she says, "I'm discerning something here. I see danger with this guy, John."

"Well, if you see danger, what should you do?" Jesus asks, referring her back to her study the night before.

"I should be prudent, seek advice, and take caution. I need to know more about this guy John. Wonder who could help me. . . ." Fran thinks for a moment. "Pat, that's who. She's been here ten years and knows everybody." She dials the extension number.

"Pat, Fran here. I need some information and figured you're the best person to talk to. What do you know about John Sims?"

"He's been with the company a long time," Pat says, "but never worked here before. He's our new vice president, right?"

"Yes, he's going to be introduced today. I met him yesterday, and he's going to spend a few days working with me, for orientation, he says. And I just wondered what the scoop is on him."

"I've got some contacts in the office he came from; I'll make some calls and see what I can find out," Pat says.

"Thanks," Fran replies. "I'd appreciate that very much."

After the departmental meeting, where John is introduced, Fran heads back to her office, but John catches up with her. "Well, I'm ready, teacher," he says with a smile. "Shall we begin our orientation now?"

Fran had hoped for a day's reprieve, but no such luck. She tries to sound cheerful. "Sure, I'm ready when you are." He follows her to her office. She explains again about her deadlines and that she really won't have much opportunity even to fill him in on the background. He assures her that is not a problem; he will learn most by observing. He moves her side chair to the same side of the desk as Fran's, positions it very close to her, and then takes a seat.

She tries to concentrate on what she's doing and truly forget he's there, but that's not easy to do. She offers many silent prayers throughout the morning. "Lord, please help me to be discerning." "Lord, please help me to be kind." "Lord, please help me to see this man the way you see him." And most important, "Lord, please help me to forget he's here!"

After they break for coffee and walk back to the office, John brushes up very closely against Fran as they both go through the door. It is the kind of touching that doesn't seem accidental. She had definitely tried to avoid the touch, but it was impossible. "Don't let your imagination run away with you, Fran," she says to herself, but nonetheless that bell goes off in her head.

"You prayed for discernment," Jesus whispers to her. ***"Don't ignore it when it comes your way."***

"You mean, I've got to watch this guy for sexual advances?" Fran whispers back to Jesus. The light is dawning; Fran is beginning to see why she needed to be prudent and shrewd.

John pulls his chair even closer as they sit down again and leans across her desk toward Fran, pretending to look at something on her computer screen. "What are you doing now, Fran?" he asks, and as he leans his knee touches her thigh. Fran immediately pulls it away and moves her chair closer to the computer, away from John. He leans close to her ear and says, "Nice legs, Fran. Very nice."

"John," she says with surprise, "please!" She is so stunned she hardly knows what to say. What has she done to give John the idea that she is that kind of woman? What's wrong with the way she's dressed today? It's a very conservative suit, nothing sexy about it at all.

"Oh, you women all pretend you don't like it, but the fact is, you love it," he says, but backs away a bit as he does.

"Excuse me?" Fran says.

"Just keep working, Fran," he replies as he leans back with a grin. "Don't worry your pretty head. I'll just admire the scenery."

Keep working? How can Fran keep working with this kind of behavior. Again she thinks, *What did I do to make him behave like this?* and she feels very ashamed and humiliated.

Because of conferences with coworkers and lots of phone calls, the rest of the morning goes without any further words between her and John. But at lunch, she gets edgy. "Listen, John, why don't you go on to lunch without me. Joyce will pick up a sandwich for me, and I'll stay here and keep working."

"Now, Fran, it's against company policy to work through your lunch. Come on, you need a break," John replies, as he gets up and starts toward the door. "I'll treat you to lunch—since I'm on an expense account," he says with a laugh, "and you can choose the restaurant."

"Well, I choose the cafeteria, and we'll go dutch," Fran says with as much finality as she can muster, and she grabs her purse. Again John positions himself beside the door in such a way that she has to walk past him. When she does, he brushes up against her again, but this time she's sure he puts his hand on her hip and gives it a quick pat.

Walking to the cafeteria, Fran is in stunned silence. Could she have imagined that? Surely a vice president would never touch a female employee in that way! Walking along beside her, he seems so professional, so intimidating, so in control. Fear starts to gnaw at Fran's stomach. She gets a small salad for lunch but finds she really can't eat even that. She tries to keep up small talk during lunch, but she can't look John in the eyes. This is one time she wishes the whole company would sit at their table, but nobody does, and she and John are alone.

"Fran," he says, as he wipes his mouth. "You're one good-looking woman, as I'm sure you know. I'm glad we've got some women in our company who look and act like women."

What's that supposed to mean? Fran thinks. "Jesus, I feel very alone here—and guilty and humiliated. What do I do?" But before she has a chance to talk to Jesus, John continues.

"A lot of women try to be one of the boys, you know what I mean? Man, I hate that. I like a woman who's a real woman—like you. Pretty face, nice legs, great shape. A woman—that's what a man likes." And he looks at her with a knowing smile.

"John," Fran stammers, truly at a loss for words, "this is not appropriate—"

"Oh, come on, don't get upset. I'm not attacking you, Fran, I'm just telling you how good looking you are. Can't be anything wrong with that, can there?" he responds before Fran can say anything.

"Somehow, John," she manages to say, "it doesn't feel like a compliment."

"Well, it is, believe me, it is," he replies. "It takes a lot in a woman to impress me, and you've got what it takes. I can see why Hank was so high on you." As he says that, he grabs his tray and heads for the exit. Fran has no option but to follow.

So he and Hank have been talking about her. Wonder what was said? She certainly had made it clear to Hank that she was not this kind of woman. What did he tell John? What was she doing to send out the wrong signals?

She is very thankful that the afternoon is taken up with a long meeting with Production, to iron out all the details for the Mitchell promotion. But even so, all afternoon she can feel John's eyes on her, and when he catches her eyes, he gives her that "We've-got-a-secret" smile. It gives her the creeps, and again she wonders if she's just imagining things.

The meeting runs late and as they head back to her office Fran notices that the place is practically empty. "Well, I'm about through for the day, John, so this would be a good time to split, I guess. Will you be with me again tomorrow?" she asks, hoping against hope that he will say no.

"Fran, I'll be with you anytime I can," he says, "and, I mean, I'd really like to be with you. Don't suppose you're free for dinner, are you?"

"No," she answers hastily, "I always go straight home to my kids."

"Yeah, that's what Hank tells me," John says. "But, who knows, one of these days you may see the incredible benefit of having dinner with me. You know, Fran, the name of the game is networking and building relationships in this business. It's not what you know; it's who you know, as they say. Couldn't hurt to get to know key people better." The tone of his voice gives a sinister meaning to the words.

"John, I don't know what you're implying, but I plan to get ahead by hard work and satisfied customers," Fran says, trying to sound calm.

"Oh, sure," he replies. "That's important. But a few good connections couldn't hurt. Just remember what I told you." He follows her to her office and walks in behind her, closing the door after himself and purposely—she is quite sure of it this time—pushing himself against her from behind. She moves away as quickly as possible and heads behind her desk, but he follows and traps her in the corner. Then he moves toward her slowly and says, "I've been looking at those lips all day and wondering what they would feel like on mine." He puts his arm around her waist and leans toward her to kiss her.

Fran struggles out of his grip and moves around him quickly, toward the door. She flings it open and says, "I think we've had enough for one day, John. Good-night."

"Oh, Fran, there you go again. Methinks thou protesteth too much, but I'll let you get by with it this once," he says with a wink as he prepares to leave. This time she makes sure he can't touch her as he walks by, with a promise to see her first thing in the morning. "By the way," he says, "if you change your mind, I'm at the Hilton downtown."

As soon as he leaves her office, Fran shuts the door and falls into her chair. She tries to assimilate in her mind what has happened, but it seems too incredible to be true. She must be imagining it; she must be blowing it up out of context. No executive in his right mind would say the things John said to her. She dials Louise's number, hoping she hasn't left yet.

"Louise," she says with an anguished voice, "I'm

so glad you're still here. Do you have plans tonight? Can you come to my house or have dinner or something?"

"What's wrong, Fran?" Louise asks. "You sound terrible."

"I need to talk to someone I can trust. Can you come over?" she asks again.

"Well, I was supposed to be at church for a committee meeting, but it doesn't start until 7:00. This sounds urgent," Louise says, "so I'll change the plans or whatever you like."

"Let's go to the coffee shop around the corner—how soon can you get away?" Fran asks.

"I can be out of here in ten minutes, I guess," Louise replies.

"Okay, I'll meet you in the lobby in ten minutes," Fran says as she hangs up. She puts her head in her hands and can feel the tears start to come. "Now, don't cry," she says to herself. "That's not going to help anything." As she reaches for a tissue, there's a knock at her door. Her heart goes into cardiac arrest, thinking it might be John again. Apprehensively she says, "Yes?" and Marilyn comes in.

"Just checking. How'd it go today? Any problems?" Marilyn asks.

"Well, he does slow me down a bit; I knew he would," Fran stumbles. "Isn't there any way you could get him off my back tomorrow?" She hopes her manager doesn't see the fear and anger in her face. But more than anything, she hopes John will become history and she'll never have to encounter him again. That would be a wonderful, simple solution.

"I tried. He came by my office saying what a good day he'd had with you and what good work you do,"

Marilyn replies, "and when I offered to let him observe some of my other good workers, he said another day or two with you would be best. I tried."

"Thanks," Fran replies wearily, and she's certain Marilyn knows something is wrong.

"Fran, are you okay?" Marilyn asks, as she shuts the door behind her.

What does she say? Fran is trying to think hard and fast and make good decisions. She sends another crisis prayer up: "Lord, what should I say? Will Marilyn believe me or think I've just overreacted? Will I harm my career by reporting that a vice president has sexually harassed me?" For the first time those words form in her mind, and she immediately understands what she's dealing with. It's that wisdom from above that she prays for all the time.

"Well," Fran begins, "it was not a comfortable day, let's put it that way." She waits to see how Marilyn reacts.

"I know John can be a dirty old man sometimes," Marilyn says, "but don't let that get to you. You know, it goes with the territory. These guys that have been around for a while—well, they're in a cultural lag, if you know what I mean. They don't want to hear about women's rights; to them a woman is still a sexual object, and they can't believe that offends us. But you just take it with a grain of salt."

"Well . . . ," Fran doesn't know what to say.

"Let's hope one more day will do it. I'll try my best to limit it to one more day, Fran, I promise," Marilyn says. "That's enough punishment for any woman. I put my time in with John when I was a rookie. Guess it happens to lots of us. Go home, forget about it. The most important thing is the Mitchell job—get it in on time."

"Okay," Fran replies meekly, as she watches Marilyn leave. In a daze she packs up her attaché and heads for the lobby to meet Louise. Louise takes one look at her and says, "Fran, you look like you've seen a ghost. What in the world has happened?"

"Let's get out of here, Louise," and they head down the street to the coffee shop.

"It must have something to do with John Sims," Louise surmises, "because I saw you eating lunch with him, and he was in your office this morning when I walked by. What's that all about?"

Fran brings Louise up to date on how John insisted on spending a few days with her for orientation and confirms that indeed, John is the problem. "Louise," she says, "I just don't know if I'm losing my mind or imagining things or what, but I believe with all my heart that I endured overt sexual harassment today."

"Oh, good grief," Louise replies. "What happened?"

They go into the coffee shop, find an empty booth, and order coffee. Then Fran pours her heart out to Louise, telling her all the details of John's behavior, his touches, his remarks, and his attempt to pin her behind the desk and kiss her. Louise shakes her head as she listens.

"You're not imagining things, Fran," Louise says. "That was classic sexual harassment."

"Are you sure?" Fran asks.

"You remember when I was laid off? The local community college had a seminar for businesswomen and I went. One of the workshops was on sexual harassment, and for some reason I decided to go to it. I learned a lot, and you need to learn, too," Louise counsels Fran.

"Sexual harassment," Louise continues, "is unwelcome sexual behavior, and usually it is repeated. What they told us in that workshop is that the goal of sexual harassment is not sexual pleasure but gaining power—it's a power play. Lots of men, especially men who've been around a while, want to put us 'up-and-coming' women in our place, and that's the way they do it. It's their way of telling us to keep our place."

"But maybe," Fran replies, "maybe I did something or gave him some wrong impression. I mean, is there anything sexy about this suit? Maybe I'm giving off signals and I don't even know it."

"Fran," Louise tells her, "you're falling into a typical response behavior. It's not dissimilar to that of an abused woman, who thinks she's done something to deserve the abuse. Certainly you're dressed very conservatively and professionally, as you always are, but even if you had a sexy, tight dress on, that doesn't give any man the right to harass you. It's the same mind-set we've battled with women who've been raped. Good decent women get raped, and good decent women are harassed."

"I guess I've always thought that if I behaved right and dressed right, it could never happen to me. I always thought that a really spiritual woman would never have to endure such treatment. But—I didn't tell you this—Hank asked me out and made it clear he wanted to have an affair with me. I had to set him straight. And now John. But John is different."

"How so?" Louise asks.

"Well, with Hank he just said up front he liked me and wanted to take me out, which was uncomfortable but not offensive. And once I told him no, that was the end of it. With John—it's humiliating, and I feel so powerless against him. He's very intimidating, Louise. And he doesn't quit."

"Fran, you're giving me textbook descriptions of sexual harassment and your reaction to it," Louise assures her. "I've still got my notes from that workshop at home. I ought to go get them and come over and talk to you because you need to take some decisive action quickly."

"But you've got a meeting tonight," Fran says.

"And they can get along without me. I belong with you tonight," she says to Fran as she takes her hand. "Now, let's go on home, you get the kids settled, forget this dirt-ball for a few hours, and I'll come over around 8:30 when the kids are ready for bed. Then we'll talk about what you should do."

"Oh, Louise, thanks so much. I don't know what I'd do without you," Fran says, and she gives her a big hug as they leave the coffee shop.

She tries to put it out of her mind. "Oh, Lord," she says to Jesus on the way home, "how I long for those wonderful days of just being a mommy. I never had to put up with this kind of stuff before. My home is a protected, safe haven, and I can't wait to get there with my two kids. Sometimes when you work in the world's environment, you just feel contaminated. I can't wait to get home where it's clean and pure. Thank you for my home."

"Yes, Fran, you're right," Jesus answers her. ***"Working and moving in this sin-infected world is not a Sunday school picnic, as they say. But, if you remember, I told my disciples that I purposely left them in this***

world. You are not of this world, but you are left in it to shine as a light for me."

"I know, Lord, and I realize how important that is," Fran replies. "I just want you to know how much I appreciate my haven away from it all."

"One of the blessings of your work experience, Fran, is that you have a much-increased appreciation for lots of things—like time and pressures and deadlines. You are much more compassionate now because you're having to deal with these issues. Before they touched your life it was hard to relate," Jesus says.

"Well, Lord, I need some help in this mess. Please carefully direct my thoughts and decisions. Help Louise and me to stay on track in our thinking and our discussion tonight," Fran asks. "Please give us wisdom—there I go again, asking for wisdom. I know I've worn that verse out in James 1:5, but—"

"No, you haven't worn it out nor have you wearied me with your asking," Jesus interrupts her. ***"I long to see my children run to me for wisdom and strength. That delights my heart; you can never overdo it!"***

"Thanks, Lord," Fran says as they pull into the driveway. She can't wait to get into the house and see her kids and feel the safety of those walls. As soon as she opens the door, she yells, "Drew, Alice, where are you? Mom's home!" They don't come running and she has to find them, upstairs in Drew's room playing a new game Grandma gave them.

"Oh, hi, Mom," Alice says, as she walks in the door. "Yeah, hi," Drew says, barely looking up.

"Come here, you two," Fran says, gathering them in her arms. "I've missed you today, and I just want to give you both a big hug." They are somewhat overwhelmed with her intensity, but she doesn't care. She needs to feel their faces and look in their eyes and remember God's goodness to her, so she can forget the cesspool she's been in all day.

Their evening goes as usual, with conversation and homework, and then it's time for bed. "Louise is coming over tonight," Fran says, and they both get excited because Louise always brings a gift, but Fran warns she probably won't tonight. However, Fran is wrong; Louise stops at the store for a special treat for both of them, which Fran insists they must keep until tomorrow.

Finally, she and Louise sit down to talk. "Fran," Louise starts, "you need to decide what you should do, but you should do something. This needs to be confronted and reported."

"Right, and if I do, guess who will be in trouble," Fran replies. "Not John—me. He'll blame me. After all, there were no witnesses, Louise. He made sure of that."

"I know, but my guess is this is a pattern with John. If he came on that strongly with you on day one, undoubtedly he's done it to other women," Louise responds. "And besides, somebody has to stand up sometime and bring this out in the open so he can't keep getting away with it. Fran, he propositioned you and virtually told you that, to get ahead, you need to sleep with him."

"Well, he didn't use those words, Louise," Fran says, "and he would just deny it and say I blew everything out of context."

"Yes, that's true, but you know and he knows exactly what his intent was," Louise argues. "He intended to get power over you through sexual threats and propositions. It's a power thing, Fran; it's his way of getting back at all these women who have invaded his male domain and taken some of those male jobs—that's the way he sees it."

"How do you know?" Fran asks.

"I don't know, but his behavior is very typical," Louise adds. "And if there is any track record, it would definitely confirm my suspicions."

"Well, I did ask Pat to check him out for me, but she didn't get back to me today. Maybe she will tomorrow," Fran says. "But I want to be careful about playing with someone's reputation and career. He has a family, and I can't be irresponsible about how I accuse someone."

"That's very true," Louise agrees, "but do you think he was being very considerate of you or your career in the propositions and suggestions he made to you?"

"No," Fran says, "but I'm a Christian, and I don't treat people the way they treat me. I treat them as Christ would treat them."

"And I agree with you again, Fran," Louise says. "But Christ stood against wrong and for right, and he didn't worry about people's reputations or hurting their feelings when he knew they deserved his condemnation. He threw out the money changers from the temple openly and abruptly."

"Yes, but that was because they were doing something harmful to lots of people," Fran answers. "In this case I'm just talking about the harm John's done to me."

"But don't you believe that if he's done it to you, he's done it to others, and he'll keep on doing it as long as he can get by with it? Don't you think we have an obligation to try to right these kinds of wrongs for the other people who come after us?"

"Yes, I believe we should take a stand against evil

and sinful things for the sake of everyone else," Fran says quietly, "but it's not easy when it's your neck in the noose."

"I know," Louise says, "and I don't want to push you into this, Fran. It's a lot easier for me to encourage you to do this than it would be for me to do it."

Fran shares with her what she's been learning from Matthew and Proverbs on being prudent and shrewd. They agree it's no accident that she's been doing this study and talk about how it relates to her situation.

The phone rings and Fran reaches to answer it. "Oh, hi, Pat. No, no, you're not interrupting me. Glad to hear from you. In fact, Louise is here, and I was just telling her that I talked with you today, so your call is well timed. You say you got some information for me?" Fran pauses. "You're kidding! Who told you that?" Fran listens further, as Louise perks up. Fran indicates Louise should pick up the extension phone in the kitchen, so she can hear, too.

"You mean, two other women have complained about John's behavior? Are you sure of your facts?" Fran asks.

Both she and Louise listen as Pat relates what she found out about John. In the last three years two other women have filed formal complaints with the company about the way he talked or acted, but nothing could be proven. So, he was not officially punished, and it was more or less overlooked. But Pat knows for a fact that there are documented records of these complaints; in addition, there are several other women who have had similar problems with John but never lodged a formal complaint.

"Well, what happened to these two women?" Fran

asks, and Pat informs her that one has left the company, and the other is still in the same job. She says that the rumor is John has been assigned to this office because the president of the subsidiary where he worked wanted to get rid of him. So he promoted him.

Pat then asks Fran, "Have you had any trouble with him yet?"

"Well," Fran hesitates, not sure how much she should share, "you might say so. But this information is very helpful. Thanks for calling me at home. That was smart of you rather than discussing it at the office."

She and Louise look at each other as they hang up the phones. "See—what did I tell you?" Louise says. "The man has a pattern of treating women as sex objects and expecting sexual favors. He's got a problem and he needs help."

"So you think I'm the one to blow the whistle," Fran remarks. "How do I get myself in these messes? You know, Marilyn gave me some indication that she's had the same kind of experience with him, but her view was that it just goes with the territory. I'm not sure she would support me if I decide to confront John with this."

"Lots of women have put up with sexual harassment for years to protect their career. It's only recently that women are beginning to feel they can come out and talk about it without losing their job or a chance of promotion," Louise says. "They gave us lots of information at that workshop about all this."

"Well, now the question is, what should I do?" Fran asks. "What did you learn at the workshop?"

For a couple of hours Fran and Louise discuss her plan of action and agree that step one is to confront John directly and hope that's the end of it. Louise encourages Fran to put it in writing, keep a copy at home, even mail a copy to herself and leave it unopened so the date can be verified. They work on the letter and finally come up with the finished product.

"Okay, read it to me all the way through," Louise says.

"Well, it begins with a detailed objective account of the offensive behavior, then a description of how that behavior made me feel, and then I tell him what I'm going to do if it continues. Here's how it goes:

> *"John,*
>
> *"Yesterday our time together made me very uncomfortable because of the way you looked at me and the sexual remarks you made. I want you to know that it is inappropriate for you to say things like 'You have nice legs' and 'I like your shape,' as you did to me yesterday.*
>
> *"Furthermore, I am convinced that you deliberately maneuvered yourself into positions so that your body contacted mine when it was totally unnecessary. And even though I moved away quickly and indicated that it was inappropriate, you took it lightly and told me, basically, that when I say no I really mean yes. Let me assure you that when I say no, that's exactly what I mean. That kind of physical contact is definitely off base.*
>
> *"Finally, your attempt to pin me in the corner of my office and kiss me after closing my office door was totally unacceptable and offensive behavior. I believe this is legally*

and morally classified as sexual harassment.

"This behavior is demeaning and humiliating, and I was unable to work at my job with my usual enthusiasm and concentration because of your presence. I want you to know that if any of this continues, even one instance of it, I will make a formal complaint through the corporate human resources office, which, along with the other complaints they've received, would undoubtedly be viewed very negatively and couldn't do you any good.

"Furthermore, if I sense that my career is negatively impacted by any input from you because of this, I will not hesitate to bring it out in the open. For the good of the company and many other women who have to deal with you as well as my own self-respect, I will not go quietly, John.

"I trust this matter is now ended and will never need to go any further. You should know, however, that I'm keeping a copy and having one time dated so there can be no question of its validity or its timing, should that need ever arise.

"Do you think it's too strong, too threatening?" Fran asks Louise for the fourth time.

"No, I don't, but that's your decision. John isn't going to listen to anything that isn't strongly stated, Fran," Louise adds. "However, you can sleep on it tonight, pray lots about it, and see how it sounds in the morning. That's always a good idea."

They spend time in prayer for the situation, praying specifically for John, recognizing that he is indeed a man with a big problem that only Jesus can solve. They pray for his family and for healing for him. That quiet peace settles in, and Fran thanks Louise again and again as she starts to leave.

Amazingly, Fran slept like a baby, and the next morning she talked further with Jesus about this plan of action. He reminded her that the wisdom from above is first of all pure; then peace-loving, considerate, submissive, full of mercy and good fruit, impartial, and sincere, as found in James 3:17. Since she continues to have peace about this and believes it to be the pure and good thing to do, she can proceed with confidence.

He reminded her that it may or may not have the desired effect; certainly there is a risk involved for Fran. Many times we do the right thing and suffer for it. But, as she's learned before, when you suffer for doing right, you are blessed. He's promised to take care of her and keep her from harm.

With that reassurance, Fran gets to the office early to type the letter on her personal computer. She does so and prints out three copies. One she puts in an envelope addressed to her, which she will personally mail at the post office on the way home. The other copy goes in her purse to take home, and the third she folds to hand to John. She deletes it from her disk to make sure there are no other copies. At this point it is strictly between her and John. Louise had offered to be present as a witness when she confronted him, but Fran decided to take a baby step before taking a giant one.

She bows her head at her desk once more to ask for peace and courage and strength.

Shortly after nine o' clock, John appears in her office with muffins he's bought at the bakery. "Well, Fran, ready to go again?" he asks in a cheerful way. "Thought we'd get the day started right with these muffins. Let's get a cup of coffee to make it complete," and he starts to head out of her office toward the coffee machine.

"John," Fran says in a voice that stops him at the door, "before we get coffee there's something I want you to read. We do need to get this day started right, and that's why you need to read this."

She hands him the letter and watches as he cautiously opens it and begins to read. As he does, his face gets redder and redder, and he looks like he's about to explode. Then, reading further, he turns from red to pale white. When he finishes, he looks at Fran and says in a low voice, "This is garbage, Fran. You can't prove anything."

"You know it's not garbage, and you know I can make it stick," Fran says without blinking an eye. Inside she's a bowl of jelly, scared to death and feeling very guilty. After all, he brought muffins in for her. But Jesus says quietly to her, ***"Ignore those emotions; they're giving you wrong signals. Keep doing what you know you should do."***

A long silence follows that feels like an eternity. Finally, John says, "I certainly don't agree to any of these accusations, but if you're so sensitive and so delicate that you have to be treated with kid gloves, I can do that, Fran. You women ask for equal rights and then don't like it when you get it."

"John, this is not a question of equal rights," Fran

replies. "I'm simply insisting that I be allowed to do my work in an environment that is free of sexual harassment. I don't harass you or anyone else, and I don't want to be harassed."

"Well, Fran, you've really messed up with this. Nobody would ever believe you, but I tell you what. To avoid a scene, I'll let this go. But don't expect your career to take off with this kind of goodie-two-shoes attitude," John says, as his voice rises in volume.

"Is that another threat, John?" Fran asks. "Are you telling me that I can't succeed in this company unless I go along with sexual advances?"

At this John stares at Fran for a long time, then says, "I can see that working with you today would be impossible. I'll tell Marilyn to reassign me," and with that he stomps out.

Fran falls into her seat like a limp dishrag as he leaves, her knees buckling beneath her. She's so glad he's gone but realizes he does have clout and could make good on his threats. He's part of the "good-ol'-boys" network at this company and is well connected in high places. They do protect each other.

But she also knows she has done the right thing. Later Marilyn walks in and says, "Wow, what'd you do to John? He couldn't wait to be reassigned to someone else today, and yesterday he wouldn't talk about it."

"Marilyn, you need to know that I confronted John over what I consider to be totally inappropriate behavior—what I believe to be sexual harassment that I had to endure yesterday," Fran replies. "He may try to damage my career as a result, but I had to do it—for myself and all the other women in this company."

Marilyn looks at her and shakes her head. "You confronted him? Well, I'll be." She pauses for a long time, then says, "Good for you, Fran. I should have done it years ago. And just let him try to do you any harm—over my dead body!" With that she walks out, and Fran smiles at Jesus.

1. Jesus refers Fran to his admonition to his disciples found in Matthew 10:16: "I am sending you out like sheep among wolves. Therefore be as shrewd as snakes and as innocent as doves." How do you think this direction from Jesus should be interpreted in our lives today? What is Jesus trying to teach Fran—and us?

2. Notice how Fran did a Bible study on her own. She saw a theme that intrigued her and began to track the verses. Of course, that study became an important resource to her in the situation with John Sims. Have you ever initiated your own Bible study in that fashion? Do you keep a journal and write things down? It can be a great help in your Christian walk.

3. What's the difference between being prudent and being a suspicious person?

4. When John makes his first overt sexual move with Fran, her first reaction is "What have I done to cause him to think I'm that kind of woman?" Can you understand her reaction? Why do you think a person often has that initial response of humiliation and guilt in these kinds of situations?

5. John's comments on her looks are not compliments. What are they? Does that mean that anytime a man comments on woman's appearance we should be

suspicious of his motives? How can we know the difference?

6. Should Fran have told Marilyn exactly what John did when she asks her how the day went? Was it smart for Fran to "test the waters," or should she have said something immediately?

7. Marilyn seems to have the attitude that sexual harassment is part of the unwritten job description and that women should not make an issue of it. Do you agree? Have you encountered men who are in "cultural lag," as Marilyn puts it? What do you think that means?

8. How does Fran's experience with Hank differ from that with John? Would you consider both to be sexual harassment?

9. Fran feels contaminated by the world and appreciates the haven of her home. Do you have a haven where you can go to get away from the world's evil environment? How important is it for us to have such a place?

10. Louise is insistent that John likely has a track record of this kind of behavior, and she is proven right. Do you think that sexual harassment is always a repetitive pattern for a man? What do you think of the idea that it is a power play more than anything else?

11. Fran chose to put her complaint in writing and then confront John with it before taking it through proper channels. Were those the right things to do, especially since she knows this is a pattern for John?

12. Should Fran be concerned about harming

John's reputation or his family? How can we be careful not to overreact to remarks that may simply be insensitive or stupid and are not actually meant to be sexual? How can you tell the difference?

15
Refusing a Promotion

The Mitchell's account is booming. Sales are up, the special offers are working, the advertising is pulling, and the client is very happy. As a result, they are increasing their advertising. Hank leaves the daily managing of the account to Fran, as he is more and more confident of her ability to handle things. He comes out once a month or so, but most of their communication is by phone, and he continues to be pleased with Fran's work. She is thankful that he is professional and fair and doesn't let their unpleasant experience influence his business judgment.

But the bad news is that Fran's work load is increasing daily; no matter how hard she works, it's impossible to keep up in a normal eight-hour day. She is strongly committed to being home by six o' clock each evening, but lately she often finds it impossible to do. When she does get home, usually she brings an attaché-full of paperwork to do after the kids go to bed.

Fran keeps thinking it'll get better, that it's just a temporary work load problem. But she's beginning to realize that is not the case. She talks to Jesus about this almost daily, trying to find out what she should do.

"Lord," she says to him this morning, "you gave me this job, and I know you want me to do good work. You've given me lots of good ideas and helped me so often, but success is killing me. I just can't keep up without working twelve-hour days consistently. And that means I have to neglect the kids. I feel very trapped."

"Yes, I certainly can understand how you feel, Fran," Jesus responds. ***"And it's true that I want you to do good work. But you also have to know what your limits are. Remember our many discussions on your tendency to want to be superwoman."***

"I have to admit," Fran replies, "that all the good press I've been getting at work feels good. Hank often tells me what a great job I'm doing, and Marilyn is very free with her compliments. But then, why shouldn't they be? I'm bringing in lots of dough for the company."

"That's right, you're making a strong contribution to the bottom line and that's always impressive. But don't lose sight of your own bottom line."

"What do you mean?" Fran asks.

"I mean, don't forget what is ultimately important. Put on those Forever Eyes every day," Jesus reminds her.

"Yes," Fran replies, "I understand that, but I have to tell you, Jesus, I really love my job. It's fun and fast-moving and really taps into my creative abilities. I know I've been able to improve my gifts greatly because of my job responsibilities, so, in that way, what I'm doing is eternally significant."

Jesus smiles at her. ***"Yes, I often use the corporate world for my training grounds,"*** he says. ***"I'm the most efficient human resource manager there ever was."***

Fran laughs. "I agree. Thank you again for this job, but please do help me keep it in perspective. I know that my children are far more important than my accomplishments at work, and I know that people are more important to you than positions and titles and paychecks."

"But the challenge is not to lose sight of that in the midst of your busy days and the lure of success," Jesus says quietly.

Fran understands and commits to him again that she wants more than anything to please him. "My goal, Lord," she says as a few tears escape, "is to hear you say to me, 'Well done, good and faithful servant.' That really is what I'm working for. I know that it gets lost sometimes underneath all the other stuff going on in my life, but please believe me, more than anything I want to please you."

"I do believe you, Fran," Jesus says, ***"because I see your heart. But I also know how your enemy wants to sidetrack you from that goal. So this is just a loving warning to be on your guard at all times. Don't forfeit the eternal for the temporal."***

After a little more time with Jesus, Fran starts her busy day by getting her two children up and ready for school.

Arriving at work, she finds Joyce has gotten there ahead of her and put a muffin and cup of coffee on her desk. She and Joyce have become good friends. Lynn carried through on her idea to invite Joyce over and has been a real help to Joyce also. She comes to church with Toby almost every Sunday now, and she told Fran she's quit drinking. Lynn believes she's very close to accepting Christ as her Savior. One thing is for sure, her attitude at work has changed 180 degrees! What a joy she is to have around, and her work is excellent.

As Fran hangs up her coat, Joyce comes in with phone messages. "Joyce, what a treat! Thank you so much for the muffin. How'd you know I'd need that this morning?" Fran asks, as she gives her a hug.

"Well, I know you've been working too hard and

too long. You know, you can't keep this up, Fran. You need more help. Already you've got two fires to put out," she says as she hands the messages to Fran.

"Ughh," Fran sighs, "just our daily crises. That's the nature of this business. It goes with the territory."

"Does burnout go with the territory?" Joyce replies. "I'm worried about you."

Fran smiles at her. "I appreciate your concern; really, I do. And you're right; I can't keep this up. But it'll get better soon, I think."

"Yeah, and I'm Donald Duck," Joyce says as she rolls her eyes and walks out of Fran's office.

One of the messages is from Marilyn: "Can you have lunch today?" "Hmm, I wonder what's up," Fran says to Jesus, as she enjoys her muffin and coffee. She confirms with Marilyn's secretary that lunch is fine and then plows into the stack of work on her desk.

The morning goes by before she realizes it, and Marilyn is standing in her doorway. "It's time for lunch, Fran," she says. "Hope you didn't forget."

"Oh, hi, Marilyn," Fran replies. "Nope, I didn't forget; just didn't realize how late it is." She puts down her work and grabs her purse. "We haven't had lunch together in weeks. Am I being called on the carpet or something?" Fran smiles at Marilyn. Their relationship has improved immensely, and they both seem to feel very comfortable with each other. The jealousy and competition Fran had once sensed from Marilyn seem to have gone away. What a difference it makes to have a good working relationship with one's boss.

"Yeah, on the carpet at Pier 22. We're going out to lunch first class," Marilyn says as she leads the way.

"Whoa," Fran says, "Pier 22. Sounds great, but let

me check the finances here. That's not in the budget." She starts to check her purse but Marilyn stops her.

"Put your money away; this is on the company," she says.

"No joke? Great, I'll enjoy every bite. They have the best seafood in town," Fran says.

They carry on the usual chitchat as Marilyn drives to the restaurant, but in the back of her mind, Fran is thinking, "What's up?" She quickly says to Jesus, "Please give me wisdom, guidance, and clear thinking for whatever it is I'm going to face."

"Yes, I will," Jesus whispers back, ***"and Forever Eyes."***

They get a private table in the back of the restaurant, and Fran orders Dover sole, her favorite. It's great not to have to look at the price when ordering, as she usually does! Once in a while the job does have a perk or two, but there's no guilt on Fran's part. She's earned every one of them, and then some!

As they munch on their rolls, waiting for the entrée, Marilyn says, "Fran, I just want you to know that the management of the company recognizes what a great job you're doing with Mitchell's. Really, the account has already exceeded projections by a large amount. I'm convinced that it's mainly due to your hard work and creativity. And I've said so to the people who count."

"Thanks, Marilyn," Fran replies, putting down her knife. "I was just thinking this morning what a pleasure it is to have a boss like you. You have been so supportive and helpful, and of course you've taught me a lot. I rely on your business judgment often; I don't deserve all the credit, you know that."

"You deserve a great deal of credit, and my pleasant duty today is to tell you that effective next month, you will be promoted to senior account rep," Marilyn says slowly, letting the effect settle in on Fran.

Fran's mouth drops open, and she is stunned. Trying to assimilate it all, she pauses for a moment, then says, "You're not kidding, are you? Wow, that's really something. Senior account rep—I never dreamed I'd get it this soon. . . ."

"It is soon. In fact, as I recollect, there are only two others who have been promoted this fast. Sam—you don't know him, he's in corporate now—and myself," she says with a smile.

"Well, I'm in very good company then. Thanks, Marilyn. Now tell me exactly what this means," Fran says.

"Well, it means that you'll be getting a 15 percent raise right off the bat. Then you'll be eligible for the yearly bonuses and profit sharing. You'll have management status, Fran," Marilyn informs her.

The smile on Fran's face won't go away. "I can sure use the money," she says.

"Well, I can imagine a single mom like you has lots of expenses," Marilyn says. "Never having had any children myself, I'm sure I don't have the financial obligations that you do."

They talk further about the bonus program and how much money that can mean to Fran. It could be significant, depending on how much Fran bills to the client and on the company's profitability. Fran's head is spinning just thinking about how nice it will be to have some extra money.

In the midst of the conversation, Jesus says quietly to Fran, ***"Ask her about added responsibilities and***

work load." It seems like an unnecessary question to Fran, but Jesus seems insistent, so she does.

"Marilyn, let me be sure I understand exactly what will be expected of me—what added responsibilities or duties will I have?" she asks.

"Well, basically you'll still be doing what you're doing with Mitchell's. There'll be some additional management meetings and responsibilities, but nothing significant, I don't think. Hank will be turning the account over to you exclusively, so all client contact will be yours to control," Marilyn informs her.

Fran puts her fork down and thinks about what Marilyn has said. Her work load will not go down; it will go up. And already she is over capacity. If she accepts this promotion, the responsibilities go with it.

"Lord, I need Forever Eyes fast," Fran breathes a prayer, and it seems as though she is given an instant capsule picture of life as a senior account rep. Frantic, hectic, tired, burned-out. And on the sidelines are her kids, waiting for her attention, taking second place to the job. Once Fran takes the promotion, she can't refuse the responsibilities. Now she must make a choice, and it's not an easy one.

"Remember, Fran," Jesus whispers to her, ***"promotions, titles, and incomes don't count for eternity. Don't be deceived by the allure of these things."***

"But, Lord," she says, "I could use the money, you know that, and . . . well, it's just not smart to turn down a promotion. They'll think I'm crazy!"

"Which is more important to you, what people think, or what I think?"

Jesus always cuts through the maze and helps Fran to see the clear-cut choice she has. She gulps and says slowly, "Marilyn, obviously I'm very honored with this promotion, and I appreciate your confidence in me more than I can say. But I need to ask you to give me a day to think it over before I accept."

"Think it over?" Marilyn asks with great surprise. "What can there be to think over? You've worked hard and earned a promotion."

"Yes, I believe I have worked hard for it," Fran agrees. "But I have to consider the impact it will have on my family. Frankly, Marilyn, lately I've had to work a lot of extra hours just to keep up, and I've been debating what to do about that if it continues. It appears to me it will continue, and now with some added responsibility—"

"Fran, you can't turn this promotion down. If you do, I don't know what will happen. I might have to reassign you—I don't know," Marilyn seems genuinely concerned and puzzled.

"I surely don't want to put you in a bind, Marilyn," Fran responds, "but I have to give this careful consideration. My priorities, because of my children, are different, and I don't apologize for that. I have to be at home in the evenings and have time and energy for my kids. They won't be young and teachable forever, and I have limited years with them. I don't want to blow those years. Nothing is worth neglecting my children."

"You know, I never even thought about the possibility that you might turn this promotion down, Fran," Marilyn says, shaking her head. "This takes me totally by surprise. I guess I'm so used to people clawing their way to the top as quickly as possible, that it's a little puzzling to meet someone who isn't hell-bent on climbing the ladder."

"Fran," Jesus says quietly, ***"here's an open door, a***

marvelous opportunity to tell Marilyn about me. Don't lose this opportunity."

The thought frightens Fran. "You know I'm not good at witnessing."

"You need to be ready to give an answer for the hope that is in you," Jesus says. ***"If you're ashamed of me, I'll be ashamed of you."***

Jesus' last comment really gets to Fran. "I'm never ashamed of you, Lord." With that she responds to her manager.

"Oh, don't get me wrong, Marilyn, I'd love to take this promotion and climb this ladder as fast as I can. I'm a very competitive person, and I like to win. I'd love to prove that I'm superwoman and can walk on water. But the fact is, I'm not. It's something I've been learning lately. In the past I've found a lot of my identity in trying to be superwoman, and that's a big mistake. So now I try to put on what I call Forever Eyes and look at each situation from a long-term perspective. It helps me to make better choices."

"Forever Eyes—that's a strange term. Part of your religious belief?" Marilyn asks.

"Yeah, I guess it is. Jesus teaches us to lay up our treasures in heaven, not on this earth, and by that I think he means not to be focused on stuff that won't last forever," Fran tries to explain in nontheological terminology. "My kids are going to last forever, and I don't want to wake up in ten years regretting the fact that I didn't give them the foundation they needed in these early years. They are eternally important; promotions are not."

"What did you say?" Marilyn asks.

"I said, my kids are eternally important, but . . . ," Fran starts to explain but is interrupted.

"I heard you but I'm just trying to understand," Marilyn says. "You are willing to give up this promotion if you feel it will negatively affect your kids in any way, is that what you're telling me?"

"Yeah, I guess you've hit it perfectly," Fran replies.

"Do you know how that kind of attitude is viewed by the male executives above us, Fran?" Marilyn asks. "They say we asked for equal treatment and equal opportunities, so we can't bail out when it calls for equal commitment and sacrifice. It doesn't help us females break through the glass ceiling when competent women like you refuse to accept promotions because of your children."

This catches Fran off guard. She hadn't thought about that, and she gets a knot in her stomach. Quickly she sends up another emergency prayer to Jesus: "Lord, I need some wisdom fast. What do I say now?"

"You don't back away from what you know is truth," Jesus responds, firmly. ***"Your enemy is trying to make you compromise. Stand firm and resist him."***

Quickly Fran prays, "In the name of Jesus, I resist you, Satan. Get out of here." In that moment, she knows what to say to Marilyn.

"Wow, that's heavy, Marilyn. I never saw myself as having that kind of responsibility. But it doesn't change my thinking because my first priority is my kids, not women in business. I believe as long as I work hard and perform well for this company, I have given everything expected and required. Furthermore, I think men should be as aware of the impact of their career decisions on their families as I am. This is not a female issue, as I see it. It's a family issue. Admittedly my decision might be different if Jim were still alive and the kids had two parents instead of one. But then again, it might not be."

At that, Marilyn puts her fork down and pushes back in her chair, looking Fran straight in the eye and shaking her head. She seems to be at a loss for words, and the silence between them lengthens. But Fran senses it's a time for her to be quiet and let Marilyn make the first move.

"You're serious about this, aren't you, Fran," Marilyn remarks. After another pause, she says, "I admire you. I really do admire you."

"You do?" Fran says with shock in her voice. "You're not mad at me?"

"No, I admire you. You've got some kind of guts," Marilyn says. "I first saw it when you refused to do the proposal the way I wanted you to—remember the Ross account?"

"How could I ever forget," Fran replies. "I almost lost my job over it."

Marilyn smiles, "Yeah, I knew then you were a different kind of cat. Then when you took on John Sims—I knew you had some kind of strength I'd never seen before. And now, to see you be willing to turn down money you need because you refuse to shortchange your kids—I'm impressed. But I'm not sure if I think you're smart or weird." Marilyn gives Fran a tongue-in-cheek look.

"Well, I think it's neither," Fran replies. "I'm certainly not extra-smart and, in the context of my commitment to Jesus Christ, my actions aren't weird. You see, Marilyn, more important than anything else in my life is my decision to commit my life to Jesus. And what I'm discovering is that he empowers me to do what I'd never want to do or be able to do otherwise."

"You know, you've tried to talk to me about that before, but frankly, it just makes me uncomfortable," Marilyn confesses. "I've never been around people who talk about Jesus as though they know him."

Fran smiles and says, "Well, I can see how that would seem weird. But when you do know him as I do, it's not weird at all. He is more real to me than you are, Marilyn. He is my best friend, my counselor, my guide. I know him and he knows me—very well!"

"See, that seems really weird. How can you know a man who doesn't exist? He's dead. I mean, I don't know—say—George Washington, because he died before I was born. How can you know Jesus?" Marilyn asks.

Fran's mind is spinning. It's like someone wrote the script for Marilyn. Fran can't believe she's got such an opening to talk about Jesus. She quickly remembers 1 Peter 3:15, which says to "be prepared to give an answer to everyone who asks you to give the reason for the hope that you have." There's no doubt that Fran must now be prepared to answer Marilyn, and again she quickly asks Jesus to help her.

"But the difference between George Washington and Jesus is that Jesus arose from the dead. He's alive; literally, physically, spiritually alive. The Bible tells me he now sits beside God in his new body, the one he had when he arose from the grave," Fran begins.

"You mean, you believe he really came back from the dead?" Marilyn asks.

For the next hour, Fran talks with Marilyn about Jesus. Marilyn knows almost nothing; it's as though she spent her life in a heathen land with no information at all about who Jesus is or what he did. So, in the simplest words possible, Fran explains, over and over again, what it means to know Jesus.

Marilyn listens intently. She really wants to know. They both lose total track of time. Nothing seems important at this point except knowing Jesus. As Fran shares how she daily communicates with Jesus and how he gives her strength, how he healed her pain and comforted her when Jim died, how he cares about her and her kids, Marilyn is very touched and tears start to roll down her cheeks.

"All my life," Marilyn says, "I've always wanted someone who just loved me for myself, and I've never had it. You know, every day of my life my mother told me I was a mistake and should not have been born, and if abortion had been available to her, she would never have had me." Marilyn is crying unashamedly at this point.

"Oh, Marilyn, I can't believe it. I'm so sorry," Fran says. "That's awful. What pain and hurt. Oh, Marilyn, Jesus understands your pain, and he loves you so much. He wants to be to you everything he is to me."

"But I'm not good like you are," Marilyn says. "I just can't live like you do."

"Marilyn, don't you understand that the reason I'm good—if I am—is because of Jesus," Fran explains. "You don't have to get cleaned up to come to Jesus. You come to Jesus to get cleaned up. He's the only one that can change you."

"But what will my friends think if I suddenly become a religious fanatic?" Marilyn looks at Fran with red, swollen eyes.

"They'll think you're weird." Fran smiles. "But they'll want to know where you got that peace and joy."

"This is scary," Marilyn says quietly, gaining her

composure. "Never before have I been so vulnerable with anyone, and I'm not sure I'm ready to make this commitment you're talking about."

"You'll never be ready," Fran says, "because you just have to come by faith. It's all one huge step of faith. It's like stepping into a black unknown, but you do it by faith. First you have to believe that Jesus is the Son of God and the only way to God. And if you can do that by faith, then you take the step into the black unknown, and you'll find solid ground beneath your feet. But you have to make the first move, Marilyn."

"How do I do it?" Marilyn asks.

"You just talk to Jesus like you talk to me. He understands English really well," Fran says with a laugh. She looks around to see that the restaurant is almost empty, and because their table is way in the back, nobody notices them, and the waiter is leaving them alone. She prays quickly that Jesus will keep it that way for a few more minutes.

"You mean, now? Talk to Jesus now?" Marilyn says.

"Why not?" Fran replies. "I'll start and then you say whatever is on your heart."

"Okay," Marilyn agrees.

Fran doesn't even bow her head. She doesn't want Marilyn to be uncomfortable or feel unnatural, and Fran knows that the position of your head or body or eyes is not important to God. He looks at the heart. She begins, "Lord, it's me, Fran, and with me, as you know, is Marilyn. She's struggling with this idea of becoming a disciple of Jesus, and, while she wants to do it, she's also scared. I know you understand that, so please calm her heart right now and give her the assurance that you do love her and you are listening to what she has to say."

After a few moment's silence, Marilyn begins, so

quietly at first that Fran can hardly hear. "God," she says, "I'm Marilyn, like Fran said, and I am indeed scared. I'm not sure I can believe everything that Fran has told me, but I know she's got something I don't have. And I also know that I need you. I'm not a good person; you know all the bad things I've done. I don't have a kind heart like Fran, but she says you'll give me one. At any rate, if this is really the truth, then I want to accept you into my life. Please forgive me for being so bad and please help me to be good. Amen."

They both sit in silence for a few moments. Then Fran says, "I know that God heard you, Marilyn, and he is faithful to his promises. He said in the Bible that anyone who comes to him in simple faith will never be rejected. I believe you are accepted. Welcome to the family. You are now my sister in Christ." And with that Fran can no longer hold back the tears. She gets more tissues out of her purse and puts her head in her hands, sobbing.

"Why are you crying?" Marilyn asks as she grabs one of her tissues.

"Because," Fran says, "all the angels in heaven are having a party right now because you accepted Jesus. Did you know that?"

"Oh, come on, get serious," Marilyn says.

"I am serious. The Bible says that when one sinner repents and comes home, all of heaven rejoices, and I'm rejoicing, too. My joy just happens to come out in tears," Fran says as she wipes her eyes again.

"You really think that did it?" Marilyn says. "That's all I have to do? No trial period? Nothing else—just ask God to forgive me?"

"That's it—simple faith and repentance," Fran assures her.

"Well, if it's so simple, why don't more people do it?" Marilyn asks.

"Because it's so simple," Fran replies. "Like you, they want to earn their way to God. But it can't be done."

They look at each other with big smiles and ruined makeup! "Hello, my sister," Marilyn says. "I have to get used to this."

"You've just made the most important decision in your life, Marilyn," Fran says. "Nothing else is as important as your relationship to Jesus, and now you are his child."

"Well, I thought maybe a lightning bolt would come crashing through and change me right here, but I look pretty much the same," Marilyn says.

"Oh, you'll see some lightning bolts, don't worry," Fran says. "But your relationship is not based on an emotional experience. It is based on God's Word and his promises. The emotions come and go, but his Word will always be there to confirm that you are indeed his child."

"I have to tell you," Marilyn replies, "that I do feel lighter. The sun seems to be shining brighter. I don't know—there's a glow. You look different, Fran."

"Well, I hope it's an improvement," she laughs. "You are different, Marilyn. You are now a new creation. The old has passed; the new has come."

They talk for a few more minutes and agree they've stretched this lunch hour as long as they can. Marilyn understands that she is a baby Christian needing much teaching and discipleship, and Fran tells her about their discipleship program at church. Marilyn is willing to do a one-on-one Bible study with another woman, and Fran offers to set it up for her.

On the way back, Marilyn says, "You know, we almost forgot the purpose of this luncheon—your promotion. Now, what am I going to do about that?"

"You do whatever you have to do, Marilyn, but I know that I can't take on any more work or responsibility that would demand more time. If that means I can't accept the promotion, so be it," Fran says.

"Well, let me think about it. I'll get back to you tomorrow," Marilyn says.

On the way home from work Fran stops at the bookstore to buy Marilyn a Bible that's easy to understand. She can hardly keep her feet on the ground as she recalls the great miracle that has taken place today. Again and again she thanks Jesus for the blessed privilege of being a part of this new birth. "Thanks, Lord, for using people like me," she says to him. She calls everyone she can think of to share the good news. Louise is especially excited to hear it.

The next morning she takes the Bible in to Marilyn's office and lays it on her desk—wrapped in a box with a special note from Fran written on the inside. Mid-morning Marilyn walks into Fran's office, shuts her door, thanks her for the Bible, and says, "I've got good news for you. I've been on the phone with Hank yesterday and today about your situation, and he's gotten approval to assign an assistant rep to you with the Mitchell's account. He says the business they're giving us warrants two people. So, you are indeed a senior account rep, with an assistant reporting to you. Can you accept the promotion under those circumstances?"

"You'd better believe it," Fran says, as she shakes Marilyn's extended hand. "Thanks—oh, Marilyn, thanks so much."

"My pleasure," she replies. "You know, Fran, I

prayed this morning that Jesus would help me get this approved. I think it worked."

"I know it worked," Fran replies. "See, you're already learning to practice the presence of Jesus in your life. I told you he'd be there for you all the time."

"This morning when I woke up," Marilyn says, "I just lay there in bed and kept saying, 'Is this real, or am I just imagining it?' I really do feel different. Like heavy burdens have been taken off my back. Is that normal?"

"Totally normal, because indeed heavy burdens *have* been taken off your back, Marilyn," Fran replies. "That burden was sin and pain and loneliness. You don't have to carry them anymore. You're free. Jesus said that when he makes someone free, they are free indeed."

"So what you're saying is that I am now a liberated woman, is that it?" Marilyn says with a laugh.

"You got that right," Fran says. "You never knew liberation until you accepted Jesus."

"Well, as you suggested, I'm going to start reading the book of John. Thanks again for the Bible."

She walks out, and Fran stands in stunned awe at what God has done. All she can say is "Thank you, Jesus; *thank you,* Jesus!"

THINK ABOUT IT!

1. Fran loves her job because she can use her creative gifts and that's fun. Is there anything wrong with loving your job? Can it be eternally significant? What if you have a job you don't love that doesn't use your gifts? Should you try to find a new job?

2. Jesus warns Fran not to forfeit the eternal for the temporal. At what times are you most tempted to do that? About what points of vulnerability do you

need to pray and ask for strength to have Forever Eyes?

3. Notice that Lynn is now involved in Joyce's life because of Fran. Is Lynn doing what Fran should be doing for Joyce? Or is this the way the body of Christ should work?

4. What a difference it makes to have a good working relationship with your boss, Fran says. Do you agree? Ever had a boss that was difficult to work for? How did you handle it? If you have a good boss, do you appreciate her or him as you should?

5. Notice that Fran is able to perceive what Jesus wants her to do and react more quickly than a couple of years ago. Why do you think this is true? In what ways do you respond with obedience more quickly than you used to?

6. Marilyn points out the harm Fran will do to the possibility of getting women into more upper-management positions if she refuses this promotion. Is that a valid consideration for Fran?

7. Fran says the impact of a business decision on the family is not a female issue and that men should be equally concerned. Do you agree? Do you know many men who feel the same way, or is there a double standard in families, in the workplace, and in our churches?

8. Fran witnesses to Marilyn and then has prayer with her right in the restaurant. Was that a good idea to do it in a public place? Does it matter?

9. Fran is very careful not to use "theological terminology" with Marilyn, who has never had any con-

tact with true Christians before. She prays very simply and directly, without any *thee*s and *thou*s. Is this a good idea, or is Fran compromising?

10. Marilyn doesn't have all her theology straight as she prays. Should Fran correct her and try to teach her everything at once? What do you think Jesus thought of Marilyn's prayer?

EPILOGUE

How does the story end? It doesn't.

Like all of us, Fran's life continues with daily struggles, high moments, scary moments, many disappointments and unfulfilled desires, and a great deal of routine and mundaneness. But Fran is learning and growing and becoming; she's not sitting on the sidelines or standing still. She's going forward.

Oh, true, there are backward steps at times, and that will undoubtedly continue to be true. She'll have to relearn some lessons many times, but in the process she is coming to understand what Paul meant in 2 Corinthians 3:18:

> *And we, who with unveiled faces all reflect the Lord's glory, are being transformed into his likeness with ever-increasing glory, which comes from the Lord, who is the Spirit.*

Every child of God should be able to see transformations in his or her life, because that's what is happening to us when the Spirit of God living within us is allowed to control us. We are "predestined to be conformed to the likeness of his Son," as we read in Romans 8:29, and we shouldn't settle for anything less than what we've been predestined to be.

Being forced into the working world has made Fran face many new problems and emotions and people that she wouldn't have faced otherwise. That has, in turn, taught her to run to Jesus all the time. He is her hiding place, and that's exactly what he wants to be. He cried over Jerusalem because he longed to gather their children together as a hen gathers her chicks under her wings, but they were not willing (Matt. 23:37). He never tires of our running to him with all our problems, all our worries, all our confusion, and looking to him for wisdom, strength, guidance, and comfort.

We need a hiding place, but often we choose the wrong ones. Some of us try to hide in denial, some in blaming others and refusing to be accountable for our own actions. Lots of people try to hide by eating or drinking too much; others by running away, working too much, or losing themselves through sex. But none of these "hiding places" work; they are, at best, temporary Band-Aids on our cancer of sin and loneliness and desperation.

Jesus has come to be our hiding place, our refuge, our Mother Hen to gather us in and protect us. But many of us have never learned to run to him—all the time, every time—and find that place of hiding that enables and empowers us to go back out there and face the world where we've been sent.

God is not nearly so interested in where we are as in who we are, and Jesus wants us to live up to everything he died for us to be. And we live up to it by giving up and allowing the power of the risen Christ to control us. Then we can be "transformed into his likeness with ever-increasing glory."

That's the process that Fran has been going through and will continue to go through. Oh, it surely didn't seem like it most of the time, and she was not aware of it except in retrospect. She was dealing with people and ethical decisions and work-load pressures and guilt and trying to be superwoman—and everything else! But those were the things that Jesus used in her life to transform her into his likeness with ever-increasing glory.

If she continues to let Jesus do that for her—a year from now, two years from now, ten years from now, if we check in with Fran—we'll find she looks more like Jesus then than she does now.

You and I have precious few years on this earth before we face Jesus and spend eternity with him, if indeed we are born from above and know him as our Savior. If we can learn to wear Forever Eyes every day, to stay in constant touch with Jesus, to saturate our life with his Word, to bring our thoughts in line with Philippians 4:8, and to obey Jesus right away every time, we'll be able to hear him say, "Well done, good and faithful servant." What else really matters?

You're not alone in your struggle to gain Christ's perspective on your various roles and responsibilities. Here are just a few of the many resources available:

Books and Magazines

"But Can She Type?" Overcoming Stereotypes in the Workplace, by Janet L. Kobobel (IVP, 1986)

Not Just a Job: Serving Christ in Your Work, by Judith Allen Shelly (IVP, 1985)

Out of the Saltshaker and into the World: Evangelism as a Way of Life, by Rebecca Manley Pippert (IVP, 1979)

Playing Hardball with Soft Skills: How to Prosper with Non-Technical Skills in a High-Tech World, by Steven J. Bennett (Bantam, 1986)

Should You Be the Working Mother? A Guide for

Making the Decision and Living with the Results, by Bee-Lan C. Wang and Richard J. Stellway (David C. Cook, 1987)

Wait a Minute, You Can Have It All: How Working Wives Can Stop Feeling Overwhelmed & Start Enjoying Life, by Shirley Sloan Fader (Jeremy Tarcher, Inc., 1993)

What Color Is Your Parachute? by Richard Nelson Bolles (Ten Speed Press, annual)

Working Mother magazine, including their annual listing "100 Best Companies for Working Mothers"

Working Moms: From Survival to Satisfaction, by Miriam Neff (Nav Press, 1992)

Organizations

- Catalyst—a national organization of resources for women, specializing in books, job information, and career counseling for those looking for work, changing jobs, or reentering the job market
- Professional women's groups in your field
- Trade organizations and unions